BY JAMES CARVILLE AND PAUL BEGALA

Buck Up, Suck Up . . . and Come Back When You Foul Up

ALSO BY JAMES CARVILLE

Had Enough?

Stickin'

. . . And the Horse He Rode In On

We're Right, They're Wrong

All's Fair
(with Mary Matalin)

ALSO BY PAUL BEGALA

It's Still the Economy, Stupid

Is Our Children Learning?

TAKE IT BACK

Our Party,
Our Country,
Our Future

JAMES CARVILLE

AND

PAUL BEGALA

Simon & Schuster

New York   London   Toronto   Sydney

SIMON & SCHUSTER
Rockefeller Center
1230 Avenue of the Americas
New York, NY 10020

SIMON & SCHUSTER and colophon are registered trademarks
of Simon & Schuster, Inc.

Designed by Elliott Beard

Manufactured in the United States of America

10 9 8 7 6 5 4 3 2 1

Library of Congress Cataloging-in-Publication Data has been applied for.

ISBN-13: 978-0-7432-7752-5
ISBN-10:   0-7432-7752-X

For information regarding special discounts for bulk purchases,
please contact Simon & Schuster Special Sales at 1-800-456-6798 or
business@simonandschuster.com

For Diane: twenty-five years after I first flirted with her
in the student lounge, she still makes my heart race.
Paul

For every man and woman in the United States Marine Corps who has
fought, is fighting, or will fight in Iraq and Afghanistan. Semper Fi.
James

Contents

Introduction

Lord Acton was right.

The British historian and philosopher of the late nineteenth century is most famous for his observation that "power corrupts, and absolute power corrupts absolutely."

The Republicans in Washington today have absolute power. They control the White House. They control the Senate. They control the House. They control the federal bureaucracy. They control the military. They control the federal judiciary. They control the money of corporate special interests. They control powerful right-wing grassroots organizations. They control a conservative media that includes radio, television, print, and websites. They control an array of right-wing think tanks.

About the only thing they can't control is their lust for power.

This absolute power has corrupted the Republicans, absolutely. This tremendous concentration of power has corrupted our democracy, degraded our military, diminished our stature in the world, damaged our environment, bankrupted our Treasury, and indentured our children to foreign debt-holders.

There is one reason and one reason only the Bush Republicans enjoy this unchallenged power:

Democrats let them win it.

By being too timid or too weak, too hesitant or too confused, Democrats have allowed Republicans to run amok. Most important, Democrats have not clearly and courageously stated what they stand for and what they stand against.

It is the goal of this book to do just that. We've spent our adult lifetimes toiling in the Democratic vineyards. We love our country and we love our party and we're determined to take them back.

If you're looking for a book that merely bashes the Republicans, this will disappoint. We take a backseat to no one in our contempt for what the GOP is doing to our country. And this book catalogs the damage in some detail. But more important, the purpose of this book is to look unflinchingly at what Democrats must do and say in order to take back our party, our country, and our future.

To be sure, we don't have all the answers. But we've got a good start on them. Not because we're geniuses—rather, because we're not. Too many Democrats over-think things. This is politics, not organic chemistry. Success has less to do with brains than with guts. The concepts are comparatively easy; it's the execution that's hard. Democrats have failed at the basics: defining their message, attacking their opponents, defending their leaders, inspiring their voters.

When we set out to write this book, we took a hard look at what the Bush-Cheney team did right and what the Kerry-Edwards team did wrong in the 2004 campaign. The short answer is, everything. Researching and writing that chapter was painful. We had to confront the reality that, in some cases, people we've considered friends for decades made terrible strategic and tactical decisions—and their failure has given us four more years of the Bush-Cheney policies we believe are ruining our country.

Some of our friends in the progressive movement believe the answer is for Democrats to rally the base, to move more squarely to the left. They see a Democratic Party that is too close to corporate special interests, too eager to please big money, too willing to sell out working people, too quick to go along with an unwise and unjust war.

On the other hand, some of our friends in the center believe the answer to the Democrats' problems is to move to the center. They see a Democratic party in thrall to Hollywood bigshots and cultural elites. They see a party too beholden to liberal pressure groups like the National Abortion and Reproductive Rights Action League, too contemptuous of people of faith, too dismissive of the middle-class values moms and dads try to pass on to their children.

They are, in our view, like the proverbial blind people examining the donkey (hey, we're Democrats; we can't very well use an elephant analogy). They're both right and they're both wrong. They each have a point and they both miss the point. Sure, we want the Democrats to stand more forcefully against corporate greed and we are still angry that so many leading Democrats believed Mr. Bush's falsehoods and supported his march to war in Iraq. At the same time, we believe some liberal pressure groups have too much influence, that some left-wing intellectual elites truly do have contempt for traditional American values. We believe Democrats should be the party of family, faith, and flag.

Here's what both sides of this false choice get wrong: the problem with the Democratic Party is not ideological, it's anatomical. We lack a backbone. Consider this book an attempt at a spinal transplant.

It's not that people know what we stand for and disagree; it's that they have no idea what we stand for, and so they think we're too weak to lead. The Bible says no one will follow an uncertain trumpet. The purpose of this book is hand the Democrats a trumpet and teach 'em to blow like Gabriel himself.

This book is focused on a set of issues that we believe have cost Democrats elections—issues that we believe we can Take Back. We believe we can Take Back national security, social issues, and taxes. We believe we can Take Back the issues of energy and the environment; we can Take Back the fairness of the media; we can Take Back the issue of health care; and we can Take Back our political system from the lobbyists and power brokers. We can Take Back all of those issues—but to do so we've got to stand up and speak out.

When the current President Bush's father was running for president in 1988, Senator Daniel Patrick Moynihan observed that if we can't beat these guys, we need to find another country. Of course, in 1988 Democrats couldn't beat Bush Sr.'s team—and we didn't find another country. We know how Moynihan must have felt, however. After all the damage of the first term of George W. Bush, it was hard to imagine how the Democrats could have lost to those guys. And yet a combination of the Bush campaign's strategic brilliance and the Democrats' lack of a clear message and a strategy for delivering it sent George W. Bush back to the White House for a second term.

We wrote this book, in short, because we're sick of watching Democrats lose. We're also sick of Democrats whining about the Republicans' hardball tactics. We want our party to toughen up, smarten up, and listen up.

The stakes could not be higher. President Bush was re-elected despite the fact that a near-majority of Americans believed he was not doing a good job. Since then his position with the American people has only deteriorated. And yet Democrats seem unable to capitalize on the Bush/GOP collapse.

The debacle of the 2004 election gave birth to this book. As we prepared to write it, we met with some of the smartest, savviest people in American politics. We talked with them about the issues that were hurting Democrats. And we thought about how to take those issues back. Those conversations were enlightening, but the one light-bulb moment Paul had actually came from his twelve-year-old son, John.

Paul and John were driving out to their farm in the Shenandoah Valley in October, 2004. It was a beautiful fall day so they decided to take the back-roads to enjoy the scenery. They passed a trailer on the side of the road. It was a little old, a little rundown. And it had a brand-new Bush-Cheney sign in the window. "Dad," John asked, "why are those folks for Bush and Cheney if you say they only care about the rich? And why are we for Kerry and Edwards if you say Democrats care about the poor? We're not poor."

We had a long talk about it. We discussed why, for many people, values trump economics. And we talked about how wrong some Democratic intellectual elites are when they denigrate working-class people who vote Republican. They condescendingly argue the Republicans have pulled the wool over their eyes; that they've been tricked into voting against their economic self-interest. We think that analysis is overblown. It just might be that these folks know full-well that the GOP doesn't represent their economic interests, but they've come to think the Democrats don't respect their culture and values and religion. Just as many rich liberals proudly vote against their economic self-interest, that working-class family living in that trailer is doing the same thing. When forced to make a choice, they go with their values, not their wallets. Why is it we celebrate prosperous progressives for voting against their economic self-interests, but denigrate poor and middle-class people who do?

The conclusion of that talk was the realization that rather than patronize poor people who put their principles ahead of their pocketbooks, Democrats need to make that choice unnecessary. We can and should represent both. Democrats need to show respect for voters' cultural concerns, while fighting for their economic interests. The problem is the values debate has been limited to a bizarre and tiny set of issues—principally abortion, gay rights and gun control. But poverty is a values issue. Lack of health care is a values issue. The minimum wage is a values issue. Lying about a war is the ultimate values issue. In this book we suggest ways both to Take Back the more narrow values issue—engage rather than ignore God, guns, and gays—and to expand the range of issues values voters should consider.

This book is a blueprint—a call to arms—for Democrats to give voice to their beliefs. To stand up proudly and speak out strongly that *both* our economic ideas and our moral values are more in line with those of most Americans than the Republicans are. Most of all, this book is an effort to take back so much of what we've lost: not just power and position in Washington, but something more important—the soul of a great party and the future of a great nation.

"Houston, We Have a Problem"

When astronaut Jim Lovell uttered those words from Apollo 13, it was one of the great understatements of American history. An explosion had ruptured an oxygen tank. The spacecraft was essentially rudderless, the crew without a road map to get back on track. As Lovell described it, "Our normal supply of electricity, light, and water was lost, and we were about two hundred thousand miles from Earth." [1]

The skinny guys in the skinny ties back at NASA knew this was most definitely a problem. And that's what made them different from the Democratic Party at the dawn of the twenty-first century.

There are still several leading Democrats who think we don't have a problem. They look at the 2000 election and point out that Al Gore won. We agree, he did—and not just the popular vote. A sensible examination of the ballots in Florida shows that Gore carried that state, and therefore the electoral college. [2]

But in the zeal to blame Ralph Nader and Katherine Harris and Chief Justice Rehnquist, Democrats (including us) failed to ask the bigger question: How could the incumbent party, running in a time of peace and prosperity, make the election close enough for the Republicans to steal?

If 2000 should have been a wake-up call, 2004 was an old-fashioned ass-kicking. And yet, say the "No Problem" Democrats, we almost won. We won the moderate vote, they say. We won the independent vote, they say. And if you add up the totals in the eighteen battleground states, apparently we won them, too. Moreover, if just sixty thousand people in Ohio (fewer than turn out for an Ohio State game) had switched sides, Senator John Kerry would be President John Kerry.

The only thing is: We lost the White House. As Casey Stengel said, "You could look it up."

This bizarre logic is like us telling our wives that if they take out their contacts, squint their eyes real tight, cock their heads, and turn off the lights, we look like George Clooney and Brad Pitt. You can do that, but it doesn't make us actually look like Clooney and Pitt.

Now open your eyes, put your contacts back in, and look at the reality. We're realists, so we know how bleak things have gotten for the Democrats of late. John Kerry's defeat at the hands of George W. Bush was a calamity for our nation and the world. But it was also a symptom of the catastrophe that has befallen the party we love. Not only did George W. Bush win on November 2, 2004, so did the Republican candidate for Senate in Oklahoma, Tom Coburn, who called for the death penalty for doctors who perform abortions. He also called his state's legislators "crapheads." And he decried "rampant lesbianism" in Oklahoma schools. He won. By 12 percent.[3] Against Democratic congressman Brad Carson, who is a Rhodes Scholar, a former Defense Department official, and a member in good standing of the First Baptist Church of Claremore, Oklahoma—not exactly a dangerous extremist.[4]

Perhaps worse, if that's possible, Jim Bunning won. The Hall of Fame pitcher with the Detroit Tigers and the Philadelphia Phillies went from being a reliable right-hander to being a flaky ultra-right-winger. He said his opponent, a respected physician named Daniel Mongiardo, looked like one of Saddam Hussein's sons. Bunning also claimed that Mongiardo, or Mongiardo's staff, roughed up his wife—with no evidence to back it up. And after promising to debate Mongiardo, Bunning refused to show up, preferring instead to debate via satellite from Washington with the aid of a teleprompter. Bunning, who isn't recognized as a senator even when he's in the halls of the Capitol, said he needed a large security detail to protect him from al Qaeda terrorists. "There may be strangers among us," he murmured darkly to a

Paducah, Kentucky, television station. It got so bad that Louisville's *Courier-Journal* hinted at mental illness: "Is his increasing belligerence an indication of something worse? Has Sen. Bunning drifted into territory that indicates a serious health concern?"[5]

And Bunning won. You know what that means? We couldn't beat an alleged nutcase in a swing state.

Or take Jim DeMint, who ran for Senate calling for a 23 percent national sales tax to replace the income tax. And he said gays and pregnant women with live-in boyfriends should be banned from teaching. Of course, since he also supported outlawing abortion, DeMint's plan would put a pregnant, unwed teacher in a hell of a bind. In DeMint's world, she couldn't have the baby—she'd lose her job for being pregnant. And she couldn't have an abortion—she'd go to jail.[6]

DeMint won. Against the popular and successful state education commissioner, Inez Tanenbaum.

We point out these victorious Republican wack jobs not to depress you, nor to amuse you. We do so to alarm you. If we can't beat these clowns, we ought to find another country to run in.

And yet we couldn't beat them.

Not because we didn't have good candidates; Carson, Mongiardo, and Tennenbaum are high-quality people who would have excelled in the Senate. Rather, we lost because, as corporate marketers would say, there's something wrong with Brand D. Brand R is strong enough to sustain even weak candidates, while Brand D is so weak even a good candidate can't win with it in a tough state.

You can blame John Kerry if it makes you feel better. But the problem is much bigger than one candidate in one campaign. The problem, in part, is that on some important issues, people think Democrats are out of step with the mainstream. But the bigger problem is that people don't know what it is the party stands for. That's a problem we must solve.

Time for the Donkeys to Kick Some Ass

It's high time—indeed, past time—for Democrats to take back the country. Democrats in the post-Clinton era have come to be a modern-day Mount Losemore, and yet, despite the failings of the past, they are positioned for a comeback. We believe that if Democrats think a little more and fight a lot more, they can be the dominant party in American politics once again—and deep into the twenty-first century.

Some of the keys to taking back power are tactical. Some of them are cultural. But most of them are existential. Democrats must say loud and clear what it is they believe in. If we want to take our country back, we must first take our party back—back from the mushy-spined mealy-mouthed wimps; back from the Pollyannas who deny there's a problem; back from the accommodationists who think being a lighter shade of Republican is the key to survival.

While we mourn the loss of House and Senate seats, the White House has always been the big enchilada of American politics. So take a look at the presidential map from 2004. The Kerry-Edwards ticket lost the entire South, most of the Midwest, and all of the Rocky Mountain States. They carried only eight states outside the Northeast.

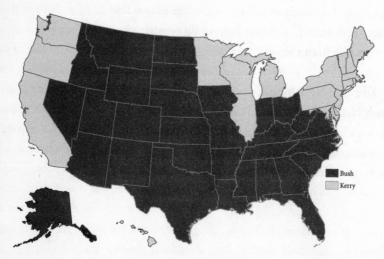

Source: http://www.cscs.umich.edu/~crshalizi/election/

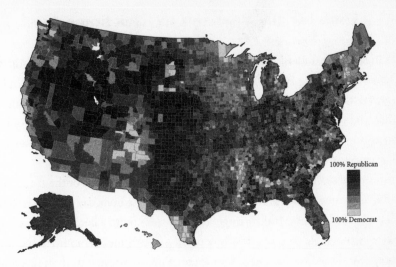

Source: http://www.cscs.umich.edu/~crshalizi/election/

And when you look closer, the picture gets worse. The county-by-county map is downright frightening.

Sure, some of that is because Bush-Cheney carried lots of counties where there are more pine trees than people. But according to an analysis by Ron Brownstein and Richard Rainey of the *Los Angeles Times,* Republicans carried 97 of the 100 fastest-growing countries.[7] Many of these counties are what demographers call "exurbs"—fast-growing places that are farther out from cities than bedroom communities. Brownstein and Rainey call them "the new frontier between suburbs and the countryside."[8] Bush carried 94 of these counties in 2000, but back then they gave him only a margin of 1.06 million votes; in 2004 they gave him a cushion of 1.7 million votes.

Why? Many of these communities are bursting at the seams with young families. The Bush campaign made these communities their top geographic priority and pitched a values-based message tailor-made for people who think their children are threatened by a culture that's out of control. The Republicans' pitch that they're "regular guys," while Democrats are cultural and intellectual elitists who look down their noses at middle-class values, has real power in these places. Robert E. Lang, director of the Metropolitan Institute at Virginia Tech, told the *L.A. Times* he thinks voters in the exurbs can be understood this way: "I think their conservatism is born out of a feeling that

Bush looks like a regular guy, and the Democrats are all snots and they are not addressing my concerns."[9]

Even in states Democrats carried, the margins were narrow, and the GOP made inroads. Take Pennsylvania, a key swing state the Democrats carried in both 2000 and 2004. But look at the results by county for the last three elections, and you see the erosion from Clinton's big blue win to Kerry's carrying just the most populous counties. Southwestern Pennsylvania has counties that went for McGovern but which Kerry lost. If the trend continues, color Pennsylvania red in the 2008 election.

When you switch the analysis from geography to demography, the results aren't any better. In 2000, George W. Bush lost to Al Gore by 11 percent among women. In 2004 he lost by only 3 percent. He did so by trouncing Kerry among married women, 55 percent to 44 percent.[10] And while Gore won a whopping 58 percent of the votes of working women, Kerry managed an anemic 51 percent. Combine Bush's improvement among women with his dominance of the male vote (which he won, 55 percent), and you see why Bush carried the popular vote in 2004.[11]

Or let's look at religion. You would think the first Catholic presidential nominee since JFK would dominate the Catholic vote as Kennedy did. You would be wrong. The Kerry-Edwards ticket could not even muster a majority, getting just 47 percent.[12]

In 1992, Clinton-Gore beat Bush-Quayle by nine points among Catholics, and in 1996 the Democratic ticket won a majority (53 percent) of Catholics.[13] In 2000 the Gore-Lieberman ticket won Catholics 50 to 47.

In 2004, however, George W. Bush combined his gains among Catholics with a solid 59 percent of the Protestant vote—a 3 percent improvement from 2000.[14]

When you look at education, it's not much better. Bush tied Kerry among college graduates but stomped him by six points (53 to 47) among noncollege folks.

All in all, there's not a lot of great news in the 2004 election returns. But there ought to be some valuable lessons.

A Very Different Map

A dozen years earlier, the map was very different.

Sure, we love our old boss Bill Clinton, but even those who hate him have to admit he's one of the great talents in American political history. In 1992 he carried thirty-two states plus the District of Columbia. He won four states in the Deep South—Georgia, Louisiana, Tennessee, and Arkansas. He beat George H. W. Bush in border states like Kentucky, West Virginia, and Missouri. He swept through midwestern states like Ohio, Iowa, and Michigan. He carried western states like Nevada, New Mexico, and Colorado. Hell, he even won Montana. Look at the map. Clinton won states in every region.

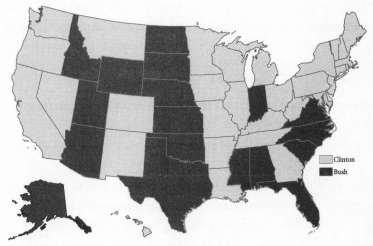

Source: http://www.gwu.edu/~action/maps9296.html

And don't believe the old line of bull about Ross Perot handing all those states to Clinton. Perot voters told the exit pollsters as they were leaving the voting booths that they were overwhelmingly disenchanted with President Bush. The fifteen-thousand-person exit poll of 1992 (which, unlike some more recent exit polls, was actually quite accurate) found that 81 percent of Perot's voters said they disapproved of Bush's handling of the economy—and they said the economy was the central issue in that election, followed by the deficit and health care.[15] Fifty-three percent of Perot's voters described themselves as moderate (as did 54 percent of Clinton's voters; Bush voters were far more conservative: Only 41 percent described themselves as moderate).[16] Perot's voters were also strikingly secular—and pro-choice.[17] In order to believe that Perot took voters from Bush, you'd have to believe that voters who thought Bush had done a terrible job on the economy; who thought the economy, the deficit, and health care were the major issues; who described themselves as moderate; and who were pro-choice would have preferred Bush—a conservative, pro-life president who was responsible for the bad economy. Nonsense. Everything we know about politics tells us that if Perot hadn't been in the race, Clinton would have done even better against Bush.

Finally—and definitively—38 percent percent of Perot voters said they would have voted for Clinton if Perot hadn't been on the ballot; 37 percent said they would have voted for Bush. Face it: Clinton would have won a slightly bigger victory if Perot hadn't been in the race.[18]

Americans Wanted to Fire George W. Bush

As much fun as it is to revel in Bill Clinton's success in 1992, let's get back to 2004.

George W. Bush is the first incumbent president since Harry Truman to be reelected with a job approval rating below 50 percent in the year he was running.[19] What's more, even as they were voting for Bush, the majority of Americans were saying the country was moving in the wrong direction. To be sure, some of the Bush voters thought the country was going in the wrong direction because of what they saw as collapsing moral values and a corrupt culture. But still, it's unheard of for a president to win when most of his fellow Americans think their country is headed in the wrong direction.

Why was Bush so vulnerable? The economic statistics read like an indictment: Eight million Americans were out of work on Election Day 2004.[20] America lost 2.7 million manufacturing jobs in George W. Bush's first term.[21] Overall, the economy lost a net of 821,000 jobs under Bush, making him the first president since Hoover to preside over a loss of jobs.[22]

Census data show that the poverty rate, which had fallen every year Clinton was in office, had risen every year under Bush;[23] the number of people without health insurance rose to a record high of 45 million; and median household income was as stagnant as one of the man-made ponds on Bush's ranch in Crawford.[24]

When he was inaugurated in 2001, George W. Bush inherited the largest budget surplus in American history. Over ten years, it was projected to be $5.6 trillion.[25] And in just four years he'd turned it into the largest deficit in history—a ten-year debt of $5.2 trillion.[26] We aren't exactly math majors, but that looks to be a $10.8 trillion reversal in just four years.

And then there's Iraq. By Election Day, 1,121 heroes had lost their lives in Bush's war. Another 8,355 had been wounded.[27] National Guard and Reserve members—and their families—were being whipsawed by extended deployments and canceled returns. The taxpayers were spending about $5 billion a month to maintain operations in Iraq.[28] On Election Day, the majority of Americans said things were going badly in Iraq.[29]

So why did Democrats lose in 2004?

You've Got to Stand for Something or You'll Fall for Anything

We believe that the lack of a clear, simple, consistent message was the greatest shortcoming of Democrats in 2004. The Bush message was everything ours wasn't. One of President Bush's top strategists told us after the election. "From day one we talked about three things: strength, trust, and values."[30] In their story, Bush embodied all of those things, and John Kerry had none of them.

President Bush's first slogan, "Steady Leadership in a Time of Change," was, a Bush strategist told us, initially conceived with an eye toward a challenge from Howard Dean.[31] Indeed, the Bush campaign secretly made an ad showing the desk in the Oval Office unoccupied. The camera slowly pushed in toward the desk as the announcer intoned that this was a dangerous world and asked whom the audience wanted sitting behind that desk if tragedy struck. But when Howard Dean flamed out and John Kerry emerged as the Democratic front-runner, a frustrated Bush campaign learned from focus groups that their ad no longer worked: Voters saw Kerry as a steady and strong presence at that Oval Office desk (whereas they did not think that about Dean).[32]

What to do? Team Bush decided to recalibrate its "Steady Leadership" message away from "steady versus crazy" (Bush versus Dean) to "steady versus changing with the political winds." Even though voters initially saw Kerry as strong and steady enough to occupy the Oval Office, the Bush campaign decided to portray Kerry as unsteady—not in the sense of being unstable but in terms of being too uncertain and too political to guide the country in a crisis.

Kerry, the winner of the Silver Star for heroism, the Bronze Star for valor, and three Purple Hearts for being wounded for his country, was caricatured as embodying the three W's—weak, waffling, and weird.

Once the Bush campaign settled on "strong and certain versus weak, waffling, and weird," the issues almost selected themselves. Hence, the question of why Kerry voted against $87 billion to fund the war in Iraq became a bigger issue than health care. Why? Because it fit into a narrative. Bush alleged that Kerry had flip-flopped on funding our troops, and that he'd done so for political reasons. If true, that would mean Kerry was both weak on defense and too weak to stand up to political pressure. And Kerry's comment about "voting for the $87 billion before I voted against it" was just fuel for the fire. When you know your message is "strong and certain versus weak, waffling, and weird," a Bush strategist told us, the ads pretty much write themselves. The image of Kerry windsurfing became a natural metaphor for tacking one way and then the next. Having a message allows voters to make sense of the specific issues. Not having a message causes issues to lose their resonance.

What was the Democrats' message? What values did Kerry embody that Bush lacked? What story was Kerry telling the American people?

Our friends who ran the Kerry campaign (and they really are our friends) continue to insist they did have a message. Proof that denial, as they say, is not just a river in Egypt. Here's what they called a message:

J-HOS.

That's right: J-HOS. (It's pronounced "Jay-Hose," by the way.) It stands for:

> **J**—Jobs
> **H**—Health Care
> **O**—Oil
> **S**—Security

That, of course, is a litany, not a narrative. Calling "J-HOS" a message is like calling a supermarket full of food a gourmet meal.

Instead of telling a story, Democrats focused on issues. They talked about the economy. They talked about health care. They talked about the environment. They talked about Iraq. They talked about prescription drugs and Social Security. They talked about equal rights and women's rights and gay rights.

They talked and they talked, but voters weren't listening or, more accurately, couldn't hear any message in the laundry list of issues. Without a message, Democrats were, if you'll pardon the expression, J-HOSED.

Presidential elections just aren't about issues, per se. Sure, ideas matter. But without context, it's hard to make sense of issues. We believe that when they're voting in a race for an executive position, voters do not walk into the booth with a tick list of issues, the way they might for a legislative position. Choosing a president is a powerful act of self-definition. It's more than the sum of specific issues; it's about the candidate and the story. Bob Dole said it pretty well in 1996 when he remarked that asking people for their vote for president is like asking them who they would rather raise their kids for them if they died. (Unfortunately for Dole, voters preferred Bill and Hillary Clinton on that score in 1996.)

President Bush and his team believed presidential elections are about character, and so they talked about values. Senator Kerry and his team believed presidential elections are about issues, and so they talked about policy proposals: Bush's team was right; Kerry's team was wrong. Democrats approached the campaign with a checklist. Bush screwed up the economy: here's our economic plan. Bush has done nothing on health care; here's our health plan. Bush has botched the war on Iraq; here are our views on foreign policy. But absent an overarching story—or a clear, specific rationale for firing Bush and hiring Kerry—the campaign's issue litany didn't have any resonance. Or, as Bush has said, "It didn't resignate with voters."[33] Sure, he mangles the nomenclature, but Bush damn sure understands the concept.

The political scientist Sam Popkin helped us understand this back in 1992, when he introduced us to his theory of low-information rationality. In laymen's terms (at least in underachieving state school terms) it's this: Voters infer. They reach broader conclusions based on the limited information they have.

Here's an example. We once had a client who was endorsed by the gay community, who was a strong environmentalist, and who was very pro-union. If we gave you that information—and nothing more—and then we asked you what you thought his position on abortion rights was, you'd say pro-choice. And you'd be wrong. That client was the late Pennsylvania governor Bob Casey. Why would you infer that he was pro-choice? None of the issues has any logical, linear connection to abortion. But (and here's where Dr. Popkin's theory comes in) you didn't simply say, "Gee, guys, you didn't give me any information about abortion." You reasoned. You inferred. You used your gut, your intuition, your common sense. You filled in the blanks. Popkin says it's like a constellation—a point here, a point there, and then you connect the dots in a way that makes sense.

We put Popkin's theory to the test in the 1992 Clinton campaign. As we began winning primaries, here was what voters knew about Clinton: He'd been accused of infidelity; he'd been accused of dodging the draft; he'd been a Rhodes Scholar; and he'd gone to Georgetown and Yale Law School. They took those stars and created a constellation of a spoiled, rich brat who never had to work for anything in his life. Voters initially thought Clinton was a product of privilege: a trust-fund baby who dodged the draft, tooled around in his daddy's convertible, and had no sense of what their lives and their struggles were all about. (Come to think of it, they thought he was George W. Bush.)

So Clinton moved quickly to put a few more stars in the constellation.

He told them about the Man from Hope—about how his poor mother had been widowed even before he was born. About how his grandparents had taken care of him while his mother studied to be a nurse. About how he'd grown up poor, worked his way through college, been inspired to public service by meeting John F. Kennedy.

In 1992 we combined the contrast of the candidates' personal stories with voter anger about a president who, we said, had no new ideas to help people in a stagnant economy. Our message was CHANGE VERSUS MORE OF THE SAME. That's what was written at the top of the sign in the Little Rock war room—above THE ECONOMY, STUPID. Clinton's 1992 campaign told a story of the need for change in the middle class. The specifics of the economy and health care were illustrations of that story, not the story itself.

The overarching message—the master narrative, if you will—must precede the specific issues. A clear message allows voters to make sense of specific issues. Not having a message causes issues to lose their resonance.

War Matters

No president has ever lost reelection in wartime.

In 1864 the nation was still battered by civil war. Lincoln had enraged conservatives with his Emancipation Proclamation and had angered liberals by reversing John C. Frémont's attempts to free the slaves in Missouri when the senator was serving as Union commander in the western United States. (How's that for a flip-flop?) Lincoln looked so vulnerable that even his vice president, Hannibal Hamlin, considered opposing him. Other Republicans were touting General Ulysses S. Grant and Treasury Secretary Salmon P. Chase.

The Democrats, meanwhile, nominated Union general George McClellan, whom Lincoln had fired. The Democrats' platform called for a cease-fire and a negotiated settlement with the South. McClellan himself merely said he'd prosecute the war more competently than Lincoln. (Sound familiar?)

But before McClellan could get up a head of steam, General William Tecumseh Sherman captured and burned Atlanta, and Lincoln was reelected on the slogan "Don't change horses in the middle of the stream."[34]

In 1900, William McKinley was running for reelection. McKinley had successfully prosecuted the Spanish-American War, which was won in just four months and was dubbed a "splendid little war." [35] But, perhaps emboldened by the support he received from his first little war, McKinley decided to launch a second war—this one to "liberate" the Philippines. By 1900, 120,000 American troops were bogged down in an occupation of the Philippines, and 4,200 American soldiers had been killed by insurgents who did not appreciate McKinley's attempt to occupy their country. (Gee, why does that sound familiar?) McKinley argued that he was trying to help the Filipinos. He told a group of his fellow Methodists gathered at the White House that he was intent on bringing Christianity to the Philippines. The astonished guests were too polite to point out to the president that the Philippines had been evangelized by the Spanish some three hundred years earlier.[36] Americans did not approve of McKinley's occupation of the Philippines, but like it or not, America was at war, and McKinley was our commander. He was reelected handily over William Jennings Bryan.[37]

In 1944, Franklin Roosevelt sought an unprecedented fourth term, even though his health was failing. The Republican nominee, Thomas Dewey, attacked the sixty-two-year-old FDR as "a tired old man." [38] Republicans also implied that FDR had known about Pearl Harbor in advance but had done nothing. At the 1944 GOP Convention, Clare Booth Luce said FDR had "lied us into war" (déjà vu all over again).[39] Republicans also questioned FDR's stance on communism and his competence as an administrator. FDR flat out stole Lincoln's slogan, "Don't change horses in midstream." And, like Lincoln, he won.[40]

In 1972 the country was bitterly divided over Vietnam. Dissatisfaction with the war had already claimed the political career of Lyndon Johnson. But Richard Nixon persuaded the country that war hero George McGovern was too weak on national security, and Republicans slammed Democrats, calling them the party of "abortion, acid and amnesty." Nixon won in one of the great landslides of American presidential history.[41]

George W. Bush and his team no doubt, were fully mindful of this history in 2004. From day one, they wanted to stress that America was at war. Like McClellan in 1864 and McGovern in 1972, John Kerry had a much more impressive military career than the incumbent president, but it didn't matter. As in 1900, even an unpopular occupation with Americans being gunned down by insurgents half a world away failed to turn voters against the incumbent. Americans just do not like changing horses in midstream.

That was why the Republicans scheduled their convention in New York City, just miles from Ground Zero and days from the anniversary of the September 11 attacks. That was why the first image in Bush's first ad featured a flag-draped body being carried from the wreckage of the World Trade Center. That was why the second sentence of his convention speech got straight to 9/11: "In the heart of this great city, we saw tragedy arrive on a quiet morning. We saw the bravery of rescuers grow with danger. We learned of passengers on a doomed plane who died with a courage that frightened their killers. We have seen a shaken economy rise to its feet. And we have seen Americans in uniform storming mountain strongholds, and charging through sandstorms, and liberating millions, with acts of valor that would make the men of Normandy proud." [42] In the middle of the speech, Bush returned to 9/11, telling his audience, "Three days after September the eleventh, I stood where Americans died, in the ruins of the Twin Towers. Workers in hard hats were shouting to me, 'Whatever it takes.' A fellow grabbed me by the arm, and he said, 'Do not let me down.' Since that day, I wake up every morning thinking about how to better protect our country. I will never relent in defending America, whatever it takes." [43] He concluded his speech with his umpteenth reference to 9/11: "My fellow Americans, for as long as our country stands, people will look to the resurrection of New York City, and they will say: 'Here buildings fell; here a nation rose.' " [44] And yet for all those references to 9/11, Bush did not mention that he'd spent precious minutes after the attack reading *The Pet Goat* to schoolchildren in Florida; nor that he'd retreated to Louisiana, then Nebraska, on that fateful day, leaving Vice President Dick Cheney to tell military pilots to shoot down civilian aircraft.

The speech was not an aberration. From the beginning of the campaign to the end, Bush used 9/11 as the answer to everything, no matter the substance of the issue. If the issue was the deficit, the president's answer was 9/11.[45] The loss of jobs? September 11. Drought in the Midwest? September

11. No matter what the question was, 9/11 was the answer. No Democrat dared mention that six weeks before 9/11, the president had been warned by American intelligence that "Bin Laden Determined to Attack Inside U.S." [46]

Voters Love Negative Campaigning

If 9/11 was Bush's shield, he made sure he also had a sword, with which he relentlessly attacked. Presidential reelection campaigns are generally referenda on the incumbent. But as the 2004 elections approached, the president's team knew that after four years of George W. Bush, voters were not convinced they wanted another four. The percentage of voters who approved of the job Bush was doing hovered dangerously below 50 percent. After all the unimaginable things we'd been through—9/11, the war in Afghanistan, the invasion of Iraq, even the Red Sox winning the World Series—voters' views of George W. Bush were right back where they'd been when the Republican-dominated Supreme Court installed him as president in 2000.

And so, from the first day to the last, Bush and Cheney attacked Kerry. Bush strategists told us it was imperative that they make the election "a choice, not a referendum." [47]

Think about that: a choice, not a referendum. With the president's approval rating below 50 percent, they knew he would lose a referendum on his leadership: In other words, if he'd been unopposed, he would have lost. And the Bush strategists were probably right. If the presidential election had been like the California gubernatorial recall vote that dumped Gray Davis, Bush likely would have met the same fate as Davis. So they made a clear-eyed, cold-blooded decision to posit the election as a choice, not a referendum.

The Bush-Cheney campaign had three priorities: attack, attack, attack. When it looked like Howard Dean would be the Democratic nominee, Bush strategists loaded up on Dean attacks. They were prepared to attack him as a liberal who signed gay civil unions into law; as a peacenik who would not defend America; as a wild-eyed hothead whose hand you wouldn't want on the rudder of the ship of state.

When Kerry surged past Dean, Team Bush simply swung their howitzers toward the man from Massachusetts. The obvious attack would have been "Massachusetts liberal." The two words are so linked in the Republican lexicon, they might as well be Eng and Chang, the original so-called Siamese twins. The Bushies could have joined Kerry at the hip with, say, Michael Dukakis, for whom he served as lieutenant governor. Or Ted Kennedy, with whom he serves in the Senate. They could have attacked Kerry's opposition to the death penalty and his support for tax increases and abortion rights: the standard Republican attack. While there was some of that, they actually took a different tack—a narrative they settled on surprisingly early and from which they rarely deviated.

In April 2003, nineteen months before the election, Bush's attack dogs were already savaging Kerry. Carefully coordinated attacks forced Kerry to spend days explaining why he'd called for "regime change" for America. But these were just minor jabs, in the manner of a fighter who prods his opponent in the early rounds to test his defenses. The Bush team didn't find much of a defense from the Democrats.

A year and a half before the election, Bush aides unveiled what was to be their main theme—their negative master narrative. They launched a massive campaign to define their opponent before he defined himself.

Their strategy was simple and deadly. One of the most powerful indictments in American politics is "He's not one of us." If a candidate is seen as someone who does not live your life, does not share your values, and is not someone you'd like to have a beer with, chances are that candidate is never going to be president. So the Bushies went to work, telling *The New York Times* that Kerry was ideologically and culturally out of step with mainstream America. Kerry was to be painted as weak, waffling, and weird. "He looks French," sniffed one Bush strategist—whatever that means.[48]

By May 2004—months before Kerry had even accepted his party's nomination—the Bush-Cheney campaign had aired an astonishing 49,050 negative ads in the top hundred media markets. The incumbent's campaign was devoting 75 percent of its advertising budget to slamming Kerry.[49]

An early Bush-Cheney ad contrasted a leader of "confidence, resolve, and hope" against someone who held the "dangerous illusion that terrorists are not plotting and outlaw regimes are no threat."[50] This was a positive ad. Or was it? Implicit is the sense that Kerry must not be a leader of "confidence, resolve, and hope." Like any successful political message, Bush's interwove the negative indictment of Kerry and the positive narrative of Bush. Every ode to Bush's strength suggested Kerry was weak; every attack on Kerry's alleged weakness harked back to Bush's strength. When you can discuss virtually any issue in a way that favors your candidate and disadvantages the opponent, you've got a message. And the Bush campaign most definitely had a message.

To be sure, there were a few small detours from "weak, waffling, and weird." Kerry was attacked on taxes—having supported gas tax increases and taxed Social Security benefits. But these were the exceptions. "Weak, waffling, and weird" was the rule.

Some of the attacks were about small things, meant to paint Kerry as an out-of-touch elitist. The Bush campaign or its allies attacked Kerry's suits, his homes, and his wealth—all intended to make Kerry look effete and elite, which is to say, both weak and weird.[51] Never mind the facts that Bush himself wears exclusive and expensive Oxxford suits (which can run up to $14,000 apiece);[52] that he owns a fifteen-hundred-acre, multimillion-dollar ranch, complete with a private lake stocked with his own private bass;[53] or that he is filthy rich.[54] Kerry was attacked for windsurfing even though a windsurfing board was a hell of a lot less expensive than the $250,000 cigarette boat (which one critic called "a penis extender") that Bush liked to zoom around in.[55]

Silliness aside, the heart of the Bush attack on Kerry—the ultimate expression of "weak, waffling, and weird"—was the flip-flop. Kerry was accused of flip-flopping on:

- the death penalty for terrorists[56]
- the Israeli security fence
- affirmative action
- releasing oil from the Strategic Petroleum Reserve
- free trade
- No Child Left Behind
- the Patriot Act
- NAFTA
- abortion
- ethanol

Of course, the most consequential flip-flop attacks centered on national security. Bush personally outlined the narrative slamming Kerry: "He voted for the use of force in Iraq and then didn't vote to fund the troops. He complained that we're not spending enough money to help in the reconstruction of Iraq, and now he's saying we're spending too much. He said it was the right decision to go into Iraq; now he calls it the wrong war." [57]

The portrait of Kerry as too weak and indecisive to lead during wartime was, as our former client Zell Miller would say, "unrelentless." This was no accident, but rather the result of careful coordination. Look at the focus and consistency of speeches from the Republican convention.

Here's what pro-choice, pro-gay-rights Republican Rudy Giuliani said at the Republican Convention:

> President Bush, a leader who is willing to stick with difficult decisions even as public opinion shifts, and John Kerry, whose record in elected office suggests a man who changes his position often even on important issues.

New York governor George Pataki certainly stayed on message:

> Well, what can we say of Senator Kerry? He was for the war and then he was against the war. Then he was for it but he wouldn't fund it. Then he'd fund it but he wasn't for it.

Here's Michael Steele, the lieutenant governor of Maryland:

> Senator Kerry's leadership is illustrated best by the senator himself when he said, "I actually voted for the $87 billion before I voted against it."

Dick Cheney also wielded the attack ax, saying,

> On Iraq, Senator Kerry has disagreed with many of his fellow Democrats. But Senator Kerry's liveliest disagreement is with himself. His back-and-forth reflects a habit of indecision and sends a message of confusion. And it is all part of a pattern.

And they were just the warm-up acts. Usually, incumbent presidents seeking reelection try to stay above the fray. They use surrogates to attack, if attacks are necessary. In 1984, Ronald Reagan ridiculed liberal ideas, but he never singled out Walter Mondale. In 1996, Bill Clinton was so confident that the American people wanted to keep him in office that he made this commitment in his convention address: "I believe that Bob Dole and Jack Kemp and Ross Perot love our country, and they have worked hard to serve it. It is legitimate, even necessary, to compare our record with theirs, our proposals for the future with theirs. And I expect them to make a vigorous effort to do the same. But I will not attack. I will not attack them personally or permit others to do it in this party if I can prevent it." [58]

Reagan and Clinton could afford to take the high road while offering contrasts between competing worldviews. Bush could not risk being so lofty. Again and again he directly attacked Kerry, either by name or as "my opponent." He portrayed himself as resolute, saying, "In the last four years, you and I have come to know each other. Even when we don't agree, at least you know what I believe and where I stand."

In his convention address, Bush returned to that theme, portraying Kerry as—you guessed it—weak, waffling, and weird:

> My opponent and I have different approaches. I proposed, and the Congress overwhelmingly passed, $87 billion in funding needed by our troops doing battle in Afghanistan and Iraq. My opponent and his running mate voted against this money for bullets, and fuel, and vehicles, and body armor. When asked to explain his vote, the senator said, "I actually did vote for the $87 billion before I voted against it." Then he said he was "proud" of that vote. Then, when pressed, he said it was a "complicated" matter. There is nothing complicated about supporting our troops in combat. . . .[59]

As strategists, we were impressed with the focus and clarity of the Republican message. They had a job to do, and they did it. It was, as the mobsters said in *The Godfather*, nothing personal. Just business.

The Democrats' Unilateral Surrender

Contrast the Republicans' attack machine with what we saw at the Democratic convention. Democrats actually had a rule that you could not attack Republicans. At the *Democratic* convention? Come on. It's like putting up a sign at Fenway Park that says, PLEASE DON'T BOO THE YANKEES. Most Americans are in the tradition of Alice Roosevelt Longworth, the daughter of President Theodore Roosevelt and the wife of House speaker Nicholas Longworth, who famously said, "If you haven't got something nice to say about someone, sit right here by me." [60]

The purpose of a political convention is to draw distinctions between your party and theirs, especially when you're out of power. FDR understood that. In 1932 he was trying to seize the White House from Herbert Hoover. In his convention address, Roosevelt noted that he was breaking the old tradition that a party's nominee should feign ignorance of the entire convention until weeks afterward, at which time he would formally accept the party's decision. Roosevelt used his break with outdated tradition as a metaphor for his candidacy—and as a club to beat the Republicans, saying, "We will break foolish traditions and leave it to the Republican leadership, far more skilled in that art, to break promises." [61]

FDR blamed the Depression squarely on the Republicans, ridiculing their defense that the whole world was in dire economic straits, and he said the Republican economic program "sees to it that a favored few are helped and hopes that some of their prosperity will leak through, sift through, to labor, to the farmer, to the small-business man. That theory belongs to the party of Toryism, and I had hoped that most of the Tories left this country in 1776." [62]

But Roosevelt's indictment of the Republicans was as much moral as economic. He decried their sinful selfishness, saying they'd given our country "a period of loose thinking, descending morals, an era of selfishness. . . . Republican leaders not only have failed in material things, they have failed in national vision, because in disaster they have held out no hope, they have pointed out no path for the people below to climb back to places of security and of safety in our American life." [63]

Harry Truman continued in Roosevelt's tradition. When he accepted the nomination in 1948, he put the wood to the GOP: "The Democratic Party is the people's party, and the Republican Party is the party of special interest, and it always has been and always will be." He vowed to "win this election and make the Republicans like it." He kept returning to the theme of a Republican Party that "favors the privileged few and not the common everyday man. Ever since its inception, that party has been under the control of special privilege." [64]

Those were the days. The tradition of Democrats playing hardball (and, by the way, winning) continued into the 1960s. In his ringing "New Frontier" address at the Democratic convention in Los Angeles, John F. Kennedy smacked Richard Nixon upside the head. Nixon, he said, "has often seemed to show charity towards none and malice for all." But Kennedy was just warming to the task: "We know it will not be easy to campaign against a man who has spoken and voted on every side of every issue. Mr. Nixon may feel that it's his turn now, after the New Deal and the Fair Deal—but before he deals, someone's going to cut the cards.

"'That 'someone' may be the millions of Americans who voted for President Eisenhower but would balk at his successor. For just as historians tell us that Richard the First was not fit to fill the shoes of the bold Henry the Second, and that Richard Cromwell was not fit to wear the mantle of his uncle, they might add in future years that Richard Nixon did not measure up to the footsteps of Dwight D. Eisenhower."

Kennedy seemed to relish mocking Nixon: "His approach is as old as McKinley. His party is the party of the past, the party of memory. His speeches are generalities from *Poor Richard's Almanac*. Their platform, made up of old, left-over Democratic planks, has the courage of our old convictions. Their pledge is to the status quo; and today there is no status quo." [65]

Throughout the rest of the 1960s, the Democratic Party was defined by Lyndon Johnson and Robert F. Kennedy. The two didn't like each other, but they hated Republicans even more. Each was accused of being ruthless.

In 2004 the Democrats weren't ruthless. They were toothless.

Lest you think this is all 20/20 hindsight, we remind you that, watching the convention in Boston, Paul got so frustrated that he publicly attacked the Democrats for not attacking, telling *Crossfire* viewers, "The Kerry campaign has decided they want to run as positive a convention as they can. I have to say, I like negative stuff, so I'm not very happy with their strategy, and I'm not participating in their strategy." [66] James went Paul one better, calling the Kerry campaign "a perpetual committee listening to a perpetual focus group." [67]

While the Republicans had a coordinated strategy of attacking, the Democrats carefully scrutinized speeches to ensure they were not too negative. One aide even tried to tell Clinton that *his* speech was too negative. Can you imagine the chutzpah (as we say down south) that took? If you recall Clinton's speech, it wasn't negative at all. It certainly offered a contrast between the competing visions of the two parties, but nothing even approaching the foam-at-the-mouth attacks of Dick Cheney's speech. As a newly wealthy man, Clinton thanked the Republicans for cutting taxes for him and his fellow rich folks. But then he described the cost of those tax cuts: kids kicked out of Head Start, cops laid off, schools without enough money, homeland security underfunded. We'd discussed the speech with him beforehand, and we were worried that it read more like a budget address than a rip-roaring convention speech. And yet the folks running the convention had the opposite fear—that Clinton would be too negative. Clinton smiled and said, "Don't worry, boys. I believe it'll work out fine."

And it did. In his warm and wonderful style, Clinton summarized the choice this way:

> We Americans must choose for president one of two strong men who both love our country but who have very different worldviews: Democrats favor shared responsibility, shared opportunity, and more global cooperation. Republicans favor concentrated wealth and power, leaving people to fend for themselves, and more unilateral action. I think we're right for two reasons: First, America works better when all people have a chance to live their dreams. Second, we live in an interdependent world in which we can't kill, jail, or occupy all our potential adversaries, so we have to both fight terror and build a world with more partners and fewer terrorists.
>
> We tried it their way for twelve years, our way for eight, and then their way for four more. By the only test that matters, whether people were better off when we finished than when we started, our way works

better—it produced over 22 million good jobs, rising incomes, and a hundred times as many people moving out of poverty into the middle class. It produced more health care, the largest increase in college aid in fifty years, record home ownership, a cleaner environment, three surpluses in a row, a modernized defense force, strong efforts against terror, and an America respected as a world leader for peace, security, and prosperity.[68]

That was too negative?

Top Kerry strategists told us they were even angrier with Jimmy Carter. Carter gave a serious, thoughtful critique of Bush's foreign policy. It had none of the derisive, contemptuous sarcasm of the speech by his fellow Georgian Zell Miller. Rather, it was classic Carter: rooted in a strong sense of morality, idealistic about America's potential to do good, and grieving for America's lost credibility. The man who was elected president because we craved decency and honor after the criminality of Richard Nixon returned to one of his most cherished themes—trust. "Truth is the foundation of our global leadership, but our credibility has been shattered and we are left increasingly isolated and vulnerable in a hostile world. Without truth—without trust—America cannot flourish. Trust is at the very heart of our democracy, the sacred covenant between the president and the people."[69] Carter did not mention George W. Bush by name. He didn't ridicule him the way the Republicans did Kerry. And yet Team Kerry was furious with Carter for being too negative. We remember thinking that if this Nobel Peace Prize winner, this pillar of rectitude and decency, was too mean for them, the Kerry folks were in real trouble.

The lack of a focused convention—and the lack of a clear reason to fire the president—denied Kerry the customary convention bounce. While most candidates gain ten points from their convention, Kerry added only a point or two.[70]

Why Didn't Democrats Attack Bush?

Democrats wrongly thought voters would be turned off by negative campaigning. Republicans understood that no matter what people say in focus groups, negative campaigning works—so long as it's seen as fair, as factual, and as being about issues rather than personal failings.

We were told by high-ranking Democratic strategists that they'd conducted focus groups in Dayton, Ohio, and the denizens of Dayton told them they didn't like negative campaigning. Our response was "And you believed them?"

Focus groups can be useful; Lord knows we've conducted and attended many. Here's how they work: You grab a dozen or so poor souls in a place like Dayton. In this case you focus on undecided voters. You sit them around a table in a room with a giant one-way mirror and microphones hanging from the ceiling, and a stranger asks them questions. You can gain valuable insights from focus groups, but you've got to know how to separate the beef from the bullshit. When the good people of Dayton said they didn't like negative campaigning, that was classic focus-group baloney. They were telling the moderator and a roomful of strangers what they thought they should say. If you'd asked them what they watched on TV, they'd have said, *MacNeil/Lehrer,* despite the fact that MacNeil hasn't hosted the show in years. None of them is going to say, "To hell with PBS. I just love *Desperate Housewives.* Nothing I like more than watching sluts in the suburbs on a Sunday night!"

But we Democrats are sometimes awfully literal. And so the edict went forth: Thou Shalt Not Attack Bush.

Let's be clear. We're not advocating willy-nilly, unfocused attacks or savage personal destruction. Far from it. What we're saying is that Democrats need a message that draws contrasts, one that says both what we're for and what we're against. There's a difference. When the radical Republicans tried to impeach President Clinton, when they attacked him personally and viciously, the attacks backfired. But that doesn't mean all attacks will backfire. Attacks on ideas and issues, attacks on policies and positions, and, most important, attacks on subjects that affect the real lives of real people—those kinds of attacks work. The distinction is important and was utterly lost on the Democrats in 2004. They were like the cat in Mark Twain's aphorism about the cat that sits on a hot stove—it will never sit on a hot stove again, but it'll never sit on a cold stove, either.

At one point James got so frustrated by the campaign's lack of a message that he tried an intervention. At a meeting with the Kerry high command he begged them to focus on a clear message. He became so upset that he broke down and cried. Paul tried, too. He commandeered a huge whiteboard in Kerry headquarters and covered it with twelve possible negative messages on Bush: from framing the election in terms of truthfulness (claiming Bush misled us about the war, the deficit, being a uniter and not a divider, funding education, and more); to casting Bush as out of touch with real people; to arguing that he's too rigid and ideological; to making the case that he was in over his head; to describing Bush as favoring the rich and special interests; to noting that he simply has the wrong priorities for America. Paul begged the campaign to pick one—any one would be better than nothing—and stick to it till the end.

Dream on. The campaign did not want a rationale to reject Bush. As one Kerry strategist lamented, "Our idea of a 'negative frame' is to say, 'Bush is taking us in the wrong direction.' Their idea of a negative frame is to say, 'Kerry is a coward, liar, and not fit to be president of the United States.' They're hitting us with a baseball bat and we're spitting on them."[71]

Bush's Brilliant Campaign

Lest this chapter become a litany of the Kerry team's failures, it's important to note that not only did our side do almost everything wrong, the other side did almost everything right. We've already shown you that they did the most important thing—choose a clear, consistent frame and then focus all their energy on it.

The Bush-Cheney '04 campaign also set a new standard for tactics. For generations Democrats have beaten Republicans at the ground game: the get-out-the-vote efforts staffed by door-knockers, phone-callers, precinct captains, and street-walkers (no, not that kind of street-walker; my goodness, you have a dirty mind).

After narrowly losing the popular vote in 2000, Bush and his strategists looked long and hard at what the Democrats had done to turn out their voters. Karl Rove had said there were four million conservative, Christian evangelicals who'd failed to turn out for Bush in 2000. He'd made it his mission to find them, motivate them, and bring them to the polls.

When we heard this, we were skeptical. Bush & Co. were proposing to change the composition of the electorate. In 2000, 54.3 percent of the eligible voting-age population turned out to vote—105.4 million voters in all. By 2004 that figure had leaped to 59.6 percent, or 120.2 million.[72] That's the largest one-cycle increase in over fifty years.[73]

The 2004 increase barely eclipsed the jump in turnout between the 1988 and 1992 presidential elections. It's easy to see why turnout surged in 1992—the economy was in bad shape, President George H. W. Bush ran a spirited campaign, H. Ross Perot, Jr., livened things up, and Bill Clinton wasn't a bad campaigner, either. But why the surge from 2000 to 2004? Both campaigns featured the Bush-Cheney ticket. Was Kerry-Edwards that much more charismatic than Gore-Lieberman? No. The war in Iraq doubtless played a major role. As did George W. Bush's uniquely polarizing effect. But a good bit of the credit for the increased turnout is due to the campaign tactics employed by Bush-Cheney '04.

First, never let any of the hand-wringers tell you negative campaigning depresses turnout: 2004 was the most negative campaign in history (at least for the winning side), yet turnout jumped way up.

Second, the Republicans excelled at targeting. Realizing that there were damned few persuadable voters, they decided to forgo the usual strategy of targeting the tiny percentage of undecided voters and chose instead to find and inspire conservatives who'd been staying home. It's hard for us to overstate how remarkable this accomplishment is. We've sat through hundreds of meetings in which Democrats pined and whined about how everything would be better if only we could persuade every American to vote. That's a common misperception. Nonvoters typically mirror voters. A survey of nonvoters in the 2000 election, for example, found them evenly split between Bush and Gore—just like voters.[74]

So, rather than target undecided voters, Bush's strategists focused most of their resources on "soft Republicans"—people who either weren't registered to vote or often just didn't show up. Team Bush did not merely target all non-voters. They targeted *conservative* nonvoters. They did this through high-tech microtargeting.

Rather than just looking at whether a neighborhood tended to vote Democratic or Republican, Bush strategists did an enormous amount of data mining. They looked at reams of consumer data and cross-referenced it with analyses of how consumer choices reveal political persuasion. For example, Volvo drivers are overwhelmingly Democratic (no surprise), while Porsche drivers are Republicans. And it's not just the car you drive that suggests your politics; it's what you drink, watch, and talk about around the watercooler. As *The Washington Post* reported after the election:

> Republican firms, including TargetPoint Consultants and National Media Inc., delved into commercial databases that pinpointed consumer buying patterns and television-watching habits to unearth such informa-tion as Coors beer and bourbon drinkers skewing Republican, brandy and cognac drinkers tilting Democratic; college football TV viewers were more Republican than those who watch professional football; viewers of Fox News were overwhelmingly committed to vote for Bush; homes with telephone caller ID tended to be Republican; people interested in gam-bling, fashion, and theater tended to be Democratic.[75]

Alex Gage of TargetPoint explained to the *Post* what the GOP did after they'd identified a potential Republican who hadn't been voting: They pissed him or her off. The more elegant term is finding "anger points." Or, as Gage said, "You used to get a tape-recorded voice of Ronald Reagan telling you how important it was to vote. That was our get-out-the-vote effort. In 2004, Gage told the *Post,* the message was much more carefully targeted—and de-signed to make you mad. If the GOP's market research said you were very likely to vote pro-life, you'd get a call telling you that 'if you don't come out and vote, the number of abortions next year is going to go up.' "[76]

The proof of Bush's superior targeting is this: While Kerry's vote exceeded Al Gore's by 6.8 million, Bush improved his 2000 vote total by a staggering 10.5 million.[77] Think about that. With the same approval rating—the same level of popularity in the country—Bush increased his vote total by 10.5 million. That's astonishing. Most presidents who are reelected win because the country concludes they've done a good job. Voters are satisfied with the direction the country's going in, and they reward the commander in chief. In 2004, George W. Bush was no more popular than he was on the day he lost the popular vote to Al Gore. And yet instead of losing the popular vote to John Kerry, he won it by more than three million.

In the chapters to come, we'll take a closer look at how individual issues—from abortion to guns to taxes to national security—affected the race. But the big-picture story of the 2004 election is that the Republicans had a message; we didn't. The Republicans attacked; we didn't. The Republicans targeted and turned out their voters; we didn't.

Houston, We Have a Solution

Let's check in with Jim Lovell, shall we? When we left him, he was (as David Bowie sang) "sitting in a tin can, far above the moon." There was nothing in the manual about guiding a crippled spaceship that had drifted forty thousand miles off course, so Lovell and his crew did what any American would do: They improvised.

They crammed into the tiny lunar module, three men in an area designed to hold two, surviving four days with little food and water. And that was the easy part. The lunar module was so cramped, and had so little oxygen, that the carbon dioxide from the astronauts' breath reached almost deadly levels. So they used duct tape and cardboard to rig an air-cleansing system. But because of the debris around the spacecraft, they couldn't see the stars to navigate. So they reckoned from the sun and the moon and used the tiny thrusters on the lunar module to ease the spaceship onto a course that brought it into the moon's orbit. Then they used the moon's gravitational force as a slingshot to launch them back to Earth. It was creative and audacious—and successful. Today Lovell and his crew—as well as the folks at NASA, in Houston—are considered heroes.[78]

Lovell had named his spaceship *Odyssey,* and what an odyssey it took him on. So let's take a little odyssey of our own. Let's squeeze into what's left of our damaged and diminished party, jettison what no longer works, improvise, create new tools and techniques, and chart a new course using the eternal, fixed constants of our Democratic solar system. Who knows? If it all works, maybe Tom Hanks will make a movie about this journey of survival and triumph, too.

Moral Values:
God Is a Liberal

For much of the twentieth century, if you'd asked voters why they preferred Democrats, chances are you'd hear "Democrats care about the
little guy." Franklin D. Roosevelt reinvented the Democratic Party as a diverse coalition gathered around one central theme: using government as an
engine of opportunity for the poor and the middle class. He was, in our esti-
mation, the greatest president of the twentieth century. Yet in many ways,
FDR had it easier than modern-day Democrats. In Roosevelt's day, racist
southern segregationists shared a party with liberal northern reformers.
From FDR to JFK, Démocrats held the coalition together in an uneasy alliance that focused on economic issues and minimized social—especially
racial—issues.

But that alliance exploded in the 1960s. When Lyndon Johnson signed
the Voting Rights Act in 1965, he lamented that he was handing the South to
the Republicans for a generation. If anything, LBJ was understating the
power of racial resentment in our beloved South. Savvy Republicans saw the
crack in the Democratic coalition and filled it with dynamite. They artfully
co-opted racial tensions, not by talking about race but by couching it in a
code that anyone born south of the Smith & Wesson Line could crack. In the
wake of riots in the African-American neighborhoods of Watts, Newark, and

31

Detroit, Richard Nixon talked of "law and order." White southerners got it. Hell, white northerners and white midwesterners got it, too.

Ronald Reagan was even less nuanced. Standing in Philadelphia, Mississippi, where civil rights workers Andrew Goodman, Michael Schwerner, and James Chaney had been murdered, he declared, "I believe in states' rights." [1] States' rights. Those two words conveyed resentment and anger—and, yes, racism—without directly using racist language, which would have offended and repulsed white moderates. Of the eleven states of the Confederacy, Reagan carried ten, even though he was running against a true son of the South, a fifth-generation Georgian named Jimmy Carter.

So effective has the Republican Southern Strategy been that in 2004, George W. Bush went Reagan one better, carrying every single southern state.

Race—along with the Democrats' embrace of civil rights—was the precipitating factor. But it was not the only one. During the Vietnam War, many on the left who rightly opposed the war wrongly attacked the working-class soldiers, sailors, airmen, and marines who were fighting it. Like race, the war split the country along class lines, with the white working people who were at the heart of the New Deal coalition feeling that Democrats looked down on them.

While race and war have been dividing lines in American politics since before the nation's founding, the pace of social change since the 1960s has been staggering. If FDR—or JFK, for that matter—were to return to the political scene today, he'd be confronted with divisive social, cultural, and religious issues that were not on any politician's radar when he was alive: abortion, gay rights, gun control, school prayer, pornography, and more.

What's interesting is that while the cultural terrain would be unrecognizable, the economic issues would be familiar: Republicans want to cut taxes for the wealthy, they pass special privileges for special interests, they oppose raising the minimum wage, they oppose unions' efforts to organize working people, they want judges who will overturn laws on everything from child labor to worker safety. FDR or JFK would recognize the Republicans today; on those issues they are indistinguishable from the Republicans Roosevelt called "economic royalists." [2]

What would puzzle Roosevelt and Kennedy is how the economic royalists have been able to run and win as cultural populists. We think FDR and JFK would marvel at how the country-club elite has won over the country-music crowd. And they would fight like hell to win those folks back. So should we.

Many liberals share the conceit that they are intellectually superior. It's not true—any movement that includes George F. Will and William F. Buckley and, well, Mary Matalin can't be dumb. But liberals—too many of them, anyway—seem to have a need to believe that they're intellectually superior to conservatives. Argue with a liberal, and before you know it, you'll hear "You're stupid." If he's a little more polite, he'll say, "Your idea is stupid."

Intellectual elitism is an arrogance that Democrats can't afford. Republicans play off it, they exaggerate it, and they use it to distract middle-class Americans from the Republican economic policies that are ripping them off. The Democrat George Wallace showed them the way. He delighted in attacking "pointy-headed intellectuals" stuck in the clouds, trying to impose their liberal notions of social engineering on salt-of-the-earth southerners. George W. Bush has picked up Wallace's anti-intellectualism (when he's not boasting of his Yale-Harvard education). When the legendary journalist Bob Woodward told Bush that people were concerned about the lack of weapons of mass destruction, he snapped, "Well, you travel in elite circles." Woodward says, "I think he feels there is an intellectual world, and he's indicated he's not a part of it . . . the fancy-pants intellectual world. What he calls the elite."[3] Too many Democrats, it seems, have the opposite desire—to be a part of and approved by the intellectual elite. They didn't seem to understand that constant attacks on Bush's intelligence merely served to make Bush look like "one of us." Liberals need to feel smarter than their opponents.

By the same token, conservatives have their own conceit: that they're morally superior. Argue with a Republican, and before you know it, she'll say, "You're wrong." Or "You're a bad Christian/a bad American/a bad parent." Or "You don't have family values."

Tellingly, Democrats have not used Republicans' sanctimony against them. We have little doubt that the same middle-class Americans who are tired of being told Democrats look down their noses at them intellectually are just as tired of Republicans who look down on them morally. Judgmentalism and sanctimony are central to the right wing's culture wars. It's time Democrats took them on.

How on earth did this happen? How did Republicans come to be seen as guardians of family values and Democrats as the enemies of those values?

There was a time when progressives spoke powerfully of their faith. Don't forget, Dr. Martin Luther King, Jr., led the Southern *Christian* Leadership Conference. Dr. King marched with priests and rabbis and Protestant ministers, all the while appealing to Americans' sense of righteousness as much as their sense of right and wrong.

Anyone who's read Thomas Frank's book *What's the Matter with Kansas?* has a sense of what happened. Republicans have conducted a decades-long campaign to win over middle-class and lower-middle-class voters with cultural populism. They stoke anger and resentment on cultural issues in order to win votes, then use the power they receive from the votes to hammer these people on economic issues.

In particular, Republicans have exploited abortion, gun control, and gay rights. These three hot-button emotional issues have probably cost more Democrats more elections in the last thirty years than anything else. Here's how Democrats can take them back.

Abortion

The U.S. abortion rate dropped significantly under President Bill Clinton. In fact, by the time Clinton left office, the abortion rate had dropped to its lowest level since 1974.[4]

That's right. The number of abortions fell under Bill Clinton's leadership. When Bill Clinton started his first term as president, there were 1.6 million abortions per year. By the end of his term, there were 1.3 million abortions per year—a drop of three hundred thousand abortions per year. This was not a function of declining fertility. Among women who got pregnant and did not have miscarriages, the percentage who had abortions dropped from 28 percent to 24.5 percent.[5] Democrats should repeat this fact like a mantra until every American knows it, internalizes it, and repeats it.

Clinton, of course, is pro-choice. So why would the abortion rate decline during his presidency when it didn't under the stridently pro-life Ronald Reagan? Some of the decline no doubt has to do with the expanding economy: Clinton's commitment to helping low-income working moms probably made having a baby a more attractive option. And some of the decline, we believe, has to do with Clinton's commitment to sex education and contraception. As Senator Hillary Rodham Clinton has noted, "Seven percent of American women who do not use contraception account for 53 percent of all unintended pregnancies."[6]

Glen Stassen, a pro-life Christian theologian and the Lewis B. Smedes Professor of Christian Ethics at Fuller Theological Seminary, in Pasadena, California, has an interesting theory: "Economic policy and abortion are not separate issues, they form one moral imperative. Rhetoric is hollow, mere tinkling brass, without health care, insurance, jobs, child care and a living wage. Pro-life in deed, not merely in word, means we need a president who will do something about jobs, health insurance and support for mothers."[7]

Abortion is, of course, a complicated issue. But the political contours have become fairly clear in the three decades since the Supreme Court ruled in *Roe* v. *Wade* that the Constitution protects a woman's right to choose to have an abortion.

The majority of Americans support a woman's right to have an abortion. In fact, 56 percent of Americans say abortion should be legal in most or all cases.[8] But from here it gets tricky. Americans are conflicted about abortion. They don't want to ban it, but they'd like to restrict it. They certainly don't want to celebrate it. Americans' support for legal abortion is contingent on the circumstances: 85 percent of Americans support abortion when a woman's life is in danger; 77 percent when her physical health is in danger; 76 percent when a pregnancy is caused by rape or incest; 66 percent support all abortions in the first three months of pregnancy; 56 percent support abortion when there's evidence that a baby may be physically or mentally impaired.[9]

At the same time, the majority of Americans support restrictions on a woman's right to have an abortion: 88 percent support requiring doctors to inform patients about alternatives to abortion; 84 percent think abortion should be illegal in the last three months of pregnancy; 78 percent support a

When Do the Majority of Americans
Support a Woman's Right to Have an Abortion?

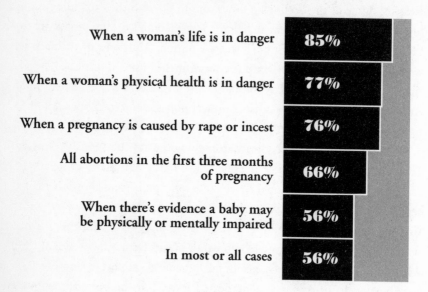

When a woman's life is in danger	85%
When a woman's physical health is in danger	77%
When a pregnancy is caused by rape or incest	76%
All abortions in the first three months of pregnancy	66%
When there's evidence a baby may be physically or mentally impaired	56%
In most or all cases	56%

twenty-four-hour waiting period before a woman has an abortion; 73 percent support a law requiring a woman under the age of eighteen to obtain her parents' consent for an abortion; 72 percent support legislation requiring women to inform their husbands if they have an abortion; and 70 percent support a ban on so-called partial-birth abortions.[10]

And yet the Democratic Party, which seeks to be the majority party in America, has somehow managed to position itself on the fringe of the issue when it should be in the mainstream.

In 2004 all eight of the Democratic candidates for president supported a woman's right to have a legal abortion. That's where the country is; that's where the party is. But that's not where the abortion rights pressure groups are. Perhaps out of conviction, perhaps out of convenience, all eight candidates went beyond simply supporting abortion rights. They publicly pledged to oppose every restriction on abortion, including the ban on late-term, or partial-birth, abortions. While so-called partial-birth abortion is supported by just 25 percent of Americans, it was supported by 100 percent of the 2004 Democratic presidential candidates.[11] In fact, the majority of Democrats

When Do the Majority of Americans
Support Restrictions on a Woman's Right to Have An Abortion?

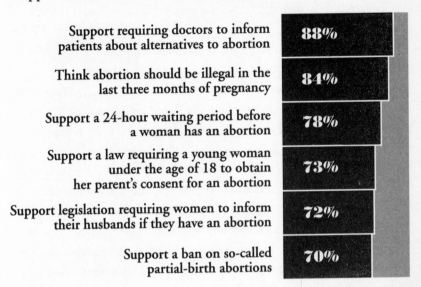

Support requiring doctors to inform patients about alternatives to abortion	**88%**
Think abortion should be illegal in the last three months of pregnancy	**84%**
Support a 24-hour waiting period before a woman has an abortion	**78%**
Support a law requiring a young woman under the age of 18 to obtain her parent's consent for an abortion	**73%**
Support legislation requiring women to inform their husbands if they have an abortion	**72%**
Support a ban on so-called partial-birth abortions	**70%**

support a ban on partial-birth abortion.[12] And yet every single Democrat running for president took a position that most Democrats oppose? That is the very definition of extremism. The Democratic candidates pledged to oppose laws to require a parent's consent before a minor can have an abortion. They opposed laws that called for parental notification, which is less than consent. Remarkable.

Some of the candidates, like John Kerry and Howard Dean, had long records in support of abortion rights. Others, like Dennis Kucinich, had been pro-life before they started running for president. Dick Gephardt had traveled a remarkable distance: from being the party's premier pro-life congressman (in his first speech on the House floor, he called for a constitutional amendment to ban all abortions); to voting in favor of the Partial Birth Abortion Act; to, finally, disavowing his previous record and embracing all abortions in all circumstances, at all times.

We're not faulting the pro-choice pressure groups; they are, by definition, special-interest groups. They put their particular issue ahead of any party. They support pro-choice Republicans. Fine. So let's not confuse them with people who have at heart the best interests of the Democratic Party. Anytime a politician is in 100 percent support of any interest group's agenda, watch out. That politician is vulnerable to the attack that he or she is merely a tool of that special interest.

Simply put, the Democratic Party has become viewed as a tool of the abortion rights interest groups, at least on the presidential level.

When Bill Clinton ran for president in 1992, he had a different attitude, one that reflected the ambivalence and conflicted feelings people have about the issue. He was giving a speech in which he mentioned his support for abortion rights, and the audience cheered. He stopped them cold: "This is not something to cheer about," he scolded. Like Jimmy Carter before him, Clinton respected and acknowledged the power of the convictions of pro-life Americans. His mantra was that abortion should be "safe, legal, and rare."

You don't have to tell us that the issue has obvious religious overtones—we're both Catholic. But sometimes religion gets overplayed by the media. We believe that many Americans see abortion as a class issue. Pro-choicers tend to be more highly educated. They tend to have higher incomes. They tend to live on the coasts. Pro-lifers know this, and they resent what they believe is the snobbery, the elitism, the supposed intellectual superiority of the pro-choicers.

The late Pennsylvania governor Bob Casey was one of the great populist liberals. You never would have seen him described that way in the press, because he was strongly pro-life. But he was also pro–gay rights and had openly gay staff members as far back as 1986. He was strongly pro-union, distrustful of corporate power, and a committed environmentalist. But it was the abortion issue—and the Democrats' increasingly strong ties to the pro-choice interest groups—that broke Casey's heart.

To understand Casey, you had to know his story. His father, Alphonsus, was a mule tender in the anthracite coal mines near Scranton. Casey used to tell us that his father's hands were gnarled from being run over by the mule carts that hauled the coal. With an iron will and a faith in the American Dream, Alphonsus Casey pulled himself out of those mines, got a law degree, and became a lawyer for mine workers. He died young, but he instilled in his son his ferocious work ethic and unquenchable faith in the American Dream. He also instilled a populist sensibility that Casey never forgot.

In 1986, Casey found himself running for governor against Bill Scranton III. It was, *Time* magazine wrote, like a John O'Hara short story: the son of a coal miner running against the scion of the family that had owned the mines. Casey approached nearly every issue—and life itself—almost with a chip on his shoulder. He viewed Republicans as elitists who looked down their noses at ordinary people. And he had a point. After he'd lost three races for governor, "the smart guys"—as Casey used to call the elites—dubbed him "the three-time loss from Holy Cross." Casey was proud that he'd gone to Holy Cross, a terrific Jesuit school. And he deeply resented being held in contempt by men who'd gone to Harvard and Yale only because their daddies had gone to Harvard and Yale.

Like so many pro-lifers, Casey believed the pro-choicers were, as he described them, "a small, well-heeled elite."[13] He believed they dismissed him as a religious fanatic from the wrong side of the tracks. And he was right. One of the darkest days in Democratic Party history was when pro-choice activists—overwhelmingly Democratic—staged a protest in front of the Governor's Mansion in Harrisburg. They chanted, "Casey: Take your rosaries off our ovaries." Others passed out buttons mockingly depicting Casey as the pope.[14]

Nice.

Can you imagine the hue and cry if right-wingers had ridiculed Joe Lieberman's profound Jewish faith?

In 1990, when he ran for reelection, Casey's pro-choice Republican opponent dismissed him as a "redneck Irishman from Scranton." The redneck Irishman from Scranton went on to win the biggest landslide in Pennsylvania history.

Republicans understand the populist power of the abortion issue and manipulate it to their advantage. Democrats ignore that power at their peril. Casey used to describe the Democrats as being like a Fuller brush man. The case might be filled with wonderful brushes—issue positions and policy proposals to address your every concern—but the lady isn't going to let you in the door if you're wearing a ragged T-shirt and sporting a purple Mohawk and a tattoo that says EAT DEATH, SCUM. That's how he believed the abortion issue worked. He saw it as a threshold issue: If Democrats didn't at least show respect for the values and beliefs that lead millions of Americans to be pro-life, they'd never hear us out on our ideas to bring them health care, jobs, and education. They'd just slam the door in our face.

Here's how Democrats can take back the abortion issue.

1. Be the Big Tent Party

There are still a lot of pro-life Democrats in America. The party should welcome them, and they are already doing so. Harry Reid, the Democratic leader in the Senate, is pro-life. Nancy Pelosi, the Democratic leader in the House, is pro-choice. Both are good Democrats; neither should be ostracized because of their position on abortion.

Governor Casey's son, Pennsylvania treasurer Bob Casey, Jr., is, at this writing, challenging Republican wing nut Rick Santorum in a hot Senate race in Pennsylvania. Casey, who is strongly pro-life, is enjoying solid support from leading pro-choice Democrats.

Democrats will always be the pro-choice party. But we should not compare the issue to civil rights. Once Kennedy and Johnson led us away from our racist heritage, you simply could not be a good Democrat and support segregation. Democrats today must recognize that you can be a good Democrat and be pro-life or pro-choice on abortion.

2. Move to the Mainstream

So-called partial-birth abortion is against the law. Period. The votes aren't there to repeal the ban, nor are they likely to materialize, given Americans' support for it. So why not recognize the obvious and either support the ban on partial-birth abortion or at least acknowledge that it won't be repealed? The pro-choice movement has lost the debate over late-term abortion. You may like it, you may not, but it's real. And it's settled. Pro-choice Democrats should deal with that reality and stop losing elections over an issue they've already lost.

In conservatism's long, dark winter—1964 to 1980—Republicans rigorously reexamined what they stood for. They moved away from being the

Are You a Fanatic on Abortion?

Here's a Carville and Begala test to determine if you're a fanatic: Do you believe someone can be a good person and hold the exact opposite position from you?

We know lots of good people—and good Democrats—who would say no on the abortion issue. Some are pro-life, some are pro-choice. Sorry, but we're just not fanatics on the issue. Growing up in the heart of red-state America, as well as in the Catholic church, we don't just *know* people who would outlaw all abortions, we love them. They're our sisters and cousins and aunts. They're some of the best people we've ever known.

The same goes for pro-choicers. Both of us have friends and relatives who are as stridently, strongly, staunchly pro-choice as the head of the National Abortion and Reproductive Rights Action League.

So we're not fanatics on abortion. We know too many good people on both sides who have deeply principled positions. Still, we can understand the fanaticism. There is one issue we are fanatics on: civil rights. We don't think you can be a good person and be for a return to segregation and Jim Crow. Other than that, there's almost no issue on which we'd flunk (or is it pass?) the Carville and Begala fanatic test.

So we understand—and respect—the passionate people on both sides of this issue. We just don't think fanaticism is good for our party.

party of the moderate corporate elite, away from being the party of defending the old ways, and into being a more dynamic, even radical party. At the same time, they made their peace with the New Deal and the Great Society. In the 1960s, Ronald Reagan opposed the Civil Rights Act, the Voting Rights Act, and the creation of Medicare. By 1980 he wasn't publicly opposing any of them. He'd made peace with them. They were, we're sure, still anathema to his ideology. But Reagan was shrewd enough to recognize that the American people wanted those programs and would not elect a president who proposed dismantling them. His public transformation was so complete that when he was accused, in his debate with Jimmy Carter of having opposed Medicare, Reagan said, "There you go again," before claiming that he'd supported a different version of the program.[15]

Do Democrats need to make peace with at least some restrictions on abortion? If they want to show the overwhelming majority of Americans who support those restrictions that they understand and respect their values, yes. If not, they will continue waging a battle they've already lost, and risk losing the war they ought to win.

3. Take the Fight to the Republicans

If Democrats had the flexibility to give a little on the margins, they could win the abortion debate in the mainstream. Rather than losing a battle for the fringe of the issue—"partial birth," parental consent, etc.—they could be winning the war. The key to winning that war is to engage it at its center: Should all abortions be outlawed, as the GOP platform calls for? Or should abortions be legally protected, as the Democratic platform calls for?

How many abortions would actually be affected by the restrictions on "partial birth" and minors' access to abortions? Our guess is damn few. But politically, giving up ground we've already lost would allow the Democrats to shift the debate away from the issues on which we look like extremists, and onto the terrain where we're strongest. No more would Republicans like George W. Bush be able to change the subject, slickly saying that they prefer adoption but that everyone can agree partial-birth abortion is wrong. No, Republicans would have to explain why they want to take what has been a constitutional right for three decades and turn it into a criminal wrong. They would have to tell us why their platform calls for a ban on abortion, even in cases of rape and incest.[16]

Tell us, O morally superior Republicans, if abortion is murder, and we should (as do most Republicans) support the death penalty for murder, shouldn't a doctor who performs an abortion be executed? Republican senator and ob-gyn Tom Coburn thinks so.[17] For that matter, so should a woman who has one. Where will you station the abortion police: in clinics? Hospitals? Doctors' offices?

Suddenly, Democrats move from defending a position on which four out of five Americans disagree with us to a position on which the majority is with us. To some highly principled supporters of abortion rights, that's going to sound like a sellout. It's not. We're not asking people to abandon their views. We're simply recognizing reality: The country is on the Democrats' side on the fundamental issue of a woman's right to choose. But too many Democrats are more insistent on losing on comparatively marginal issues than on winning on the broader issue.

It's called being pragmatic. If you're strongly pro-choice, do you really think it's worth fighting against every restriction on abortion and losing—in which case the Republicans will win elections, seize power, and ultimately outlaw all abortions? Or does it make more sense to stage a tactical retreat where you're weak and then fight where you're strong?

4. Stand Up to the Pressure Groups

The kind of shift we're talking about will require pressure groups to ease up on the pressure. This is not such a ridiculous request. The Falwell wing of the Republican Party doesn't demand that Republicans parade in front of them and give red-faced, eyes-bulging speeches about how abortion is mass murder. Why not? Because Jerry Falwell and his cronies already know the deal. They understand the game. They get the gig. As Al Davis used to say, Just win, baby. Just win. So they grin and bear it as Bush pretends he doesn't have a litmus test on judicial nominations. Of course he does. And they cheer approvingly as the Republican convention highlights pro-choice speakers like Rudy Giuliani and Arnold Schwarzenegger, relegating pro-life Republicans to introducing the delegates from American Samoa at four A.M. on C-SPAN.

5. Agree that the Goal Should Be to Reduce Abortions

Democrats routinely say they're not pro-abortion; they're pro-choice. If that's the case, they should act like it. They should speak of abortion the way Jimmy Carter did in an interview with *The American Prospect:* "I have always been against abortion; it's not possible for me in my own concept of Christ to believe that Jesus would favor abortion. But at the same time, I have supported the Supreme Court ruling of our country as the law of the land. And the present arrangement, whereby a woman is authorized to have an abortion in the first trimester of the pregnancy, or when the pregnancy is caused by rape or incest—these are the things that moderates who have beliefs like mine can accept as the present circumstances in our country." [18] Similarly, Bill Clinton said he thought abortion should be "safe, legal, and rare."

Both of these positions concede a vital point—that abortion is bad. Will Saletan, who has written thoughtfully and at great length on abortion, argues that this concession is vital to winning the debate over abortion rights. Hillary Clinton seems to agree. In a speech to abortion rights supporters commemorating the anniversary of *Roe* v. *Wade,* Senator Clinton called abortion "a sad, even tragic, choice to many, many women. . . . There is no reason why government cannot do more to educate and inform and provide assistance so that the choice guaranteed under our Constitution either does not ever have to be exercised or only in very rare circumstances." [19] In analyzing her speech, Saletan argues that Hillary has it right. "Once you embrace that truth—that the ideal number of abortions is zero," Saletan writes, "voters open their ears." [20]

Hillary has it right. Pro-choice Americans should make common cause with pro-life Americans to reduce—and God willing, eliminate—the need for abortions. Such an approach has the potential to drain some of the venom from one of the most bitter and divisive issues on the political scene.

That's the last thing our Republican friends want. If middle-class folks aren't getting jacked up about abortion, they might pay attention to how the GOP is robbing them blind on economic issues.

A group of pro-life Democrats called, appropriately enough, Democrats for Life, has come up with what it calls the 95-10 Initiative. Its goal is to reduce abortions by 95 percent in ten years. The 95-10 Initiative has been championed in the House of Representatives by Tim Ryan, a bright and engaging congressman from Ohio. One of the youngest members of Congress, Ryan was fed up with extremists on both sides who endlessly debated *Roe* v. *Wade* without doing anything constructive to reduce the need for or number of abortions. The 95-10 Initiative is built around seventeen concrete policy proposals that would reduce the number of abortions. In announcing their plan, the pro-life Democrats said their goals are to empower women, to defend pregnant women, and to protect unborn children.[21] The pro-life Democrats have concluded that the thirty-two-year fight to overturn *Roe* v. *Wade* hasn't stopped a single abortion. So they've decided to change tactics. Rather than trying to reduce the number of abortions by making an abortion more *difficult* to have, they want to reduce the number of abortions by making abortions less *necessary* to have. Instead of changing the Constitution, they want to change circumstances.

The policy programs outlined in the 95-10 Initiative include encouraging adoption by making the adoption tax credit permanent, and giving women with unplanned pregnancies counseling information on adoption. They would expand the Women, Infants, and Children program (WIC), which gives nutritional support to new moms and their babies. The pro-lifers would seek to limit the number of unplanned pregnancies by requiring insurance companies to cover contraceptives. They would also expand age-appropriate pregnancy prevention education in schools.

Some on the far right will find particulars to quibble with. Economic right-wingers, being the social Darwinists that they are, will oppose spending more money to feed hungry moms and babies. But Jesus said, "Feed my lambs," so let the Republican tightwads take up their argument with the Lord. (Or, if it makes them feel better, the Republicans can pretend the money's going to wealthy heiresses like Paris Hilton instead of poor newborn babies.) No doubt some Republicans, at the behest of the big insurance companies, will rail against the contraception provision. Those on the Falwell fringe will complain about pregnancy prevention education. Too bad. We believe these proposals would do more to prevent abortions than all the speeches, all the marches, and all the campaign ads pro-lifers have used over the last thirty years.

Unlike, say, partial-birth abortion, these are the fights Democrats should want. They're the fights we need. Democrats should challenge Republicans who do nothing more than give lip service to pro-lifers to put some policy behind their speeches. This is both good politics and, we think, good policy. If Republicans who call themselve anti-abortion oppose these commonsense steps to reduce the number of abortions, it will be clear they're more interested in demagoguing the issue than in actually protecting the unborn and reducing abortions.

6. Be Prepared to Take the Fight to the States

Harry Blackmun, the Justice who wrote the majority opinion in *Roe* v. *Wade,* famously predicted that the Court would one day overturn *Roe.* In 1989, when abortion rights barely survived the challenge of *Webster* v. *Reproductive Services,* Blackmun noted, "For today, the women of this Nation still retain the liberty to control their destinies. But the signs are evident and very ominous, and a chill wind blows." [22] A generation later, *Roe* is still the law of the land. Was Blackmun wrong? No. If anything, overturning *Roe* is more likely now than when Blackmun first felt the chill wind.

Let's say the Court, reshaped by President Bush, does the unthinkable. It overturns three decades of precedent and says *Roe* was decided wrongly. What happens then? Abortion is not automatically outlawed in all cases, for all time. Instead, the issue reverts to the states, where it was before *Roe* declared that abortion is a constitutionally protected right.

The Center for Reproductive Rights, a pro-choice interest group, has estimated that thirty states are poised to outlaw abortion as soon as the Supreme Court gives them the go-ahead. Some of these states have vestigial statutes that had outlawed or restricted abortion before *Roe.* Others have passed so-called fail-safe statutes that will outlaw abortion if and when *Roe* is overturned. And still others, the center's analysis says, have anti-abortion majorities in the legislature that would outlaw abortion if given the chance.[23]

We think the center's analysis is sound, as far as it goes. But what it doesn't take into account are the dynamic repercussions of a Court decision overturning *Roe*. The political energy in the abortion issue is entirely on the negative side. One of the reasons Democrats lose elections on abortion is not because most Americans are pro-life; as we've established, they're not. It's because people who support abortion rights are happy, and people don't vote on issues they're happy about. Take away *Roe,* and the pro-choice majority in this country becomes unhappy. Very unhappy. Thus Democrats, as the pro-choice party, stand to dominate elections in a post-*Roe* era. Pro-choice voters who have voted Republican because they liked lower taxes, or because they supported the war in Iraq, or because their family has always been Republican, will flee from the GOP like the devil runs from holy water. They'll be hunting down Republicans with dogs.

In short, the conservatives' fondest dream—overturning *Roe*—will be the Republicans' worst nightmare.

Gun Control

Gun control is another cultural issue Republicans use to divide Americans and distract them from how they're being hammered by GOP economics. Republicans are damn good at it, too. They understand that all across America there are people—mostly men—with an NRA card in their pocket, right next to their union card. The Republicans capture these guys' votes by persuading them that their gun is more at risk than their job.

It's time for Democrats to take back the gun issue.

The fundamental political reality about gun control is that the two sides are at a standoff. There aren't the votes in Congress to repeal the gun-control laws passed under President Clinton. The Brady Bill and other Clinton-era gun laws are strongly supported by the American people and by America's cops. It's been estimated that the Brady Bill has kept guns out of the hands of a hundred thousand felons a year since it was signed into law in 1993.[24]

The gun-control laws currently on the books have not restricted the rights of law-abiding citizens to own guns. The National Rifle Association scare tactics were wrong. There's been no slippery slope; no black helicopters have swooped in to confiscate the weapons of law-abiding citizens. It was a massive con job, a total lie, pure horse hockey.

And it worked.

No, it didn't work to defeat the Brady Bill, but it convinced millions of red-blooded, red-state gun owners that Democrats were the enemy. This is an issue on which polling can be misleading—and seductive for Democrats. The majority of Americans support gun control, but at the same time, 72 percent say the Second Amendment guarantees each individual an inalienable right to own a gun.[25]

We once worked on a poll in which we measured support for banning assault weapons; it was overwhelming. But then, on the advice of the genius strategist Mike Donilon, we added this statement to the poll: "When I hear a politician talk about gun control, it makes me think he doesn't share my values." Boom. The same people who said they were for banning assault weapons also said they thought a politician who was for gun control didn't share their values. That's because gun control is more about culture than about crime, especially in noncoastal America. There, a gun is seen not as a dangerous and deadly weapon for urban criminals but as something that unifies generations, part of a heritage of hunting passed down from fathers to sons (and, very often, from mothers to daughters). For a generation, Republicans have told gun owners that Democrats look down their noses at them. And for a generation, gun owners have believed it. The result is that when a Democrat takes a position on gun control—even a position that most folks agree with—millions of Americans resent them and worry about whether the position is really an attack on their culture.

So how do Democrats take back the gun issue?

1. Acknowledge the Standoff

Here's how the National Rifle Association states its public position: "For years NRA has said that the best way to fight illegal gun use is to enforce the laws already on the books, not pass more laws."[26] Keep in mind that "the laws already on the books" were all opposed by the NRA. But now, rather than calling for the repeal of the Clinton-era gun laws, the NRA implicitly praises them. Why? Because they know they don't have the votes to repeal them. They also know those laws are popular—and they work. Since the Brady Bill took effect in 1994, it has kept guns out of the hands of eight hundred thousand felons, fugitives, and wife-beaters, without burdening a single decent, law-abiding American.[27] So rather than rail against the Clinton gun-control laws—rather than continue fighting a battle they lost a decade ago—the NRA wisely says it supports those laws.

Just as there aren't enough votes to repeal any existing gun laws, there aren't enough votes to pass any new ones. The most talked-about new gun-control law is to close the gun-show loophole. Sponsored by Senators Joe Lieberman (D-CT) and John McCain (R-AZ), the bill would require that people who buy guns at gun shows pass the same background check required for purchases made in stores. Okay. Sounds reasonable. But what is the political cost-benefit analysis? A study by the Clinton Justice Department showed that just 1.7 percent of criminals who used guns in the commission of a crime obtained their gun from a gun show.[28] By extending the Brady Bill to catch such a small percentage of transactions, Democrats risk inflaming and alienating millions of voters who might otherwise be open to voting Democratic. But once guns are in the mix, once someone believes his gun rights are threatened, he shuts down.

Howard Dean gets this. Although some see him as a model of liberal elitism, Dean campaigned for president against new federal gun legislation. Dean said Washington should not "inflict regulations" on states such as Montana and Vermont, where gun crime is not a big problem. New York and California, he said, "can have as much gun control as they want"; but states, not the federal government, should decide how much gun control they want.[29] Dean has a substantive as well as a political point. Eighteen states—including three of the top five gun-owning states—have already enacted their own legislation closing the gun-show loophole.[30]

Dean was being a realist. Gun control played a major role in the defeat of congressional Democrats in 1994.[31] It was no doubt part of the reason Al Gore lost states he'd carried when he was on the ticket with Bill Clinton:

southern states like Arkansas, Tennessee, and Louisiana, and border states like Missouri, Kentucky, and West Virginia. So Dean tried to defuse the issue. More Democrats should follow his lead.

2. Enforce the Laws Already on the Books

The NRA was not the first group to call for strict enforcement of America's gun laws. Janet Reno's Justice Department beat the gun lobby to the punch. Project Exile was created by S. David Schiller, an assistant U.S. attorney in Richmond, Virginia, during the Clinton administration. Project Exile moved gun crimes from the state to the federal system, where bail is harder to get and sentences are longer. According to *The New York Times,* Schiller claimed Project Exile "led to the recovery of 475 illegal guns, indictments against 404 people on gun charges, a conviction rate of 86 percent through trials and plea bargains, and an average prison term of more than four and a half years." [32] There were critics, including federal judges, who worried that routine gun cases would clog their dockets. Tough. Routine gun cases are better than routine gun violence. We pay federal judges $162,100 a year. [33] If they can't find the time to hear gun cases, let them leave the bench and go back to writing wills.

Other critics of Project Exile noted that the NRA had strongly supported it. So what? We're not exactly fans of the gun lobby, but is that really the best way to judge the merit of an idea? You shouldn't reflexively support Project Exile just because it originated with a Clinton administration official, nor should you oppose it just because the NRA likes it. It's a good idea, it's tough on crime, it's reducing gun violence, and it calls the NRA's bluff.

3. Respect Gun Owners

We believe gun control hurts Democrats because voters are offended by what they perceive as judgmentalism and elitism by gun-control advocates. About four in ten Americans own guns, including both authors of this book.[34] We're not all toothless, ignorant, inbred rednecks. Granted, there are some real wack jobs out there. But most gun owners are good people, with strong values. For hunters especially, gun ownership is a link from one generation to another. Paul has a gun his father gave him; he's bought guns for his sons. Paul's brother Dave has given Paul's boys three guns. And every one of those guns is under lock and key, as they should be.

John Kerry was much ridiculed for going goose hunting in Ohio during the presidential campaign. In truth, Kerry is a hunter; not long after the election, he went quail hunting—without any cameras. He is more than a photo-op hunter. So why did his goose-hunting trip backfire? In part because his campaign seemed so ambivalent about hunting, as about almost everything else. Yes, Kerry went hunting. And, yes, he shot a goose. But no, he would not carry the dead goose in front of the cameras. And he rarely talked about his views on guns. His handlers apparently didn't want to show him as comfortable with guns, which he is, or as a hunter, which he is. They made ads showing Kerry carrying a gun in combat in Vietnam, but they allowed him to portray himself as a hunter only in that lone photo op. Other than that, the Kerry campaign's strategy seemed to be to ignore the issue and hope it would go away. It didn't. One of the enduring images we have from Election Day is the photo from Virginia's Shenandoah County, where working people were lined up along the street to vote. They stood under two billboards: One accused Kerry of wanting to take their guns; the other accused him of wanting to outlaw their ammunition. Bush won 69 percent of the vote in Shenandoah County.[35]

Democrats should feel comfortable saying they support the Second Amendment. After all, you can't say you support the Bill of Rights if you don't support the Second Amendment. Democrats should make it clear they respect the rights of hunters. They should tell voters about their own connection to guns and hunting. For Kerry, that would have been easy. He's not only used guns in mortal combat, he uses them for sporting purposes as well. We recall Hillary Clinton telling us about her one foray into Arkansas duck hunting. If Hillary Clinton can be comfortable with talking about wielding a twelve-gauge, so can you. Democrats don't have to pretend to be something they're not, the way President Bush pretends to be a rancher. They just have to show respect for gun owners and an understanding of what guns mean to so many millions of Americans.

Gay Rights

When he was pondering a run for the White House, George W. Bush told a friend, "I'm not going to kick gays, because I'm a sinner. How can I differentiate sin?" [36] But he also told the same friend, former Assemblies of God minister and evangelical activist Doug Wead, that he shared the right wing's view on its most important gay-bashing issue: "Gay marriage. I am against that. Special rights. I am against that." [37]

So Governor Bush was trying to have it both ways. Slick George. In truth, and in private, he was merely stating the Democratic position. Most Democrats oppose gay marriage, but they also oppose efforts by right-wing pressure groups to demonize gays. What Bush meant about "special rights" is beyond us. What most Democrats support is equal rights. We're not asking that gay Americans be given preferential treatment. No gay American is asking that she be given affirmative action, as other victims of discrimination have requested. Gays are merely insisting on the right to be treated the same way their straight brothers and sisters are.

Of course, President Bush proved more—how shall we say this delicately?—flexible than Governor Bush. When his 2004 reelection was in trouble, he was more than happy to rely on the most virulent anti-gay bigots to deliver his victory. If not for the purposeful manipulation of anti-gay attitudes in swing states, George W. Bush might be clearing brush in Crawford full-time right now. Indeed, he acknowledged his win-at-all-costs mentality in the same conversations in which he said he would not bash gays, telling Doug Wead, "I may have to get a little rough for a while, but that is what the old man had to do with Dukakis, remember?" [38]

Boy, do we remember. In 1988, George H. W. Bush successfully used divisive social issues to portray Massachusetts moderate Michael Dukakis as a left-wing wimp. Dukakis was slammed for vetoing a bill requiring teachers to recite the Pledge of Allegiance, for belonging to the American Civil Liberties

Union, for a Massachusetts furlough program that allowed a convict named Willie Horton to have a weekend pass, and for his opposition to the death penalty.

Dukakis's former media adviser, Dan Payne, predicted in May 2004 that George W. Bush would use the Massachusetts gay-marriage controversy the same way Bush's father used the death penalty, Willie Horton, and the Pledge.[39] Payne was right. As they used to say on the old cop shows, "They always return to the scene of the crime."

How did Democrats let them get away with it again?

Keep in mind that since mainstream America didn't think the president was doing a good job, the Bush-Cheney campaign had to expand the electorate by bringing more right-wing conservatives to the polls. Also recall that the Bush team decided the best way to boost right-wing turnout was not by appealing to conservatives' love for President Bush but, rather, by prodding conservatives' "anger points."[40] And it doesn't take Karl Rove to figure out that gay rights anger and scare right-wingers. Presto.

The argument that the gay-marriage issue won Bush the presidency is disputed. Republicans put anti-gay-marriage initiatives on eleven state ballots. All eleven passed overwhelmingly. But the presidential campaign was a different story in those states. Four of them—Arkansas, Georgia, Mississippi, and Oklahoma—were in the South. Although Bill Clinton carried Arkansas and Georgia in 1992, none of the four was considered up for grabs in 2004. Three others—Montana, North Dakota, and Utah—are rock-solid Republican in presidential elections. The Bush-Cheney ticket was already assured of their combined eleven electoral votes. The other four—Kentucky, Michigan, Ohio, and Oregon—were crucial swing states. Bush and Kerry split them, with Bush carrying Kentucky and Ohio, while Kerry captured Oregon and Michigan.

So, while Bush did carry most of the states with anti-gay-marriage initiatives on the ballot, he would have carried most of them under virtually any scenario. Indeed, two political science professors at MIT, Stephen Ansolabehere and Charles Stewart III, have argued that the anti-gay initiatives actually *hurt* Bush.[41] They posited that Bush and Cheney improved their vote more in states that did not have anti-gay initiatives on the ballot than in states that were voting on gay rights. "Marriage referenda," they said, "mobilized voters on both sides, not just the conservatives, and the net result may have been to John Kerry's benefit."[42]

We don't go as far as the good professors. The anti-gay initiative in Ohio may have pulled enough previously nonvoting conservatives to the polls to swing the Buckeye State, and thus the presidency, to Bush. But we believe that Democrats shouldn't be panicked by gay rights. Here are some facts on Americans' opinions about gay rights—some hopeful, some not.

When asked if a gay marriage in Massachusetts should be recognized in other states, Americans are split. Forty-six percent say yes, 50 percent say no.[43] Americans are also evenly divided on a constitutional amendment prohibiting gay marriage and on whether they want their state to outlaw gay marriage. And they narrowly support (46 percent to 41 percent) allowing gays to enter into civil unions. That is not exactly a disaster for pro-gay-rights Democrats. But in the same poll, voters say they disapprove of gays and lesbians being allowed to marry at all, by a 50 to 37 margin.[44] Other polls have shown an even more overwhelming rejection of gay marriage, by as much as 65 to 31.[45]

The Republican right uses gay-bashing to divide Americans, to frighten people, and, most important, to distract them from their common economic concerns. When the Vermont Supreme Court recognized gay relationships, former GOP presidential candidate Gary Bauer said, "I think what the Vermont Supreme Court did last week was in some ways worse than terrorism."[46] Fred Phelps, the right-wing leader of the Westboro Baptist Church, took a group of conservatives to the funeral of Matthew Shepard, the young gay man who was savagely murdered in Wyoming. They carried signs proclaiming NO FAGS IN HEAVEN and GOD HATES FAGS.[47] And now this right-wing group has a website on which Matthew's picture is engulfed in flames and you can "hear" a message from Matthew in hell.

Nice.

It's not just the lunatic fringe that spouts anti-gay hate. We already mentioned that Rick Santorum, the number three Republican in the Senate, compared gay Americans to people who practice something he called "man on dog." Senator Trent Lott of Mississippi compared gays to alcoholics and kleptomaniacs.[48] The platform of the Texas Republican Party, long dominated by President Bush, reads, in part: "Homosexual behavior is contrary to the fundamental, unchanging truths that have been ordained by God, recognized by our country's founders, and shared by the majority of Texans. Homosexuality must not be presented as an acceptable 'alternative' lifestyle in our public education and policy, nor should 'family' be redefined to include homosexual 'couples.' " The Texas Republicans also call for a federal anti-sodomy law, despite the fact that the Supreme Court has ruled the Texas anti-sodomy law unconstitutional.[49]

Seems like every time the GOP has its back up against the wall, they gay-bait. When President Bush's job was on the line in 2004, men in drag (bad drag, according to reports) held up pro-gay-marriage signs and shouted, "Gay marriage!" as they hassled voters outside polling places across the country. In Wisconsin and other states, swing voters received automated calls on which the taped voice claimed to be from the Kerry campaign and told people, "A vote for Kerry is a vote for gay marriage—it's our time."[50] *LA Weekly,* which reported the stunt, could not ascertain who was behind it. But does anyone doubt it was a right-wing dirty trick?

Clearly, not responding when the Republicans whipped up this anti-gay frenzy didn't work for the Democrats. Here's how Democrats can take back the issue of gay rights.

1. Broaden the Debate

Right-wingers always want to fight the gay-rights issues on the fringes, where they can make us look extreme. That's why they jumped Clinton on gays in the military. James, as a former marine, has always maintained that it's more important whether a marine shoots straight than whether he or she *is* straight. Moreover, how many people are in the military? Two and a half million[51] out of a population of 300 million.[52] So, the whole universe of Americans in the military constitutes 0.8 percent—eight tenths of one percent—of our citizenry. And of that 0.8 percent, how many are gay? Obviously, we don't know. We don't ask and they don't tell. But let's assume the rule of thumb of 10 percent is true—that 10 percent of the total population is gay, and that they're represented equally in the military. That means 10 percent of 0.8 percent—or 0.08 percent of the total population: eight one hundredths of one percent—is directly affected by the issue of gays in the military. Each case of a deserving, courageous person drummed out of the military is tragic. But Democrats would be better off trying to move the debate to issues that affect more people.

Same with gay marriage. Right-wingers target gay marriage because it's emotional and fraught with religious overtones. But what they don't talk about—and what we should talk more about—is employment nondiscrimination. It's a much bigger issue. While perhaps only a fraction of gay Americans wants to join the military or get married, virtually every gay American wants to be able to hold down a job. And yet today, in America, it is perfectly legal to fire someone for being gay. That is simply un-American.

Democrats should speak out more strongly in support of the Employment Non-Discrimination Act, or ENDA. We should ask our friends who are queasy about marriage and the military whether they believe people should be fired on account of whom they fall in love with. We ought to shift the debate away from the more divisive terrain for now and advance on fronts where the American people are moving our way. In 1977 just 56 percent of Americans said gays should be treated equally in terms of opportunity; by 2001 that number had soared to 85 percent.[53] Success breeds success. So start with employment and go from there.

Too many Democrats want to ignore the issue of gay rights entirely, hoping instead to win folks over with their ideas on health care, jobs, and education. We think that's a bridge too far. If a Democrat is asked about gay marriage and she answers in terms of health care, it looks like a dodge. That's because it *is* a dodge. It's far better simply to broaden the debate by saying something like "I believe marriage is between one man and one woman. But I do not support people being fired from their job for being gay. Did you know that it's legal under federal law to fire someone for being gay? That's wrong. That's why I support the Employment Non-Discrimination Act."

Focusing on employment will put the monkey on the Republicans' back. The more craven Republican politicians will be torn between fealty to the fanatic fringe and a desire to appeal to the mainstream. They won't know whether to wind their asses or scratch their watches.

Besides the strategic advantage we get from focusing on ending employment discrimination, it's the right thing to do—morally and economically.

Our brilliant and brave friends at the Human Rights Campaign, the premier gay-rights organization in Washington, point out that a woman in Georgia who was an award-winning cook was fired when her company adopted a written policy against employing gay Americans.[54] A teacher in Kansas (who happened to be straight) was fired because someone *suggested* he was gay.[55] And when a postal worker in Michigan was beaten at work because coworkers thought he was gay, the federal courts ruled his civil rights had not been violated, because "homosexuality is not an impermissible criteria on which to discriminate" under Title VII of the 1964 Civil Rights Act.[56]

Our favorite example of employment discrimination is one that shows the stunning, staggering hypocrisy of Republican politicians. Mike Bowers, the homophobic former attorney general of Georgia, rescinded a job offer to attorney Robin Shahar when he learned she'd had a ceremony celebrating her commitment to her lesbian partner. Bowers told ABC News that, yes, America is a free country, "but that doesn't mean they [gays] can do whatever they want to, no more than I can."[57] Ah, but Mike, you did do whatever you wanted. While piously preening about morality, you were having a ten-year affair with a woman who worked under you in the attorney general's office.[58]

The bottom line here is that employment discrimination against gays is a reality. Democrats should fight against it.

2. Go Beyond the "Inborn Versus Choice" Debate

For some, this issue pivots on the question of whether homosexuality is an immutable characteristic or a lifestyle choice. We know that we never chose to be straight. Both James's wife, Mary, and Paul's wife, Diane, have brothers who are perfectly attractive. Neither of us ever even considered dating them. No, we were drawn to females by something powerful and innate. In fact, we don't know anyone who sat down with a legal pad and wrote out the pros and cons of being gay versus straight. (What would it be? "Hmmmm . . . on the one hand, I'd have a better fashion sense. But on the other hand, some adulterous Republican hypocrite could fire me for being gay. . . .") This debate matters, because if being gay is an immutable characteristic, like skin color, then to discriminate on that basis is wrong. We don't countenance discrimination based on a characteristic we're powerless to control.

Right-wing culture warriors are certain that being gay is a choice, not something we're born with. In fact, the right-wing nutballs at Focus on the Family host a conference called Love Won Out where they preach the nonsense that homosexuality can be "cured." "Homosexuality is preventable and treatable," they bleat, trying to make being gay sound like a disease.[59] But the American Psychiatric Association, the American Psychological Association, the American Counseling Association, the American Academy of Pediatrics, and the National Association of School Psychologists all say homosexuality is not a mental disorder. It's not something to be "treated" and "cured."[60]

Republican National Committee chairman Ken Mehlman was asked how he felt about this by NBC's Tim Russert on *Meet the Press*. Mehlman is a skilled operative, a well-educated attorney who oversaw one of the most brilliant campaigns in American history. Yet he had no idea how to answer Russert's simple question: "Do you believe homosexuality is a choice?" Mehlman said, "I don't know the answer to that question. I don't think it matters to the fundamental question here, because at bottom, this president believes in nondiscrimination. He believes in equal treatment. He believes in respect for all. . . ."

At this point we believed we were going to throw up. We were thinking, "If, as you say, Ken, at bottom President Bush believes in nondiscrimination, why doesn't he support, at bottom, the Employment Non-Discrimination Act? It's even in the name, Ken: *Non-Discrimination*." Russert, undeterred by Mehlman's spin, tried again:

RUSSERT: But the Log Cabin Republicans will say if you're born gay, it's a biological determination, not a matter of choice.

MEHLMAN: And that's— That may be, but the fact is that's irrelevant to the question of the public definition of marriage. They're two totally different issues.[61]

Huh? Mehlman began by saying the president doesn't support discrimination. Then he went on to say Bush does support discrimination. "They're two totally different issues." No, they're two totally different positions on the same issue. That's called hypocrisy.

To his credit, Mehlman didn't endorse the right-wing claptrap about homosexuality being a choice. But he didn't repudiate it, either. Then he said it didn't matter. In a way, he's right. It doesn't matter whether being gay is innate or a choice. For the sake of argument, let's stipulate that homosexuality *is* a choice. So what? There are some choices in life that are so central to our identity, our happiness, our freedom, that we protect them in law. Our choice of religion, for one. America's civil rights laws say your employer can't fire you because of your choice of religion. The boss cannot walk up to your cubicle tomorrow and say, "Jenkins, you're fired for being a Lutheran." Jenkins chose to be a Lutheran—religious denomination is not, obviously, innate. But it's a choice that is so central to our personal integrity, our freedom, the pursuit of happiness, that we have decided to honor and protect that choice.

Democrats can probably win the debate over whether folks choose to be gay or are born that way, but we should stress that even if it is a choice, it's not a valid basis for discrimination. The analogy to religion is apt, because it shows respect for religion—something we need when we're debating against people who oppose gay rights based on their interpretation of their religion.

3. Personalize the Discussion

As more gays come out of the closet, more of us realize we have gay friends, gay relatives, gay children, and gay neighbors. Prejudice relies on stereotypes. Stereotypes rely on ignorance. Ignorance melts away in the face of firsthand experience. Democrats should speak proudly of their gay relatives and point out that if voters are looking for someone who's going to try to put good old Cousin Ralph in prison just because he's gay, they'll have to look elsewhere. Family values start with loyalty to family. People respect that. Most right-wing Republicans love Dick Cheney, despite the fact that he pointedly opposes President Bush's cynical attempt to amend the Constitution to outlaw gay marriage. Why? Because they know Vice President and Mrs. Cheney have a gay daughter. Democrats shouldn't use Mary Cheney as a political prop. But referring to your own willing and out gay relative personalizes the debate.

4. Repeat After Us: Dick Cheney Is Right

Speaking of Dick Cheney, he has articulated the liberal position on gay rights pretty effectively. In his debate with Joe Lieberman in 2000, Cheney was asked about gay rights, specifically marriage and civil unions. This is what he said:

"The fact of the matter is we live in a free society, and freedom means freedom for everybody. We shouldn't be able to choose and say you get to live free and you don't. That means people should be free to enter into any kind of relationship they want to enter into. It's no one's business in terms of regulating behavior in that regard." Cheney went on to say he opposes gay marriage, per se, but: "I think we ought to do everything we can to tolerate and accommodate whatever kind of relationships people want to enter into." [62]

In five sentences, Cheney said it all: that this is an issue of personal freedom (an argument that appeals to Americans' bias against government intrusion); that who you fall in love with is no one's business (a libertarian notion); and that you can oppose gay marriage while acknowledging that love relationships deserve some legal protection. Good for you, Dick.

The Cheneys deserve enormous credit for publicly embracing their lesbian daughter. Some on the far right blame parents for children's homosexuality, viewing it as a "gender-identity disorder," caused by insufficient attention from the parent of that child's gender. [63]

What a load of crap. From what we can see, the Cheneys are model parents and model grandparents. But we can only imagine the grief they took from their so-called allies on the right. Tony Perkins of the Orwellian-named Family Research Council blasted Cheney: "I find it hard to believe the vice president would stray from the administration's position on defense policy or tax policy. For many pro-family voters, protecting traditional marriage ranks ahead of the economy and job creation as a campaign issue." [64]

And yet, to his credit, Cheney didn't back off an inch. He acknowledged that President Bush was calling for an anti-gay constitutional amendment and, while observing that Bush sets policy in the administration, he noted that he opposes such an amendment.

Democrats can—and should—hide behind Cheney. Make the Republicans say that we're anti-family for taking the same position as Dick Cheney. If our position is a threat to the sanctity of marriage (an argument we find comical), then Dick Cheney is an even bigger threat. And if they don't know our vice president is pro-gay-rights, they don't know Dick.

5. Slow Down

Democrats need to respect Americans who are a bit dizzy from the pace of social change, especially in the area of gay rights. Representative Barney Frank of Massachusetts, one of the party's smartest strategic thinkers, pointedly and publicly criticized San Francisco mayor Gavin Newsom's move to marry gays and lesbians in defiance of California law. Frank is hardly anti-gay. He's a practical realist—and a lawyer. "When you're in a real struggle, San Francisco making a symbolic point becomes a diversion," he said.[65] Frank has made the point that the time-consuming process of amending the Massachusetts constitution works in favor of gay-rights defenders. It will take years for opponents to change the Massachusetts constitution, and during that time, folks will be able to see for themselves that gay unions haven't been a threat to anyone's marriage.

This kind of strategic smarts is essential. We need to be for progress, not perfection. The gay-rights movement is, after all, a movement. As long as it's moving in the right direction, we should be happy. But if the pace of change outruns people's ability to process, digest, and accept it, a backlash will ensue.

Dr. Martin Luther King, Jr., got this. Knowing that much of the anti–civil rights fervor was fed by bigots who played on fears of interracial marriage, he defused the issue, saying, "I want to be the white man's brother, not his brother-in-law."[66] If someone said this today, he'd be called a racist. Interracial marriage was declared a constitutionally protected right five years after Dr. King uttered those words. But America needed those five years, and Dr. King understood that.

Gay-rights advocates need to understand it as well. Democrats must recognize and respect that the pace of social change can be overwhelming to some. Understanding that pace helped make Dr. King one of the great moral leaders of American history. Laudably, gay-rights activists have learned Dr. King's lesson.

6. Attack the Republicans for Dividing Americans and Distracting Us from Common Challenges

A CNN–*USA TODAY*–Gallup poll in 2005 asked Americans to rank nine issues in the order of their importance. Terrorism and Iraq, health care, and the economy all clustered at the top in basically a four-way tie. Education, Social Security, and taxes trailed the top-tier issues. Limiting lawsuits is a much lower priority—28 percent lower than Iraq and terror. And then comes limiting gay marriage. Over twice as many Americans say Iraq and terrorism—or the economy and education—are the most important issues, as compared to those who say limiting gay marriage should be the government's most important priority.[67]

The question is, Why are Republicans spending so much time on an issue that's clearly one of the least important issues in America? Because they have a strategy of division, distraction, and diversion. If they can make people turn away for a moment from the debacle in Iraq or the export of American jobs, they can win elections. Democrats should call them on this by pointing out that the Republicans are doing to the whole country what they don't want two men to do in the privacy of their own home.

God

How the hell (oops!) did Republicans claim God as the private property of the GOP? We've checked, and God is not a registered Republican. And yet Republicans yap so much about their deep love for God, and God's deep love for them, that you half expect to see the Almighty wearing one of those goofy elephant hats.

So, how did this happen? First, the Republicans made a conscious effort to bring conservative, churchgoing Americans into their ranks. Up until the 1970s, fundamentalist Protestants eschewed taking an active role in politics. Many believed they should be "in the world, not of the world." Indeed, to be "worldly" was a bad thing. Thus, many evangelicals up to the 1970s were politically inactive.

At the same time, the left was openly religious. One of Dr. King's most important epistles—his Letter from Birmingham Jail—was addressed to the clergy. John F. Kennedy had to parry charges that since he was a Catholic, his policies as president would be dictated by the pope in Rome—essentially a charge that he was too religious. Despite those fears, Kennedy closed his Inaugural Address with these words: "Let us go forth to lead the land we love, asking His blessing and His help, but knowing that here on earth, God's work must truly be our own." [68] In the last speech he ever wrote, a speech he did not survive to deliver, Franklin Roosevelt exhorted his fellow Americans to "move forward with a strong and active faith." [69]

As happens from time to time in American politics, the two parties essentially switched sides. The social changes of the 1960s and '70s galvanized religious conservatives and helped draw them into the political system. Many right-wing Protestants, including Reverend Jerry Falwell, opposed racial integration. Indeed, Falwell hosted Governor George Wallace, America's foremost race-baiter, on the *Old Time Gospel Hour* in 1972.[70] Race may have begun the shift, but it was hardly the only issue that propelled conservative Protestant evangelicals into the vortex of politics. Birth control and abortion were legalized by the Supreme Court. Forced school prayer was found to be unconstitutional. College students with long hair were protesting the war in Vietnam. Women were burning their bras. Drug use became commonplace, even among the children of the pillars of the establishment. In the blink of an eye, the cutting edge of rock and roll went from the Beatles singing "I Wanna Hold Your Hand" to the Rolling Stones screaming "Let's Spend the Night Together."

In other words, stuff happened.

With the world seemingly spinning out of control, Republicans moved quickly. As Paul Weyrich, one of the pioneers of the self-described religious right, recalls, in the late 1970s he was having a hard time persuading conservative Christian ministers to engage in politics. So he took a poll, and in a secret meeting with some of the leading lights of evangelism, Weyrich has written, "the survey was revealed. It showed that not only would the followers of their ministries not leave, their followers were anxious for their ministries to get active politically. And here was the zinger . . . the survey showed that people would be willing to contribute to political activity in addition to contributing to the ministries. That was it."[71] That was it, indeed. God and mammon, joined together.

As fate would have it, at the very point when these preachers were predisposed to lead their congregants into right-wing politics, there emerged a charismatic political leader ready to ease the transition into worldly politics: Ronald Wilson Reagan. Just after securing the GOP nomination in 1980, Reagan told a convention of twenty thousand evangelicals gathered in Dallas that he understood their reluctance to get too publicly active in politics, but with a wink and a nod he sealed the deal: "I know you can't endorse me, but I endorse you."[72]

As Weyrich, Falwell, Reagan, and others were herding conservative evangelicals into the GOP, liberals seemed to be losing their religious roots. In the name of pluralism and tolerance, they sent signals that were seen as hostile to religion. The leftist writer Christopher Hitchens attacked Mother Teresa in a book with the charming title *Missionary Position*. (It should be noted that Hitchens has undergone something of a political metamorphosis, becoming a semi-professional Clinton-hater. He is now one of the chief cheerleaders for Bush's war in Iraq. Note to our right-wing friends: You can have Hitchens. We don't want him.) CNN founder Ted Turner, at an Ash Wednesday retirement party for the legendary anchor Bernard Shaw, noticed the ashes on many of his CNNers' foreheads and said, "What are you, a bunch of Jesus freaks? You ought to be working for FOX."[73]

Keep in mind that both Hitchens and Turner are members of the media, not the Democratic Party. As a rule, Democrats are too tolerant—and too P.C.—to make fun of anybody. But what many leading Democrats did was just as damaging. They stopped talking about religion and refused to acknowledge the role faith plays in their lives. As one Democratic aide told the perceptive Amy Sullivan of *The Washington Monthly,* "Democrats worry about talking about religion in a way that endorses a particular faith or offends anyone. So they've just decided not to talk about religion around other people, and that's hurting them."[74]

Sullivan notes that in the 2004 campaign, Dick Gephardt, a devout Baptist, usually mentioned his religion only when he said he'd gotten a scholarship from his church. Joe Lieberman, one of the most openly religious Democrats, eased off on the religious rhetoric in 2004, telling fellow Jews that his support for President Bush's faith-based initiative was rooted more in liberalism than in Judaism.[75] John Kerry, who was an altar boy, was caught in a time warp. When asked about his faith, Kerry usually repeated a variation of JFK's line that the church would not control him. While we agree that no politician should surrender his or her conscience and conviction, it looked to us like Kerry hadn't appreciated the tectonic shift since JFK's time. In 1960, Kennedy had to reassure nervous Protestants that he wasn't too Catholic. In 2004, Kerry had to reassure his coreligionists that he was Catholic enough. Thus, when Kerry gave the JFK answer, this deeply religious man unwittingly reaffirmed many people's concerns.

As Republicans became more openly religious and Democrats became more reticent about their faith, the right wing opened a new front. In the classic American tradition, they claimed victim status, posing themselves as an oppressed minority.

Say what?

How can Christians be an oppressed minority when 83 percent of Americans say they're Christian?[76] Right-wingers seem to have adopted one of the more distasteful tactics of the old left: whining. And why not? Every single American president has been Christian, and Christians are the colossal majority in Congress, in the courts, in the bureaucracy, in business, the military, academia, sports, and just about every other facet of American life. In fact, about the only place in America not run by Christians is the synagogue.

And yet somehow millions of Christians—especially conservative white Christians—see themselves as an oppressed minority. Republican congressman John Hostetler of Indiana somehow turned the tables during a House debate on an amendment that would require the Pentagon to investigate allegations of evangelical Christians mistreating non-Christians at the Air

Force Academy. Although the topic was allegations that Christians were abusing non-Christians, Hostetler said, "The long war on Christianity in America continues today on the floor of the House of Representatives." He alleged that this war—waged against 83 percent of Americans—"continues unabated with aid and comfort to those who would eradicate any vestige of our Christian heritage being supplied by the usual suspects, the Democrats. Like a moth to a flame, Democrats can't help themselves when it comes to denigrating and demonizing Christians."[77]

Hostetler's outburst was typical. When Democrats tried to block seven well-heeled, highly educated, privileged lawyers from the federal bench, Republicans saw anti-Christian bigotry there, too. A collection of wing nuts organized by the Family Research Council organized a church-based right-wing political rally called Justice Sunday. The name sounded to us like a new flavor from Ben & Jerry's, but the wingers were serious—and seriously aggrieved. They'd somehow cracked the code. Democrats, they alleged, weren't blocking the Bush Seven because they disagreed with their judicial philosophy. No, it was their religion. See if you can follow this: Democrats had by then confirmed two hundred Bush judges. If we're anti-religious, then what were the two hundred: atheists? Pagans? Druids? Undeterred by the facts, the wingers drew a parallel to the civil rights movement (which many conservative Christians opposed in a most un-Christian way). "The filibuster was once abused to protect racial bias," their flyer read. "And it is now being used against people of faith."[78] The poor, benighted Christian conservatives never did explain how the Democrats even knew what the religion of the nominees was; only a few had listed their religion on the Justice Department's website biographies. For example, Bush's nominee for the D.C. Circuit Court, Janice Rogers Brown, listed no religious affiliation on her official Justice Department biography.[79] Same with Bill Pryor, Bush's nominee for the Eleventh Circuit.[80] But wait! Judge Priscilla Owen, the Texas Supreme Court Justice whom President Bush put on the Fifth Circuit, slipped up. Her official bio says she's—gasp!—an Episcopalian.[81] Of all the religious denominations, we daresay the least discriminated against is Episcopalian. George Washington was an Episcopalian of sorts.[82] Ten other presidents were Episcopalian, including one of the Roosevelts (Franklin) and one of the Bushes (George

H.W.)[83] Not bad for a religion whose adherents constitute just 1.7 percent of the country's population.[84]

Besides, just whom are we supposed to be prejudiced against? Baptists? Hardly. Jimmy Carter, Bill Clinton, and Al Gore, the last three Democrats to win presidential elections (no, we haven't gotten over 2000), are Baptists. How 'bout Methodists? President Bush is a Methodist. Maybe that's whom Democrats hate. But wait. Hillary Clinton is a Methodist, and a devout one at that. Okay, scratch the Methodists. What about Mormons—Latter-day Saints? Orrin Hatch, one of the most influential Republican senators on judicial nominations, is LDS. Sorry, so is Harry Reid, the Senate Democratic leader. If we were prejudiced against LDS, we never would have made Reid our leader. Okay, Catholics. Justices Clarence Thomas and Antonin Scalia are Catholic, and liberals can't abide them. Your humble authors are Catholic, and not the self-loathing kind. So is John Kerry. So are Ted Kennedy, Pat Leahy, and Dick Durbin, three of the senior Democrats on the Senate Judiciary Committee. That leaves the Jews. Let's face it, if any religion truly has faced discrimination in America, it's Judaism. But we don't think any of the judicial nominees whom the Democrats opposed were Jewish. But Joe Lieberman, our party's 2000 nominee for vice president, is Jewish. Jews vote overwhelmingly Democratic, and no political party hates its most loyal voters.

It's all pretty amusing. Or it would be if not for all the good, faithful, religious Americans who believe this horse hockey. There's something in the right-wing character that needs to feel oppressed. In his landmark 1964 essay, "The Paranoid Style in American Politics," Richard Hofstadter quotes Norman Cohn's description of paranoids from millennial sects in Europe from the eleventh to sixteenth centuries: "The megalomaniac view of oneself as the Elect, wholly good, abominably persecuted, yet assured of ultimate triumph; the attribution of gigantic and demonic powers to the adversary; the refusal to accept the ineluctable limitations and imperfections of human existence, such as transience, dissention, conflict, fallibility whether intellectual or moral; the obsession with inerrable prophecies . . . systematized misinterpretations, always gross and often grotesque."[85]

Sound familiar? Think we're exaggerating when we say those on the far fringes of the self-proclaimed Christian right have a "megalomaniacal view of [themselves] as the Elect, wholly good [and] abominably persecuted"? Reverend Pat Robertson, the right-wing Republican preacher who said 9/11 was God's punishment for America's sinfulness, has also accused liberals of an all-out assault on Christianity. In his book *Courting Disaster,* he claims that Democrat-appointed judges are the most serious threat America has faced in nearly four hundred years of history.

And we thought we were masters of hyperbole. Perhaps, you might think, Robertson is just saying this for dramatic (if overstated) effect. An incredulous George Stephanopoulos of ABC News confronted Robertson about it, asking him if he really believed that liberal judges are a "more serious [threat] than Al Qaeda, more serious than Nazi Germany and Japan, more serious than the Civil War?" Robertson didn't bat an eye. "George," he said. "I really believe that."[86]

Now, *that's* saying something. The founder of the Christian Coalition says Democrats and the judges they appoint are a greater threat to America than the Nazis? Than the terrorists? Than the slave masters and the segregationists? It is so paranoid, so delusional, that one wants to dismiss it as an insane rant.

And yet it is widely believed.

Why else would conservatives complain that in a country that is 83 percent Christian, it is somehow impermissible to wish someone "Merry Christmas"? But that's what the Committee to Save Merry Christmas thinks. The California-based group called for a boycott of Macy's, claiming the department-store chain replaced MERRY CHRISTMAS signs with banners reading (we hope you're sitting down; this is shocking) HAPPY HOLIDAYS or (gee whiz, we hope kids aren't reading this) SEASON'S GREETINGS.[87]

There's only one problem. Macy's says it isn't true. It says the folks who run each store are free to hang whatever signs they feel are appropriate, and that its ads commonly use the phrase "Merry Christmas."[88] Another paranoid story claims UPS drivers were instructed not to wish their customers "Merry Christmas." UPS says the claim is, "silly on its face and just not true."[89]

Yeah, but it's such a *good* story.

Why does this stuff work? Why would sensible people believe that 83 percent of Americans are being oppressed by the other 17 percent? We believe culture and class are at the heart of the answer.

First the culture. Reverend Jim Wallis, the progressive evangelical minister who wrote the best-selling book *God's Politics,* says his most consistent applause line is "Raising children in today's society is a counter-cultural activity." Audiences—including liberal audiences—respond to the notion that today's culture is hostile to raising children with strong values. Conservatives see things like the broadening acceptance of gay rights, the failure to outlaw abortion, and lawsuits seeking to remove "under God" from the Pledge of Allegiance, and they believe their traditional values are under assault. At the same time, liberals think materialism, intolerance, and the politics of personal destruction are just as damaging. Both sides feel frustrated by their inability to turn back what they see as a dangerous tide of cultural waste. That frustration makes them prime targets for an argument that they're a victimized, oppressed minority. Clever right-wing propagandists are making that argument to disaffected conservatives. No one is making the parallel argument to liberals. Hence, millions of Christian Americans have been conned into thinking they're under assault.

We say "conned" because the conservative big shots who are advocating the culture of victimization are actually in the best position to do something about it. If the honchos at FOX News were truly concerned about the hyper-sexuality of prime-time television, all they'd have to do is walk down the hall to FOX Entertainment, where the programming is so explicit, so sexual, so sordid that we can't even watch a Saturday-afternoon ball game on FOX without covering our kids' ears and eyes during the promos for the network's prime-time shows. FOX's entertainment division creates highly profitable sleaze, and FOX's news division creates highly profitable talk shows on which the hosts decry indecency in the entertainment industry. What a racket.

Or how about those endless (and pathetic) ads for wiener drugs? You know, Viagra, Cialis, Levitra. The folks who are exposing our children to erectile-dysfunction ads are the same pharmaceutical-industry executives who give millions to the Republicans. Who, in turn, tell TV viewers that they should express their anger over those Republican-leaning pharmaceutical companies' ads . . . by voting Republican. (Here's a free Carville-Begala parenting tip on how to explain those gross ads to your kids. When one of our children asks, "Daddy, what's erectile dysfunction?," we tell them, "You don't have to worry about it. It's a disease that only affects Republican men.")

Class is as much a part of this as culture. Thomas Frank has it right. In *What's the Matter with Kansas?*, he documents the class-based resentments nursed by lower- and middle-income Americans. What's stunning is that, rather than rage bitterly against the millionaire moguls who have stacked the deck against them, they fume about supposedly liberal "cultural elites." Of course, Michael Moore didn't force overstressed and hard-pressed parents into working two jobs—or three. Barbra Streisand didn't rig the economic deck so that most families require Mom to work outside the home. Steven Spielberg doesn't make dirty movies or sleazy TV shows. Republican economic and social policies have created the culture that so repulses Christian conservatives. But that's not how the conservative elites pitch their message. "Joe Six-Pack doesn't understand," says Gary Bauer, one of the savviest leaders of the far right, "why the world and his culture are changing and why he doesn't have a say in it."[90]

Dr. Frank notes that conservatives masterfully fed class-based resentment against John Kerry. He cites an anti-Kerry pamphlet published by the American Conservative Union that says, "Like many children of affluent parents, John Kerry joined the so-called New Left in its relentless attack on America."

Huh?

Can you imagine the chutzpah it took to write something like that? First, John Kerry's parents were actually not very well off. Second, rather than joining the "New Left" and attacking America, Kerry joined the U.S. Navy and fought against Communists in Vietnam. Perhaps just as important, George W. Bush truly was a child of privilege who did all he could to avoid fighting in Vietnam. But he's not a liberal, so in the conservative mind, he's not an elite. Class, Frank has written, "is a matter of cultural authenticity rather than material interests." In touring West Virginia before the 2004 election, Frank says he "spotted Bush posters adorning even the humblest of dwellings and mobile homes." Voters there said they were voting for Bush because of abortion or gun control.[91]

We've already discussed abortion and gun control. But how do we reconnect with voters who believe God is on the Republicans' side—or at least that Republicans are on God's side? Here's how to Take Back the issue of faith.

1. Give Voice to Our Faith

When, in a 2000 debate, George W. Bush was asked to name his favorite political philosopher, he responded instantly, "Christ. Because he changed my
heart." Some of the devout, hearing that, were appalled. Jesus Christ was the
Son of God and presumably had a leg up on human philosophers. Naming
Christ as our favorite philosopher is kind of like saying He was the greatest
winemaker ever, or the finest fisherman, or the best doctor. It's almost blas-
phemous.

Still, Bush's target audience got the point. They overlooked the implicit
rejection of Christ's divinity and focused instead on the larger point that
Bush credits Christ with turning his life around. Throughout his presidency,
Bush has employed evangelical verbiage. In his 2003 State of the Union address, he said, "There is power—wonder-working power—in the goodness
and idealism and faith of the American people." Nonbelievers heard a nicely
turned phrase, but Christians heard their president quoting an evangelical
hymn whose actual words are "There is . . . wonder-working power in the
blood of the Lamb."[92]

There's no reason Democrats of faith can't do the same thing. To be sure,
faith informs and influences the policy positions of lots of Democrats, at
least as much as faith drives Republicans. After all, we don't believe Jesus
would have protected tobacco companies that marketed poison to children.
We don't think the Holy Spirit was behind the accounting miracles at Enron.
We refuse to believe that God wants more mercury in the water, more car-
cinogens in the air, more dioxin in the ground.

Democrats simply must be more comfortable alluding to their faith in
public. We respect the profoundly private faith many Democrats have, but in
the current climate, if people don't hear a candidate referring to her faith,
they presume she has none. When asked by the *Ladies' Home Journal* whether
President Bush invoked his faith too often, Kerry said, "I personally would
not choose—though I'm a person of faith—to insert it as much as this president does. I think it crosses a line, and it sort of squeezes the diversity that the
president is supposed to embrace."[93] That's a reasonable and nuanced position. But during a campaign in which the far right was desperate to declare

Kerry an infidel, the words got mangled and misunderstood. Conservative columnist Brent Bozell jumped immediately. He was kind enough to translate Kerry's words, claiming that what the senator had meant to say was "I'm a Catholic, I'm a legislator, but by God I'm not a Catholic legislator." [94]

So forget nuance. Democrats need to hit voters where they live—or, rather, where they pray. That's the message of Jim Wallis. In a 2003 *New York Times* op-ed, he begged Democrats to give voice to their faith. Imagine how different the election might have been if Democrats had heeded Wallis's plea:

> It is indeed possible (and necessary) to express one's faith and convictions about public policy while still respecting the pluralism of American democracy. Rather than suggesting that we not talk about "God," Democrats should be arguing—on moral and even religious grounds—that all Americans should have economic security, health care, and educational opportunity, and that true faith results in a compassionate concern for those on the margins.
>
> God is always personal, but never private. The Democrats are wrong to restrict religion to the private sphere—just as the Republicans are wrong to define it solely in terms of individual moral choices and sexual ethics. Allowing the right to decide what is a religious issue would be both a moral and political tragedy.

Amen, Brother Jim. Amen.

Instead of simply opposing savage budget cuts for the poor in order to preserve massive tax cuts for the rich, we ought to tell folks that our priorities are different—and closer to Jesus'. In the Sermon on the Mount, Jesus said this about setting priorities: "For where your treasure is, there will your heart be also" (Matthew 6:21). Democrats should say: "Look at where the Republicans put our treasure, and we'll know where their heart is. Their heart is with the overprivileged, with the special interests, that's why they put our treasure there."

Or progressive taxation? Instead of explaining why it's the right economic or fiscal policy, we should unapologetically quote Christ: "From everyone who has been given much, much will be required; and to whom they entrusted much, of him they will ask all the more" (Luke 12:48).

Jesus, of course, predated capitalism. But He had strong views about the rich. When He was asked if there was anything a believer had to do other than obey the Commandments, the Gospel tells, "Looking at him, Jesus felt a love for him and said to him, 'One thing you lack: go and sell all you possess and give to the poor, and you will have treasure in heaven; and come, follow Me. But at these words he was saddened, and he went away grieving, for he was one who owned much property. And Jesus, looking around, said to His disciples, 'How hard it will be for those who are wealthy to enter the kingdom of God!'

"The disciples were amazed at His words. But Jesus answered again and said to them, 'Children, how hard it is to enter the kingdom of God! It is easier for a camel to go through the eye of a needle than for a rich man to enter the kingdom of God'" (Mark 10:21–25).

We're certainly not biblical scholars. We were lucky to get through Sunday school. But this seems pretty clear: Jesus wasn't a fan of the rich. We've heard some apologists for the rich say that Jesus was speaking metaphorically. Could be. We hope so, since we've been pretty lucky financially. But if Jesus was speaking metaphorically about camels and needles, we think John the Baptist was being literal when he said, "He that hath two coats, let him impart to him that hath none; and he that hath meat, let him do likewise" (Luke 3:11).

Jesus' followers got the message. After He was resurrected, "all that believed were together, and had all things common; And sold their possessions and goods, and parted them to all men, as every man had need" (Acts 2:44–45).

If a Democrat called for an economic policy in which everyone with two coats gave one to the poor, in which no one owned possessions but everyone owned everything in common, in which everyone received what she or he needed, Republicans from Rush Limbaugh to the Chamber of Commerce would be calling him a Commie. Let's face it: Jesus would be a pariah in the Republican Party.

Consider school prayer: James went to Catholic school in Louisiana, so prayer was never an issue there. Paul went to John Foster Dulles Junior High and John Foster Dulles High School in Sugar Land, Texas. (They weren't very creative in their choice of names, and though there's no record that

Dulles ever set foot in Sugar Land, the city fathers had a pretty good idea he was anti-Communist, and that was good enough for them.) In Sugar Land, Paul saw the only two Jewish kids in his school get up and stand in the hall each morning as the principal read a fundamentalist Christian morning devotional. Funny, the devotional never quoted Matthew 6:5–6: "When you pray, you are not to be like the hypocrites; for they love to stand and pray in the synagogues and on the street corners so that they may be seen by men. Truly I say to you, they have their reward in full. But you, when you pray, go into your inner room, close your door and pray to your Father who is in secret, and your Father who sees what is done in secret will reward you."

When we read the painful story about then-governor Bush mocking Karla Fay Tucker's last desperate plea for life—a plea that Pat Robertson and other evangelicals took heed of—or when we watched Bush smirk and giggle as he was asked about death-penalty cases in which lawyers slept while their clients were condemned to die, we turned to John 8:4–5: "They said unto him, Master, this woman was taken in adultery, in the very act. Now Moses in the law commanded us, that such should be stoned: but what sayest thou?" Jesus stopped the lawful execution of a person guilty of a capital offense, saying, "He that is without sin among you, let him first cast a stone at her."

How about the environment? Our evidently faithful Christian in the White House asks for regulations that would allow more arsenic in our drinking water, more mercury in our air, more logging in our national forests, more drilling in our national wilderness, more mining in our national parks. Has he not read Revelation 7:3: "Hurt not the earth, neither the sea, nor the trees"?

Too often, when Democrats discuss the poor, they talk like sociologists. They ought to talk like preachers and priests, rabbis and imams. When Republicans—with the help of shameless Democratic sellouts—pass a bankruptcy bill that all but brings back Dickensian debtors' prisons; when Republicans—with the help of other shameless Democratic sellouts—pass tax cuts that favor the greedy and hurt the needy; when Republicans—with the help of still other shameless Democratic sellouts—kill the minimum wage, cut health care for the poor, and slash anti-poverty programs, Democrats—real Democrats—should roar like God Almighty did in the Book of Malachi:

"I will draw near to you for judgment; and I will be a swift witness against
. . . those who oppress the wage earner in his wages, the widow and the or-
phan, and those who turn aside the alien and do not fear Me" (Malachi 3:5).

Why don't Democrats talk this way? Okay, so our examples are a little
overdrawn. We're not suggesting the Democratic Party become the Christian
Democratic Party, citing the Bible for our position on global warming. But
what's wrong with pointing to our faith as the source of our values? Republicans certainly do it. And the Jesus they yammer about is almost entirely absent from the Gospels. To hear the right-wingers tell it, Jesus spent His
ministry railing against homos and fornicators. They'd have us believe Jesus
took a whip to gays and feminists, rather than to the money changers in the
temple. In reality, Jim Wallis says he's found three thousand verses in the
Bible dealing with the need to take care of the poor.[95] Jesus, especially, focused on the moral imperative of caring for the poor—and to our knowledge, he never once mentioned homosexuality.

Like Lincoln (a Republican who'd actually read the Gospels), we're not
saying God's on our side; we're just praying that we're on God's side.

It is no accident that the last two presidents our party has produced were
openly, explicitly religious. Jimmy Carter based his presidential campaign on
the simple but profound power of his integrity, vowing, "I'll never lie to you."
After years of Richard Nixon's lies, the Sunday-school teacher from Plains,
Georgia, had just the right message. Bill Clinton's appeal was much less
rooted in a call for moral cleansing, but he was utterly comfortable in his faith
tradition. Young Bill Clinton attended a Billy Graham revival in 1959,[96] and
he later recalled how impressed he'd been that Graham, a southerner through
and through, refused to preach at a whites-only, segregated revival. Just as
Bush sprinkles his speeches with references to evangelical hymns, Clinton
called his signature idea of a government that rewards those who work hard
and play by the rules the "New Covenant," the words Jesus used to describe
the pact He sealed with mankind at the Last Supper (Luke 22:20).

Let's be clear. We don't think Democrats should ape the Republicans'
sanctimony. We do not think Democrats who don't have faith should suddenly adopt one—or, worse, fake it. What we're saying is that Democrats of
faith should not hide their light under a basket.

2. Challenge the Right Wing's Definition of "Values"

Our friends on the right have the oddest sense of what's important. Jerry Falwell famously accused the character Tinky Winky from the children's show *Teletubbies* of being gay.[97] The Traditional Values Coalition found gay propaganda in *Shrek 2*.[98] A North Carolina preacher has alleged that Bert and Ernie of *Sesame Street* are gay.[99]

This obsession with kiddy characters leading our children into temptation is not, sad to say, limited to wack-job preachers. The first major public act performed by Margaret Spellings upon assuming the post of secretary of education was not to address test scores, nor drug use in schools, nor even the crumbling classrooms all across America. No, Secretary Spellings had her priorities right—or, should we say, ultra-right. The first thing she did was go after Buster the Bunny. Buster is the star of PBS's *Postcards from Buster,* wherein an animated *Oryctolagus cuniculus* visits families in various parts of America. The ever-vigilant Spellings learned that Buster was planning to visit a lesbian couple in Vermont. Instantly, she leaped into action, threatened Buster's funding, and got the offending broadcast banned in much of America.[100]

When they're not hyperventilating about the sexuality of puppets and cartoon characters, conservatives piously lecture the rest of us about other carnal issues: birth control (bad), premarital sex (very bad), abortion (very, very bad), and human homosexuality (so bad I think I'm gonna faint). While the self-righteous right has an almost perverse fixation on matters sexual, most Americans define moral values more expansively. When the poorly worded 2004 presidential exit poll revealed that "moral values" had been the force behind one fifth of the vote, pollster John Zogby decided to probe more deeply. What, after all, do people mean when they talk about moral values? Abortion and gay rights were doubtless important in targeted constituencies. But when Zogby asked people what they mean by "moral values," he came up with some interesting findings.

"The Zogby poll shows that when voters were asked to list the moral issue that most affected their vote, the Iraq war topped the list (42 percent)—

more than triple the number that chose abortion (13 percent) or gay marriage (9 percent). Also, when asked to choose the most urgent moral crisis facing the U.S., voters chose 'greed and materialism' (33 percent) and 'poverty and economic justice' (31 percent) twice as often as abortion (16 percent) and gay marriage (12 percent)." [101]

So, if the war in Iraq is the most important moral issue, and if greed and materialism pose the most urgent moral crisis facing the U.S., why is it that Republicans—the party of greed—keep kicking Democrats' butts?

Because Democrats rarely cast their qualms about the Iraq war in moral terms. And they almost never talk about greed and materialism as examples of spiritual poverty. They ought to start.

Opponents of stem cell research are in the minority in America; six in ten Americans think stem cell research should be not only legal but funded by the federal government. [102] But opponents of embryonic stem cell research believe it's an issue of morality. "Once we succumb to the false principle that medical benefits justify exploitative research," says Dr. David Stevens, executive director of the Christian Medical Association, "there will be an ever-expanding group who will become targets of harmful research in the name of medical progress." [103] Note that Stevens doesn't argue the efficacy of embryonic stem cell research. He argues the morality.

On the other side of the issue, John Kerry also speaks in moral terms. At the second presidential debate in St. Louis, Kerry was asked by a member of the audience why he didn't advocate harvesting stem cells from umbilical cord blood, which does not require the destruction of an embryo. Kerry showed deep respect for the questioner's evident faith, and then he answered her moral concerns about performing embryonic stem cell research with his own moral concerns about *not* doing the research. He said a man with Parkinson's disease had come up to him in New Hampshire. "And this fellow stood up, and he was quivering," Kerry said. "His whole body was shaking from the nerve disease, the muscular disease that he had. And he said to me and to the whole hall, he said, 'You know, don't take away my hope, because my hope is what keeps me going.' . . . Now, I think we can do ethically guided stem cell research." [104] In fact, Kerry cast his support of stem cell research as a life-affirming moral choice: "I think it is respecting life to reach for that cure. I think it is respecting life to do it in an ethical way." [105]

President Bush, on the other hand, is morally incoherent on the subject. On the one hand, he sounds like the Christian Medical Association, saying in the same debate that he believes "embryonic stem cell research requires the destruction of life to create a stem cell." [106] Okay. Fair enough. Embryonic stem cell research is, in Bush's mind, killing. But *in the very next sentence,* Bush boasted, "I'm the first president ever to allow funding—federal funding—for embryonic stem cell research. I did to because I too hope that we'll discover cures from the stem cells and from the research derived." [107] What? It's killing—murder, really. And I'm the first president to allow federal funding for something I think is murder.

If Bush and other opponents of embryonic stem cell research really believe that destroying those blastocysts is killing, then they have a moral obligation to stop the creation of those embryos. That means outlawing in vitro fertilization. About four hundred thousand embryos (which are six-day-old fertilized eggs) lie frozen today in fertility clinics across America.[108] Because doctors routinely create a surplus of fertilized eggs for couples, nearly all are ultimately destined for destruction. Kerry and most Democrats believe that if the eggs are going to be destroyed anyway, they should be destroyed in the furtherance of life-affirming medical research, rather than simply being dumped in the trash. Democrats should press the moral point on stem cell research and challenge the Republicans who oppose embryonic stem cell research to carry their position to its moral conclusion: making criminals out of every loving couple who use in vitro fertilization to have a baby.

Too many Democrats think the way to counter the right's moral arguments is with pragmatic arguments. That strategy sends the signal that we don't care about morality. Democrats should follow Kerry's lead and answer the GOP's moral arguments against stem cell research with their own arguments for it.

3. Organize the Religious Left

Yes, Virginia, there is a religious left in America. Though neither as vibrant nor as visible as they were in Martin Luther King's or Dorothy Day's time, religious progressives are still alive and well. Reverend Jim Wallis says, "Since when did believing in God and having moral values make you pro-war, pro-rich, and pro-Republican? And since when did promoting and pursuing a progressive social agenda with a concern for economic security, health care, and educational opportunity mean you had to put faith in God aside?" [109]

Wallis is right. And yet too many Democrats seem to think the better way to combat the power of the religious right is to attack religion. But how can Democrats of conscience attack Republicans for organizing white Christians to vote Republican when they're simply copying (and improving on) the tactics Democrats used to organize African-American Christians to vote Democratic?

Wallis is the force behind Call to Renewal, a faith-based movement to combat poverty. Although no one checks their ideology, most of the leaders of Call to Renewal would probably place themselves on the progressive end of the political spectrum. Similarly, millions of American Catholics support progressive anti-hunger, anti-poverty, and social justice organizations like the Catholic Campaign for Human Development, Pax Christi, and the U.S. Conference of Catholic Bishops' Department of Social Development and World Peace. American Jews have long been known for their commitment to philanthropy and social justice. Rabbi Jacob M. Rothschild was a strong, early supporter of Dr. King's call for equality, and he remained so after his temple was bombed in October 1958. [110]

Sadly, too many progressives have no idea of the scope and reach of the religious left. According to the Zogby poll, progressive faith-based groups reached 38 percent of the voters in the 2004 election; the religious right reached 71 percent. Democrats need to work hard to close the God Gap. [111] If religious progressives are successful, they have the capacity to change the face of American politics.

4. Fight Back

The Republican National Committee sent a flyer to voters in West Virginia and Arkansas that said if Democrats were to win, they'd ban the Bible. [112] The Democrats responded swiftly.

They issued a press release. Calling on President Bush to apologize.

Wow.

Yep, John Edwards, in a written statement, said Mr. Bush "should condemn the practice immediately and tell everyone associated with the campaign to never use tactics like this again." [113]

That showed 'em.

To be fair, Senators Blanche Lincoln of Arkansas and Robert Byrd of West Virginia also attacked the flyer. But a couple of speeches and a press release hardly match the power of a mass mailing. Mostly, the Democrats acted like they just wanted it to go away.

WWCD? (What would Clinton do?) Just asking the question probably brings a smile to your face, doesn't it? Can't you just see him in Morgantown, waving his family Bible over his head, biting that lower lip. "I couldn't make it one day without this good book," he might say. "I read it every day. And Lord knows every day I fall short of the glory of God. But this book has a happy ending. It says we don't have to be perfect; just forgiven. But Lord, I'm having a hard time forgiving our Republican brothers and sisters for accusing us of bannin' the Bible. Haven't they read the Ninth Commandment? Let me read it to them. It's right here: Exodus 20:16, 'Thou shalt not bear false witness against thy neighbor.' Before God Almighty, and with the Bible in my hand, I swear to you we will never let anyone ban the Bible. And let me warn you: If we get four more years of Republican economic policies; four more years of plants closing; four more years of jobs going overseas; four more years of tax cuts for the idle rich and more burden for the forgotten middle class, you're going to need that Bible more than ever. Because we're all going to be praying for deliverance from these economic policies. We're all going to be praying for food to eat, a roof over our heads, and health care for our kids. So I will never, ever allow anyone to ban this Bible."

We believe that in their tepid, timid response, Democrats said volumes about themselves. They looked like wimps and acted like they thought in their heart of hearts the charge was true.

In his terrific new book, *How the Republicans Stole Christmas,* our buddy Bill Press, who was once a Catholic seminarian, demonstrates how Democrats of faith can break what he calls "the Republican Party's Declared Monopoly on Religion." [114] The first step is to stand up and speak out on moral issues from a progressive perspective.

The Kerry campaign failed to do that.

At eleven-thirty P.M. on election night, as it became apparent that the presidency was slipping away from John Kerry, Paul called President Clinton and asked a simple question: What happened? Before any of the pundits or political scientists had time to stroke their chins, Clinton had a strong sense of what had gone wrong. "You can't be elected president," he told Paul, "without some of these cultural conservatives. John Kerry didn't relate to people on those cultural issues. You can't ignore God and gays and guns and win. You can't win on just the secular stuff.

"Look at Barack Obama," Clinton said. "He went all over the state with his preacher. He didn't pretend to be a cultural conservative, but he didn't walk away from those cultural issues, either. Denial is not an option. You've got to find a way to argue these issues. You cannot ignore them. They're going to beat us every time until we find a way to argue our case. Keep in mind: Values trump economics."

4. Challenge the Republicans' Self-Proclaimed Moral Superiority

Just as Republicans have succeeded in baiting middle-class Americans into resenting the Democrats' intellectual elitism, so should Democrats express their resentment toward the GOP's unbearable moral preening. There is no better example than Rick Santorum, maybe the most sanctimonious senator of all.

We told you about Senator Sanctimonious earlier. But we didn't tell you that he has been the link between the GOP Senate majority and the corporate lobbying establishment on K Street in Washington. In fact, he is intimately involved in the K Street Project, through which GOP politicians like Santorum pressure corporations into hiring only Republican lobbyists, who in turn reward the politicians with campaign contributions. The politicians then reward the lobbyists with special-interest legislation. And the whole corrupt circle remains unbroken.

Santorum also charged a small-town school district in Pennsylvania $100,000 to pay for homeschooling his children, who happen to live in

Virginia. After pledging not to support or accept congressional pay raises, Santorum voted three times to raise his own pay—by a total of $14,000. In short, in a city filled with venal, greedy politicians, Rick Santorum stands out.

And yet Santorum loves nothing better than lecturing people about how moral he is and how immoral they are. A good example is how he loves to stand in moral judgment of others. He sees himself as more than a senator; he's the grand inquisitor. In a famous interview, he compared gay Americans to people who had sex with dogs.[115] Really, Rick? Lots of American families have a gay member. Damn few have one who has sex with dogs.

In the same interview, Santorum said he didn't approve of the Supreme Court's decision in *Griswold* v. *Connecticut,* which said states could not make criminals of married couples who use birth control.[116] Santorum is comfortable passing moral and religious judgment on the beloved John F. Kennedy, telling *The New York Times Magazine* that JFK wasn't a real Catholic. As the *Times* paraphrased Santorum's view, "in a political sense, Kennedy shed his Catholicism." [117] Santorum went on to stand in moral judgment "of a people that strive to be both religious and nonjudgmental." [118] The *Times* was too polite—or perhaps too wimpy—to note that there is a name for people who strive to be both religious and nonjudgmental. They call themselves Christians. Jesus Christ directly instructed His people in Luke 6:37 to be both faithful and nonjudgmental: "Do not judge, and you will not be judged; and do not condemn, and you will not be condemned; pardon, and you will be pardoned."

In the Gospel According to St. Rick, working moms are selfish and greedy; they're bad parents (despite the fact that Rick's own mother worked outside the home—paging Dr. Freud). Santorum believes moms work outside the home because of some interpretation of feminist ideology. Most moms who work do so because they have to—because Beltway Republicans like Rick Santorum have stacked the economic deck against them. Santorum has supported economic policies that have allowed the costs of health insurance, prescription drugs, and gasoline to go through the roof. So when moms (and dads) work harder to provide those things for their kids, Senator Sanctimonious calls them selfish. Rick doesn't have that problem. In addition to taking $100,000 he didn't deserve to pay for his kids' education, Rick accepts generous government-provided health insurance. That sure takes a lot of pressure off the paycheck. (Of course, Rick has voted against increasing tax-payer-provided health insurance . . . for veterans.)[119]

While Rick votes for a raise for himself, he's voted against raising the minimum wage for hardworking moms and dads—the very parents he thinks are immoral for working. He thinks he's worth $162,000, but a working man or woman in Pennsylvania isn't worth $7.25 an hour.[120]

After Hurricane Katrina destroyed much of the Gulf Coast region of Louisiana, Mississippi, and Alabama, thousands of Americans were stranded—without a car, without bus service, without trains. Some were disabled or elderly or mentally ill. Others were just too poor to jump in an SUV and head for higher ground. It seems to us that these folks—poor and frail and injured and ill—were precisely whom Jesus was talking about when He spoke of the need to care for "the least of these" (Matthew 25:40).

Santorum looked at them and did not see his brothers. He saw criminals. That's right: crooks. Not the looters and the shooters—the scum who took advantage of the tragedy. Obviously, they were crooks, and if the Bush administration had moved in to restore order, those thugs would not have been roaming the streets. But Santorum declared that anyone who had been unable to evacuate was a criminal. "There may be a need," he said, "to look at tougher penalties on those who decide to ride a hurricane out and understand that there are consequences to not leaving." [121]

For that comment, Keith Olbermann, MSNBC's brilliant and darkly hilarious anchor, named Santorum "The Worst Person in the World," noting, "That's right, Senator. And don't forget to prosecute all those dead people in New Orleans." [122]

Imagine the gall, the arrogance, the elitism it takes for someone to lecture his fellow Americans like that. Where Rick Santorum finds the brass to declare himself morally superior to anyone, we'll never know. But we do know Democrats ought to call him on it.

Santorum may be the most powerful Republican hypocrite in Washington, but he's not the worst. Our runner-up for the worst is Spokane mayor Jim West. For two decades in the Washington legislature, West was one of the most ardent, reactionary, and strident anti-gay crusaders. He supported legislation to bar gays and lesbians from working in schools, day-care centers, and parts of state government. As Senate majority leader, he killed a bill that would have outlawed discrimination against gay Americans. When he became mayor of Spokane, he threatened to veto legislation providing equal benefits to the domestic partners of gay and lesbian city employees. He was, in short, the most self-righteous anti-gay politician in Washington. So it was front-page news when West admitted that, as mayor, he had offered enticements and inducements—gifts, favors, and coveted internships at city hall—to young men he'd met in online sex chat rooms.[123]

We can take back moral values. We can take back cultural issues. And we can take back faith. All we need are a little more spine, a little more brains, and a little more heart.

National Security

Let's say this just as clearly as we can: We Democrats have a national security problem. Americans just don't trust us with protecting the security of our nation. And as long as that is true, we're not going to win another presidential election.

Now, admittedly, some will say that's a bit of an exaggeration. But not much. Look at the numbers. Two years into the disastrous Iraq war, with the number of terrorist attacks rising and America's great army and proud marines stretched to the breaking point, President Bush and the Republicans still hold a massive advantage on what national security geeks like to call "hard" issues—what the rest of us call guns, terrorists, homeland security, and big, scary weapons.

None of this should come as a surprise to Democrats. While it would be tempting to say that it's all a frightening (and successful) Republican plot—and we have to give them some credit for selling themselves as more patriotic, more pro-military, and just plain stronger—this lack of trust is deeply rooted in recent history. It's taken our party about forty years to get here: forty years of people identifying Democrats as opponents of the Vietnam War (and, in turn, of the military); enemies of defense budgets; responsible for helicopters crashing in the Iranian desert instead of rescuing hostages; boycotting Olympics in a futile gesture; watching as the Black Hawk went down in Mogadishu, Somalia, and our boys' bodies were dragged through the streets.

When things were relatively calm on the foreign front—say in the 1992, 1996, and 2000 elections—this perceived weakness was okay. Or rather, it wasn't politically fatal. But after the terrorist attacks of 9/11, the new litmus test is whether you trust a political party or a presidential candidate to protect your family. The terrible events of that clear September morning introduced a new, strong note of uncertainty and insecurity into American life. Yes, voters will continue to tell the pollsters that their top concern is the economy and jobs, just as they did in 2004. And no, voters have never given the nod to someone they felt was simply incapable of protecting them. But the impact of the national security factor in presidential elections is stronger and more pervasive than at any time since the end of the Cold War.

We don't think that's about to change. And, as Karl Rove's staging of the Republican convention and campaign themes of 2004 so well demonstrated, neither do they. If we're ever going to come back strong on national security issues, we have to "take the fight to them," as Eliot Ness (Kevin Costner) says in Brian De Palma's *The Untouchables*. Before all is said and done, we'll even have to adopt a few of the tough-guy tactics from that movie. And while we're not advocating that Democrats go around brandishing baseball bats and whacking open the skulls of those who don't seem to get it, we are arguing against the kind of unilateral disarmament that has marked the party's approach to national security politics to date. If we're not tough enough to take on Republicans who are damaging our national security, who's going to think we're tough enough to take on external threats to our security? In other words, if you're not tough enough to fight Dick Cheney, you're not tough enough to fight Osama bin Laden.

A forty-year period of trouble is not going to be changed overnight. But we better start now, unless we enjoy watching George W. Bush and the Republicans destroy our nation and reputation and threaten the stability of the world. The stakes here are big. To quote Sean Connery in the movie, we've got to stop bringing knives to a gunfight.

How We Got Here

For much of the last century, Democrats were seen as the more hawkish party. In 1976, when he was Gerald Ford's running mate, Bob Dole snapped, "I figured up the other day, if we added up the killed and wounded in Democrat wars in this century, it'd be about one point six million Americans—enough to fill the city of Detroit."[1]

That line has gone down in history for its nastiness. But what's forgotten is that it was in response to a question about whether Ford's pardon of Richard Nixon was an appropriate issue to raise. Why would Dole, one of the sharpest minds we've ever seen in the Senate, respond with such a stunning non sequitur? Because as the "hatchet man" of the Ford-Dole ticket, he knew it was his job to attack.* He obviously knew Ford was vulnerable on the pardon; the questioner in the debate, Walter Mears of the Associated Press, noted in his question that Dole himself had criticized the pardon.[3] Rather than explain why he thought the president was wrong, Dole, ever the loyal soldier, took the bullet and counterattacked, answering a question on his ticket's biggest weakness with a shot at what he believed was the Democrats' biggest weakness: their warmongering foreign policy.

It's astonishing, isn't it? Thirty years ago Republicans were attacking Democrats for being trigger-happy. How did Democrats go from warmongers to wimps?

The truth is, Bob Dole was behind the curve in 1976. The demonizing of Democrats as weak had already been under way for several years by the time Dole reached back for the old talking point of Democrats as loose cannons. In the previous presidential election, Richard Nixon had attacked George McGovern as weak. Years later, McGovern recalled that Nixon "pounded me night and day as weak on defense, weak on crime, weak on not standing up to abuses in the welfare system."[4]

---

* In an interview with Jim Lehrer, Dole recalled: "My role in that campaign was to go out and try to go to the edge, you know, to keep pushing the Mondale-Carter group, and I guess some referred to me as a hatchet man, but maybe that was correct. But Ford had sort of the rose garden strategy and I was out in the briar patch."[2]

The Vietnam Legacy—and Legend

Richard Nixon spent World War II as a navy supply officer in the Pacific.[5] Better than drinking beer and missing Guard duty in Alabama, to be sure. But a far cry from George McGovern's remarkable war record. As a nineteen-year-old, McGovern volunteered for the army immediately after Pearl Harbor. He piloted a B-24 bomber through thirty-five harrowing missions in Europe, earning the Distinguished Flying Cross. McGovern's heroism has been chronicled by the historian Steven Ambrose in *The Wild Blue: The Men and Boys Who Flew the B-24s Over Germany 1944–45*.[6] No historian has yet chronicled Nixon's heroic efforts to keep the PX stocked with toilet paper.

But in 1972, Richard Nixon made McGovern look like a wimp. Sound familiar?

It was a bold strategy. In 1968, Nixon could not have attacked Hubert Humphrey as weak. As LBJ's vice president, Humphrey was chief cheerleader for the war in Vietnam. In 1960, JFK had attacked Nixon for being weak. Kennedy alleged that under the Eisenhower-Nixon administration, a "missile gap" had developed vis-à-vis the Soviet Union—and the two previous Democratic presidents were FDR and Harry Truman. FDR had led us through World War II; Truman had dropped the atomic bomb on Japan. But in 1972, Nixon was ready. There was no way another war hero would make Nixon look like a wimp.

Vietnam had changed everything. Nixon had been elected in 1968 saying he had a "secret plan" to end the war. Four years later, America was still mired in Vietnam. McGovern pointed out that America had lost twenty thousand lives in Vietnam since Nixon took office, claiming that "10% to 15% of our Vietnam GI's became addicted to heroin while serving there." As the election approached, Nixon drew down American troop strength in Vietnam, but 140,000 American troops were still there. McGovern pointed out that he'd opposed America's military role in Vietnam since 1963, and pledged that he would "withdraw all our military forces and aid and bring home all our POW's" in the first ninety days of his presidency.[7]

McGovern, of course, was right. After the election, Nixon withdrew U.S. troops, Vietnam went Communist, and America wasn't harmed or threatened in the least. In fact, the Communists in Vietnam today drink Pepsi and stay in Hyatt hotels. Some of them even work for Dow Chemical, which produced napalm.[8]

The American people still haven't forgiven the left for being right about Vietnam. The war was a defeat for the United States, and many Americans felt as if the Democrats had been rooting against America. Americans resented that.

Worse, some on the activist left moved from principled opposition to the war to unfair attacks on the soldiers who fought it. Some veterans were called "baby killers." They were portrayed in films as deranged and dangerous. Damn few were given the recognition and respect they'd earned. James served in the Marine Corps, and though he never went to Vietnam, his brother Bill did. Those guys served in a hellhole with honor. The fact that their sacrifice wasn't recognized back home galls him still.

To this day, stories persist about Vietnam veterans being spat upon by anti-war protestors. But according to Jerry Lembcke, an associate professor of sociology at Holy Cross College, it didn't happen. In his exhaustively researched book *The Spitting Image: Myth, Memory, and the Legacy of Vietnam*. Lembcke notes that a 1970 Harris poll showed that 90 percent of veterans reported a friendly homecoming. And he could not find one news article, not one news report, not even one confirmable example of a vet being spat upon. "The persistence of spat-upon Vietnam veteran stories suggests that they continue to fill a need in American culture," Lembcke writes. "The image of spat-upon veterans is the icon through which many people remember the loss of the war, the centerpiece of a betrayal narrative that understands the war to have been lost because of treason on the home front."[9]

Our point here is not to diminish the pain of our unheralded heroes from Vietnam. Rather, we note the exaggeration of the left's mistreatment of veterans, because in our business, the image is sometimes more important than the reality. As the crusty newspaper publisher Maxwell Scott says to cub reporter Ransom Stoddard in the John Wayne classic *The Man Who Shot Liberty Valance*, "When the legend becomes fact, print the legend."[10]

It doesn't matter that many Vietnam veterans were welcomed into the anti-war movement. Nor does it matter that the last two Democratic presidential nominees were Vietnam veterans, and the Republicans have never nominated a Vietnam vet. The legend of liberals—and Democrats—hating our troops lingers. And it hurts.

9/11

The attacks of September 11, 2001, were the bloodiest day on American soil since Antietam. (Indeed, more people were killed on 9/11 than Union soldiers were at Antietam: 2,108 Union soldiers and 1,512 Confederate soldiers lost their lives at Antietam.) Even now Americans have not fully worked through all the implications of that day, in terms of security, psychology, civil liberties, and more. But the Republicans sure have figured out the politics of 9/11 and how to exploit the tragedy for their ideological and partisan purposes.

The Wall Street Journal editorial page, lowering its nearly nonexistent standards of decency, even begged President Bush to use the attacks to advance a hard-right-wing agenda. Just eight days after the attack, with Ground Zero still smoldering and bodies still trapped in the rubble, the *Journal*'s editorial page urged Bush to "spend his windfall of political capital." [11] On what, pray tell? Acknowledging that he was napping and vacationing through warnings that "bin Laden [was] determined to strike in America"? No. The *Journal* urged Mr. Bush to leverage the rare moment of national unity and raw emotion to—you guessed it—cut taxes for the rich. "The phony 'trust fund' constraints on fiscal policy," the *Journal* wrote, "have fallen with the Trade Center towers, opening up as much as $150 billion a year in surplus for pro-growth tax cuts." [12] Think about just how sick that imagery is. The Towers didn't just "fall," as the *Journal* passively suggests. They were knocked down, by men whom James famously described on-air at CNN as "assholes." Notice, though, that it's the *Journal* editorialists who are suggesting we knock down the walls of fiscal restraint. They're depicting themselves as fiscal Mohamed Attas, cynically celebrating the collapse of America's fiscal discipline.

The *Journal* didn't stop there. "The transformed political landscape should also boost other Bush initiatives," it thundered. The paper's editorial writers actually advised the president to use the solidarity surrounding the terror attacks to force through legislation allowing oil companies to drill in the Alaskan wilderness, expand free-trade authority, and confirm a bunch of right-wing nominees.[13]

Anticipating (perhaps even dictating) future Bush strategy, the *Journal* argued that if we didn't cut taxes for the rich, drill in the Alaskan wilderness, ship jobs overseas, and appoint right-wing lawyers to the federal courts, the terrorists would have won. Keep in mind, this argument was made just *eight days* after the attacks. We hadn't even buried the dead, and the right wing was trying to use the tragedy to resurrect its partisan political agenda.

The message was startling—breathtaking, really—in its audacity. It was so slimy, so selfish, so cynical, so transparently scummy, so transcendentally sleazy, that you just knew it would appeal to the Republicans. They immediately started putting the *Journal*'s editorial into action.

From that day to this, Bush has used the 9/11 attacks the way a frightened drunk uses a cheap handgun in a bar fight. Bush used 9/11 to justify the war in Afghanistan—which is only right. He used 9/11 to justify the Patriot Act—fair enough, although the usefulness of its more intrusive provisions is debatable. He used 9/11 to justify his expensive, unworkable missile defense plan (which truly is faith-based missile defense), saying, "The case is more strong today than it was on Sept. 10 that the Anti-Ballistic Missile Treaty is outmoded."[14] No, it isn't, sir. Even the strongest supporters of Star Wars don't claim it would protect us from terrorists wielding box cutters and turning commercial aircraft into guided missiles.

But at least missile defense is related to defending America. Bush also invoked 9/11 to justify spending $170 million of special-interest money in his primary campaign for reelection—a primary in which he did not have an opponent. Reporters asked him why he felt the need to spend such an astronomical sum to win primaries in which he was unopposed. Bush said, "Every day, I'm reminded about what 9/11 means to America."[15]

And he didn't stop there. When questioned about tax cuts, Bush had a ready reply: 9/11. Just twenty-four days after the attacks, Bush stood in the Rose Garden and—with a straight face—told a shocked and grieving nation that he was calling on Congress to, "as quickly as possible, pass tax relief equal to or a little bit greater than the monies that we have already appropriated" for 9/11 relief aid. In the wake of the disaster, Congress and the president sent emergency aid to New York and other affected areas. Now the president was using that aid as a benchmark for cutting taxes for the wealthy and for corporations. He called this giveaway to the rich and the corporate special interests "the best way to make sure that America recovers from the terrorist attack of September the 11th."[16]

In the same vein, Bush had a ready answer when asked why the deficit exploded after his tax cuts: 9/11. Speaking to the Fiscal Responsibility Coalition—a phony-baloney pro-Bush group created to support the pro-deficit economic policies—the president said, "I remember when I was campaigning. I said, would you ever deficit spend? And I said, yes, only if there were a time of war, or recession, or a national emergency. Never thought we'd get— (Laughter and applause.) And so we have a temporary deficit in our budget, because we are at war, we're recovering, our economy is recovering, and we've had a national emergency. Never did I dream we'd have the trifecta. (Laughter.)"[17]

Yuk, yuk.

But what Bush didn't tell his audience is that the story wasn't true. He'd never made any such claim while campaigning. The indefatigable Tim Russert confronted Bush's budget director on *Meet the Press* noting that Bush often claimed to have made the "trifecta" statement while campaigning in Chicago in 2000, "We have checked everywhere, and we've even called the White House as to when the president said that when he was campaigning in Chicago, and it didn't happen. The closest he came was when he was asked, 'Would you give up part of your tax cut in order to ensure a balanced budget?' And he said, 'No.' But no one ever talked about a war, a recession, or an emergency, the Bush trifecta."[18]

September 11 also came in handy when Bush was called to account for being the first president since Herbert Hoover to preside over a loss of jobs. "We had an attack on 9/11 where we lost over a million jobs in just about three months," said Suzy DeFrancis, Bush's deputy assistant for communications. By the way, Bush's own Department of Labor estimated the job losses directly or indirectly associated with 9/11 to be 125,637. So the Bush White House's estimate was off by 875,000.[19]

More grave, President Bush repeatedly used 9/11 to justify his attack on

Iraq. Again and again—and again—Bush sought to link Saddam Hussein and Osama bin Laden, despite scant evidence linking the intensely secular madman (Saddam) with the intensely Islamic fascist (Osama). Bush never directly blamed Saddam for 9/11, preferring to suggest the link by juxtaposition. In a prime-time news conference just weeks before he invaded Iraq, Bush mentioned September 11 eight different times. As *The Christian Science Monitor* reported, Bush "referred to Saddam Hussein many more times than that, often in the same breath with Sept. 11. Bush never pinned blame for the attacks directly on the Iraqi president. Still, the overall effect was to reinforce an impression that persists among much of the American public: that the Iraqi dictator did play a direct role in the attacks." [20]

In fact, after Bush's relentless effort to link Iraq with 9/11, a stunning 69 percent of Americans said they believed Saddam was personally involved in the 9/11 attacks.[21] No wonder. If Bush was even a bit sly, Dick Cheney was, as usual, more blunt. In the weeks after the 9/11 attacks, Cheney said it was "pretty well confirmed" that 9/11 ringleader Mohamed Atta had met with a senior Iraqi intelligence official in Prague.[22] That charge was at best fantasy and at worst a purposeful falsehood.

Cheney was referring to a story that purportedly placed Atta in a meeting in Prague with an Iraqi named Ahmed Khalil Ibrahim Samir al-Ani. This story was apparently based on one source: a student who claimed he recognized Atta after seeing his picture following the 9/11 attacks. Shortly thereafter, *The Washington Post* reports, Czech officials distanced themselves from the charge. They said the informant was untested, of dubious credibility. Czech president Vaclav Havel personally told the Bush White House there was no evidence to confirm the Atta–al-Ani meeting. The *Post* reported, "The Czechs had reviewed records using Atta's name and his seven known aliases provided by the CIA and found nothing to confirm the April 2001 trip. Meanwhile, CIA and FBI officials were running down thousands of leads on Atta and the other 18 hijackers involved in the Sept. 11 plot. U.S. records showed Atta living in Virginia Beach in April 2001, and they could find no indication he had left Virginia or traveled outside the United States." [23]

So the Czech authorities said the story was false, and yet Cheney repeated it. Hell, the *American* authorities said it was false, and Cheney still repeated it. Even after everyone who knew anything about the alleged Atta-Iraqi meeting had declared it was false, Cheney kept repeating it. Why? How else are you going to get 69 percent of Americans to believe something that's flat-out false? Repetition, repetition, repetition. Cheney even claimed Iraq was "the geographic base of the terrorists who have had us under assault for many years, but most especially on 9/11."[24] He said this even though he knew (or should have known) that nearly all the 9/11 hijackers had come from Saudi Arabia; none had come from Iraq. He said this even though all of the 9/11 hijackers had received support from Afghanistan; none had received support from Iraq. Cheney said this because he knew Mark Twain was right when he said a lie gets halfway around the world before the truth even puts its boots on. (Nowadays we suspect Twain would say that a lie covers half of cyber-space before the truth even boots up.)

Here are the facts. The exhaustive 520-page 9/11 Commission report said investigators found no evidence that any "contacts [between Saddam Hussein's regime and al Qaeda] ever developed into a collaborative opera-tional relationship. Nor have we seen evidence indicating that Iraq cooper-ated with al Qaeda in developing or carrying out any attacks against the United States," it said. In fact, the 9/11 Commission found, Osama bin Laden was sponsoring anti-Saddam fighters based in the Kurdish-controlled northern part of Iraq. Bin Laden, far from being Saddam's ally, was actually his enemy.[25]

Tom Kean, the Republican chairman of the 9/11 panel, was forthright when asked about the alleged connection between Iraq and 9/11: "There is no credible evidence that we can discover, after a long investigation, that Iraq and Saddam Hussein in any way were part of the attack on the United States."[26]

John Kerry's Finest Hour

Democrats have been too tame and too timid about critiquing President Bush's shortcomings in the war on terror. One notable exception was John Kerry.

In December 2001 bin Laden was cornered in the mountains of Tora Bora, in Afghanistan. The president had at his disposal the 10th Mountain Division, among the most famous and heroic mountain fighters in history. But he didn't deploy them. Instead, Bush, in Kerry's words, "outsourced" the hunt for bin Laden to a ragtag group of local mercenaries.

"It was wrong," Kerry said, "to outsource the job of capturing them [bin Laden and his lieutenants] to Afghan warlords who a week earlier were fighting against us, instead of using the best-trained troops in the world who wanted to avenge America for what happened in New York and Pennsylvania and Washington." [27]

Kerry was right. Citing after-action reports from the military, *The Washington Post* reported, "In the fight for Tora Bora, corrupt local militias did not live up to promises to seal off the mountain redoubt, and some colluded in the escape of fleeing al Qaeda fighters." [28]

One senior official with direct responsibilities in counterterrorism told the *Post,* "We [messed] up by not getting into Tora Bora sooner and letting the Afghans do all the work. Clearly a decision point came when we started bombing Tora Bora and we decided just to bomb, because that's when he [bin Laden] escaped. . . . We didn't put U.S. forces on the ground, despite all the brave talk, and that is what we have had to change since then." [29]

Over two years after those comments, just before Election Day 2004, the Bush administration was singing a different song. When Osama bin Laden released a videotape in the closing days of the campaign, Kerry criticized Bush for the blown opportunity to capture or kill bin Laden. Bush struck back: "This is an unjustified and harsh criticism of our military commanders in the field. This is the worst kind of Monday-morning quarterbacking." [30]

The Bush campaign pulled out the heavy artillery. Dick Cheney, showing that he's not much of a stand-up guy, tried to pin it on the local commanders. He said the U.S. commander on the ground "stated repeatedly it was not at all certain that bin Laden was in Tora Bora. He might have been there or in Pakistan or even Kashmir," the disputed region bordering Pakistan and India.[31] Bush said much the same thing in the closing days of the campaign—that no one really knew whether bin Laden was at Tora Bora.

Well, we knew bin Laden wasn't in Toledo. In truth, there is ample evidence that Bush's team did believe bin Laden was in Tora Bora when they allowed local yokels to let him escape. In fact, over two years before Cheney made that statement, the Bush administration's intelligence officials compiled what was described as "decisive evidence, from contemporary and subsequent interrogations and intercepted communications," that bin Laden was in Tora Bora as the battle began. The Bush administration experts concluded that "bin Laden slipped away [from Tora Bora] in the first 10 days of December."[32] According to *The Washington Post*, "a common view among those interviewed outside the U.S. Central Command is that Army Gen. Tommy R. Franks, the war's operational commander, misjudged the interests of putative Afghan allies and let pass the best chance to capture or kill al Qaeda's leader."

Bush and Cheney were engaged in what James's fellow marines used to call "a CYA operation." But their posteriors still weren't fully covered. In 2005 the top CIA field commander at Tora Bora, Gary Berntsen, revealed that bin Laden was indeed at Tora Bora, and that U.S. commanders knew it. Berntsen claims he had "definitive intelligence that bin Laden was holed up at Tora Bora—intelligence operatives had tracked him—and could have been caught."[33]

What Would Gore Have Done?

During the national trauma that followed the 9/11 attacks, a few people in Washington tried to comfort themselves by pretending they were glad George W. Bush was in the White House that terrible day instead of Al Gore. Psychologists could probably do a better job of explaining why anyone would have preferred the less intelligent, less experienced Bush over Gore. But whatever prompted the feeling, there it was. A few weeks after the attacks, a former Gore aide told Howard Fineman of *Newsweek*, "I'm glad Bush is in there and Gore is not."[34] Democratic congressman Jim Moran of Virginia said, "Even though I'm a Democrat and think the Supreme Court selected our president, I don't think it's to our disadvantage to have George Bush as president. Sometimes you need a certain amount of braggadocio in your leaders."[35]

We're no longer shell-shocked, so perhaps it's worth a sober reassessment of that dopey bit of conventional wisdom. Just what do you suppose President Gore would have done? And, just as instructively, what do you suppose a Republican opposition would have done to Gore in the aftermath of the 9/11 attack?

Let us stipulate that this is pure conjecture, but it is informed by the record. First, could President Gore have prevented the attacks of 9/11? Tom Kean, the Republican former governor of New Jersey who was appointed by Bush to chair the bipartisan 9/11 Commission, has said that the attacks could have been prevented.[36]

But "could have" and "would have" are two very different things. Would President Gore have prevented the attacks? We think so. It is 2001, the first year of the Gore administration. It's August, so the new president is spending it where he spent most of his childhood summers—on the farm in Carthage, Tennessee. On the morning of August 6, he's sipping coffee with Tipper, who's up early with their new grandbaby. The CIA briefer comes in, the family leaves, and Gore switches from relaxed grandpa to intense wonk. The president's daily brief for that day has a real grabber for a headline: BIN LADEN DETERMINED TO STRIKE IN U.S.[37]

This jolts Gore even more wide awake than the coffee. He furrows his brow and reads the memo closely. It refers to a definite increase in "chatter"—intelligence intercepts—indicating a possible attack in the U.S. Nothing specific, but President Gore has been receiving security briefings for over twenty years. He knows they don't come wrapped up in a bow; the time, place, and manner of an attack are almost never specified. A combination of diligence and luck helped the Clinton-Gore administration break up an al Qaeda plot to launch a 9/11–style attack on December 31, 1999. The plan included terrorist bombings at Los Angeles International Airport, various Christian holy sites in Israel (when they were likely to be packed with American Christian pilgrims); and the Radisson Hotel in Amman, Jordan.[38]

Given his deep experience, President Gore knows this intelligence is nothing to be shrugged off. One comment especially catches his eye: Some of the unconfirmed chatter suggested "bin Laden wanted to hijack a U.S. aircraft."[39]

This is not news to President Gore. Back when he was vice president the Clinton-Gore administration arrested Ramzi Yousef, an al Qaeda terrorist. Yousef was planning to hijack eleven American airplanes and blow them up over the Pacific Ocean.[40] Yousef also had a scheme to hijack airliners and crash them into the Pentagon and the CIA headquarters.[41] By August 6, 2001, lots of people have foreseen an al Qaeda attempt to use commercial jets as guided missiles, and President Gore knows all too well that this is serious. Deadly serious. With a sigh (you know he would've sighed), he calls Tipper back in the room. "Vacation's over," he says. "I've got to go back to the White House."

Gore moves into action. And he knows just what to do. You see, aviation security is one of the issues Al Gore is an expert on. After TWA Flight 800 crashed in 1996, Clinton appointed Gore to chair a special commission on aviation security. In typically earnest Al Gore fashion, the vice president made himself an expert on the subject. This is what the Gore Commission said in its final report: "The federal government should consider aviation security as a national security issue. . . . The Commission believes that terrorist attacks on civil aviation are directed at the United States, and that there should be an ongoing federal commitment to reducing the threats that they pose."[42] Gore proposed a series of security improvements, including "use of Explosive Detection System (EDS) machines, training programs for security personnel, use of automated bag match technology, development of profiling programs (manual and automated), and deployment of explosive detection canine teams." Gore also recommended improving the training and professionalism of airport screeners, including creating a nationwide nonprofit corporation to handle security—years before the Transportation Security Administration.[43]

Sadly, congressional Republicans, under pressure from airline industry lobbyists, killed many of Gore's proposed reforms. Why? The folks at Democrats.com did a little digging and found out that eight of the nine Republicans serving on the Senate Aviation Subcommittee had received airline PAC contributions in 1996. (By comparison, only one of the eight Democrats on the panel did.)[44] The snotty attitude of one TWA lobbyist was typical. He sniffed at Gore's recommendations to safeguard our planes from terrorists, claiming, "TWA last year carried 21 million people and we didn't have a single plane blown out of the sky by someone who carried a bomb on the plane through security. . . . I don't see it as an issue. The reality is, it hasn't occurred."[45]

Even though most of his recommendations were killed by the GOP Congress, Al Gore has retained that deep knowledge of the issue of aviation security. So on August 6, 2001, President Gore moves decisively. He pushes the bureaucracy and the industry, he puts airports on high alert, he (in the words of former counterterrorism czar Richard Clarke) "shake[s] the trees," calling the CIA and the DIA and the NSA and the Pentagon and the FBI and ordering them to track down all leads. Bureaucracies respond to pressure from above. Without it, they fall into institutional inertia. When President Gore shakes the trees, Zacarias Moussaoui falls out.

Responding to pressure from President Gore, the FBI high command in Washington in turn puts pressure on all of its offices to step up surveillance and reporting on potential terror threats. This is music to the ears of Minneapolis special agent Colleen Rowley. Rowley and her fellow Minnesota FBI agents have arrested Moussaoui, a French Moroccan, holding him on immigration charges after he raised their suspicions while taking flying lessons. On the basis of information gleaned from French authorities, Rowley was convinced Moussaoui was a dangerous terrorist taking flight lessons so he could hijack an airplane.[46]

Rowley is able to get her urgent message through the FBI bureaucracy because the higher-ups want to please President Gore, and because the new president has fired Clinton's FBI director, Louis Freeh, for his massive incompetence. Under Freeh the FBI was using 1980s technology. Under Freeh, two thirds of the FBI's terrorism analysts were unqualified. And under Freeh, the FBI never once offered a comprehensive analysis of the terrorist threat against America. So President Gore did what Clinton should have done but failed to do: He put someone in charge of the FBI whose first priority was protecting Americans from terrorism, rather than protecting himself from bad press.[47]

Would all of President Gore's efforts have been enough? Who knows? We do know this: After receiving that briefing, President Gore would have done more than play golf. He would have done more than "instruct" his vice president to chair a review of the terrorist threat—a panel that did not even meet with Cheney until after the 9/11 attacks.

Then again, it might not have come to that. There's a good chance that Osama bin Laden would have been playing checkers in hell with Hitler long before August 6, 2001.

For years Gore and his predecessor had a near-obsession with capturing or killing Osama bin Laden. As far back as 1998, Bob Woodward and Vernon Loeb of *The Washington Post* have reported, "The CIA has been authorized . . . to use covert means to disrupt and preempt terrorist operations planned abroad by Saudi extremist Osama Bin Laden under a directive signed by President Bill Clinton. . . ."[48]

As Richard Clarke has written, the Clinton-Gore administration gave the incoming Bush administration direct warnings about bin Laden. The outgoing national security adviser, Sandy Berger, told the incoming NSA, Condoleezza Rice, that he wanted to brief her personally on only one issue: the terror threat. "I'm coming to this briefing," Berger told Rice, "to underscore how important I think this subject is." Berger then made a chilling prediction: "I believe that the Bush Administration will spend more time on terrorism generally, and on al-Qaeda specifically, than any other subject."[49]

After receiving conclusive proof that the October 2000 attack on the U.S.S. *Cole* was carried out by al Qaeda, the Clinton-Gore national security team produced a comprehensive plan to attack al Qaeda in Afghanistan. The plan, devised by Clarke, was presented to the Cabinet-level "principles meeting" on December 20, 2000, just a month before George W. Bush was to be inaugurated. The Clinton Cabinet officials, perhaps recalling how President George H. W. Bush had committed America to a quagmire in Somalia just months before Clinton took office, decided to leave the final decision to Bush. "We would be handing [the Bush administration] a war when they took office on Jan. 20," recalls a former senior Clinton aide. "That wasn't going to happen."[50]

President Bush, tragically, never acted on the Clinton plan to attack al Qaeda. Condoleezza Rice put it in bureaucratic limbo, where it gathered dust until she finally received it back on her desk—on September 10, 2001. A senior Bush administration official later admitted to *Time* magazine that the Clinton-era plan was a strong and effective one. It included, the official said, "everything we've done since 9/11."[51]

Would President Gore have shelved the plan the way President Bush did?

No chance. Like Bill Clinton, Al Gore had looked into the eyes of families who'd lost loved ones in the al Qaeda attacks on America's embassies in Kenya and Tanzania. He knew and trusted Clarke; they had worked together for years. And while he would have been, as he said, "my own man," he never would have shelved a plan simply because it had been drafted under Bill Clinton.

The new Bush administration had different priorities. One of them, amazingly, was cozying up to the Taliban—the medieval, misogynistic monsters who ran Afghanistan and gave safe haven to bin Laden. Clinton had bombed Afghanistan in an attempt to kill bin Laden. Instead of sending cruise missiles, George W. Bush tried sending checks. In 2001 he sent the Taliban $43 million of American foreign aid.[52]

The Gore administration also would have acknowledged Clarke's plan because it would have recognized the validity of Gary Hart and Warren Rudman's report. Hart and Rudman had been charged by Clinton—and the Gingrich-led GOP Congress—to investigate America's vulnerability to a terrorist attack. Their final report, delivered to Bush in July 2001, could not have been more clear: "The combination of unconventional weapon proliferation with the persistence of international terrorism will end the relative invulnerability of the U.S. homeland to catastrophic attack. A direct attack against American citizens on American soil is likely over the next quarter century. . . . In the face of this threat, our nation has no coherent or integrated governmental structures."[53]

Let's go back to our dream of Al Gore in the Oval Office, shall we? President Gore, ever the policy wonk, spends hours with Hart and Rudman, his former Senate colleagues. He assures them he will personally remain vigilant, active, engaged. So when Richard Clarke presents his comprehensive plan to attack al Qaeda in early 2001, he finds an eager audience in the commander in chief. When Clarke gets to slide fourteen of his PowerPoint presentation, which reads, "Response to al Qaeda: Roll back," President Gore presses him: "How? Where, Dick? What specific military, political, economic, and diplomatic actions do you propose?" Clarke has a long list. His goal is the breakup of al Qaeda—smashing its cells and arresting its people. The most important way to do that is through an enormous increase in covert operations in Afghanistan, to—in Clarke's words—"eliminate the sanctuary" that bin

Laden and his murderers received there. Clarke also has bold proposals to cut off the financing for al Qaeda, freezing funding and breaking up the phony charities funneling money to the terrorists. Finally, other nations where al Qaeda operates—Uzbekistan, Yemen, the Philippines—will be given training and assistance in hunting down and killing or capturing the terrorists in their territory.[54]

President Gore gives the go-ahead to Clarke. He also checks on the status of an innovative Clinton initiative: to arm the unmanned Predator drone with Hellfire missiles and use it to kill bin Laden. Frustrated by his inability to kill bin Laden with cruise missiles—which took six hours from the time the order was given to the time they hit their target, thus giving bin Laden ample time to escape—President Clinton pushed hard for more and better options. On November 7, 2000, Sandy Berger pushed Defense Secretary William Cohen, telling him, "We've been hit many times, and we'll be hit again. Yet we have no option beyond cruise missiles."[55] Berger pressed for "boots on the ground" in Afghanistan, but there was another option. The Predator drone had taken video images of bin Laden. If the Predator could get close enough to shoot pictures, the reasoning went, why couldn't it shoot missiles? The air force said it would take three years to arm and test such a radical modification in the Predator's mission. Dick Clarke pushed them so hard they had it done in three months.[56]

In June 2001 the air force and the CIA built a four-bedroom brick house in the Nevada desert that closely approximated bin Laden's home in Kandahar, Afghanistan. Then they had the Predator launch Hellfire missiles at the house. Bingo. Bomb damage assessments made it clear no one in that house could have survived the attack.[57]

Rather than dither and let the Predator sit on the shelf (as Team Bush did), President Gore gives the order. The war on terror is fully operational on all fronts. And Mohamed Atta and his thugs still have not boarded those planes.

Where Gore likely would have taken Clinton's obsession with al Qaeda to another level, the Bushies were more concerned with Star Wars, their faith-based missile defense system.

But suppose we're wrong. Suppose Al Gore had done exactly what George W. Bush did. How do you think the Republicans would have acted?

Would they have rallied around our stumbling, staggering, stuttering, stammering president, or would they have eviscerated him?

Suppose Gore had missed the warning signs the way Bush did. And suppose that on that peaceful Tuesday morning in September, President Gore had been reading *The Pet Goat* to a classroom full of children at Emma E. Booker Elementary School in Sarasota when he received word that terrorists had crashed planes into the World Trade Center. Do you really think Al Gore would have frozen, unable to get up from the classroom for seven long minutes? We don't.

And we don't think he would have chased his tail across the country, from Florida to Louisiana to Nebraska, while our nation's capital and its largest city were under attack. Nor do we think Al Gore would have called the terrorist murderers "folks," as Bush did.[58]

But again, what if he had? What would Republicans in Washington and the right-wing media have done? It may well be that they would have behaved as the Democrats did—setting partisanship aside and rallying 'round the president. It may be that House Republican leader Tom DeLay would have embraced President Gore's response to the tragedy the way House Democratic leader Dick Gephardt endorsed President Bush's war in Iraq.

Right.

If Al Gore had been president on 9/11, and if he had panicked as Bush did—freezing in a classroom, avoiding the nation's capital for twelve hours, giving bug-eyed speeches that looked like a hostage tape—the radical Republicans in Washington would have tried to impeach him. Even though the attack occurred on Bush's watch, and after Bush and his team ignored the warning signs, the right wing tried to blame Clinton and Gore. Does anyone seriously doubt that the Republicans would have hammered Gore relentlessly if the attacks had occurred on *his* watch?

Keep in mind that when Bill Clinton launched sixty cruise missiles in a furious attack on Osama bin Laden—which narrowly missed killing him—some Republicans accused Clinton of trying to distract the nation from the Monica Lewinsky scandal. Republican senator Dan Coats of Indiana questioned the timing, asking, "Why did he wait until now?," and suggested the scandal was the reason. Republican Pennsylvania senator Arlen Specter made similar scandalous inferences.[59] The answer to "Why now?" is that just thirteen days before, bin Laden's murderers had blown up American embassies in Dar es Salaam, Tanzania, and Nairobi, Kenya. (President Bush waited nearly a month to strike Afghanistan in retaliation for the 9/11 attacks.)

Similarly, when Clinton led America into war to stop ethnic cleansing in Kosovo, Republicans undermined him at every turn. Tom DeLay, who never met a war he didn't like, finally did. He called the war a "Balkan quagmire" and called for America to withdraw its forces.[60] Even the normally level-headed Senator Richard Lugar (R-IN), chairman of the Senate Foreign Relations Committee, turned vicious. "This is President Clinton's war," he grunted, "and when he falls on his face, that's his problem."[61] The governor of Texas, George W. Bush, also refused to support the war effort, saying, "Victory means exit strategy. And it's important for the president to explain to us what the exit strategy is."[62]

Today the Texas governor who was worried about a hawkish president committing troops without an exit strategy is himself a hawkish president who has committed troops without an exit strategy.

The contrast is striking. For Democrats, politics generally still stops at the water's edge. But for the Republican power brokers in Washington, war is just another political issue. When a Democratic president is waging war, the Republicans are peaceniks calling for an exit strategy and callously rooting for failure. But when a Republican president goes to war—even if that war devolves into a quagmire with no exit strategy—most Republicans simply fall in line.

Iraq: Bush's "Brain Fart"

President Bush's war in Iraq is Exhibit A in the contrast between the two parties' approaches on national security. The only Republican in the Senate to oppose giving President Bush authority to attack Iraq was Rhode Island senator Lincoln Chafee.[63] The GOP was just as disciplined in the House, where just six Republicans opposed the war resolution.[64]

The Democrats, on the other hand, were in disarray. Joe Lieberman had been agitating for war against Iraq for years and was an eager sponsor of

Bush's war authorization. No surprise there. What surprised us—and lots of other grassroots Democrats who opposed the rush to war in Iraq—was how many Democrats jumped on the war wagon. While most House Democrats opposed the use-of-force resolution, the majority of Democrats in the Senate voted for the war.[65]

As opposition to the war has grown, some of the Democrats who supported it began to claim their vote was to put pressure on Iraq—that they voted merely to give the president the *option* to go to war. Bunk. The war resolution was a blank check. Senator Robert Byrd told his colleagues during debate on the resolution that they were "handing the president unchecked authority."[66] The language of the resolution could not be clearer: "The President is authorized to use the Armed Forces of the United States as he determines to be necessary and appropriate" against Iraq.[67] As if that weren't enough, the war resolution included some of President Bush's hall-of-fame fibs—among them, that Iraq was hosting al Qaeda terrorists (in truth, there were some al Qaeda terrorists in Iraq, but they were operating in the northern part of the country, which Saddam didn't control), as well as five separate references to September 11, 2001. The resolution conflated Iraq and 9/11 directly, asserting that attacking Iraq was somehow related to avenging the terrorist attacks.[68]

And so, with bipartisan support, Bush got his war. Or, rather, we got his war. Thousands of Americans have been killed in that war. Untold numbers of Iraqis have died as well. The number of Americans injured in action is well over fifteen thousand. The war costs our Treasury $186 million *a day.* That's $5.6 billion per month—slightly more than the inflation-adjusted monthly cost of the war in Vietnam. (Although, to be fair, as a percentage of GDP, Iraq only costs one sixth as much per month as Vietnam did.)[69] Perhaps that's why General Anthony Zinni, a four-star marine who ran Central Command, called Iraq a "Brain Fart."[70]

The cost in blood is paid by military families, most of them middle-class, most of them unrelated to the congressional big shots and Washington pundits who led the cheers for this war. But the cost in treasure is going to be paid by everyone. And how. For the first time in American history, we have a president and a Congress who have cut taxes in a time of war. George Washington didn't ask for a tax cut when his men were freezing at Valley Forge.

Lincoln didn't call for a capital-gains tax cut at Gettysburg. FDR didn't cut taxes while thousands of soldiers were dying at the Battle of the Bulge. But President Bush is made of sterner stuff. Soldiers in Iraq may lack body armor, but millionaires in tuxedos will not lack for tax cuts. Young heroes may drive Humvees in the desert without armor plating, but fat cats in gated communities will be driving sparkling new Jaguars.

Here again, Democrats bear some culpability. In addition to supporting the war, a troubling number of Democrats also supported the Bush tax cuts for the rich. We recall being in meetings with key Democratic strategists before the 2002 midterm elections. The strategists told us that Democrats didn't want to debate Iraq—they wanted that off the table, so they voted for it. They also wanted taxes off the table, so they voted for the tax cuts. We responded by pointing out that it is the job of busboys to take things off tables; it's the job of a political party to put things *on* the table. The notion that we could go into an election after nullifying the most important foreign policy issue (Iraq) and the most important domestic policy issue (taxes) was catastrophic. Without principled opposition to the president's wrongheaded priorities, and without a competing agenda of their own, Democrats floundered. Bush shamelessly manipulated the debate over the creation of the Department of Homeland Security. Despite the fact that Democrats had proposed creating the department, and Bush had initially opposed it, the GOP was able to paint Democrats as insufficiently committed to homeland security, because Democrats wanted civil-service protections for DHS employees. Without a clear debate on the war or tax cuts, the election turned on the comparatively minor issue of what civil-service rights the employees of the new department would have. That's what happens when you take big issues off the table.

Now, nearly three years and thousands of lives later, it is Bush's war in Iraq, not the union-organizing rights of DHS employees, that holds center stage. But only because the cost and the carnage have put it there.

Trashing the Warriors

From President Bush and Vice President Dick Cheney on down, the Republican elites in Washington fancy themselves tough guys. They talk like Dirty Harry, but when it came time for them to fight in Vietnam, they acted like Barney Fife. So it's been interesting to see how Team Bush acts when confronted with bona fide war heroes.

Bill Clinton was not exactly Audie Murphy, either, and he defeated two World War II heroes, George H. W. Bush and Bob Dole. But Clinton never had the audacity or the lack of class to try and trash the war records or impugn the courage of his opponents.

One of the hallmarks of the Republican Party in the Age of Bush has been a pattern of brazenly attacking war heroes. War heroes who happen to oppose the president's policies, that is.

In the 2000 South Carolina primary, George W. Bush was in a tough battle against John McCain. McCain, as you may know, was held as a POW for five and a half years in North Vietnam. Both his arms were broken. His leg was so badly broken that his right knee was twisted at a 90-degree angle—the wrong way. After he'd spent over two years in solitary confinement, the North Vietnamese offered to release him. McCain refused as a matter of honor. He knew that the release of an admiral's son before men who had been held longer would be devastating for morale. And so, again and again, McCain refused to accept release. He was tortured. He was beaten savagely and repeatedly. His arm was broken—again. But he toughed it out. He is a hero.[71]

But in that South Carolina primary, Bush stood on a platform in Sumter, South Carolina, with a man named J. Thomas Burch, Jr., described by the local Democrats as "a fringe-element vet whose suspicions of McCain extend a good distance toward Manchuria."[72] Burch savaged McCain, accusing him of betraying veterans. Bush shook Burch's hand in gratitude for the smear, saying, "Thanks, buddy."[73] When challenged to defend Burch's preposterous claim, Bush said he was "proud" to be supported by Burch's fringe group.[74]

Attacking McCain's support for veterans was the least of it.

According to the local Democrats, someone (hmmmm, we wonder who?) did push-polling, calling voters and pretending to be a legitimate pollster. The fake pollsters told voters that McCain's adopted daughter, who's from Bangladesh and dark-skinned, was his illegitimate child. A professor from the notoriously bigoted Bob Jones University (where Bush spoke, praising the racist, anti-Catholic institution) sent an e-mail saying McCain "chose to sire children outside of marriage." When confronted about the charge, the professor said, "Can you prove there aren't any [illegitimate children]?"

The attacks on McCain didn't stop there. A man distributed flyers outside a McCain campaign event accusing McCain's wife of being a drug addict and a "weirdo."[75]

The attacks worked. The hero, McCain, lost the South Carolina primary—and the GOP presidential nomination—to Bush.

If that's what the Bushies will do to one of their fellow Republicans, you can imagine what they're willing to do to someone in the Democratic Party.

Max Cleland is one of our favorite politicians. We became friends with him when he was secretary of state of Georgia. He's an impressive man with an easy laugh, a quick bear hug, and a heart as big as the heart of a Morgan horse. He went off to Vietnam as a strapping, strong young army captain, and he returned a triple amputee: Max lost both of his legs and one of his arms. He was awarded both the Silver Star and the Bronze Star for valor in action, braving enemy fire to save the lives of his wounded comrades-in-arms. He is one of the most courageous men we have ever known.

He was up for reelection to the Senate in 2002. His opponent, Saxby Chambliss, did not serve in Vietnam. He claimed he had a bad knee.[76] You would think chickenhawk Saxby would not dare question the courage of a Silver Star, Bronze Star, triple-amputee war hero. Ahh, but you underestimate Saxby. In perhaps the slimiest ad in years (and that's saying something), Chambliss attacked Cleland's courage. The ad showed images of Saddam Hussein and Osama bin Laden while accusing Cleland of lacking "the courage to lead."[77]

Why would a guy who's never shot off anything bigger than his mouth question Max Cleland's courage? Because Max supported the Democratic version of legislation creating a Department of Homeland Security, instead of supporting the Republican version. It could be that one or the other was superior, but supporting one is hardly an issue of courage. And showing images of Saddam and bin Laden while questioning Max Cleland's courage was beyond the pale.

Finally, there's the case of Lieutenant (jg) John Kerry, who, as we've said, earned the Silver Star "for conspicuous gallantry and intrepidity in action" in Vietnam. Before the spin doctors and sleaze merchants started trashing John Kerry the presidential candidate, the real record, created by the navy decades earlier, said this about John Kerry the navy lieutenant:

> As [Kerry's] force approached the target area on the narrow Dong Chung River, all units came under intense automatic weapons and small arms fire from an entrenched enemy force less than fifty feet away. Unhesitatingly Lieutenant (junior grade) Kerry ordered his boat to attack as all units opened fire and beached directly in front of the enemy ambushers. This daring and courageous tactic surprised the enemy and succeeded in routing a score of enemy soldiers. . . . After proceeding approximately eight hundred yards, the boats were again taken under fire from a heavily foliated area and B-40 rockets exploded close aboard PCF 94; with utter disregard for his own safety and the enemy rockets, he again ordered a charge on the enemy, beached his boat only ten feet from the VC rocket position, and personally led a landing party ashore in pursuit of the enemy. Upon sweeping the area an immediate search uncovered an enemy rest and supply area which was destroyed. The extraordinary daring and personal courage of Lieutenant (junior grade) Kerry in attacking a numerically superior force in the face of intense fire were responsible for the highly successful mission. His actions were in keeping with the highest traditions of the United States Naval Service.[78]

"Extraordinary daring and personal courage." That's what the navy said of John Kerry at the time. And yet, with the approval of President Bush and Vice President Cheney, right-wing hacks trashed Kerry's war record. No one on the Democratic side tried to discredit the medals earned by Bush or Cheney. Because they didn't earn any. They were happy to allow John Kerry and others to do the fighting for them in Vietnam. (Cheney famously said, "I had other priorities in the '60s than military service.")[79] And, just as they did during Vietnam, Bush and Cheney allowed others to do the difficult, dirty, and dangerous fighting for them in their campaign.

The right wing's treatment of Kerry's war heroism was disgraceful. And yet it worked.

As strategists, we believe McCain and Cleland and Kerry could have and should have responded more forcefully. But there's something about these war heroes that makes them reluctant to talk about their heroism. The Bush Republicans are made of sterner stuff. They've been more than happy to allow and encourage their hatchet men to trash the heroism of John McCain, Max Cleland, and John Kerry.

So how do Democrats take back issues of national security?

1. Be Strong

President Clinton famously said the American people would rather have a president who was "strong and wrong" than "weak and right." We agree. America has been targeted by terrorists. We need a strong leader.

It's important to understand that security is a threshold issue. If voters don't think a leader is strong enough to protect them, that usually ends the inquiry. No matter how good your plan on health insurance, most folks aren't going to vote for you if you're too weak to fight the bad guys. Thus, the Democrats' first point has to be strength. This is not just a rhetorical matter. We believe deeply that both Al Gore and John Kerry are strong leaders. We know them both and are absolutely certain they would act swiftly and strongly to protect America. Without revealing any confidential conversations, suffice it to say Vice President Gore never blinked when President Clinton asked him about using deadly force against America's enemies. And Senator Kerry has, as they say, "been there, done that." In his heroic service in Vietnam, he was required to take human lives—directly, personally. Not in the clinical and cynical way that, say, a death-penalty-happy governor might approve the execution of a woman and laugh about it later.

And yet the GOP successfully painted Kerry (and, to a lesser extent, Gore) as weak. Why? How?

First, strength does not come from supporting every weapons system and every war that comes up. Rather, strength begins with *conviction*. Senator Paul Wellstone, we believe, showed more strength in voting against Bush's war in Iraq than a lot of Democrats showed in voting for it. Why? Because, we think, a lot of the Democrats who voted for the war did so against their better judgment. Some reluctantly went along because at the end of the day, they believed in giving the president more options. Others reluctantly went along because they were worried about being wrong substantively and politically if they voted no. With all due respect, those are weak reasons for voting to invade a country, kill untold thousands of its citizens, and send brave young Americans to their deaths.

The Republicans, ever eager to make partisan hay from war, pressed for a vote just one month before the 2002 elections. Paul Wellstone was in a tough reelection battle against the mayor of St. Paul, Norm Coleman (who had been a Democrat until he saw an opportunity to take on Wellstone as a Republican). The "smart" thing would have been to go along with the war. Many people, no doubt, advised Wellstone to do just that. Be strong, be bold, be patriotic. But Wellstone understood politics on a deeper level. He knew voters would see a calculated political move on a matter of life and death as weak, small, and craven.

And so, on October 3, 2002, Paul Wellstone spoke out on the Senate floor. He must have known his political future was hanging in the balance, but he sure didn't act like it.

When the lives of the sons and daughters of average Americans could be risked and lost, their voices must be heard by Congress before we make decisions about military action. Right now, despite a desire to support our president, I believe many Americans still have profound questions about the wisdom of relying too heavily on a preemptive, go-it-alone military approach. . . .

There have been questions raised about the nature and urgency of Iraq's threat, our response to that threat, and against whom, exactly, that threat is directed. What is the best course of action that the U.S. could take to address the threat? What are the economic, political, and national security consequences of possible U.S. or U.S.-British invasion of Iraq?

There have been questions raised about the consequences of our actions abroad, including its effects on the continuing war on terrorism, our ongoing efforts to stabilize and rebuild Afghanistan, and efforts to calm the intensifying Middle East crisis, especially the Israeli-Palestinian conflict.

And there have been questions raised about the consequences of our actions here at home. Of first and greatest concern, obviously, are the questions raised about the possible loss of life that could result from our actions. The United States could send tens of thousands of U.S. troops to fight in Iraq, and in so doing we could risk countless lives, of U.S. soldiers and innocent Iraqis.

There are other questions, about the impact of an attack in relation to our economy. The United States could face soaring oil prices and could spend billions both on a war and on a years-long effort to stabilize Iraq after an invasion.[80]

Wellstone was strong and right. He accurately, tragically predicted the consequences of Bush's war. And he opposed that war . . . strongly. We have no doubt that Wellstone's strength in opposing the war would have carried him to victory over the unprincipled weasel Norm Coleman. Coleman, who had been Bill Clinton's state co-chair in 1996, was running as a pro-Bush, pro-war Republican in 2002. Although 54 percent of Minnesotans supported invading Iraq, they respected Wellstone's strength and courage. Mary Ann Johnson of suburban St. Paul told a reporter she supported the invasion, but said of Wellstone, "If he's standing up for what he thinks, I think it will be OK. I think a lot of people support him."[81]

Americans admire conviction in politicians, and they can't stand a wimp. Moreover, the Democrats' hide-under-the-table strategy on issues separate from the war also projected a sense of weakness. Some Democrats were so cowed by President Bush's post–9/11 poll numbers, you could almost hear them moo. So when the Republican attack machine starting sliming Senate Democratic leader Tom Daschle, precious few Democrats came to his defense. Voters saw that and didn't like it. Reasonably, they inferred that a party that can't be trusted to defend its leaders shouldn't be trusted to defend America.

2. Respect the Military

One of the most critical strategic mistakes of the anti–Vietnam War movement was confusing the war with the warriors. No more. This is easy for James—he was a marine. Paul never even finished the Boy Scouts, but his grandfather was decorated in World War I, his cousin was a marine sniper in the first Gulf War, and his father-in-law was a career army officer, retiring as a lieutenant colonel after two combat tours in Vietnam. When we look at the men and women in uniform, we see our family.

Today's anti-war movement has certainly learned those lessons. No one we know of is alleging widespread atrocities or blaming enlisted personnel for the outrages of Abu Ghraib. It was Democrats who stood and fought when the Bush administration tried to eliminate imminent-danger pay and family-separation pay for the 148,000 troops in Iraq. They were being attacked every day, and yet the Bush administration wanted to deny them imminent-danger pay. They were thousands of miles from home, and yet Bush wanted to deny them family-separation pay.

Congresswoman Ellen Tauscher of California and her Democratic colleagues rode to the troops' rescue. "You can't put a price tag on their service and sacrifice," she said, "but one of the priorities of this [defense appropriations] bill has got to be ensuring our servicemen and women in imminent danger are compensated for it."[82] Thanks to the Democrats, the Bushies were shamed into restoring the extra pay our soldiers in Iraq and Afghanistan had earned.

3. It's Our Flag, Too

One of the most incendiary moments of the Bush war in Iraq occurred not in Baghdad or Mosul or Basra but in Crawford, Texas. A right-wing jerk ran his pickup truck over hundreds of crosses bearing the names of heroic Americans killed in Iraq. He also took out scores of American flags in the process. The crosses and flags had been put there by supporters of Cindy Sheehan, the Gold Star Mother who camped in Crawford to protest the war that had taken her son's life. Police say the perp was Larry Chad Northern, a Waco real estate agent. Northern is entitled to the presumption of innocence, despite the fact that the local sheriff's office says Ol' Larry Chad was spotted at nine-thirty P.M. on the night in question, changing a tire on his pickup truck. Citing sheriff's office reports, the *Waco Tribune-Herald* reported, "Small white crosses were found stuck in the truck's undercarriage."

Nice, Larry Chad. Real nice.

We don't think they taught Larry Chad to desecrate crosses at the Columbus Avenue Baptist Church. And we doubt his army buddies from Vietnam are proud to see him running over American flags and disrespecting a memorial for the war dead.

So what could drive a true-blue—or should we say Bush-red—American to commit such a heinous act?

Such is the hatefulness of the far right at the dawn of the twenty-first century. And how the worm has turned. Now it is the left invoking faith, flag, and family while the right destroys crosses. Now it is the left that honors the war dead, raises up a Gold Star Mother, and publicly prays for our troops, while the right viciously attacks a woman who gave her country everything. Now it is the left that patiently and peacefully respects the office of the presidency, while the right diminishes the office by claiming it's more important for the president to go bike riding with a sports hero than to hear the concerns of the mother of a war hero.

What would Republicans have done if liberal anti-war protestors had desecrated the flag? Destroyed the cross?

But what of the Democrats? Why didn't they pounce on this travesty? Perhaps they didn't want to infringe on Larry Chad's freedom of expression. Hogwash. His freedom to express himself does not require us to gag ourselves.

We felt the same sense of frustration when Vice President Cheney, a few days after the crosses and flags were desecrated, addressed the Military Order of the Purple Heart. Cheney, we have noted, helped himself to five draft deferments during Vietnam. He did not earn a Purple Heart. John Kerry did. Actually, he earned three of them. But this symbol of heroic sacrifice was mocked by the Republicans in the 2004 campaign.

At the 2004 Republican National Convention, Morton Blackwell, one of President Bush's most prominent supporters in Virginia, handed out Band-Aids with purple hearts on them.[83] Apparently the idea was to mock Kerry's wounds, suggesting they weren't all that bad. They were worse than Dick Cheney's, that's for sure.

Democrats whined, but they didn't hit the GOP as hard as Republicans would have hit them if they'd mocked wounded soldiers—especially at a time when thousands of troops have been wounded in Iraq.

And that's how, just days after the flags and crosses were desecrated in Crawford, Cheney found himself addressing the Military Order of the Purple Heart. He did not apologize for the shameful behavior at his party's convention. Instead, securely surrounded by bodyguards who gladly would give their lives for him, Dick Cheney wrapped himself in the flag. A flag Larry Chad Northern wrapped around his axle on Prairie Chapel Road.

If Democrats are going to take back national security, they'll have to fight to reclaim the icons of freedom.

4. Challenge Bush to Win in Iraq

Only in the minds of the Bush Republicans (and the national media) does it make sense to fault Democrats for not having the solution to the mess in Iraq. Democrats do not control the White House. They do not control the House or the Senate. And they sure don't control the Pentagon. And yet *we're* supposed to clean up this mess?

The truth is, most Democrats opposed the war. If the politicians in Washington had listened to the Democrats in America (or the two Democrats on *Crossfire*), we never would have invaded the place.

And even Republicans who supported the invasion are aghast at the abject incompetence of Bush's handling of the occupation. David L. Phillips was a senior Iraq policy official in the Bush administration. He was part of the Bush State Department's Future of Iraq group, which produced an impressive set of plans for postwar Iraq, plans that were entirely ignored by the White House and the Pentagon. In his book *Losing Iraq: Inside the Postwar Reconstruction Fiasco,* Phillips reveals that just a few weeks before Bush invaded Iraq, he had no idea of the differences between the Shiites, Sunnis, and Kurds in Iraq. We are not making this up. Here's Phillips's account: "Bush was apparently unaware of the animosity between Iraqi factions. Less than a month after the [London] conference [of anti-Saddam Iraqi opposition leaders in late 2002], Kanan [Makiya, a dissident Iraqi intellectual who supported a U.S.-led invasion of Iraq] was invited to watch the Super Bowl at the White House; he told me later that he had to explain to the president of the United States the differences between Arab Shi'a, Arab Sunnis, and Kurds." [84]

Stunning ignorance. Staggering incompetence. Surely Democrats can do better. Lord knows we couldn't do worse.

But just what is it that Democrats should do about Iraq? We are not foreign policy experts, nor are we military strategists. But there are two options in Iraq: staying or leaving. Both stink. It reminds us of the classic lyrics by the Clash: "If I go there will be trouble / And if I stay it will be double."

If we stay, we risk being bogged down in the middle of a low-intensity civil war. Our presence may well be inflaming the Muslim world and providing a recruiting tool for al Qaeda. We're spending $5 billion a month, and worse, we're losing lives.

But if we go, we risk abandoning Iraq to a full-blown civil war—one that's unlikely to be won by the "good guys." Without the stabilizing effect of U.S. troops, Iraq could descend into a Hobbesian war of all against all.

Still, Congressman Walter Jones of North Carolina has introduced legislation calling on President Bush to begin withdrawing troops from Iraq in 2006.[85] Walter Jones is not a liberal Democrat. He's not even a conservative Democrat. He's a conservative Republican whose district includes Camp Lejeune, home of the United States Marine Expeditionary Forces in Readiness. Jones's previous claim to fame was insisting that the House cafeteria rename french fries "freedom fries." Jones uses the folksy imagery of football to assert that the war in Iraq is like a football game without a playbook—even without a clear goal line. "All we are asking for is that the president develop a strategy for the fourth quarter," Jones told his constitutents. "I have spent over a year evolving to this position: If you don't have a fourth-quarter strategy, then you aren't going to win the game. We are not asking the president to have a fourth-quarter strategy for certain. But what is victory? We've got to have victory, but let us get a better understanding of what victory is." Jones says he changed his mind after reading James Bamford's book *A Pretext to War*.[86] He now says the reasons for invading have been proved false.[87]

Jones is not the only Republican expressing concern about the Bush policy in Iraq. Nebraska senator Chuck Hagel is a decorated veteran of the Vietnam War and a life member of the American Legion. He told his fellow veterans, "I think we are losing in Iraq." Hagel said Bush's rationale for the war has evaporated. "We went into Iraq and it was all about regime change, weapons of mass destruction, and that Saddam was not complying with UN mandates," Hagel said. "Now the objective is to fight terrorists. That wasn't the objective when we went in. There were no terrorists. . . . Terrorism wasn't even an issue when we went into Iraq. Now terrorism is the objective in Iraq. We have to be clear about what the objective is. What is the objective?" [88]

After Hagel's blistering attack on Bush's war, the American Legion of Nebraska—a conservative veterans' group in a conservative state—gave him a standing ovation.

Unlike Jones, Hagel has not called for a timetable to withdraw troops. But if leading Republicans, patriots like Walter Jones and Chuck Hagel, can criticize the president's misbegotten war in Iraq, why can't Democrats?

Democrats can, should, and do criticize the Bush policy (or lack thereof) in Iraq. But it's unrealistic to expect them to solve Bush's problems in a sound bite. It's as if the Republicans are saying, "Because we've screwed up so badly in Iraq, there really is no good solution, which means you don't have a solution, either. So, because you don't have a solution, leave us in charge, even though we screwed it up in the first place."

President Bush says he has a strategy: "As Iraqis stand up, we will stand down." [89] In reality, that's a slogan, not a strategy. And a pretty depressing slogan at that.

There's one statistic every Democrat should memorize and repeat in every discussion of Bush's war in Iraq. And that statistic is one. 1. Uno. That's how many Iraqi battalions are capable of standing and fighting on their own. One. In September 2005, General George Casey, America's top general in Iraq, told the Senate that only one Iraqi battalion is ready to engage in combat without American troops holding their hands. [90] That's down, believe it or not, from three battalions a few months earlier. An Iraqi battalion has 500 to 600 troops. America has 148,000 troops in Iraq. So, presuming that Iraq will need an army at least as large as ours (and presuming the wildly optimistic scenario in which every single Iraqi battalion, once stood up, becomes self-perpetuating and that we lose none of those battalions), the Iraqis will have an army as large as the American force in Iraq . . . in 269 years.

The good news is that, after 269 years, when the Iraqi army is fully capable of standing up on its own, Bush promises we'll leave. So our mission in Iraq will last 269 years, "not one day longer." [91]

America can do better. Democrats should set the bar for Bush in Iraq: victory. They should support any request for funding for our troops in the field. But they need not be shamed into silence merely because they don't have a silver bullet for a problem that has no obvious solution.

5. Redefine the War on Terror

Americans love declaring war. Not in the sense of Congress issuing a formal declaration of hostilities the way it did in World War II, but in the metaphorical sense. We've had a war on poverty, a war on cancer, a war on drugs. We declared that the energy crisis of the 1970s was the "moral equivalent of war" (which William Safire brilliantly turned into the acronym "MEOW"). Right-wingers who didn't like President Clinton's policies of preserving and protecting western lands complained of a "war on the West."

And now we have the war on terror. But unlike the metaphorical wars, this one involves real shooting and real killing. And yet the term is in part inapt. War is between nation-states. The United States and its allies defeated Germany and its allies in World War II. Terrorism is not a nation-state. It's not a people or an ideology or a religion. Terrorism is a tactic. Former national security adviser Zbigniew Brzezinski argues that the very phrase "war on terror" is meaningless. He says it makes no sense to "talk about 'terrorism' or 'terror' as if it was some abstract, generalized, unified global evil."[92]

Terrorism, at its heart, is the use of force against civilians to intimidate governments into recognizing political, religious, ethnic, or ideological aims.

Narco-traffickers use terrorism. So do the Basque separatists in Spain. So do right-wing Americans like Timothy McVeigh and Eric Rudolph. Surely our president has not committed America to a shooting war against every sect and cell that uses terrorism. Surely he just got carried away—or, rather, his speechwriters did—when he said, "My administration has a job to do and we're going to do it. We will rid the world of the evil-doers."[93] Huh? Rid the world of evil-doers? That kind of sloppy thinking is indicative of a president with no clear goal, no real vision, and no sound plan for victory. Democrats must do better. We must think more clearly, speak more sensibly, and plan more thoroughly.

General Richard Myers, President Bush's Chair of the Joint Chiefs of Staff, has said he doesn't like using the phrase "war on terrorism" because it suggests that soldiers are the solution to the problem. Terror, Myers has noted, isn't the enemy. Violent extremists are. Terror is the tactic they use.[94] Apparently Myers hasn't been able to persuade the president on this score.

We think that, while Myers is right, Democrats shouldn't waste too much time arguing about nomenclature. This is a war; it's an all-out effort, using the military to kill the enemy (and, tragically, inflict unintentional civilian casualties). But what's the endgame? To rid the world of evil-doers? So long as there are lobbyists, there will be evil-doers. Besides, at another point Bush declared that we can't win the war on terror. In an interview with NBC's Matt Lauer, our president said, "I don't think you can win it."[95] So on the one hand, our president says the goal is to rid the entire world of evil-doers. On the other hand, he says we can't win. He is incoherent. His lack of clear language is not a charming Everyman failing. Lack of clear language be-speaks a lack of clear thinking.

Democrats should explain that the war on terror is a new kind of war. It is not—or should not be—America's huge army rolling over another country's army. There are old-fashioned military components, like invading Afghanistan and driving out the Taliban after 9/11. But the Afghanistan model should be the exception, not the rule. That is why Bush's invasion of Iraq has been so counterproductive. It applied an out-of-date model to a new challenge. While evil, Saddam Hussein did not pose a terrorist threat—or any real threat at all—to the United States. He was contained, boxed in by no-fly zones and sanctions and inspections and bombings. Democrats should note that America would be much safer today if we had used a fraction of the blood and treasure we've expended in Iraq to quietly, ruthlessly, and effectively hunt down and kill the senior leadership of al Qaeda.

So while this is indeed a war, it is one that must be fought with new tactics on new terms. Bush does not seem to get this. Democrats must explain it. Abraham Lincoln could have been speaking of the need for a new strategy against terrorism when he wrote to Congress in 1862: "The dogmas of the quiet past are inadequate to the stormy present. The occasion is piled high with difficulty, and we must rise with the occasion. As our case is new, so we must think anew, and act anew. We must disenthrall ourselves, and then we shall save our country."[96] Today it is the Democratic Party that must persuade the country to disenthrall itself from the dogmas of the quiet past.

The need to think anew about how to fight terrorism is deadly serious. Former counterterrorism chief Richard Clarke has revealed that, in the hours after the attacks of September 11, Defense Secretary Donald Rumsfeld was already calling for an attack on Iraq. Clarke recalls that at first he thought the Pentagon chief was joking—what a lively sense of humor that Rummy has. But then it dawned on Clarke that Rumsfeld was serious. "Rumsfeld was saying that we needed to bomb Iraq," Clarke recalled. "And we all said . . . no, no. Al-Qaeda is in Afghanistan. We need to bomb Afghanistan. And Rumsfeld said there aren't any good targets in Afghanistan. And there are lots of good targets in Iraq. I said, 'Well, there are lots of good targets in lots of places, but Iraq had nothing to do with it.' "[97] In the moment of crisis, Rumsfeld was incapable of grasping the changed reality. Today, mired in Iraq, while al Qaeda regroups and plans more attacks on America, the Bush administration is reaping the consequences of its inability to think anew.

At the same time, the Bush high command's nation-against-nation concept of warfare has hampered its ability to adapt to the insurgency in Iraq. One month after Bush's famous "Mission Accomplished" speech, the CIA told him he was facing a guerrilla war—an insurgency—in Iraq. Rumsfeld dismissed the intelligence. "I guess the reason I don't use the term guerrilla war," he said, "is that it isn't . . . anything like a guerrilla war or an organized resistance." He characterized the insurgency as a bunch of ragtag "looters, criminals, remnants of the Baathist regime."[98] Saddam had fallen. We'd torn down the statue. George W. Bush had landed on an aircraft carrier. Hung up a banner saying, "Mission Accomplished." Game over, right? After all, that's how wars are won, isn't it? No, Rummy, it's not. Not when you're dealing with a new kind of war—precisely the kind of war our undermanned army of occupation was unable to deal with.

The Bush administration chose not to listen to experts like Army Chief of Staff General Eric Shinseki, who said occupying Iraq would take "several hundred thousand soldiers." Stating what should have been obvious, except to the ideologues in the White House, Shinseki said Iraq is "a piece of geography that's fairly significant." Compounding the geographic challenge,

Shinseki told the Senate Armed Services Committee, the occupying force would have to be large enough to secure a nation rife with "ethnic tensions that could lead to other problems."[99] The Bushies were furious at Shinseki's candor. Paul Wolfowitz, the pointy-headed intellectual who was Rumsfeld's number two, rebuked the army's top general in public, calling him "wildly off the mark."[100] Imagine the arrogance. Shinseki, who had commanded the NATO stabilization force in Bosnia-Herzegovina, knew something about maintaining security in a region fraught with ethnic tensions. (We did not lose one soldier in the occupation Shinseki led.) Wolfowitz has never occupied anything bigger than an office. Shinseki was educated at West Point, earned his master's at Duke, and was trained at the Armor Officer Advanced Course, the United States Army Command and General Staff College, and the National War College. Wolfowitz has an undergraduate degree in mathematics from Cornell and a Ph.D. in political science from the University of Chicago.

Shinseki fought and was wounded in Vietnam; Wolfowitz taught at Yale. He was not wounded there (although paper cuts are a persistent occupational hazard in the Ivy League).

Shinseki has been awarded the Defense Distinguished Service Medal, Distinguished Service Medal, Legion of Merit (with Oak Leaf Clusters), Bronze Star Medal with "V" Device (with two Oak Leaf Clusters), Purple Heart (with Oak Leaf Cluster), Meritorious Service Medal (with two Oak Leaf Clusters), Air Medal, Army Commendation Medal (with Oak Leaf Cluster), Army Achievement Medal, Parachutist Badge, Ranger Tab, Office of the Secretary of Defense Identification Badge, Joint Chiefs of Staff Identification Badge, and Army Staff Identification Badge.[101]

Wolfowitz didn't earn any of those decorations. But his official bio does note that he was an intern at the Bureau of the Budget, and we all know how bloody those budget battles can be.[102]

All of this is not to disparage Wolfowitz's intellect—Lord knows he's a lot smarter than we are. But he doesn't know everything. Some people know more about some things. And Shinseki knew more about what it takes to occupy a large country than Wolfowitz. But because Shinseki dared to speak his mind—and because his advice was at odds with the Bush administration's ideological agenda—he was insulted and undermined.

Not only did the Bush administration leave our troops short-handed and ill equipped to fight a new style of war, it also set priorities that undermined our chances to defeat the insurgents. Remember weapons of mass destruction? Turns out there weren't any. President Bush famously joked about this with Washington elites, snickering at a black-tie dinner while showing slides of him crawling under desks and tables looking for WMD in the White House. But the lack of WMD was no joke to the troops on the ground. Dr. David Kay was sent in to find the WMD. As you can imagine, it's kind of difficult to find something that doesn't exist, but Dr. Kay tried his hardest. And the Bush administration made the fruitless search for WMD its highest postwar priority. Not securing the country. Not protecting U.S. forces. Not wiping out the nascent insurgency. The search for WMD.

Case in point: *Time* magazine's Joe Klein has reported that the Iraq Survey Group (ISG) had twelve hundred intelligence officers and support staff assigned to search for WMD. They had exclusive access to literally tons of documents collected from Saddam's office, intelligence services, and ministries after the regime fell. Kay clashed repeatedly with U.S. military leaders who wanted access not only to the documents but also to some of the resources—analysts, translators, field agents—at his disposal. "I was in meetings where [General John] Abizaid was pounding on the table trying to get some help," says a senior military officer. "But Kay wouldn't budge."

Twelve hundred intelligence officers and support staff to search for weapons that did not exist, while Bush's men ignored an insurgency that did exist. By contrast, Klein reports, the army at that time had fewer than thirty intelligence experts trying to figure out just who and what the insurgency was.

"Indeed," Klein wrote, "a covert-intelligence officer working for the ISG told *Time* correspondent Brian Bennett that he had been ordered in August 2003 to 'terminate' contact with Iraqi sources not working on WMD. As a result, the officer says, he stopped meeting with a dozen Iraqis who were providing information—maps, photographs and addresses of former Baathist militants, safe houses and stockpiles of explosives—about the insurgency in the Mosul area." [103]

We will never win the battle against the Iraqi insurgents, or the broader war on terrorism, until we have leaders who understand and describe the true

nature of the threat. A recently retired four-star general with experience serving in the Middle East summarized Bush's conceptual failure this way:
"We're good at fighting armies, but we don't know how to do this. We don't
have enough intelligence analysts working on this problem. The Defense Intelligence Agency puts most of its emphasis and its assets on Iran, North
Korea, and China. The Iraqi insurgency is simply not top priority, and that's
a damn shame."

Bush & Co. remind us of a story President Kennedy used to tell. A man
was seen crawling under a lamppost at night, obviously looking for something. A passerby asked him what he was looking for. "My keys," he said. "I
dropped them getting out of my car." He pointed across the street to where
his car was parked. "So, why are you looking over here if you dropped them
across the street?" the passerby asked. "Because," the man said, "the light's
better over here."

Democrats must describe the threat that exists and design strategies to
meet it and defeat it. So long as Republicans remain enthralled to the old
ways and the old days, America will remain vulnerable.

6. Call for America to Lead the World Again

Democrats, as John Kerry said in his campaign, can lead a more effective,
more lethal, and less costly war on terror. It will likely mean fewer tanks and
fewer troops invading countries, less emphasis on occupying countries we
have invaded, and more focus on intelligence, covert action, stealth, special
forces, and—yes—allies.

It was our allies in Pakistan who arrested Khalid Shaikh Mohammed, the
mastermind of the 9/11 attacks; Ramzi Binalshibh, whose help was behind
the bombing of the U.S.S. *Cole;* and top al Qaeda operative Abu Zubaydah.
It was our allies in the Philippines and Pakistan who led to the arrest of the
terrorist Ramzi Yousef. Our allies in France (and yes, they are our allies, despite the claptrap from the Republican right) gave us crucial evidence against
the twentieth hijacker, Zacarias Moussaoui. Our allies in Germany helped us
understand al Qaeda's Hamburg cell, where Mohamed Atta and other terror-

ists resided. The plain truth is, although America is the most powerful nation in human history, it cannot possibly defeat what some have called "Islamo fascists who use terror" without the help of allies.

General Francis X. Taylor, a thirty-one-year veteran of the air force currently serving as assistant secretary of state for diplomatic security, is an expert on terrorism. He has said there are six principles for winning the war on terrorism: "Cooperate, cooperate, cooperate; communicate, communicate, communicate." [104] Taylor is right. But if a liberal Democrat had said such a thing, the right-wing thugs would have pounced. They'd have called the Democrat too softheaded and softhearted. But Democrats must fight through that flak.

Al Qaeda is a global network, not a country. We cannot possibly invade and occupy every country where al Qaeda operates. We must have allies. We need their intelligence assets, their military assets, their assistance in cutting off terrorist financing and travel. Given that reality, America's standing in the world is one of the most important weapons we have in the war on terror. Democrats should explain that cooperating with other countries is a sign of strength, not weakness. As former secretary of state Madeleine Albright has said, America should lead—alone when it must, with allies when it can. [105] The Bushies seem to have this backward. They prefer to go it alone when they can and want to work with allies only when they must.

Democrats must insist that leadership requires, well, leading. And (not to belabor the point) leading requires followers. And followers are allies. It was a point of pride during the Cold War that each American president, from Truman to Reagan, was known as the Leader of the Free World. No one could keep a straight face while calling George W. Bush the Leader of the Free World. This has real consequences. American power is enhanced by America's prestige. The respect we have in the world is, in military parlance, a force multiplier.

Zbigniew Brzezinski cites a telling example of this power: "When President Kennedy faced the Cuban missile crisis, he sent [former secretary of state] Dean Acheson to Europe to talk to [French president Charles] de Gaulle to tell him there are Soviet rockets with nuclear weapons targeted on the United States, and the U.S. would use force to remove them if necessary, which means massive nuclear war between the West and the East. When he finished making that presentation, Acheson said to de Gaulle, 'Let me now show you the evidence.' De Gaulle responded by saying, 'I don't want to see your evidence. I trust the president of the United States. Tell him we stand with him.' Would any foreign leader do that today? Probably not. That's an actual detraction from our power." [106]

It is vital that Democrats advocate multilateralism only in the context of strength. We cannot afford to look like wimpy hand-wringers playing "Mother May I" with the United Nations. Keep in mind that President Bush's best attack line of the 2004 campaign was delivered in the least political—and most presidential—setting imaginable: the 2004 State of the Union Address. In that speech, Bush declared, "America will never seek a permission slip to defend the security of our country." [107]

Democrats cannot be the party of the permission slip. We must demonstrate that, in damaging the credibility and respect the world accords us, it is President Bush who has let America's power slip.

7. Be Tough on Terrorism and Tough on the Causes of Terrorism

When Tony Blair was shadow home secretary, formulating domestic policy for the opposition Labour Party, he said Labour should be "tough on crime; tough on the causes of crime." [108] It was Blair's way of saying that Labour would not abandon its commitment to social justice, but that under New Labour, public safety would come first. Labour had been seen as weak, soft, coddling. Blair changed all that.

On issues of national security, Democrats have a similar problem. That's why our first piece of advice for Democrats on national security is to be strong. Strong in their convictions but also unflinching in their willingness to use force to defend America's interests.

At the same time, Democrats should argue that under the Republicans, America has not been tough enough on terrorism or on the causes of terrorism. Not tough enough on terrorism because, as we've mentioned earlier, President Bush wimped out on capturing or killing Osama bin Laden at Tora Bora. Bush also took his eye off the ball when he invaded Iraq, which has allowed al Qaeda to regroup and recruit new killers. But what of the causes of terrorism? This is an area in which Bush has proved to be spectacularly—indeed, dangerously—ignorant. In his well-received speech to a Joint Session of Congress on September 20, 2001, he asked the rhetorical question, "Americans are asking, Why do they hate us?" It was the question on everyone's mind. But the president's answer left a lot to be desired: "They hate what we see right here in this chamber. A democratically elected government. Their leaders are self-appointed. They hate our freedoms—our freedom of religion, our freedom of speech, our freedom to vote and assemble and disagree with each other."

Garbanzo beans. Does our president really believe the terrorists crashed jumbo jets into buildings because they don't like the House Ways and Means Committee or the Iowa caucuses or a tough letter to the editor? We sure hope not. To his credit, Bush went on to list more realistic motivations for the terrorists: "They want to overthrow existing governments in many Muslim countries, such as Egypt, Saudi Arabia, and Jordan. They want to drive Israel out of the Middle East. They want to drive Christians and Jews out of vast regions of Asia and Africa." Okay. We can deal with that. They don't really hate our freedoms. They hate their governments, and they hate America's role in the Middle East. They hate Israel, and they hate America's support for Israel.

Bush apparently can't decide whether the terrorists' rationale is rational or loony. Democrats should point out that the terrorists, while profoundly evil, are motivated by a set of policy and political goals. Goals with which we disagree, to be sure. But defining the enemy's goals clearly and realistically heightens our chances of victory. We can never "rid the world of evil-doers." But we can defeat those who want America to abandon Israel or withdraw from the Middle East.

So why does Bush insist on describing the terrorists' motivation so inaccurately? Michael Scheuer has a theory. Scheuer is a twenty-two-year veteran of the CIA. For the last three years, he's been the chief of the agency's Osama bin Laden Unit. He's written a book—published anonymously—called *Imperial Hubris: Why the West Is Losing the War on Terror.* "It's much easier to rally the American people," Scheuer says, "to defend their liberties, their lifestyle and their freedom than to say we're going to fight because we need oil from the Persian Gulf, and so your sons and daughters in the military may die in order to allow the Royal Family in Saudi Arabia to continue stealing most of the oil revenues from their citizens." [109]

That analysis, while a little harsh and cynical for us, is worth considering. Democrats must be clear-eyed about who our enemy is and why he does what he does.

8. Provide for the Common Defense

One by one, President Bush's justifications for invading Iraq have evaporated. There were no WMDs. No imminent threat. No links to al Qaeda. No nuclear weapons program. The invasion has not spread democracy through the Middle East. And so we're left with this: We have to fight the terrorists in Baghdad so we won't have to fight them in Brooklyn.

But no less an expert than President Bush has proved this to be a fraud. In his speech to the nation on October 6, 2005, he revealed this startling fact: We have disrupted ten al Qaeda terrorist attacks since September 11, 2001, three of them in the United States itself.[110] So we are already fighting them here, at the same time we're fighting them there. Moreover, even as terrorists swarm into Iraq, and al Qaeda recruitment grows as a result of resentment over Bush's invasion and occupation, bin Laden's murderous minions have managed to commit terrorist atrocities all around the world: in Afghanistan, in Bali, Indonesia, in London, in Madrid, in Riyadh, Sharm el-Sheik, Egypt, and in Amman, Jordan.

Clearly, the terrorists are proving themselves capable of fighting in Iraq and around the world. Why aren't we doing the same? Over four years after 9/11, homeland security in the Age of Bush is a joke, and a bad one at that. At some level, it's a matter of priorities. For the years 2001 through 2006, Bush and the Republicans have invested $206 billion of your money in tax cuts for the wealthiest 1 percent of Americans—just the wealthiest 1 percent. But during the same five-year period, they want to increase funding for homeland security by just $62 billion.[111]

Those priorities are crazy. They are dangerous. They may prove deadly. With nuclear power plants poorly guarded, with chemical plants vulnerable, with bridges and tunnels and mass transit poorly protected—it is more important for Bush and the Republicans to give Paris Hilton another tax cut? I suppose their theory is that if, because of their neglect of homeland security, you're killed by terrorists, your children will take comfort in not having to pay taxes on your multimillion-dollar estate.

Democrats should call for getting serious about homeland security. The first job of the federal government is to protect its people. President Bush and the Republicans have failed in that solemn obligation.

If you have any doubts, look at the administration's chaos and incompetence in the wake of Hurricane Katrina. Or the botched attempt at evacuating Houston when Hurricane Rita was threatening. The federal government left American citizens in Louisiana stranded on their rooftops, begging for their lives. And Houstonians spent ten to twelve hours on clogged highways, sitting ducks if Rita hadn't changed course.

Now, imagine that instead of a storm for which we had days of warning, the threat is from a sudden, explosive terrorist attack. Or a chemical, biological, or radiological attack. Ask your mayor or county officials, your police chief or sheriff if the feds have given them a detailed plan for communications, command, and control in the event of a terrorist attack. Are we supposed to evacuate? If so, to where? Or are we supposed to shelter in place? Where? For how long? Should we try to get our kids out of school or leave them there? What do you suppose your local hospital's emergency room is going to look like if the attack comes in the form of a dangerous chemical or a biological agent like anthrax or plague or smallpox?

Consider this: On June 9, 2004, Kentucky governor Ernie Fletcher was flying into Washington on a small plane. Like hundreds of other dignitaries, he was coming to D.C. for Ronald Reagan's funeral. He'd been given special permission to land at Reagan National Airport, where private planes have been banned since 9/11. But Fletcher's transponder was broken, so folks on the ground were unable to confirm its identity. All they knew was that it had flown into restricted airspace.

Washington freaked out. The Capitol and Supreme Court buildings were evacuated. "Ladies and gentlemen, let's move like our lives depend on it. I mean it!" screamed the police officers who were ordered to evacuate the buildings. And so lobbyists and law clerks, tourists and tour guides, senators and staffers—all of them were sent into a panic and out into the streets.

Women tossed their high-heeled shoes and ran barefoot. Careful congressional comb-overs were flapping wildly in the wind. Corpulent, corrupt corporate lobbyists wheezed as they finally confronted a problem they couldn't bribe or buy their way out of.[112]

All because of Ernie Fletcher's little twin-engine prop plane. The whole scene was pathetic. And scary. And dangerous. Turns out that if ol' Ernie had been a terrorist, he'd have been likely to do much more damage because of the chaos of the evacuation. Unlike a 747 loaded with jet fuel, a small prop plane doesn't make a great guided missile. But it does make a damn good potential poison-purveyor. Had a terrorist been spraying a chemical or biological agent from that plane, sending thousands of people screaming and running into the streets was the worst possible thing to do. Sheltering in place would have been a much better, safer option.

If Bush and the Republicans can't protect the Capitol from Ernie Fletcher's prop plane, how the heck are they going to protect us from a real threat?

Since the Republicans have proven themselves dangerously unserious about securing the homeland, Democrats must step up to the plate.

9. Be Certain of Victory

For all of his bluster, President Bush often seems like a man who doesn't believe we can actually defeat the terrorists. In fact, he's said as much. But terrorism has never succeeded. Democrats should note that the British have largely defeated the terrorists in the Irish Republican Army; the Germans have defeated the terrorists of the Baader-Meinhof gang; the Italians defeated the Red Brigade terrorists; the Peruvians defeated Shining Path. But not one of those victories—not one—was achieved by military might alone. There was bloodshed, to be sure, but what made those victories possible was coordinated military, police, political, economic, and diplomatic effort. The governments that have defeated and destroyed terrorist networks have done so by using every instrument in the orchestra. So should we.

That is why the previous point, on being clear about our enemy's goals, is so important. Clinton is right when he says we can't kill, jail, or occupy everyone who opposes us, that we need a world with more allies and fewer terrorists. The solution to terrorism is as much political as military. President Bush is right—yes, and we should say so—when he announces that greater freedom and democracy in the Middle East are the ultimate answer to terrorism. But here's the problem: The president's invasion of Iraq has given democracy a black eye in much of the Muslim world. Bush has linked a good thing—democracy—with a bad thing—his invasion and occupation.

That said, Democrats must be committed to a political as well as a military solution. A lasting peace between Israel and the Palestinians—which will look a lot like Clinton's final proposal—combined with increased democracy in the Arab Muslim world, will do at least as much as even the most effective military strategy to win the war on terrorism.

We're not naive. But we truly believe that an aggressive, enlightened, tough Democrat—or a succession of them—can defeat terrorism.

10. Help with Military Recruitment

Despite the weak economy and the increase in poverty, all branches of the military are having a hard time recruiting people. In 2005 the army missed its recruiting target for the first time in years. The navy and air force and National Guard aren't doing any better. Even James's beloved marines are having a hard time finding a few good men. Our friend Barry McCaffrey, a retired four-star army general, wrote, "The U.S. Army and the Marines are too under-manned and under-resourced to sustain this security policy beyond next fall." Because of this lack of manpower, McCaffrey says, the army and marines "are starting to unravel." [113]

Why is it that young men and women suddenly no longer want to serve their country, despite tens of thousands of dollars in bonuses, tuition assistance, and other benefits? Joe Satterthwaite may have the answer. Joe is a sixteen-year-old in Kingston, Massachusetts. He says, "It doesn't seem fun or interesting to be going over to Iraq to fight people and kill them. And the whole thought of dying when you're 18 sounds pretty bad." [114]

We think we have the answer to the Pentagon's recruiting problem. Throwing money at the problem doesn't work—at least that's what our conservative friends say when we want to throw money at, say, hungry children or sick senior citizens. The problem is that the war is unpopular, and the Commander in Chief is untrustworthy. Moms and dads don't want their children to enlist, and the kids don't seem too wild about it, either. But not all the kids. There are tens of thousands of ready recruits out there. We've just got to mobilize them.

Michael Moore had a good start. In his film *Fahrenheit 9/11,* Moore confronted congressmen and asked them to sign their kids up for military service. But we should go beyond that. We should go to all the gung-ho young country-and-western singers, like Darryl Worley, whose hit song "Have You Forgotten?" seeks to build support for the war in Iraq by asking people if they've already forgotten about 9/11. Apparently Worley has forgotten that Iraq had nothing to do with 9/11—and that the terrorist behind 9/11, Osama bin Laden, still walks the earth and is using the war in Iraq as a recruiting tool. Still, sign ol' Darryl up. Judging from the studly picture on his album cover, complete with American flag, Darryl is buff and ready to kick some Iraqi tail. So, instead of making a fortune exploiting other people's patriotism, Darryl, sign up.

Same goes for Clint Black and Toby Keith and all the other Coca-Cola cowboys getting rich off their pro-war songs while better, braver young men are getting blown apart. (Thank God for Merle Haggard. The guy who wrote "Okie from Muskogee" and "The Fightin' Side of Me" because he was so disgusted with the anti-war movement of the 1960s is now so disgusted with Bush's war that he's written a terrific anti-war song, "That's the News." As lifelong country-music fans, we'll take the Hag over these clowns any day.)

But we shouldn't stop with country singers. Let's put Britney Spears in uniform. When asked about Bush's war in an interview with our pal Tucker Carlson, Britney smacked her gum and declared, "Honestly, I think we should just trust our president in every decision he makes and should just support that, you know, and be faithful in what happens." [115]

But, let's face it, has-been pop stars and never-was country singers are not going to fill our military. That's where the College Republicans come in. There are 120,000 College Republicans in this country. [116] That's enough to fill six divisions—more than enough to meet our needs. Maybe we should let them form their own divisions: the Fighting Frat Boys or the 102nd Trust-Funders.

As a public service, here's a recruiting form. If you support this war, don't just slap a "Support Our Troops" sticker on your SUV. No, get some skin in the game. And if you're too old, how 'bout signing up your son? Or your granddaughter? It seems to us that this is the acid test. If the war isn't worth risking your own child's life, how can it be worth risking anyone else's child's life?

It's important here for us to make special mention of Matthew and Daniel Dowd. Matthew is a good friend of Paul's. He was also President Bush's chief strategist in both the 2000 and 2004 campaigns. Toward the end of the 2004 campaign, Matthew's nineteen-year-old son, Daniel, enlisted in the army. He's studying Arabic at the Defense Language Institute in Monterey, California, and with those skills, it's a good bet he won't spend this war shoveling crap in Louisiana. Godspeed to him and to all the young men and women in this thing, as well as to all their families. We know what it's like to have someone you love in harm's way. No matter which side of this war you're on, everyone is on Daniel Dowd's side.

In sum, the way for Democrats to win on national security issues is really not strategically different from how we feel Democrats should fight on other issues: Be strong, be smart, be patriotic, be optimistic.

College Republicans: Here's Your Chance to Enlist!

ENLISTMENT/REENLISTMENT DOCUMENT
ARMED FORCES OF THE UNITED STATES

PRIVACY ACT STATEMENT

AUTHORITY: 5 USC 3331; 32 USC 708; 44 USC 708 and 3101; 10 USC 133, 265, 275, 504, 508, 510, 591, 672(d), 678, 837, 1007, 1071 through 1087; 1168, 1169, 1475 through 1480, 1553, 2107, 2122, 3012, 5031, 8012, 8033, 8496, and 9411; 14 USC 351 and 632; and Executive Order 9397, November 1943 (SSN).

PRINCIPAL PURPOSE(S): To record enlistment or reenlistment into the U.S. Armed Forces. This information becomes a part of the subject's military personnel records which are used to document promotion, reassignment, training, medical support, and other personnel management actions. The purpose of soliciting the SSN is for positive identification.

ROUTINE USE(S): This form becomes a part of the Service's Enlisted Master File and Field Personnel File. All uses of the form are internal to the relevant Service.

DISCLOSURE: Voluntary; however, failure to furnish personal identification information may negate the enlistment/reenlistment application.

A. ENLISTEE/REENLISTEE IDENTIFICATION DATA

1. NAME *(Last, First, Middle)*		2. SOCIAL SECURITY NUMBER		
3. HOME OF RECORD *(Street, City, State, ZIP Code)*		4. PLACE OF ENLISTMENT/REENLISTMENT *(Mil. Installation, City, State)*		
5. DATE OF ENLISTMENT/ REENLISTMENT *(YYYYMMDD)*	6. DATE OF BIRTH *(YYYYMMDD)*	7. PREV MIL SVC UPON ENL/REENLIST	YEARS	MONTHS	DAYS
		a. TOTAL ACTIVE MILITARY SERVICE			
		b. TOTAL INACTIVE MILITARY SERVICE			

B. AGREEMENTS

8. I am enlisting/reenlisting in the United States *(list branch of service)* _____
this date for _____ years and _____ weeks beginning in pay grade _____ .
The additional details of my enlistment/reenlistment are in Section C and Annex(es)

_____ .

a. **FOR ENLISTMENT IN A DELAYED ENTRY/ENLISTMENT PROGRAM (DEP):**
   I understand that I will be ordered to active duty as a Reservist unless I report to the place shown in item 4 above by *(list date (YYYYMMDD))*_____ for enlistment in the Regular component of the United States *(list branch of service)* _____ for not less than _____ years and _____ weeks. My enlistment in the DEP is in a nonpay status. I understand that my period in the DEP is **NOT** creditable for pay purposes upon entry into a pay status. However, I also understand that this time is counted toward fulfillment of my military service obligation or commitment. I must maintain my current qualifications and keep my recruiter informed of any changes in my physical or dependency status, moral qualifications, and mailing address.

b. **REMARKS:** *(If none, so state.)*

c. The agreements in this section and attached annex(es) are all the promises made to me by the Government. ANYTHING ELSE ANYONE HAS PROMISED ME IS NOT VALID AND WILL NOT BE HONORED.

(Initials of Enlistee/Reenlistee) _____

(Continued on reverse side.)

DD FORM 4/1, JAN 2001   PREVIOUS EDITION MAY BE USED.

Fill Out This Form, Send It to the Pentagon, and You Could Be on Your Way to Iraq in No Time!

NAME OF ENLISTEE/REENLISTEE *(Last, First, Middle)*	SOCIAL SECURITY NO. OF ENLISTEE/REENLISTEE

F. DISCHARGE FROM/DELAYED ENTRY/ENLISTMENT PROGRAM

20a. I request to be discharged from the Delayed Entry/Enlistment Program (DEP) and enlisted in the Regular

Component of the United States *(list branch of service)* _____ for a period of

_____ years and _____ weeks. No changes have been made to my enlistment options **OR**

if changes were made they are recorded on Annex(es) _____

_____ which replace(s) Annex(es) _____

b. SIGNATURE OF DELAYED ENTRY/ENLISTMENT PROGRAM ENLISTEE	c. DATE SIGNED *(YYYYMMDD)*

G. APPROVAL AND ACCEPTANCE BY SERVICE REPRESENTATIVE

21. SERVICE REPRESENTATIVE CERTIFICATION

a. This enlistee is discharged from the Reserve Component shown in item 8 and is accepted for enlistment in the

Regular Component of the United States *(list branch of service)* _____ in pay grade _____

b. NAME *(Last, First, Middle)*	c. PAY GRADE	d. UNIT/COMMAND NAME
e. SIGNATURE	f. DATE SIGNED *(YYYYMMDD)*	g. UNIT/COMMAND ADDRESS *(City, State, ZIP Code)*

H. CONFIRMATION OF ENLISTMENT OR REENLISTMENT

22a. IN A REGULAR COMPONENT OF THE ARMED FORCES:

I, _____ , do solemnly swear (or affirm) that I will support and

defend the Constitution of the United States against all enemies, foreign and domestic; that I will bear true faith

and allegiance to the same; and that I will obey the orders of the President of the United States and the orders of

the officers appointed over me, according to regulations and the Uniform Code of Military Justice. So help me

God.

b. SIGNATURE OF ENLISTEE/REENLISTEE	b. DATE SIGNED *(YYYYMMDD)*

23. ENLISTMENT OFFICER CERTIFICATION

a. The above oath was administered, subscribed, and duly sworn to (or affirmed) before me this date.

b. NAME *(Last, First, Middle)*	c. PAY GRADE	d. UNIT/COMMAND NAME
e. SIGNATURE	f. DATE SIGNED *(YYYYMMDD)*	g. UNIT/COMMAND ADDRESS *(City, State, ZIP Code)*

DD FORM 4/3, JAN 2001   PREVIOUS EDITION MAY BE USED.

"Look, Skip—a War! Let's Sign Up All the Guys at the Deke House! This Will Be Loads More Fun Than a Chi Omega Mixer!"

Don't Just "Clean Up" Washington; Fumigate It

George W. Bush ran for president pledging to "restore honor and integrity to the White House." This was a not too subtle shot at Bill Clinton's marital infidelity. And while we trust it's true that Bush has neither cheated on his wife nor lied about it, we believe honor and integrity require more than marital fidelity.

George W. Bush and the Washington Republicans have presided over the most corrupt reign since Richard Nixon and his Watergate crooks were driven from Washington in disgrace.

The CIA Leak Scandal

It may be that no Bush scandal has done more damage to America than his aides' blowing the cover of a CIA operative. When Bush White House aides told reporters that Valerie Plame Wilson was with the CIA, it didn't take long for America's enemies to connect the dots. Wilson had been designated "NOC," or no official cover, which means she did her clandestine work without the benefit of a cover-story government job. Some undercover CIA agents pose as diplomats overseas. That way, if they're caught, diplomatic immunity requires the country that catches them to return them to the United States. It's a good deal, having an official cover. The trouble with it is, the folks we're spying on tend to be wary of anyone with an official diplomatic job overseas. So, while the official cover can protect the agent, it can hinder the ability to gather intelligence.

So Valerie Plame Wilson was sent out without any official cover. If she'd been caught, she would have been subject to the tender mercies of local laws. But her work—trying to protect America from weapons of mass destruction—was vital to national security. And folks who served with her said she excelled at it. So the CIA gave her a cover. She was to be an energy consultant for the fictitious firm of Brewster Jennings. That way, she could meet with sources in foreign countries, pretending to be working on energy deals, and gather information that would help protect Americans from weapons of mass destruction.

That all changed on July 14, 2003. Our old *Crossfire* colleague Bob Novak wrote this: "[Ambassador Joseph] Wilson never worked for the CIA, but his wife, Valerie Plame, is an Agency operative on weapons of mass destruction. Two senior administration officials told me Wilson's wife suggested sending him to Niger to investigate the Italian report. The CIA says its counter-proliferation officials selected Wilson and asked his wife to contact him. 'I will not answer any question about my wife,' Wilson told me." [1]

The description of Ambassador Wilson's wife as "an Agency operative on weapons of mass destruction" was in paragraph six of a ten-paragraph column. It did not initially cause a major controversy. The only person we know of who publicly raised the issue—except Wilson himself—was David Corn of *The Nation*. Alone among journalists, he jumped on the story. Two days after Novak's column, Corn wrote a piece called "A White House Smear." It began like this: "Did senior Bush officials blow the cover of a U.S. intelligence officer working covertly in a field of vital importance to national security—and break the law—in order to strike at a Bush administration critic and intimidate others? It sure looks that way, if conservative journalist Bob Novak can be trusted." [2]

Corn pointed out that Wilson had embarrassed the White House, after which his wife's identity had been revealed. Corn called it "a thuggish act" and called for an investigation. While the rest of us were napping, David Corn had the vision and the guts to see the smear for what it was.

When the Bush White House blew that cover, it ruined Valerie Plame's career. It also unmasked Brewster Jennings, thus outing any other CIA operatives who may have been using it as their cover. Beyond that, any foreign source—the intelligence community calls such sources "assets"—who'd been meeting with anyone from Brewster Jennings was exposed, and their governments were aware of the cover story as well. We shudder to think what they might have done to anyone who was helping Plame, Brewster Jennings, and the United States of America.

This is a big deal. National security was compromised. As Larry Johnson, a former undercover CIA agent who trained with Valerie Plame, has said, "Protecting the identities of intelligence officers, whether they are working under official or non-official cover, is part of national defense. To compromise these identities is to commit an act of treason. . . . What was done to the wife of Ambassador Joe Wilson was more than a rough game of inside-the-beltway hardball. Karl Rove told Chris Matthews that 'Wilson's wife is fair game.' Not only was she an unfair target, but in going after her the White House political crew unwittingly exposed several intelligence assets and caused the loss of intelligence assets overseas. . . . The best thing [special prosecutor] Patrick Fitzgerald can do is to send a clear message to politicians in both parties that when it comes to political hardball, intelligence assets must be kept out of the game. At the end of the day our nation's security is no game, it is a matter of life and death." [3]

All of this damage was done in an effort to trash Plame's husband. Wilson had the temerity to write an op-ed article debunking the president's claim, in the 2003 State of the Union Address, that Iraq had tried to purchase yellowcake uranium in Africa. The Bush White House later admitted that the charge was based on faulty intelligence; indeed, the CIA had warned the Bush White House months before the State of the Union Address not to use the charge. [4]

A federal grand jury has indicted I. Lewis "Scooter" Libby, Vice President Dick Cheney's chief of staff, for perjury, obstruction of justice, and making false statements to federal investigators. The indictment alleges that Libby told journalists that Plame works for the CIA, then lied about it. The indictment further alleges that someone it refers to as "Official A" discussed Plame's status as a CIA employee with our right-wing colleague Bob Novak. "Official A," it was later revealed, was top Bush aide Karl Rove.[5]

That means the Bush White House lied to the American people. As the scandal was beginning, Joe Wilson, a former United States ambassador who was praised by President George H. W. Bush for his courage in standing up to Saddam Hussein in the early 1990s, pointed the finger at Karl Rove. Wilson said he wanted to see Rove "frog-marched out of the White House."[6]

The White House hit back hard. Through his spokesman, Scott McClellan, President Bush denied that Rove had been involved in telling journalists that Plame worked for the CIA. McClellan said it was "ridiculous" to blame Rove.[7] The presidential press secretary said he had contacted Rove and Libby."I've spoken with each of them individually," McClellan said. "They said they were not involved in leaking classified information, nor did they condone it."[8] McClellan said the president of the United States of America would personally vouch for Rove: "[Rove] wasn't involved. The president knows he wasn't involved."[9]

Rove's attorney was just as emphatic, saying his client "did not tell any reporter that Valerie Plame worked for the CIA."[10]

Like a fool, Paul gave Karl Rove the benefit of the doubt. He'd known Rove since the 1980s and had always gotten along with him. Besides, to him this leak seemed more likely to have come from some bitter national security wonk than from a political adviser. Why would the president's political adviser even know who was a CIA operative? But Paul had no idea how completely the national security apparatus and the political apparatus had been merged in the Bush White House.

The president himself weighed in. A journalist asked him, "Yesterday we were told that Karl Rove had no role in it. Have you talked to Karl, and do you have confidence in him?" Bush replied, "Listen, I know of nobody—I don't know of anybody in my administration who leaked classified information. If somebody did leak classified information, I'd like to know, and we'll take the appropriate action."[11]

We're not so sure the president really wanted to know the truth, because he poured cold water on the notion that we'd ever know who leaked Plame's identity. A reporter asked Bush if he believed the Justice Department investigation would reveal the perpetrator. His answer was revealing: "You tell me. How many sources have you had that's leaked information that you've exposed or had been exposed? Probably none. . . . And I don't know if we're going to find out the senior administration official. . . . I have no idea whether we'll find out who the leaker is, partially because, in all due respect to your profession, you do a very good job of protecting the leakers. But we'll find out." [12] That's an astonishingly blasé attitude about a potential crime that damaged America's war on terrorism. Bush's father, a former CIA director, has said that anyone who reveals the identity of a CIA agent is "a traitor to our country." [13]

As new facts come to light, the Bush White House keeps changing its story. When it became apparent that Rove had in fact discussed Plame with Matt Cooper of *Time* magazine, as well as with Novak; and when it became known that Libby had discussed Plame with Judy Miller of *The New York Times,* the White House line shifted. Rove's attorney said, "Karl has truthfully told everyone who's asked him that he did not circulate Valerie Plame's name to punish her husband, Joe Wilson." [14] Bush's mouthpiece was reduced to a horde of weasel words. Rove didn't "*circulate* Valerie Plame's *name*" in order to "*punish*" her husband.

Right.

We'll let the legal system sort out whether senior officials in the Bush White House are criminals. We already know this: Senior officials in the Bush White House are liars. They told us they had nothing to do with smearing Joe Wilson and outing his wife when in truth they had everything to do with it.

Eliminate the Middleman:
Put the Lobbyists in Charge of the Government

If you were to believe the civics books, you'd think Republican politicians control the House, the Senate, and the White House. After all, they won (or, in the case of the White House in 2000, nearly won) all three at the ballot box.

But while Republican politicians currently *occupy* the House, the Senate,

and the White House, they don't actually control them. Special-interest lobbyists do. On economic issues, corporate lobbyists have turned your national
government into their own private country club, members only. And on social issues, pressure groups from the kook right are firmly in charge.

Enron's breathtaking influence was, it turns out, the template for a fundamental shift in how Washington works. For generations, lobbyists have
had influence; now they have power. Here's the difference: In the old days,
lobbyists tried to affect how a policy maker acted. Ever the efficient Harvard-
trained MBA, President Bush has eliminated the middleman. He's just made
the lobbyists the policy makers.

Take Daniel Troy. Please. As the top lawyer for the Food and Drug Administration, he's supposed to protect you from dangerous side effects caused
by medicines. But as Anne Mulkern of *The Denver Post* reported in a remarkably thorough and courageous exposé, Troy publicly pledged to defend
pharmaceutical firms against consumers. In a mid-December speech to
pharmaceutical executives at the posh Plaza Hotel in New York, Troy told
them he was willing to side with them and against consumers in lawsuits,
without even knowing the facts, even if a drug's side effects were devastating.
The prospect of the federal government switching its role from protecting
patients to protecting the profits of pharmaceutical corporations is shocking.
But it shouldn't have been. Before he was made chief attorney for the FDA,
Daniel Troy represented pharmaceutical firms.[15] In volunteering to side with
industry against consumers in lawsuits, Troy broke with long-standing practice. Before the Bush administration, neither Democratic nor Republican
administrations joined lawsuits unless requested to by a judge.[16] Troy in effect put the power and prestige of the federal government in service to corporate special interests and against the very American taxpayers who pay his
salary.

Troy is one of more than a hundred corporate lobbyists whom President
Bush has put in charge of regulating the very industries they've lobbied for.
By contrast, as Mulkern reported, "only a handful of registered lobbyists
worked for [President Bill] Clinton." Bush named Anne Marie Lynch, a lobbyist for the Pharmaceutical Research and Manufacturers of America who
had lobbied against price controls on prescription drugs, to a top job in the
Department of Health and Human Services. There, she used her govern-

mental power to oppose efforts to bring down the skyrocketing cost of prescription drugs.[17]

Similarly, Bush named Tom Scully, a health care lobbyist, to run Medicare. There, he was accused of threatening to fire Medicare's chief actuary, Rick Foster, if Foster gave Congress an accurate projection of the cost of Bush's Medicare prescription-drug plan. Democrats were warning that the plan was little more than a taxpayer-financed giveaway to giant, profitable pharmaceutical firms. But when Foster determined that the cost of the Bush plan was twice what the White House had told Congress, Scully sent Foster an e-mail warning that "the consequences for insubordination are extremely severe."[18] Foster did not give Congress the more accurate numbers. Congress passed the Bush plan by one vote. Scully has since left the Bush administration. He's once again a lobbyist for the health care industry.[19]

With the help of the lobbyists Bush has put in charge of these issues, the costs of energy and health care have exploded under the Republicans. But it's not just energy and health care that have been turned over to lobbyists; food safety has been as well. Charles Lambert, a lobbyist for the cattle industry for fifteen years, was named by Bush to serve as the Agriculture Department's undersecretary for marketing and regulatory programs. When he took the job, Lambert pledged in writing that for a full year he would not "participate personally and substantially in any particular matter involving specific parties in which [Cattlemen's] is a party or represents a party, unless I am authorized to participate." But during that year, *The Denver Post* reported, he met at least twelve times with his former bosses at the Cattlemen's Association, or with former members of Cattlemen's.[20]

As a lobbyist for the beef industry, Lambert had opposed labeling beef so consumers could know what country it came from. Consumers and public health experts wanted the country-of-origin label in order to reduce the risk that beef could enter America from a country battling mad cow disease. No worries, Lambert told Congress. At a congressional hearing, he had this exchange with Representative Joe Baca, a Democrat from California:

BACA: Is there a possibility that it [beef from a country with a mad cow outbreak] could get through?
LAMBERT: No, sir.

BACA: None at all?

LAMBERT: No.

BACA: You would bet your life on it—your job on it, right?

LAMBERT: Yes, sir.

Six months later, a cow with mad cow disease was found to have been imported into America from Canada. "I overstated my case," Lambert said.[21]

In addition to putting lobbyists in charge of protecting the energy you use, the medicine you take, and the food you eat, Bush has put corporate special interests in charge of the air you breathe and the water you drink. In 2001, Bush named Stephen Holmstead assistant administrator of the Environmental Protection Agency, in charge of air and radiation. Before that, Holmstead had been an attorney at Latham and Watkins, where he represented power companies, some of the biggest sources of air pollution in America.

When the EPA proposed new rules on air pollution, something about them struck Martha Keating as funny. Funny strange, not funny ha-ha. Keating, a scientist with the environmental organization Clean the Air, noted that fully twelve paragraphs of the new EPA rule had been copied almost word for word from an industry proposal. The proposal had been written by none other than the law firm of Latham and Watkins.

The new rules (should we call them the Bush rules or the industry-written rules? Since they're the same, it's hard to tell which is the more accurate description) slowed down requirements to clean up mercury by as much as eleven years. This despite the fact that mercury in air pollution falls to the earth in rain, where it poisons fish. It's gotten so bad that forty-three states have issued advisories against eating fish.[22] Mercury is toxic to the developing nervous systems of unborn babies. The Environmental Working Group says, "Exposure to mercury in the womb can cause learning deficits, delay the mental development of children, and cause other neurological problems."[23]

You would think that our ostentatiously pro-life president and his self-proclaimed pro-life party would be aghast at the notion of foot-dragging on cleaning up a toxin that is poisoning the brains of helpless unborn babies.

But you would be wrong. "Pro-life" is a handy label for some Republicans, but "pro-lobbyist" is their real religion.

Finally, let us ponder the case of J. Steven Griles, who became the number two person at the Interior Department in 2001. A protégé of the anti-environmental wack job James Watt, Griles once bragged that he wanted to "turn the lights out" on the office that regulates the mining industry. In examining Griles, one journalist concluded that his "20-plus-year career as an industry-friendly political appointee and high-powered industry lobbyist . . . appears to have had one primary focus: get government out of the regulation business—and when you can't do that, get mining executives into government regulation." [24]

So when Bush gave Griles the power to do just that, he didn't waste time. He was a key player in the effort to allow mountaintop coal removal. It's a simple process, really. You just lop the top off a mountain, dump the debris—tons of toxic sludge—into the riverbed below, dig what you need out of the hole, then walk away. Under Griles, twelve hundred miles of Appalachian streambeds were buried in toxic sludge by this technique. "Griles allowed the coal industry to rape the people and the environment of Appalachia," says Judy Bonds, director of the West Virginia environmental group Coal River Mountain Watch. "He either thinks we're second-class citizens or he doesn't even know we exist." [25]

Perhaps a bigshot Washington Republican like Griles did in fact see folks in Appalachia as second-class citizens. He sure saw the corporate bigwigs as first-class people. Despite Griles's pledge not to involve himself in issues affecting his former clients, two of his underlings pushed for $2 million in no-bid contracts for Advanced Power Technologies, a former Griles client. And Griles reached across bureaucratic lines to pressure the EPA not to block a plan to open eight million acres in Wyoming and Montana for drilling—a plan that included no fewer than six of Griles's former clients. [26]

The Interior Department's inspector general called Griles's tenure "an ethical quagmire. . . . His lax understanding of the ethics agreement and attendant recusals . . . combined with the lax dispensation of ethics advice given to him, results in lax constraint over matters in which the deputy secretary involved himself." [27] All sounds pretty lax-ative to us.

Eliminate the Middle Man II—
The K Street Project

With all these lobbyists running the government, you'd think there'd be no one left to actually work as a lobbyist. You might even think there would be no need to be a lobbyist. Ahh, but you would be wrong. In the Age of Bush, special-interest lobbying has been one of the few growth industries in America; one of the few places where Bush has been a job generator. Since George W. Bush took over from Bill Clinton, the number of lobbyists in Washington has doubled. There are now almost thirty-five thousand registered lobbyists in Washington.[28] That's almost fifty times the total population of Crawford, Texas.[29] Not only is the number of lobbyists up by 100 percent, the fees they charge their corporate special-interest clients are up 100 percent as well. The nonpartisan Center for Public Integrity reports that since 1998, $13 billion has been spent to lobby the federal government.[30] Why the explosion in lobbying? One corporate big shot, John D. Hassell, the director of government affairs for Hewlett-Packard, was candid: "We're trying to take advantage of the fact that Republicans control the House, the Senate and the White House," he told *The Washington Post.*[31]

Let's get this straight. The Bush administration has been depleting the lobbyists' corps by bringing them into the government, and yet the number of professional lobbyists keeps growing. Where do they come from? From Republican politicians. In the ultimate case of the revolving door, GOP aides from Capitol Hill, the White House, and the myriad federal agencies controlled by the GOP have swung out of government and into high-paying jobs as lobbyists.

This is part of a plan. In fact, the plan has a name: the K Street Project. K Street is the downtown Washington power corridor where powerful, pricey lobbyists hang their hats. For years, influential Republican politicians in Washington have used their power to coerce businesses into hiring Republicans. These hires in turn channel more special-interest money to Republican politicians, who in turn pass legislation favorable to said special interests.

This is not some left-wing conspiracy theory. We know about the K Street Project because the Republicans have been brazenly open about it. Every Tuesday, Rick Santorum, the moralistic Republican senator from

Pennsylvania, sets aside his ostentatious religiosity and presides over a takeover of the temple of democracy by the money changers. At the meeting, which often includes other powerful Republicans from the White House, as well as the House and the Senate, the discussion is about jobs. Not the jobs we're shipping overseas thanks to GOP economic policies. Not the jobs that are disappearing as Washington Republicans dismantle manufacturing in America. Not the jobs that are lacking in benefits or retirement. No, the talk at Santorum's K Street Project meetings is about lobbying jobs.

Journalist Nicholas Confessore reported on this sleazy enterprise for the wonderful, tough progressive magazine *Washington Monthly.* "Every week," he wrote, "the lobbyists present pass around a list of the jobs available and discuss whom to support. Santorum's responsibility is to make sure each one is filled by a loyal Republican—a senator's chief of staff, for instance, or a top White House aide, or another lobbyist whose reliability has been demonstrated. After Santorum settles on a candidate, the lobbyists present make sure it is known whom the Republican leadership favors. 'The underlying theme was [to] place Republicans in key positions on K Street. Everybody taking part was a Republican and understood that that was the purpose of what we were doing,' says Rod Chandler, a retired congressman and lobbyist who has participated in the Santorum meetings. 'It's been a very successful effort.' "[32]

The K Street Project is led by Santorum in the Senate. In the House, it's managed by Tom DeLay (R-Indicted) and Roy Blunt (R–Philip Morris). DeLay has reportedly developed a list of who, in his mind, has been naughty and who has been nice. It makes Nixon's enemies list look amateurish. DeLay has analyzed the four hundred largest political action committees in Washington, looking at the amount and percentage of money they donate to each political party. Based on DeLay's list, lobbyists are assigned to either the "friendly" or "unfriendly" column. "If you want to play in our revolution," DeLay said, "you have to live by our rules."[33]

The intimidation has worked. A dozen years ago, as Bill Clinton was coming into office and Democrats controlled the House and Senate, nineteen major industries analyzed by the Center for Responsive Politics—such as defense, pharmaceuticals, banking, and accounting—split their donations evenly between the Republicans and Democrats. Now the Republicans have a two-to-one advantage across those industries. And pharmaceuticals, one of the biggest and wealthiest lobbies in Washington, now gives 80 percent of its contributions to Republicans.[34]

The GOP's K Street Project has been controversial. In 1998 the Electronics Industries Alliance had the temerity to hire former Democratic congressman Dave McCurdy as its chief lobbyist. Tom DeLay did not like this. So he pulled off the House floor an intellectual property bill that was vital to the high-tech industry. This was too much even for the Republican-controlled House Ethics Committee, which privately reprimanded DeLay. But the Hammer was unapologetic and unbowed.[35]

Jack Abramoff: The King of Republican Sleaze

To be sure, some lobbyists are decent people—maybe even lots of them. Maybe even most of them. But let's face it: Some of them are real dirtbags, too. You've got to be one cold SOB to lobby for more mercury in the water, knowing it causes unborn babies to be brain-damaged. But of all the scoundrels and scalawags plying Washington's oldest profession, one stands out. One man towers above the rest. One man stands like a sequoia above the merely sleazy and the simply greedy.

That man is Jack Abramoff.

Like so many of the kleptocrats and sleaze merchants in Washington these days, Abramoff got his start in the College Republicans. He served as chairman of the group in 1981, as the Age of Reagan was dawning. At the time, Democrats were complaining about the "Sleaze Factor" that surrounded the Gipper. Now those days look like *Leave It to Beaver,* compared to the scummy conduct that's par for the course in George W. Bush's Washington.

After a turn as a producer in Hollywood, where he made the Dolph Lundgren dog *Red Scorpion* ("The movie's reflective moments belong to Mr. Lundgren's sweaty chest," wrote Stephen Holden in *The New York Times*),[36] Abramoff returned to Washington as the Gingrich Revolution was ascendant. He quickly parlayed his long-standing GOP contacts into wealth and power. In the course of his career, he has helped get a visa for the spectacularly corrupt Zairean dictator, Mobutu Sese Seko, and represented just about anyone who would pay him. But his big score came from Indian gaming interests. He soon lined up a stable of American Indian gaming clients who paid Abramoff and his associates an astonishing $66 million—clients whom Abramoff has by turns called "monkeys," "idiots," and "troglodytes."[37]

Even in Washington—even in George W. Bush's Washington—$66 million is, as we say back home, a right smart o' money. What did the Indians—principally the Mississippi Band of Choctaw Indians and the Coushatta Tribe of Louisiana—get for their millions? First, they got access. The tribes wanted to meet President Bush, probably to discuss more than the latest trades by the Texas Rangers. But Bush is a busy man. He has hurricanes to ignore and intelligence briefings to ignore and deficits to ignore. And then there's his inviolable daily workout schedule. And don't forget the nap. On top of that, he's famously home and asleep by nine P.M. So that doesn't leave a lot of time to meet with a bunch of—ugggh—citizens.

But these citizens were represented by Jack Abramoff, the King of Republican Sleaze. Abramoff reportedly advised the tribes to donate $25,000 apiece to Grover Norquist's Americans for Tax Reform to underwrite a 2001 event. Norquist, a friend of Abramoff's since their College Republican days, is at the epicenter of the Abramoff scandal and nearly every other major piece of Republican chicanery in Washington these days. "The exposure would be incredible and would be very helpful," wrote Abramoff to a lawyer for one of the tribes. "One of the things we need to do is get the leaders of the tribe (ideally the chief) in front of the president as much as possible." The Indians wrote the checks, and the chiefs got to meet the commander in chief.[38]

That was just the beginning. The Choctaws have, for example, reportedly given millions, at Abramoff's direction, to a host of right-wing groups. In addition, according to Abramoff, the Choctaw and other clients have made over $10 million in unreported donations to the conservative movement.[39]

What did they get for their money, other than the thrill of meeting the president? Well, Representative Dale Kildee, a Democrat from Minnesota, says the Choctaws enjoy an "unprecedented" exemption from national regulations on gaming. They are apparently the only tribe allowed to regulate its own gaming operations. And why not? If you can't trust a tribe that pays millions to a fine man like Jack Abramoff, whom can you trust?

Like any business, the Indian gaming industry wants to restrict its competition. Here's where the story gets interesting. Abramoff allied himself with one Michael Scanlon, former spokesman for the ethically impaired House Republican leader Tom DeLay. Together, the two pro-gambling lobbyists funneled millions to anti-gambling organizations of the religious right. The religious right killed the casino, aiding the existing casinos of Abramoff's clients. And then—here's the beauty part—Abramoff and Scanlon turned around and signed up the Indians *whose casino they'd just secretly killed,* promising to use their influence to correct this "gross indignity." All for a mere $4.2 million.[40]

Even among the scummiest of scumbags, this was a slimy deal.

Here's how they pulled it off. You see, the Tigua Indians of Texas had opened a casino. Charming place called Speaking Rock in El Paso. The casino was hot, bringing in $60 million a year. But it was controversial, what with Paul's home state of Texas being such a moral place and all. However, God's people can sometimes be disorganized and distracted. So Abramoff and Scanlon hired God's own lobbyist, Ralph Reed, former director of the Christian Coalition, to help some gambling casinos by closing other gambling casinos. Reed was happy to do the Lord's work. For $4 million, that is.[41]

Reed went to work. He organized a coalition of folks who honestly, ethically, morally, and religiously opposed gambling. They didn't oppose the casinos for $4 million; they opposed them because they thought they were sinful. Our boy Reed, however, needed the $4 million to motivate his anti-gambling fervor. (We should note that Reed claims ignorance of the fact that his millions for opposing gambling were in fact coming from gambling interests. Right, Ralph. Who'd you think had a $4 million stake in stopping gambling? The Little Sisters of the Poor?)

Reed and his team pressured John Cornyn, then the Texas attorney general, now a U.S. senator. Cornyn, ever eager to court the religious right, ruled that the casino violated Texas law, and he shut it down. Cornyn later said he was "unaware" of Ralph Reed's involvement in the effort.[42]

Please. Ralph Reed is one of the most well-known and influential figures in right-wing politics. He was a consultant to Enron and an adviser to

George W. Bush.[43] And we're supposed to believe an aggressive, ambitious Texas right-wing Republican doesn't know Ralph Reed is organizing ministers in support of a move that Cornyn later described as one of the proudest moments of his career as attorney general? Ralph sure claimed he was in contact with Cornyn. In an e-mail he wrote on November 12, 2001, Reed told Abramoff, "Great work. Get me details so I can alert Cornyn and let him know what we are doing to help him."[44] Cornyn stands by his story that he had no contact with Reed. We guess that depends on what the definition of "contact" is.

Regardless of which right-wing moralist is lying here, it is apparent from the record that Ralph Reed took time away from counting his ill-gotten gains to wage and win the fight against the Tiguas' casino. On February 8, 2002, Cornyn shut the Tiguas down. Seeing this coming, Abramoff was already pitching the tribe—the same one he was screwing, mind you—to hire him. "I'm on the phone with Tigua!" he e-mailed Scanlon two days before Cornyn shuttered Speaking Rock. "Fire up the jet, baby, we're going to El Paso!!" A week later, Abramoff sent Scanlon another e-mail, noting that a Tigua consultant was pushing to hire the despicable duo. "This guy NEEDS us to save his ass!!" When the *El Paso Times* ran a story about massive layoffs at the casino, Abramoff was filled with the milk of human kindness. Scanlon e-mailed the news account to Abramoff, with a note saying, "This is on the front page of todays [*sic*] paper while they will be voting on our plan!"

"Is life great or what!!!" responded Abramoff.[45]

It sure is, Jack!!!

In another e-mail, Abramoff wrote to a representative of the tribe and offered to persuade Republicans in Washington to correct the "gross indignity perpetrated by the Texas state authorities." He assured his desperate potential client that he had "a couple of Senators willing to ram this through."[46]

It worked. The Tiguas signed up, agreeing to pay Abramoff's law firm as much as $175,000 a month.[47] At the same time he was seducing the Tiguas, Abramoff was insulting them. On February 11, 2002, he e-mailed Reed, "I wish those moronic Tiguas were smarter in their political contributions. I'd love us to get our mitts on that moolah!! Oh well, stupid folks get wiped out."[48]

That may or may not be true, but here's hoping greedy, duplicitous, hypocritical right-wing Republican lobbyists get wiped out.

Lest you think Abramoff's sleaze is limited to Tom DeLay and other GOP congressmen, you should know Abramoff's slime has penetrated the Bush White House as well. David H. Safavian, President Bush's top procurement officer, has been indicted on charges that he obstructed justice and made false statements to federal investigators who were looking into his dealings with Abramoff.

In the indictment, the Justice Department charges that Safavian (whom Bush's close friend and deputy budget chief Clay Johnson called "the most qualified person" to oversee federal procurement) did not disclose that Abramoff had business before the General Services Administration when Safavian was seeking permission to accept an Abramoff-paid luxury golf outing in Scotland. (What is it with these Republican sleaze balls and golf? You notice they all talk NASCAR but live country club.) At the time, Safavian was the chief of staff to the head of the GSA, which controls an enormous amount of federal real estate. Abramoff was trying to buy some of that real estate and, the feds allege, Safavian knew it. As you can imagine, it's not exactly proper under federal ethics rules to fly to Scotland and play golf with someone who's trying to get something out of your agency.[49]

Abramoff himself is under indictment. A federal grand jury in Florida indicted him in August 2005, charging him with five counts of wire fraud and conspiracy related to the purchase of SunCruz Casinos, a fleet of gambling cruise ships. The indictment alleges that Abramoff and his associates agreed to pay Konstantinos "Gus" Boulis $147.5 million for SunCruz, but faked a wire transfer of $23 million. The assistant U.S. attorney in Fort Lauderdale, Alexander Acosta, called the Abramoff wire transfer "counterfeit. The defendants never transferred the funds. And [they] never made a cash equity contribution toward the purchase of SunCruz."[50]

As Abramoff was wooing Boulis, he persuaded Tom DeLay to give Boulis a flag that had flown over our nation's Capitol. Abramoff also brought one of the financiers to a DeLay fund-raiser at a skybox during a Monday-night football game between the Washington Redskins and the Dallas Cowboys.[51] (Incidentally, Don Imus is the only media person we know of who has had the guts to point out the hypocrisy of Abramoff using Indians' money to rent a skybox at a *Redskins* game.)

On loan papers, Abramoff listed Tony Rudy, one of DeLay's closest aides, and California Republican congressman Dana Rohrabacher as references. He also fired up the SunCruz jet and flew members of DeLay's staff to the Super Bowl in Tampa.[52]

Despite all of Abramoff's powerful connections, federal prosecutors allege, he didn't come through with the money. You would think that as nice as it is to have a flag flown over the Capitol, it would annoy Boulis to be stiffed out of millions of dollars. But we haven't heard a peep from him. That's because on February 6, 2001, Boulis was driving home from a business meeting when someone fired three hollow-point bullets into his chest. No one has ever been arrested for the murder.[53]

Tom DeLay

If Jack Abramoff is the scummiest lobbyist in town, you won't be surprised that the scummiest congressman in town, Tom DeLay, has called Abramoff "one of my closest and dearest friends."[54] We can't figure out which is the parasite and which is the host, but these two dirtbags have been living off and feeding each other for years. In short, here's the deal: Abramoff raises special-interest money and flies DeLay to luxurious and exotic destinations; DeLay passes (or kills) legislation for Abramoff's clients. "To the casual observer, it was a pretty simple deal," one former GOP House leadership aide told the *National Journal*. "Jack raised money for the pet projects of DeLay and took care of his top staff. In turn, they granted him tremendous access and allowed him to freely trade on DeLay's name."[55]

That's unfair. Probably just a jealous lobbying competitor. Tom and Jack have more than a mutually beneficial financial and political alliance. They're buddies. Pals. Like Starsky and Hutch, or Abbott and Costello, or Butch Cassidy and the Sundance Kid. Or Sacco and Vanzetti, or Sears and Roebuck, or Stalin and Trotsky—of course, without the ice pick in Trotsky's head (so far).

They're soul mates, really, the devout Christian (just ask him) DeLay and the devout Orthodox Jew (just ask him) Abramoff. "We are the same politically and philosophically," Abramoff has said. "Tom's goal is specific—to keep Republicans in power and advance the conservative movement. I have Tom's goal precisely." [56] It warms our hearts to see those boys so close. Maybe they can go from being soul mates to being cell mates.

Oh, sure, the cynical liberal press points out that Abramoff and his wife have personally donated $40,000 to DeLay and ARMPAC, DeLay's disgraced money machine. And at least two of the tribes Abramoff represented—the Louisiana Coushattas and the Saginaw Chippewas—donated $38,000 to ARMPAC. [57]

So close are these two that DeLay, the profoundly pious Christian, set aside his moral and religious opposition to gambling in order to kill a proposed federal tax on Indian gambling revenues that was in a nonbinding budget resolution in 1995. "Regardless of what you feel about gaming," Abramoff said, using the industry's favored euphemism for gambling, "what you are creating here is a tax on these people, and conservatives should never be in favor of new taxes." [58]

We're sure that was a tough call for DeLay. As a fundamentalist Christian, he opposes gambling. But as a supply-side Republican, he opposes taxes. So what do you do when two values collide? If you're Tom DeLay, you follow the money. And Jack Abramoff definitely had the money. One gets the feeling that if Abramoff represented the hookers of Las Vegas, DeLay would support a ban on the pernicious Nookie Tax. As a matter of principle, naturally.

DeLay probably didn't wrestle long with whether to help out another Abramoff client—Tyco, headed up by the felon Dennis Kozlowski. He led the fight to kill a proposal to stop federal contracts from going to Benedict Arnold corporations—corporate traitors (like Tyco) who incorporate in Bermuda and other overseas venues in order to avoid paying their share of American taxes. [59] Sure, DeLay loves his country—though not enough to serve in Vietnam. (He once said all the military positions had been taken by minority youths, so there was no room for him in the army during Vietnam.) [60] In this case, DeLay was able to rise above patriotism to help his lobbyist "best friend" help a traitor.

One of the (many) things that has DeLay in trouble is the allegation that he accepted free trips paid for by a lobbyist. Which lobbyist, pray tell? If you have to ask, we're wondering whether you've been paying attention. DeLay has been accused of accepting luxurious trips paid for by Abramoff.

Something called the National Center for Public Policy Research financed a DeLay trip to London and Scotland (including golf at St. Andrews—isn't life great, Jack!!!). Abramoff was on the board of the center. The center was also a client of Abramoff's. According to the *National Journal,* "Abramoff listed, among other things, a $4,285 hotel bill for DeLay and his wife, Christine, during a trip to London and Scotland in the spring of 2000 with the DeLays and some of the congressman's former staff members."[61] So, did the center pay for the trip, or did Abramoff? Inquiring minds want to know. Why does it matter? Because members of Congress may accept trips from nonprofit groups like the center, but they may not receive them from lobbyists.

DeLay also says the center paid for a $57,000 trip to Moscow. But reports published in both *The New York Times* and *The Washington Post* claim the trip was financed by business interests that were lobbying DeLay to support the Russian government.[62] The papers' sources told them the trip was set up by lobbyists and paid for by a shadowy Bahamian corporation called Chelsea Commercial Enterprises, Ltd. (Isn't it always a shadowy Bahamian corporation, or have we just read too many John Grisham novels?) There has been speculation that Chelsea (the supposedly sleazy Bahamian corporation, not the delightful and completely ethical presidential daughter) may have been a front for Russian corporations with ties to the Russky security forces. Chelsea, the story goes, was in cahoots with a Russian oil and gas company called NaftaSib, which has business ties with Russian security institutions. Again, why does this matter? First, because it's important to know if a powerful congressman is in bed (figuratively speaking, that is) with shadowy Russians. And second, because members of Congress cannot accept travel from foreign agents.

If this is starting to make your head hurt, we're going to tell you about only one more sleazy DeLay trip, then we'll tell you about his alleged money laundering and how he shot a man in Reno just to watch him die. (One of those charges is real, the other we just made up; in cable TV, it's called a tease, designed to hold your interest during the ad for Depends.)

Mark Shields, who ascended to the position of Conscience of Washington upon the death of Mary McGrory, has written that Tom DeLay's intervention on behalf of sweatshops in Saipan is the sleaziest thing he's ever done. Choosing DeLay's sleaziest action is like trying to pick Hank Williams's most painful song. But we think Shields is right. Saipan, for those who got C's in geography, is the capital city of the Northern Marianas Islands. The Northern Marianas, in turn, are a United States territory, so garments made there get to have a "Made in the U.S.A." label, which makes us feel better about buying them. In addition to the label, clothes sewn in the Northern Marianas can come into the United States tariff-free and quota-free. It's a good deal.

Trouble is, as Shields points out, manufacturers in the Northern Marianas are not subject to U.S. wage and worker protection laws. Workers there are paid half the U.S. minimum wage and, according to Shields, live "behind barbed wire in squalid shacks minus plumbing, [and] work 12 hours a day, often seven days a week, without any of the legal protections U.S. workers are guaranteed." [63]

The conditions are so bad that even ultra-conservatives like Alaska's Frank Murkowski—then a senator, now the governor; then and now a deep-red conservative—were so moved they passed a bill through the Senate extending U.S. labor and wage protections to the poor souls stitching away in the Northern Marianas' sweatshops. Murkowski, with a 0 rating from organized labor and a perfect 100 from the Chamber of Commerce, was moved to say, "The last time we heard a justification that economic advances would be jeopardized if workers were treated properly was shortly before Appomattox." The bill passed the Republican Senate unanimously. [64]

Then the Abramoff-DeLay alliance got into the game. Corporate interests in the Northern Marianas paid Abramoff millions to protect their right to treat people in a U.S. territory like prisoners in a Communist Chinese gulag. Abramoff arranged for DeLay to travel to Saipan, where he played golf on a championship eighteen-hole golf course, swam, and snorkeled in crystal-clear waters amid what one tourism website calls "lush, living reefs with hundreds of tropical fish, coral, sponges and crustaceans." [65]

Between golf outings and frolicking in the ocean (we know: the idea of DeLay frolicking is nauseating), Tom spoke to a gathering of Abramoff's well-heeled clients. He told the sweatshop owners—the folks who caged their employees like animals and paid them peanuts—that they were his heroes. "You are a shining light for what is happening to the Republican Party, and you represent everything that is good about what we are trying to do in

America and leading the world in the free-market system." DeLay also described the Dickensian conditions in the Marianas in Utopian terms, telling *The Washington Post,* the place is "a perfect Petri dish of capitalism. It's like my Galapagos Island."[66] Set aside your outrage, your moral revulsion, for a minute; just a minute. Focus instead on Tom DeLay citing with approval the Galapagos Islands—the place where Charles Darwin was inspired to formulate the theory of evolution. And laugh to keep from crying.

Murkowski's bill never came up for a vote in the House. Tom DeLay saw to it that it died.

And then there's the alleged money laundering. As we write this, Tom DeLay is under indictment by two Texas grand juries. The charge, essentially, is that DeLay and his money machine conspired to evade Texas's law against corporate contributions in the state's political races. The grand juries charge that DeLay and two associates conspired to launder the corporate money this way: A DeLay-established political action committee, TRMPAC, raised corporate money. Because TRMPAC could not in turn give that corporate money to Texas campaigns (which DeLay wanted to influence so he could redraw congressional districts and increase the GOP majority in Congress), TRMPAC sent $190,000 in corporate money to the Republican National Committee. Two days later, the RNC just happened to send—you wanna guess how much?—you got it: $190,000 to Republican candidates for the Texas legislature.[67]

DeLay says the prosecutor, Democrat Ronnie Earle, is on a partisan witch hunt. But of the fifteen politicians Earle has prosecuted, twelve have been Democrats. Still, even a moral reprobate like DeLay is entitled to the presumption of innocence. That's a legal matter. As a moral and ethical—and political—matter, we are at a loss to explain why the party of Lincoln has chosen as its leader a man who has been admonished more frequently by the Ethics Committee than any other member of Congress. A man who called the Environmental Protection Agency "the Gestapo of government."[68] A man who said the Columbine killings were the result of "working parents who put their kids into daycare, the teaching of evolution in the schools, and working mothers who take birth control pills."[69] A man who believes that "judges need to be intimidated."[70] A man who visited boys who'd lost everything in Hurricane Katrina—their homes, their pets, their friends, their family members, their schools and teachers and classmates—and looked at them as they sat on cots in the Astrodome, then said, "Now, tell me the truth, boys, is this kind of fun?"[71]

This is the man to whom the Republicans look for leadership.

Roy Blunt

When it looked like Tom DeLay was going to be indicted, he moved quickly. Not to clean up his act, mind you, but to repeal a House rule that said indicted members of Congress could not serve in the leadership. Speaker Dennis Hastert, a loyal DeLay toady, rammed through the rule change. But a public outcry forced the Republicans to back down. And so, when Tom DeLay was indicted, Roy Blunt became the majority leader.

As you may have gathered from the preceding pages, we don't like Tom DeLay. Don't like him one bit. But we've got to admit, we like Roy Blunt. He's a nice man, decent and engaging to us every time we've met him. When we were hosting *Crossfire*, Blunt was the number three Republican in the House. Tom DeLay was trying to enforce a GOP boycott of our show. (Apparently, our feelings toward him are reciprocated.) But Roy Blunt appeared on the show anyway. He was always pleasant, represented his side well, and projected a sense of ethics that was a welcome respite from DeLay.

So we were pained—and we're not being sarcastic—to read in *The Washington Post* that Blunt had been an enthusiastic participant in the DeLay-era sleaze.

Just hours after being elected Republican whip, as the House was about to vote on the massive bill creating the Department of Homeland Security, Blunt slipped in a secret provision. So secret even Tom DeLay and Toady Hastert didn't know about it. The provision had little or nothing to do with homeland security, and everything to do with the institutional corruption so typical of Washington under the Republicans. The unnoticed codicil was designed to benefit one corporation—one that's very important to Roy Blunt: Philip Morris.[72]

Philip Morris is America's biggest cigarette company. That means its products kill more Americans than any other corporation. Well, sure, they're a corporate killer, but didn't Mama always tell you to try to be the best at whatever it is you choose to do? The provision would have boosted Philip Morris's profits by making it harder to sell tobacco over the Internet and by cracking down on what the media called "contraband tobacco." (Tobacco is deadly even when it's legal, so the notion of "contraband" tobacco puzzles us.) Fearing bad publicity if they were caught sneaking a pro-tobacco provision in the homeland security bill, House leaders removed Blunt's Philip Morris provision.

Why would Blunt use his newfound power to force a secret provision helping Philip Morris into the homeland security bill? Let's try a couple of theories.

Theory one: Follow the money—always a good place to start. And here we hit pay dirt. Philip Morris is the single largest donor to Roy Blunt, giving political committees connected to him a staggering $270,000.[73]

Theory two: Follow your heart—here again, bingo. In 2003, when Blunt inserted the offending provision, his marriage of thirty-one years had ended in divorce, and he was dating Abigail Perlman, a lobbyist for . . . three guesses . . . you got it—Philip Morris. Today Ms. Perlman is Mrs. Roy Blunt.[74]

Theory three: Family values—far be it from us to cast aspersions on someone for being divorced. (Although Republicans were more than happy to pass judgment on Bill and Hillary Clinton's marriage, and last time we looked, they were still married.) Blunt has another family tie to Philip Morris: his son, Andrew, is a lobbyist for the company on state issues in Missouri.[75]

If you guessed any of those three theories, you'd be right. If you guessed all three, then you already know that Roy Blunt is a worthy successor to Tom DeLay.

Blunt helped another of Andrew's clients, UPS, when he added a provision to the $79 billion emergency appropriation to pay for the war in Iraq. This provision effectively blocked foreign-owned shipping companies from carrying military cargo. We're all for buying American, but if the Blunt provision had merit, it should have passed through the committee process in the clear light of day. Incidentally, UPS and fellow domestic cargo company

FedEx have contributed $58,000 to Blunt since 2001. Looks like ol' Roy delivers about as well as UPS or FedEx do.[76]

Like his predecessor, Blunt was close to State-of-the-Art Scumbag Jack Abramoff. As the reformers at Citizens for Responsibility and Ethics in Washington (CREW) report, "Rep. Blunt and his staff have close connections to uber-lobbyist Jack Abramoff, who is the subject of criminal and congressional probes. In June 2003, Mr. Abramoff persuaded Majority Leader Tom DeLay to organize a letter, co-signed by Speaker Hastert, Whip Roy Blunt, and Deputy Whip Eric Cantor, that endorsed a view of gambling law benefiting Mr. Abramoff's client, the Louisiana Coushatta, by blocking gambling competition by another tribe. Mr. Abramoff has donated $8,500 to Rep. Blunt's leadership PAC, Rely on Your Beliefs."

Again, we give you this information on Blunt more in sadness than in anger. We think he's a nice guy. But even nice guys have become hopelessly compromised in the ethical miasma of Washington as it's being run by the Republicans.

Bill Frist

As if in a perverse race to the bottom, at the same time House Majority Leader Tom DeLay was indicted, Senate Majority Leader Bill Frist was being investigated by the U.S. attorney for insider trading. First is the scion of the founder of Hospital Corporation of America. HCA is a big, profitable, and controversial corporation. It is the largest for-profit hospital chain in America.

Frist, elected to the Senate in 1994, has long held HCA stock. He placed it in what passes in Republican Washington for a "blind trust," but in reality Frist knew exactly what was in that trust—lots and lots of HCA stock. From time to time, ethics watchdogs have called on Frist to divest the HCA stock, since, as a senator, he deals with health care issues that affect HCA's bottom line nearly every day. But Frist—with the backing of the oxymoronically named Senate Ethics Committee—maintained that his massive multimillion-dollar holdings in HCA were not a conflict of interest in 1995. Nor in 1996. Or 1997, or '98, or '99, or 2000. 2001? Nope, still no conflict.

Same with 2002. 2003 proved to be no conflict at all. 2004 was a piece of cake. But one day, one very special day in 2005, Bill Frist decided the conflict had become unbearable. He just had to dump that HCA stock.

That day was June 13, 2005. Frist's trusts are worth as much as $35 million,[77] and he had his trustees sell all his HCA stock. And all his wife's HCA stock. And his kids,' too—you can't have the kids owning stock that's suddenly a conflict of interest for you. All that selling took time, but by July 8 the deed was done.[78]

Not a moment too soon. Coincidentally, just days after Frist shed the ethical burden of owning all that HCA stock, the stock tanked. Cratered. Dropped like a gift from a seagull. HCA made an announcement that, due to bad debt, high levels of unpaid patient bills, and higher admissions of uninsured patients, its second-quarter operating earnings would probably be below analysts' estimates. This was a surprise to many, since a few weeks earlier—right as Frist was selling, as it happens—the stock hit its fifty-two-week high of $58.60. After the announcement, the stock fell almost 9 percent.[79]

But rather than applaud Frist for finally recognizing his conflict of interest—a conflict he hadn't been able to detect for ten years, a conflict he hadn't seen when the stock was in the twenties or thirties or forties but which became glaringly apparent when it hit $58; a conflict that peaked just as the stock peaked—the Securities and Exchange Commission and the U.S. attorney for the Southern District of New York decided to investigate him for insider trading.[80]

When he became a senator, Frist said he could vote on health care legislation without a conflict of interest because he had set up blind trusts in which he placed his HCA stock. If that was true, then why dump the stock days before it cratered? Moreover, it turns out Frist owned some HCA stock outside of the blind trusts.[81]

We're not securities lawyers, so we won't hazard a guess as to whether Frist is guilty of insider trading. But we do know this: Bill Frist is a liar. In 2002 he said, "Right now, I don't know if I own HCA because it's a qualified blind trust."[82]

But four months earlier his trustees had informed him that his trusts had received up to $1.5 million in HCA stock.[83]

Similarly, in January 2003, Frist said, "As far as I know, I own no HCA stock. I have no idea. And I hope—as far as I know—I don't have any." But just a month before he made that statement, his trustees had informed him he'd acquired another block of HCA stock—up to $50,000 worth.[84]

Dr. Frist's problem is that a liar needs a better memory.

Randy "Duke" Cunningham

We didn't want to put Republican congressman Duke Cunningham of California in this chapter. In many ways, he's our kind of guy: profane and headstrong, with a short temper and an iconoclastic attitude. The fact that he's a right-wing lunatic—a stone troglodyte who used to hint darkly that Bill Clinton's student backpacking trip to Moscow was somehow treasonous—is fine. While we don't exactly share his views, it's not like he sucked up to fat cats who were enslaving working people in Saipan, like Tom DeLay did. Cunningham was just another Clinton-hating, right-wing wack job. And a fairly amusing one at that.

Besides, Duke Cunningham was a war hero. The first ace of the Vietnam War, he was a real-life Top Gun. He shot down three enemy MiGs in one day, before he himself was shot down. Regardless of whether you supported or opposed that war, anyone who served is entitled, we think, to a high degree of respect.

But we cannot escape the fact that Duke Cunningham is a poster boy for Republican sleaze. This guy's ethics stink. And that's just fine with his Republican colleagues.

Duke, who was aghast at Bill Clinton's personal indiscretions, has had some pretty slimy bedfellows himself, at least in the metaphorical (and financial) sense. In 2003, Cunningham sold his home to Mitchell Wade, the president of MZM, Inc. MZM is a defense contractor with a lot of business before the Appropriations Committee, and Duke happens to be an influential member of that powerful committee. So Duke sold his house to Wade for a lot of money: $1.65 million.[85] According to local real estate records, similar-sized homes in the area sold for $500,000 less. A year later, Wade sold the house, but he could get only $975,000 for it. California real estate is hot, so it's odd that Wade lost $700,000 on a house there—unless he overpaid for it, big-time.[86]

But Wade didn't seem bitter about the deal. In fact, he remained friends with Duke. Even let Duke live rent-free on his yacht, named the *Duke-Stir*. (Duke paid dock fees and other fees, but no rent.)[87]

The friendship wasn't a one-way street. Cunningham has acknowledged using his position on the House Appropriations Committee to help MZM obtain government contracts. Of the $112 million MZM has received in government contracts since 2002, at least $104 million has come through a 2002 noncompetitive five-year blanket purchase agreement, which the Pentagon recently halted. According to Copley News, MZM received $41 million in defense contracts in 2003. In 2004, MZM had $66 million in revenues, tripling revenues since the beginning of the year and increasing staff by 285 percent.[88]

MZM's Wade isn't the only special interest Duke was in bed with (he must have a very big bed—metaphorically speaking, of course). Thomas Kontogiannis is a major GOP donor and New York real estate developer who has a record of bid-rigging. In 1997, Duke bought Representative Sonny Callahan's yacht for $200,000. Five years later, Duke sold it to Kontogiannis for $600,000, which Citizens for Responsibility and Ethics in Washington says is "considerably more than the vessel was worth." Oddly, the sale is not recorded in the official Coast Guard records. The records show that Duke still owns the yacht.[89]

In 2003, when Cunningham bought a $2.55 million home in exclusive Rancho Santa Fe, California, the congressman asked a mortgage company owned by Kontogiannis's relatives to finance the purchase at a slightly lower rate than regular mortgages. Kontogiannis also says that he paid off Cunningham's second $500,000 mortgage—at Duke's request—with money he owed Duke for the yacht.[90]

Duke Cunningham is a crook. In November 2005 he pleaded guilty to conspiracy and tax evasion for taking $2.4 million worth of bribes, including a yacht, a Rolls-Royce and a $7,200 nineteenth-century Louis-Philippe commode. He is the perfect embodiment of the Bush Republicans—an arrogant, greedy, corrupt bully.

Enron

The Bush Republicans' ties to the most corrupt and discredited corporation in recent history are well documented. George W. Bush himself once reportedly lobbied for Enron. In 1988, when George W.'s father was Ronald Reagan's vice president, the minister of public works and services of Argentina says W. lobbied him on behalf of a controversial Enron pipeline proposal. (It should be noted that Bush has denied lobbying for Enron, but the minister, Rodolfo Terragno, stands by his story.)[91]

Throughout Bush's career, Enron and its CEO, Ken Lay, have been his most generous patrons. And they got their money's worth. Bush is—how shall we say this respectfully?—not exactly known as a man of letters. And yet he and his bestest buddy, "Kenny Boy" Lay, exchanged dozens of letters. Reading them, it's hard to tell who's sucking up to whom, so effusive is each correspondence.[92]

Being pen pals is one thing. Making the federal government a wholly owned subsidiary of Enron is quite another. When Bush seized the White House (thanks in part to Enron donations to his campaign, to the Republican National Committee, and to his recount legal fund), he promptly turned the reins of government over to Kenny Boy. Several senior administration officials came straight from Enron. Thirty-four others owned stock.[93] Enron was ubiquitous. Kenny Boy played a central role in choosing who would regulate his company.[94] Enron had extraordinary access to Vice President Cheney's energy task force, and played a central role in shaping its proposals. As Representative Henry Waxman has revealed through his investigation, "there are at least 17 policies in the White House energy plan that were advocated by Enron or that benefited Enron."[95]

Waxman may be undercounting, since Cheney fought all the way to the Supreme Court to prevent you from knowing just how much influence Enron and other energy lobbyists had on his task force. But you can book this: He wouldn't have fought so hard to keep it secret if it had been a pretty picture.

How to Take Back Reform

1. Choose Which Side You're On

Democrats must stand for reform. They must stand for a more open, honest, and ethical government. Believe it or not, this is a matter of some debate among Washington Democrats. It's not an open debate; you'll never turn on *Hardball* and see two Democratic congressmen debating whether or not Democrats should advocate cleaning up the corruption in Washington. And yet the disagreement is real.

On one side are those who have bought in to the dominant Washington culture. We call them the Remainderists. They believe that a GOP collapse is imminent and that they will inherit the power—and the money—that the Republicans have amassed. On the other are the Reformers, those who truly believe the Republicans have soiled and degraded representative democracy, and who have bold new ideas to clean it up.

We know which side we're on. If Democrats don't stand for reform—if gaining power is about nothing more than sweeping out Republican lobbyists and replacing them with Democratic lobbyists—they will not deserve to govern.

You'll know which side has won this debate as you watch Democrats campaigning to take control of Congress. If the Democrats run on an agenda that includes cleaning up the cesspool that Washington has become, you'll know the Reformers have won the debate. If Democrats are silent about reform, you'll know the Remainderists are in charge.

2. Put the Lobbyists on a Leash

One of the chief Reformers in the Democratic Party is an old pal from the Clinton White House, Rahm Emanuel. Emanuel is a congressman from Chicago, representing the district once served by Dan Rostenkowski. Now, given all the jokes and stereotypes about Chicago politics, you'd think Rahm might be an unlikely leader for the Reform movement. But after two decades in politics—as a fund-raiser, a strategist, and a White House official—Emanuel has seen it all, and he's seen enough.

"When the Speaker's gavel comes down, it's intended to open the People's House, and lately it's looking like the Auction House," says Emanuel. "Whether it's an energy bill that gives $8 billion to the oil and gas interests while oil's at $64 a barrel, whether it's a corporate tax bill solving a $5 billion problem with a $150 billion solution, whether it's a pharmaceutical, prescription drug bill where the industry gave $132 million and walked away with $135 billion in additional profits."[96]

Along with Representative Marty Meehan (D-MA), Emanuel has proposed legislation to reduce the power of lobbyists. Their package of reforms would:

- Require lobbyists to divulge how private groups pay for congressional travel.
- Force lawmakers to disclose their ties to nonprofit groups.
- Double the time that retiring lawmakers and staff would have to wait before lobbying, to two years.
- Count grassroots activities (designed to influence congressmen and senators by stirring up their constituents) as lobbying.
- Make lobbyists report in more detail about who they have worked for on Capitol Hill.
- Require that financial disclosure forms be filed four times a year instead of twice.
- Increase the fine for lobbyists who fail to disclose clients from $50,000 to $100,000.
- Give the Government Accounting Office oversight of the House and Senate clerks' offices, which enforce the lobbying rules.
- Change the House Code of Official Conduct to include a K Street Project provision, which would put an end to the practice of legislators taking steps to place their former staff members and their former House and Senate colleagues in lobbying jobs.[97]

The Emanuel-Meehan reforms would go a long way toward curbing the obscene influence of dirtbag lobbyists like Jack Abramoff and bagman-politicians like Tom DeLay. Still, we'd go even further.

3. Disclose All Contacts with Lobbyists

Members of the House and Senate should be required to disclose every conversation or correspondence with a lobbyist in which a policy or legislative
matter is discussed. Filings should be electronic, monthly, and public, so we
know with whom our public officials are meeting and where they're getting
their information. Even a few years ago, such a requirement would have been
onerous. But with technology, it's not only possible, it's relatively easy. Most
politicians today carry BlackBerries or Treos or other handheld devices.
Nearly all of them are accompanied by staffers nearly all the time.

De minimis contact—casually chatting with a lobbyist at the Little
League game—would not have to be disclosed. But if the conversation
turned away from the infield fly rule and toward the highway bill, it would
have to be reported. It's easy to tell the difference. It's kind of like those
movies in hotel rooms. After a certain amount of time, it's no longer a pre-
view; it's on your bill. Under our lobbying disclosure rule, if the conversation
turns to policy or legislation, it's got to be disclosed. All we're trying to do is
put into practice Justice Brandeis's old rule: Sunshine is the best disinfectant.

4. Disclose Pork, Perks, and Loopholes

As mentioned previously, Congressman Roy Blunt was able to sneak a special
provision for Philip Morris into the homeland security bill. Sadly, this practice is as common as it is pernicious. Powerful congressmen and senators routinely slip fine print into legislation—especially spending and tax bills—that
benefits corporations or interest groups. The secret provisions are rarely
reviewed by committees, examined by experts, or voted on separately by
the House or the Senate. They're generally inserted into legislation late in the
process, unbeknownst even to most members of Congress. Sometimes the
provision exempts a corporation from regulation, sometimes it spends billions of dollars on pet projects, other times it conveys special tax breaks to
corporate special interests.

Often the loopholes benefit only one company and are so opaque that even if you found the language buried in the bill, you wouldn't know which corporation would benefit. (The language will typically say the provision applies to, for example, "any Delaware corporation incorporated on June 22, 1921, and having 2003 revenues of not more than $1.25 billion and not less than $1.24 billion. . . .")

Democrats should change the rules of the House and the Senate and require any special provision to be clearly disclosed. The disclosure should name the member who inserted it, the corporations or interest groups that benefit from it, and the cost to taxpayers of the provision. It should apply to all legislation, appropriations, and tax bills.

If members of the House or Senate want to practice whorehouse politics, let them at least walk the streets in public, so we know who the happy hookers of Congress are.

5. Radically Reform Campaign Finance

"Money," the legendary California politician Jess Unruh famously said, "is the mother's milk of politics." That it is, but in the last few years, Mama's milk has been juiced with steroids.

The bipartisan McCain-Feingold Bill, which was reluctantly signed into law by President Bush in 2002, was an honest effort to limit the influence of big money in politics. But it has not succeeded. Politicians are spending more time than ever scrambling for money. And the law's restrictions on late attack ads strike many observers as an infringement of freedom of speech.

The biggest problem with the status quo of campaign fund-raising is that it puts good people in a bad system. Nearly every member of the House and Senate, whether sinner or saint, spends a spectacular amount of time raising money. The very process of raising money distorts the politicians' perspective. You try spending six hours a day, six days a week, in a cramped room calling people and sucking up for money. If the only people you ever talk to are people with the wherewithal to contribute thousands of dollars to your campaign, that's bound to affect you. You don't hear much about the minimum wage from folks who can write a check for $2,000. Nor do you spend a lot of time calling people who don't have health insurance or who can't afford their prescription drugs.

Back in 1997, James offered a radical proposal that would fundamentally and radically reform the way campaigns are financed. His proposal combines the fondest dream of liberal reformers—public financing of campaigns— with the fondest dream of conservative and libertarian reformers—no restrictions at all on donations from American citizens. The goal is to put a little distance between power and money. Federal officeholders have power but need money. Special interests have money but need power. When the two come together, trading money for power, bad things happen.

Here's how our plan would work:

First, we raise congressional pay—big-time. Pay 'em what we pay the president: $400,000. That's a huge increase from the $162,000 congressmen and senators currently make. Paul, especially, has been a critic of congressional pay increases. But he's willing to more than double politicians' pay in order to get some of the corrupt campaign money out of the system. You see, the pay raise comes with a catch. In return, we get a simple piece of legislation that says members of Congress cannot take anything of value from anyone other than a family member. No lunches. No taxi rides. No charter flights. No golf games. No ski trips. No nothing.

And when it's campaign time, incumbents would be under a complete ban on raising money. You read that right. No president or member of Congress could accept a single red cent from individuals, corporations, or special interests. Period.

Challengers, on the other hand, would be allowed to raise money in any amount from any individual American citizen or political action committee. No limits, just as the free-market conservatives have always wanted. But here's the catch: Within twenty-four hours of receiving a contribution, the challenger would have to report it electronically to the Federal Election Commission, which would post it for the public to see. That way, if you wanted to accept $1 million from, say, Paris Hilton, go for it. But be prepared for voters and reporters to ask what you promised her in exchange.

The day after you disclose Paris's million bucks, the U.S. Treasury would credit the incumbent's campaign account with a comparable sum—say 80 percent of the contribution to the challenger, to take into account the cost of all the canapés and chardonnay the challenger had to buy to raise his funds, as well as the incumbent's advantage. So if Paris gave the challenger a mill, the Treasury would wire $800,000 to the incumbent. It couldn't be a whole lot simpler. You might even call it the flat tax of campaign laws.

The penalties for violations would be swift. If an incumbent accepts so much as a postage stamp, he loses his seat. If a challenger doesn't report contributions, he loses his shot. If you cheat, you're out on your ass.

What if the incumbent wants to spend her own money? After all, the Supreme Court has made it clear that the Constitution does not allow restrictions on how much money a candidate—challenger or incumbent—can spend. No problem. Uncle Sam would write the challenger a check for an equivalent amount. Unlike today, no one would have the upper hand simply because they were loaded.

What if a sitting congressman wants to run for senator, or a senator wants to run for president? Would he be allowed to raise funds? Sure. He'd just have to do what Bob Dole eventually did—resign his Senate seat and hit the campaign trail like a regular citizen. If you want to run for a higher office, you have to get off your current pedestal first.

The idea is to change fundamentally the role and responsibilities of incumbency. Under our plan, incumbents have to live by Thomas Jefferson's maxim: "When a man assumes a public trust, he should consider himself as public property." [98] (We know, we know, the language is archaically sexist. But we're not going to edit Mr. Jefferson.) Once you assume an elected office, you achieve a new status. You are no longer a campaigner. You are a public servant. As such, you should not be in the fund-raising business. You should be in the exclusive business of making policy.

Today more than 90 percent of all senators and representatives are reelected. Under current law, incumbents almost always have a huge money advantage. Our wager is that a majority of incumbents would be willing to give up that advantage in exchange for higher pay and no time spent fundraising. Think about it. Not only would they be bringing in a much larger salary, they'd never have to kiss up to another rich donor. You should never underestimate how much these folks hate spending half their time—or more—sniveling for money. Nor should you underestimate how damaging and distorting it is to require federal officeholders to spend that time raising money. No wonder they vote on so much legislation without even reading it.

And what about the public? We haven't seen the final data for 2004, but in all the federal races in 2000—congressional, senatorial, and presidential—candidates spent a total of $1.6 billion.[99] Half of that, which is what taxpayers would have had to shell out under our plan, would be a lot of money: $800 million. But that's nothing compared to what the current system costs us. Those special interests who pour money into politicians' campaigns get something in return. Actually, they get a lot in return. Special tax breaks, special loopholes, special funding of pork barrel projects, maybe even a no-bid contract or two. The energy bill passed in 2005 handed $2 billion in subsidies to the ethanol industry—you know, the fine folks at Archer Daniels Midland.[100] It gave makers of the controversial fuel additive MTBE another $2 billion, and another $8.1 billion in tax breaks for oil, coal, and electric utilities.[101] In all, that one bill cost you $80.8 billion.

All of a sudden $800 million—1 percent of the cost of one bill—doesn't seem like very much money, does it?

We know our plan's not perfect. Some will argue over whether salary increases for politicians are justified. Some will argue over whether the plan favors incumbents or challengers. Some will argue over whether it favors Democrats or Republicans. But at its core, this plan does something no one will argue with: It forever divorces the corrosive—and sometimes corruptive—effect of campaign cash from members of Congress and presidents. When American citizens look at their Congress and White House, they will say what Alexander Hamilton said to a visitor to the newly constructed U.S. Capitol: "Here, sir, the people govern."[102]

Too bad that's such a radical notion.

A Declaration of
Energy Independence

Might as Well Face It, We're Addicted to Oil

There is only one fact you need to know when it comes to America's energy situation, and it is this: America holds 2 percent of the world's known remaining oil reserves, but we consume 25 percent of the world's energy.

That one fact leads directly to this one conclusion: We could drill for oil in everybody's backyard, but there is no way we're ever going to drill our way to energy independence.

Now consider some other facts.

Right now over half of the oil we consume—58 percent—comes from foreign countries.[1]

And if we continue on our current pace of energy usage, that number is going to grow to 68 percent by 2025.

Meanwhile, the world is going to start consuming more energy than it has in the past—by some estimates, world consumption will increase by 40 percent in the next fifteen years, with most of that increase coming from places like China and India.

As world demand goes up, world supply is going down: Oil production is in decline in thirty-three of the forty-eight largest oil-producing countries.

173

So even if the oil is there for us to buy, there will be other buyers bidding up the price—which means that we could be looking back at the gas prices we're seeing today and remembering fondly how cheap it was.

By the way, what are the places where there might be some promising *future* oil fields? In order of future promise, Saudi Arabia (which gave us fifteen of the nineteen September 11 hijackers), Iran (charter member of the axis of evil), Iraq (where two thousand U.S. soldiers have lost their lives as of this writing), United Arab Emirates (which gave us two of the remaining four September 11 hijackers), Kuwait (which we have already fought one war to protect), and Venezuela (whose leader, Hugo Chavez, has threatened us with another war).

Face it: The Good Lord just didn't put oil in places where folks like Americans. There's no doubt the two facts are related, and have been for a century. Then again, thanks to President Bush, fewer and fewer places feel that kindly about us anyway, which means that protecting our oil supply comes at a price, and it's not cheap. It's been estimated that the cost of keeping our oil supplies safe adds ten cents to the cost of every gallon of gasoline.[2]

At the same time, we are running the largest trade deficit in our country's history, and half of that trade deficit—half—comes from our purchase of foreign oil.

Because we're running huge deficits and buying oil from some dangerous regimes, we're actually borrowing money from our economic competitors in order to indirectly subsidize some of the very people we're asking our soldiers to fight.

Is It Hot in Here, or Is It Just Global Warming?

There's one element of our ridiculously flawed energy policy that may have even worse consequences, and that's global warming.

Let's pause here to state the obvious: Yes, Virginia, there is global warming. We won't go through all of the science here, but when the American Association for the Advancement of Science met in 2005, they looked at millions of ocean temperature readings made by the U.S. National Oceanic and Atmospheric Administration and found steady ocean warming. Tim Barnett of the Scripps Institution of Oceanography summed up the findings this way: "Could a climate system simply do this on its own? The answer is clearly no." He then concluded, "The debate over whether or not there is a global warming signal is now over, at least for rational people."[3]

Well, rational people, meet today's Republican Party, specifically James Inhofe, the Oklahoma Republican who is the chairman of the Senate Committee on the Environment. Senator Inhofe has called global warming "the greatest hoax ever perpetrated on the American people."

Senator Inhofe recently found a kindred spirit in the novelist Michael Crichton, who wrote a book called *State of Fear,* which said that the science on global warming was mixed. So Senator Inhofe called Michael Crichton to testify before his committee. Now, we love Michael Crichton, and Paul's boys loved *Jurassic Park,* but, like *Congo* and *The Andromeda Strain, State of Fear* is *fiction.* When Republicans wanted an "expert" to testify to the fallacy of global warming, the best they could come up with is a guy who writes fiction. Enough said.

Why should we care about global warming? Take a look at Hurricane Katrina (discussed more thoroughly in "The Flood") to see what rising sea levels can do, and then consider that the State Department released a report predicting that an increase in temperatures would cause rising sea levels to threaten the coastal areas where 53 percent of all Americans live: more frequent and severe storms, the widespread destruction of ecosystems, and more frequent heat waves and drought in the country's interior.[4] The Pentagon commissioned a report that went even further, saying that climate should "be elevated beyond a scientific debate to a U.S. national security concern," because climate change "would challenge United States national security in ways that should be considered immediately."[5]

The Natural Resources Defense Council summarizes our views on climate change perfectly:

"Higher temperatures threaten dangerous consequences: drought, disease, floods, lost ecosystems. And from sweltering heat to rising seas, global warming's effects have already begun. But solutions are in sight. We know where most heat-trapping gases come from: power plants and vehicles. And we know how to curb their emissions: modern technologies and stronger laws. NRDC is working to put these fixes in place. By shifting the perception of global warming from abstract threat to pressing reality, and promoting on-line activism. By pressing businesses to use less energy and build more efficient products. And by fighting for laws that will speed these advances."[6]

Amen. We need to get away from an oil-based system of energy, because it threatens our national security, because it weakens us economically, and because it is destroying our planet. If we screw this one up, there's no fix. If we get it wrong, our children and grandchildren will live such a different—and diminished—life that they will be the first generation in American history to be less well off than those who came before them. Ignoring climate change will condemn our kids to economic stagnation and environmental chaos; to a shorter, less happy, and more dangerous life. If that's not worth getting off your butt and working on, we don't know what is.

The Republican Approach:
A Big Windfall for Big Oil

Back in January 2004, George W. Bush went looking for great projects to unify America as he began his campaign for reelection. What did he come up with? Sending Americans back to the moon[7]—something we first did back in 1969, and then four times after that. Why did we stop going to the moon? Because while it was the culmination of a great national sense of mission, we had done what we set out to do, and there wasn't really much to see there.

Never, in thinking about great national missions, did it occur to George W. Bush that we could find a unifying sense of national purpose in the challenge of achieving energy independence. This shouldn't be too much of a surprise, given that, for this administration, energy policy is little more than an opportunity to advance the interests of the oil business. Just take a look at the two energy bills that have been rammed through Congress by Republicans.

This summer Congress passed the Energy Policy Act of 2005. It didn't reduce our dependence on fossil fuels, didn't make our environment cleaner, didn't take on global warming, and didn't bring down gas prices. It didn't even try. What it did do was provide $6 billion in new incentives to burn coal for electricity. It gave $1.7 billion in new tax breaks and over $2.3 billion in additional spending to the oil and gas industry, and it said that they didn't need to worry about complying with some provisions of the Clean Water Act.[8]

In October, when Hurricane Katrina knocked out a lot of our refining capacity and drove gas prices even higher, Republicans saw an opportunity— not to reduce gas prices but to jam into a new energy bill all of the special-interest treats that were too objectionable to make it into the first one. This bill was called the GAS Act, and it would have been a lot better if all it contained was a bunch of hot air. Instead, it gave the EPA the authority to loosen state deadlines for meeting smog emission standards. It exempted certain parts of the country from regulations that require the use of "blended" fuels, which reduce air pollution. It restricted the government's capacity to prosecute utilities or refineries whose overall emissions become too high. But it also said that if an oil company finds itself in a lawsuit over a permit application, the American taxpayer will have to chip in to help pay the company's legal fees. These guys don't believe in legal aid for poor people, but the most profitable companies in America get federally funded counsel. Now, that's Texas justice.[9]

Give credit where credit is due, though. Getting all of this done wasn't easy for the Republicans. They had to twist some arms to get the votes in the House. The vote was supposed to take only five minutes. But after five minutes, they were losing. So they kept the vote open and worked over their boys something good. Even the indicted Tom DeLay—who isn't supposed to be the majority leader anymore—got in the game. After forty-five minutes, they had a two-vote margin, after which they promptly closed the vote.[10]

The Republican energy bill gave $80.8 billion of your money to Big Oil and other energy interests.[11] As this book went to press, oil companies reported an estimated $96 billion in profits.[12] Why would Republicans give billions in government subsidies to an industry that's showing a $96 billion profit? We can't think of one good reason. But we can think of 38 million bad reasons: The energy industry gave $38 million to Republicans in the last election. (They gave over $12 million to Democrats.)[13]

To be fair, that Republican bill is not the sum and substance of the Bush Republicans' position on energy. In addition to bailouts for hugely rich oil companies, President Bush strongly supports more hand-holding for the Saudis and other Middle Eastern energy producers. He has been photographed holding hands—in a more than friendly but less than gay way—with Saudi Arabia's crown prince (now king) Abdullah. No wonder Bush is so lovey-dovey with the Saudis. Bob Woodward reported that before President Bush invaded Iraq, he gave a top-secret briefing—one that was not supposed to be seen by foreigners—to Saudi Arabia's ambassador, Prince Bandar. According to CBS News, "Woodward says that Bandar understood that economic conditions were key before a presidential election: 'They're [oil prices are] high. And they could go down very quickly. That's the Saudi pledge. Certainly over the summer, or as we get closer to the election, they could increase production several million barrels a day and the price would drop significantly.' " [14]

When the world's largest oil producer is promising to manipulate the price of oil in order to help your reelection, it's kind of hard to crack down on them for price gouging.

The Bush/Republican energy policy can be summed up thus: Suck up all the energy you can; suck up to the big oil companies; and suck up to the Saudis.

Pardon us for saying so, but as a national energy policy, that sucks.

But rather than rant and rail at this absolute dog of an energy policy, we should take the Republicans at face value. They care deeply about enriching their friends in the oil and power industries. We should say our goal is energy independence, pure and simple, and in getting there, every option is on the table.

Here's how Democrats can take back the issues of energy and the environment.

1. A Declaration of Energy Independence

Sometimes good politics and good policy coincide, and this is one of those cases. Take a look at what the American people had to say about energy independence in a Democracy Corps poll conducted in mid-2005—*before* Hurricane Katrina hit, and *before* gas prices skyrocketed.

In the poll, Democracy Corps asked voters if they'd be more or less likely to support a candidate who ran for office and said this: "With gas prices and oil imports rising, our nation's security and prosperity require that we launch a concerted drive for energy independence. We should mobilize the scientific community, promote production of fuel-efficient cars, invest in more efficient factories and appliances, and expand the development of alternative energy sources—like wind, solar, and biofuels." Bingo. Fully 83 percent of voters surveyed said they'd be more likely to vote for someone who talked about energy that way.

This makes absolute sense. The benefits from energy independence are almost too many to mention: reduction in greenhouse gases, more jobs created by new technology, a stronger economy from exporting that technology, less money going to authoritarian regimes, significant declines in the price of oil because the less you use, the more you've got, and the more you've got, the cheaper it is. You name it, it's all there. And at a very core level, people understand this.

Embracing the absolute necessity for our country to undertake an immediate and comprehensive program toward conservation and energy independence is a winning strategy for America, so why isn't it a winning issue (yet) for Democrats? Perhaps because they're not really running on it.

We believe a Declaration of Energy Independence—a new national commitment to greater energy independence—can be just as captivating and compelling as President Kennedy's call for a moon shot. But President Bush is wrong in trying to revive JFK's sense of great national mission by repeating JFK's pledge to go to the moon. The current challenge is closer at home. And, as President Kennedy himself said, "Here on earth, God's work must truly be our own."

At every turn, the Bush Republicans have squandered opportunities to move us toward energy independence and instead rewarded their friends and contributors. Name one thing George W. Bush has done to make us less reliant on foreign oil. Can't think of anything? Neither can we. We shouldn't be so surprised. Remember, his energy policy when he ran for president was basically "I'll get OPEC to be nice to us. I can talk to them. They're my friends."

We think America's strength shouldn't rely on the kindness of sheiks, especially when they're more than happy to have us over a barrel.

2. Greenhouse Gases:
Deal with Them or Die

In August 2004 the Bush White House released a report on global warming that didn't cite Michael Crichton but finally admitted the obvious: "Human action from driving automobiles to running power plants helped cause global warming." It stated that the "severe drought that has affected the United States since 1998 is part of a consistent climate pattern," and that carbon dioxide is "more of a curse than a blessing for farmers and ranchers." [15]

What did they do in the face of such findings? Nothing. James Mahoney, director of the White House's climate-change science program, said the report was "not a significant science finding or policy finding." [16]

We know that loyalty is the keystone of the Bush administration. So we know that anyone who lets cold, hard facts trump an allegiance to well-heated ideology is a traitor.

We believe that nothing is more pro-American than identifying a challenge and then taking it on. When Republicans won't, Democrats must.

A lot of those experts have some proposals on what to do about climate change. Do we understand the intricacies of all of them? Absolutely not. But are a lot of them worth getting behind? Absolutely.

Let's review a few.

Some people have proposed creating a system for reducing emissions that looks like this: The government creates caps to control carbon dioxide and other greenhouse gas emissions. When an industrial plant makes reductions below those caps, they get a credit—like an allowance—that they can sell to other companies that haven't been able to meet those standards. The idea is simple: Companies have tangible, bottom-line incentives to reduce their emissions. Republicans love the market; they should love a market-based approach to cleaning up our air.

There are other things government can do. In 2002 the state of California enacted legislation that requires automakers to sell vehicles with lower greenhouse gas emissions by 2009—an action that would cut average emissions from new cars and light trucks about 22 percent by 2012, and 30 percent by 2016. Democrats should get behind a national system like the one

California has created. It will mean money—$325 per vehicle by 2012 and about $1,000 by 2016—but that would be offset by savings at the pump.

The big brains at the Center for American Progress have put together a whole bunch of proposals, like having Congress fund more research and development to get carbon dioxide out of coal-fired power plants, and creating a task force to reengage in international dialogue on climate change. We like that last idea. We think a global problem requires a global solution.

3. Set Priorities

It seems to us that when we talk about energy and the environment, there are two priorities that should dwarf all others: global warming and energy independence.

We're all for the Endangered Species Act, all against drilling in the Arctic National Wildlife Refuge (ANWR). Heck, the first cause Paul worked on in politics was a referendum against nuclear power. These are all important things. But not all issues are created equal, and leadership is about setting priorities.

One of the right's criticisms of Democrats on the environment is that we tend to cry wolf. It's not that, say, preserving the Alaska wilderness isn't important; it is. But how many Americans does it affect directly? Paul happens to be one of them. He loves to fish for salmon and trout in Alaska and doesn't trust George W. Bush and Dick Cheney to protect the wilderness. But most of us don't have the time and the money to fly to Alaska to fish. And so Republicans use the ANWR issue to paint us as elitists who worry about a place most Americans will never see.

Let's be clear: We are not arguing for a surrender—or even a retreat—on drilling in Alaska. We should fight them and beat them on ANWR. What we're arguing for is setting clear priorities. To the limited extent that we have the power to set the agenda, we should be directing it toward climate change and energy independence at every turn.

When we look at the Bush Republicans' record on the environment, we feel like mosquitoes in a nudist colony—anywhere we land is going to be a big, fat, juicy target. They're bad on everything—they want to log the national forests, drill in the national wilderness, mine in the national parks, and allow more arsenic in the water (arsenic, for God's sake!), and more pollution in the air, more subsidies for Big Oil—all while we cut back on regulations for toxic polluters. Lord, we could go on and on. And that's the problem: These guys are so bad on the environment we risk overwhelming folks.

What we need to do, as a party, is try our best to focus on those two issues, energy independence and global warming, above the other environmental and energy issues out there. Don't abandon the others. But keep in mind that the marquee battles are energy independence and climate change.

That laser-beam focus will not only help Democrats win elections; we'll also go a long way toward saving our nation—and the planet. All in all, not a bad way to spend your time.

4. Jobs, Jobs, Jobs

One of the things our Republican friends don't seem to understand is that a policy of putting America in the forefront of energy efficiency and greenhouse gas reductions would create jobs. Lots of jobs. Al Gore used to call this the "Green/Green Solution": green as in environmentally friendly; and green as in money.

Think we're kidding? Consider this: In May 2005, Jeffrey Immelt, the CEO of GE, announced a $1.5 billion investment in environmentally clean technologies over the next five years. He also said that by 2010, GE would double its revenues from products that provide "significant and measurable environmental performance advantages to customers." This is not small potatoes. In 2004, GE was already making $10 billion a year from such products and services, ranging from renewable energy to water purification and cleaner transportation. Immelt also pledged to reduce GE's global warming emissions by 1 percent in 2012. We know, you're thinking, "Wow. One percent. Big whoop." But it is a big whoop. Without Immelt's pledge, GE's global warming emissions would have increased by 40 percent in that same time period.[17]

We can assure you that GE has not been taken over by the Natural Resources Defense Council (although NRDC praised GE for taking these steps). No, GE and Immelt are taking the lead on these environmental issues because they believe they'll make money off them.

We'll admit it: There are times when Democrats can be preachy and prissy and sanctimonious and scornful when talking about energy and the environment. We tend to sneer at people who drive SUVs and at companies that create jobs but also contribute to global warming. Worse, some Democratic environmentalists tend to be almost self-loathing about America's energy consumption. Instead, we should celebrate the entrepreneurial spirit of America; we should embrace the profit motive that is driving more and more corporate leaders to the Green/Green Solution. And we should position the Republicans as the sourpusses who are too wedded to their ideology to do the things we need to do to create more jobs and make more money for American businesses.

5. Increase Fuel Economy for Cars and Trucks

The only way to truly get us to energy independence is to produce more and to use less. And one of the best ways to use less is to make sure that our cars do the same work on less gas.

Back in 1975, Congress enacted something called Corporate Average Fuel Economy (CAFE) standards for two categories of vehicles: cars and light trucks. The result was that the average fuel economy increased by half in light trucks and nearly doubled for cars. Today those standards save the United States over 55 billion gallons of fuel annually, and without them, carbon dioxide emissions (a major contributor to global warming) would be 10 percent higher than they are now. At the time, the normal band of naysayers made a lot of the same arguments that you hear today—the standards compromise performance, decrease safety, require smaller cars. None of those things came to pass. In fact, over the past twenty-five years, while fuel economy has increased, highway fatalities per mile driven have substantially decreased.

Congressional action has frozen CAFE standards since fiscal year 1996, and the fuel economy of the combined light-duty fleet has dropped to 24 mpg from its 1986–87 high of 25.9 mpg. Because SUVs are held to the less stringent light-truck standard, their growing popularity has led to the decline in average fuel economy for the entire passenger fleet.

The Bush administration tried to do something about fuel economy in August 2005. They proposed replacing CAFE standards for light trucks with a new regulatory system that sets different mileage targets for six sizes of vehicles, as opposed to just two. By calculating fuel economy for these six categories, Transportation Secretary Norman Mineta said, we'd be able to save 10 billion gallons of gasoline. Sounds like a lot, doesn't it? Try looking at it this way: The Bush plan would save 10 billion gallons over as long as *fifteen years*—and American drivers used nearly 140 billion gallons of gas during the last year alone.[18] That is the very definition of peeing in the ocean. We can do better.

Raising CAFE standards by 5 percent annually until 2012 and by 3 percent per year thereafter could save 1.5 million barrels of oil per day (MBD) by 2010; 4.7 MBD by 2020; and 67 billion barrels of oil over the next forty years.[19] By the way, this is ten to twenty times more than the potential oil supply from the Arctic National Wildlife Refuge.[20]

Closing the loophole that currently holds SUVs to lower standards than cars, as a bipartisan group of senators proposed in August, would result in a 10 percent reduction in oil imports and would prevent 240 million tons of carbon dioxide from being released into the atmosphere. It would also save consumers $5 billion at the pump.[21]

Better fuel economy also means more jobs for Americans. According to the Union of Concerned Scientists, if U.S. automakers produced a fleet of cars and trucks that reached 40 mpg by 2015, more than 40,800 new jobs would be created in the automotive sector alone. The country's wages and salaries could increase by $8.6 billion. Up the ante to 55 mpg by 2025, and it translates to nearly 60,000 new jobs in the automotive industry, and national wages and salaries up by almost $25 billion.[22] Increasing the fuel economy of cars and light trucks is the single most effective energy-saving policy the federal government could adopt. So why don't we?

In part because we don't want to hurt our domestic auto industry. So let's help it. Democrats should call for expanding and increasing not only the fuel economy standards but also the tax incentives for consumers to buy high-mileage, low-emissions cars.

6. Conservation: More Than Just a Sign of "Personal Virtue"

Nothing represented the Bush administration's attitude toward the environment and energy better than when Dick Cheney called conservation "a sign of personal virtue, but not a sufficient basis for a sound comprehensive energy policy."

That statement isn't just ignorant, it's wrong. Conservation helps us be more efficient, save money, clean our air, keep our kids healthy. It has the potential to dramatically reduce our dependence on foreign oil, and to release us from our marriage of convenience with Saudi Arabia. Doing those things isn't personal, it's patriotic, and that's how we should frame it.

Consider this: If you replaced just four 100-watt incandescent bulbs that burn four or more hours a day in your home with four 23-watt fluorescent bulbs, you'd get the same amount of light but, over three years, you'd also save at least 452 kilowatt-hours of electricity and $82. That's a personal virtue, yes. But if every household in America did the same, we'd save as much energy as is consumed by seven million cars in one year.[23]

That's a policy.

Or consider this: A refrigerator sold today uses 70 percent less energy than one built in the 1970s. Are you giving up anything by not using your orange refrigerator from 1970? Is your nice new fridge a personal virtue?

Or consider this: Simple standards to improve the efficiency of air conditioners, to reduce energy consumption in new buildings and houses, and to improve the efficiency of existing buildings would keep us from having to build 473 new power plants.[24]

What could the overall impact of conservation be? A study commissioned for the Pentagon found that investing $180 billion over the next ten years to eliminate oil dependence could save $70 billion every year.[25]

The only people who don't benefit from this so-called personal virtue are the energy companies at whose altar Dick Cheney and George Bush prostrate themselves. Apparently, conservation isn't a personal virtue, but sucking up to oil companies for campaign contributions in return for sweetheart energy deals is. A true commonsense conservation initiative doesn't mean turning off all your lights or wearing sweaters at home, it means doing the little things that can make a big difference, and that's what we need to encourage.

We can do this. The last time America made a real, sustained commitment to reducing our energy dependence, it was in response to the Arab oil embargo in the 1970s. We managed to cut our energy use by 17 percent and reduce oil imports by half (and imports from the Persian Gulf by 87 percent). While all of this happened, our GDP grew by 27 percent.[26]

7. Natural Gas: It's Not Something You Get from a Bean Burrito, Mr. President

We have to be honest with ourselves: We need to increase supply as well. Over the next twenty years, demand for natural gas will increase by over 50 percent. Natural gas is the cleanest fossil fuel, and it's something America has a lot of. Until recently, we just haven't had many ways to get at it.

Right now there are 35 trillion cubic feet of known natural gas reserves on the North Slope of Alaska that we're literally pumping back into the ground because we can't get it to the people who need it. There's now a proposal for a pipeline to bring it to the lower forty-eight. This gas pipeline would create an estimated four hundred thousand jobs, use a huge amount of U.S. steel, and ensure that we don't become dependent on imported liquefied natural gas from the Middle East. Energy for America, jobs and opportunity for steelworkers, and no damage to sensitive environmental areas—*this* is the type of pro-development, pro-jobs energy project Democrats should be encouraging.

But we need to do more than get at fossil fuels. We need to encourage new ones, like wind, solar, and biomass, which is a fancy term for things we grow and things animals expel, which is why we need to . . .

8. Make a Real Commitment to Alternative Fuels

Democrats like Representative Jay Inslee (D-WA) have for years championed a New Apollo Energy Act. The Republican-controlled House rejected it in 2005, but we think Democrats ought to embrace it. Inslee and his colleagues would provide $49 billion in federal loan guarantees for the construction of clean-energy power plants that use alternative fuels ranging from biomass to solar, as well as wind, geothermal, and coal with new carbon-sequestration technology. The New Apollo legislation would also commit $10.5 billion in research and development tax credits for clean energy.

Keep in mind that these are loan guarantees and tax incentives, not government-controlled bureaucratic spending. Democrats should make it a point to harness the creativity and dynamism of the private sector. They should, in the words of David Osborne and Ted Gaebler from their seminal book, *Reinventing Government,* make sure the government steers, not rows. That is, government should set the great national goal but then let the private sector reach that goal in the most efficient and effective manner.

One area the government can control is where the government acts as a consumer. The federal government has millions of cars and trucks. We believe Democrats should call for the civilian branches of government to greatly expand their purchase of alternative-fuel vehicles. In the early 1990s, the state of Texas—yes, Texas—passed clean air legislation that required agencies to buy cars, trucks, buses, and vans capable of using alternative fuels. Today the Texas Department of Transportation alone has more than five thousand alternative-fuel vehicles.[27] If alternative fuels are good enough for Texas, by God, they're good enough for America.

9. Be People-Environmentalists, Not Species-Environmentalists

Republicans often claim that Democratic environmentalists care more about obscure species than they do about people. We can't let the Republicans get away with that. The fact is, the species most threatened by the Republican policies of more mercury in the air and water, more toxins in the air, and the baking of our planet is *Homo sapiens*.

We should make that clear when we talk about the environment. Rather than stressing the plight of the snail darter, we should talk about people: the little girl in New Jersey who's fighting cancer and just happens to live near a corporate toxic waste site. The boy in California whose parents have to rush him to the emergency room with asthma because he routinely breathes so much pollution. The stunning number of women who live near a chemical plant and all develop breast cancer.

Robert F. Kennedy, Jr., gets it. As chief prosecuting attorney for River-keepers, a crusading environmental group in New York, he's done more than anyone we know to protect the water supply of New York City. He's gone after governments and corporations alike for polluting the Hudson River and the Long Island Sound. He's sued treatment plants to force them to comply with the Clean Water Act, and he's fought to expand people's access to the shorelines. To be sure, Kennedy's work has saved innumerable fish and birds and deer. But at the end of the day, it's all about that moment when a little girl wakes up her mama and daddy late at night and asks for a glass of water. At that moment, all of Kennedy's work comes together. He focuses on ensuring that those parents are not slowly, unwittingly poisoning their own daughter.

Kennedy has written a brave and scathing account of the Bush environmental policies called *Crimes Against Nature*. Its point is that when the Republicans attack nature, they are inevitably attacking humanity. One of the first things Bush did upon taking office, Kennedy argues, is drop seventy-five Clinton-initiated lawsuits against the worst coal-fired power plants—the worst air polluters in America. "As a result, 18,000 Americans are killed a year," he said. "This should be front page headlines of every newspaper every day. . . . We're living a science-fiction nightmare, where asthmatic children are born into a world with poisons in the air because somebody paid money to a politician." [28]

10. Reach Out to the "Hook-and-Bullet" Crowd

In an environmental meeting in the Clinton White House, Paul spoke up about how the decline in habitat for wildlife is making it more difficult for hunters and fishermen to find places to, well, hunt and fish. One of Paul's colleagues called him "part of the hook-and-bullet crowd." He'd never heard the phrase before, but he liked it. Paul is now a proud hook-and-bullet environmentalist. We think Democrats ought to reach out to more of them.

One of the problems with the environmental movement is that, as on so many issues, the right has caricatured us as elitist. The opposite is the case. Democrats should couch their commitment to wilderness preservation, clean air, and clean water in order to reach those populist hunters, fishermen, and outdoorsmen and -women who need to use public land. It's a populist issue. If you're a multimillionaire like George W. Bush, you can buy your own 1,583-acre private ranch. And if the river that runs through your land is the Middle Bosque River, and if that river is polluted—which it is[29]—you can afford to build your own eleven-acre lake. You can also afford to build a second pond in case you want a little variety. You can also afford to stock it with your own private bass. But what if you didn't make millions from sweetheart deals? What if you're just an average Bubba and you want to take your kid fishing?

Sorry, Bubba, you're out of luck. As public rivers and streams become more and more polluted, as wildlife habitat is killed off by polluters and developers, hunting and fishing are becoming the exclusive province of the very rich. Sort of like a gated community or a country club. Then again, Republicans are always more happy and comfortable when they keep the riffraff out.

11. Praise the Lord and Protect the Environment

In "Taking Back Moral Values," we argue that Democrats should bring their faith to bear on their public policy positions. The environment is one of them. As people of faith, we believe the earth is God's creation and that human beings are his most wondrous creations. Isn't it a sin, then, to degrade and destroy God's creation? You bet it is, and Democrats should say so.

David certainly said so. Throughout the Psalms, he sings God's praises for the natural, environmental beauty of God's creation. Typical is Psalm 104:

> O LORD, how many are Your works!
> In wisdom You have made them all;
> The earth is full of Your possessions.
> There is the sea, great and broad,
> In which are swarms without number,
> Animals both small and great. . . .
> You send forth Your Spirit, they are created;
> And You renew the face of the ground. (Psalm 104:24–25, 30)

In the book of Deuteronomy, God tells the people of Israel that, even when they are laying siege to a city, they must care for the environment in and around that city: "When you besiege a city a long time, to make war against it in order to capture it, you shall not destroy its trees by swinging an axe against them; for you may eat from them, and you shall not cut them down. For is the tree of the field a man, that it should be besieged by you? Only the trees which you know are not fruit trees you shall destroy and cut down, that you may construct siegeworks against the city that is making war with you until it falls" (Deuteronomy 20:19–20). Sounds to us like God is a tree-hugger.

He's serious about it, too. In the Book of Numbers, God instructs the people of Israel to be environmentalists: "You shall not pollute the land in which you are. . . . You shall not defile the land in which you live, in the midst of which I dwell; for I the LORD am dwelling in the midst of the sons of Israel" (Numbers 35:33–34).

Jesus, too, taught that God loves and cares for the world He created. In the Gospel, Jesus teaches that God knows and cares even if a sparrow falls (Matthew 10:29).

That means that, if anything, Robert F. Kennedy, Jr., is understating the problem. Republican environmental policies are not only a "crime against nature"; they're a sin against God.

12. Tax Windfall Oil Profits, Invest in Energy Independence

The reason oil company profits have soared to almost $100 billion is not because the companies have become more innovative or efficient. It's because Hurricanes Rita and Katrina—and jitters over President Bush's Iraq Policy—caused the price of oil to skyrocket. That's the very definition of a windfall profit.

Democrats like Senator Byron Dorgan (D-ND) and Senator Chris Dodd (D-CT) have proposed a 50 percent tax on the sale of oil over $40 a barrel. We think that's a great idea, and we'd plow the proceeds into making America more energy independent.

Sure, Big Oil will howl. But they'll still have enormous profits. If they're looking to cut expenses, maybe they could cut out the tens of millions of dollars they donate to politicians.

We can take back our energy and environmental policy from the polluters and the plutocrats and the petro-bandits. We can create more jobs—well-paid jobs—right here at home. We can save energy, save fuel, and be more efficient and productive. We can issue a Declaration of Energy Independence and tell the sheiks who are sticking us up at the pump just where they can stick it.

Oh, yeah. We can save the planet, too. All in all, not a bad day's work.

Work the Refs

One of the most impressive successes the right has had over the past several decades did not occur at the ballot box; nor did it occur in Congress. We can't think of a victory more complete and more important than the right wing's victory over the media.

The game may be a rout now, but in the 1970s it was a different story. On August 23, 1971, Lewis F. Powell, a Richmond, Virginia, attorney who in two months would be named to the Supreme Court, wrote a memo to the U.S. Chamber of Commerce. The eight-page memo, titled "Attack on American Free Enterprise System," has achieved legendary status and is credited by some with being the intellectual underpinning of the right's assault on opinion makers.

Powell began by asserting, "No thoughtful person can question that the American economic system is under broad attack." Keep in mind that this was during the Nixon administration. Still, Powell saw an attack coming from "Communists, New Leftists and other revolutionaries who would destroy the entire system." Powell argued that "much of the media—for varying motives and in varying degree—either voluntarily accords unique publicity to these 'attackers,' or at least allows them to exploit the media for their purposes. This is especially true of television, which now plays such a

193

predominant role in shaping the thinking, attitudes and emotions of our people." Powell claimed that leaders of the business community "have responded—if at all—by appeasement, ineptitude and ignoring the problem."

To defend against this supposed attack, Powell advised the Chamber to mount a massive campaign to sway public opinion. He called for a remarkably broad campaign to influence public opinion in favor of a pro-business perspective. He recommended targeting high schools and college campuses, academics, textbooks, faculty, and guest lecturers. He also advised big business to pressure the media. He thought the Chamber should monitor the media, complain about bias to the FCC, demand equal time from broadcasters, and use paid advertising to communicate a conservative message.[1]

What's striking, thirty-four years later, is that all Powell called for has come to pass—and more. For over three decades, the right has run a well-funded campaign to influence the media. It has involved monitoring and complaints about bias, as Powell suggested. But the right has taken the campaign against the media much further than the gentlemanly Justice Powell could have anticipated.

Attacking the press has become a staple of the right. Former Republican National Committee chairman Rich Bond committed the sin of candor when he dropped the charade of complaining about the "liberal press" and admitted, "There is some strategy to it [bashing the 'liberal' media] . . . If you watch any great coach, what they try to do is work the refs.' Maybe the ref will cut you a little slack on the next one."[2]

As Eric Alterman argues persuasively in his important book, *What Liberal Media?*, several honest conservatives have admitted, like Bond, that liberal bias is a myth, and that attacking this so-called bias is nothing more than a strategy designed to pressure the media into a pro-conservative bias. Bill Kristol, the thoughtful editor of *The Weekly Standard*, has told a reporter, "I admit it. . . . The liberal media were never that powerful, and the whole thing was often used as an excuse by conservatives for conservative failures."[3] Kristol has also said, "The press isn't quite as biased and liberal. They're actually conservative sometimes."[4] As Alterman notes, no less an expert on mastering the media than James A. Baker III has confessed that, during his time in the Reagan administration, "There were days and times and events we might have had some complaints [but] on balance I don't think we had anything to complain about."[5] And Patrick J. Buchanan, one of the great media bashers on the right, had to admit that the coverage the press gave his boss, Richard Nixon, in the presidential campaign of 1972 "was extraordinarily fair and balanced."[6]

So why does the right perpetuate this myth of a liberal media? Two reasons: first, because it sells; second, because it works.

Media Bashing Sells

First, the good ol' capitalist reason. Right-wingers love to buy books about the liberal media. Bernard Goldberg went from being an obscure television reporter to being an obnoxious media whiner (although we wager he was pretty obnoxious when he was obscure, too). His book, *Bias,* is a collection of anecdotes seeking to illustrate that the media are liberal. No facts, no stats, just stories. Fair enough, he's a blow-dried TV reporter. What did you expect, *The Metaphysics of Morals*? But even Goldberg's stories are silly. He notes that a CBS producer once called Gary Bauer "that little nut from that Christian group." (Gary is a good guy and a friend of ours. He's certainly not a nut, and he has more intellectual integrity in his diminutive pinky than Goldberg has in his entire body.) The comment was not made on the air, and we suspect Bauer had a lot worse said about him by the Bush campaign when he ran against George W. Bush in the 2000 primaries.

Goldberg's other "examples" are just as ludicrous. He attacks NBC's Tom Brokaw (who wrote that leftist tract *The Greatest Generation*) for allegedly not covering the story of a defective General Electric jet engine. Even if that's true, it's hardly evidence of liberal bias. More like pro-corporate bias. No one has ever accused GE of being a liberal outfit.

The book has its laugh lines, like when Goldberg says that if CBS were a prison, most of the vice presidents at the network would be Dan Rather's "bitches." Good one, Bernie. But the notion of a powerful network anchor making network toadies quake is not evidence of liberal bias.

Goldberg is bizarrely selective in where he aims his vitriol. Since he spent over three decades at CBS, it stands to reason that most of his stories come from the Tiffany Network. And, predictably, page after page of the book contains bile about Rather. But there's not a mention—not one—of the right's other Great Satan of CBS, Bryant Gumbel. When Gumbel joined CBS after a long stint at NBC's *Today* show, the right-wing Media Research Center's Brent Bozell said of Gumbel, "For fifteen years, Mr. Gumbel used [NBC's] morning program as a daily platform for personal liberal bias masquerading as news and commentary." MRC's vice president, Brent Baker, piled on: "Short of Geraldo Rivera, few have done as much as Bryant Gumbel to lower the standards of professional TV journalism. As an interviewer, he can't even pose a question without stumbling over his own liberal bias."[7] Of course, Geraldo is now part of FOX News, so he's no longer a whipping boy of the right. But Gumbel is. My goodness, how the right-wing media critics hate him. Though we don't know Gumbel well, our experiences with him have all been fair. Though we haven't always liked what he's reported, we admire and respect his professionalism. But we feel that way about Brokaw and Rather and all the other pros Goldberg attacks. So why do you suppose Goldberg gives Gumbel a pass?

Guess who hired Bernie after he left CBS? You got it. Bryant Gumbel. Gumbel put Goldberg to work on his outstanding HBO sports program, *Real Sports.* Bernie Goldberg may be a right-wing clown, but he's no fool. His media-bashing books have been best sellers, but that steady paycheck from Gumbel must come in handy, too.

Goldberg may be the most intellectually dishonest of the media bashers, but he's small beer compared to some of the giants of the anti-media right. Apparently, there is a vast market for right-wing attacks on the media. The aforementioned Brent Bozell of the Media Research Center has been feeding that appetite for years. MRC has sixty professional staffers and a $60 million annual budget. Its news division tracks media, recording broadcasts, scanning papers, sleuthing across the Web, all on the lookout for liberal bias. Its Free Market Project promotes a pro-business message in much the way Justice Powell urged in 1971. MRC's Conservative Communications Center trains conservatives in how to use the media, and its Cybercast News Service "covers" news events. (We put "cover" in quotation marks because CNS is not a legitimate news organization; it's avowedly right-wing.)

MRC is able to generate thousands of e-mails to pressure the media to reflect a right-wing perspective. It provides other conservative media critics a veneer of academic credibility, in that MRC gathers statistics as well as anecdotes. This is a far cry from the silly, seemingly random gripes Goldberg belches out.

Media Bashing Works

For right-wingers, bashing the media is a twofer: Either it pulls the media toward their ideological agenda, or it rallies the troops against an enemy. And sometimes both. As Eric Alterman points out in *What Liberal Media?*, a 1999 study in the scholarly journal *Communications Research* showed a 400 percent increase in the number of Americans surveyed who say they detect a liberal bias in the media. Hmmm. Maybe the wingers are right. More and more Americans certainly think so.

But wait. The same scholars painstakingly collected and analyzed twelve years of news coverage and found no correlation whatsoever. So what's up? The study's authors, Alterman reports, concluded the increase in the public's perception of media bias comes from "increasing news coverage of liberal bias media claims, which have been increasingly emanating from Republican Party candidates and officials."[8]

Despite the candid admission from many of the leaders of the conservative movement that there is no liberal media bias, the campaign to shoot the messenger is working. As Brent Bozell said in 1992, "We have learned that many in the media are quite open to the conservative perspective if it is presented properly. We provide journalists with the conservative argument on a given issue, lead them to the organization expert in it, and recommend qualified spokesmen. . . . It is amazing how very receptive some journalists are to this assistance."[9]

The Media Whipped Bill Clinton
Like a Borrowed Mule

One of our favorite myths about the press is that the media went easy on Bill Clinton when he ran for president. We were fairly deeply involved in Clinton's 1992 campaign, and we've never seen any presidential candidate receive rougher treatment in the press. Reporters pressed him about whether he'd ever used drugs, prompting the infamous "I didn't inhale" comment when Clinton tried to describe his furtive, failed attempts to smoke pot. When George W. Bush was running, on the other hand, journalists generally respected his desire to refuse to answer questions about alleged prior drug use—and we defended Bush's right to refuse to answer those questions.

As Clinton was campaigning for president, otherwise serious, sober journalists were knocking one another over to print the latest salacious scandal from the tabloids. Perhaps that's why Bozell was comfortable in bragging that he was bending the media to his will, because he was. In fact, at the midpoint of the Clinton presidency, Bozell had to admit, "You cannot fault the *Los Angeles Times, The New York Times, USA TODAY* . . . with a media bias in favor of Bill Clinton."

Journalists, goaded by conservative activists and semi-pro Clinton haters from Arkansas, made a federal case—literally—of a failed land deal called Whitewater. With the exception of the media's ludicrous and long-ago attempt to investigate Jimmy Carter's peanut warehouse, Whitewater was the only time in memory that the media decided after an election to relitigate charges against a president from his distant, pre-presidential past.

On and on it went. From Whitewater to Travelgate to Cattlegate; from Filegate to Billing-Records-Gate to Nannygate; from Helicoptergate to Coffeegate to Lincoln-Bedroom-Gate to Chinese-Fund-Raising-Gate. And the press, egged on by the right, didn't stop there. They speculated that the suicide of Clinton friend and White House deputy counsel Vince Foster was somehow related to Whitewater—although there was no evident connection, and the fragmentary notes Foster left behind suggested he was more worried about the cost of the new White House drapes than about Whitewater.

Throughout all of this, we had the tawdry specter of otherwise respectable journalists being spoon-fed by right-wing Clinton-hating hacks.

Chris Vlasto, a producer from supposedly liberal ABC News, called the liberal journalist Joe Conason after Conason and Murray Waas penned a column accusing Ken Starr of conflicts of interest. "After swiftly dismissing our story," Conason recalled, "Vlasto proceeded to berate me for criticizing Starr, and condescended to inform me that the corrupt liars were in the White House, not the independent counsel's office." [10]

Liberal media, indeed. The country, according to every public opinion poll, had a much higher opinion of Bill Clinton than it did of Ken Starr. But Vlasto was so out of step—whether motivated by ideology or not, we don't know—that he refused to entertain the notion that both Clinton and Starr deserved skeptical coverage.

In June 1998 the inaugural edition of *Brill's Content* featured a twenty-five-thousand-word exposé of the Starr-press axis entitled "Pressgate." While *Brill's Content* is no longer with us, this exhaustive account remains a reminder that the president wasn't the only one having an unethical affair. Every journalist in bed with Ken Starr was, too.

But why? Why was the press so rough on Clinton? After all, in one of the most-cited statistics of the media-bashing right, a survey of 139 Washington bureau chiefs and congressional correspondents showed that 89 percent voted for Clinton in 1992. [11]

Conason has a theory, at least to explain why *The Washington Post* and *The New York Times* were so rough on Clinton: "At the *Washington Post*, for instance," Conason wrote, "there is a palpable desire to relive the glorious Watergate experience of deposing a president. At the *New York Times*, there is an equally powerful impulse to even the old score with the *Post*, which beat the paper of record badly during Nixon's final days. And at both papers, there exists a feeling of indebtedness to Starr, who helped the *Times* and the *Post* escape libel judgments in the not-so-distant past." [12]

It never ended. Even when Clinton was leaving office, he was hounded and pounded by the press. First for some ill-advised pardons—which deserved critical coverage, but, we hasten to add, when President Clinton's predecessor pardoned a raft of alleged Iran-Contra criminals just before leaving office, the press was remarkably restrained. Then, in the midst of the (admittedly legitimate) coverage of Clinton's pardons, came Furnituregate. And Vandalismgate. And Officegate. All of which were bull. The president didn't steal furniture; the supposed vandalism by Clinton's staff, which the Bush staff pledged to document, photograph, and catalog, never happened; and the former president rented relatively low-cost office space in Harlem.

Still, the supposedly liberal *New York Times* ran a vicious post-presidential editorial, savaging Clinton as someone "who seemed to make a redoubled effort in the last moments of his presidency to plunge further and further beneath the already low expectations of his cynical critics and most world-weary friends." [13]

If nothing else, the brutal, unfair, and often unethical treatment Bill and Hillary Clinton got from the press should put to rest for all time the notion that the press is liberal. Or rather, as Howard Kurtz, who covers the media for *The Washington Post,* said of the press, "The stereotype—they're liberal, and therefore they work overtime to stick it to Republicans—doesn't hold up. Some journalists clearly liked Clinton during the '92 campaign, but anyone who thinks the Clinton administration got good coverage from the press— remember that Whitewater, Travelgate, illegal fundraising, Paula Jones, Kathleen Willey, Monica Lewinsky and the Marc Rich pardon were all press-driven stories—is seriously misguided. Relations between the Clinton team and the Fourth Estate were incredibly tense in '98 and '99." [14]

Even Ari Fleischer, President Bush's press secretary, who spread the un-true story of vandalism by Clinton aides, admits in his book, "No one can claim with a straight face that the White House press corps were easy on for-mer President Bill Clinton." [15]

The Vast Right-Wing Media Conspiracy, aka "The Puke Funnel"

In the mid-1990s, with the media in full-blown frenzy over a host of Clinton "scandals" like Whitewater and the suicide of Vince Foster, James decided he'd had enough. Working with the Democratic National Committee and former White House aide Mark Fabiani, he helped produce a 330-page re-port documenting how right-wing activists had manipulated the media. Rather than start at the more respectable, reputable journals, they started at the bottom and worked their way up the media food chain. The document described a phenomenon called the "Communication Stream of Conspiracy Commerce."

James had a more earthy term for it: the Puke Funnel.

Here's how the report described the funnel:

"The Communication Stream of Conspiracy Commerce refers to the mode of communication employed by the right wing to convey their fringe stories into legitimate subjects of coverage by the mainstream media. This is how the stream works. First, well funded right wing think tanks and individuals underwrite conservative newsletters and newspapers such as the Western Journalism Center, the *American Spectator* and the *Pittsburgh Tribune Review*. Next, the stories are reprinted on the internet where they are bounced all over the world. From the internet, the . . . story will be picked up by the British tabloids and covered as a major story, from which the American right-of-center mainstream media (i.e. the Wall Street Journal, Washington Times and New York Post) will then pick the story up. . . ." [16]

Keep in mind that this was years before Hillary Clinton spoke of "a vast right-wing conspiracy." At the time of his report, James was dismissed by Beltway elites as a crackpot. At a contentious breakfast with leading political reporters and editors in April 1994, James produced a chart describing how some of the most influential journalists in America had been duped by ultra-conservative activists. To put it mildly, he was not well received. Over a decade later, his observations seem obvious and commonplace. David Brock and others have detailed precisely how the media food chain was used by Clinton's enemies to sneak their sleazy stories into the mainstream.

Al Gore Got Shafted by the Press

Lest you think the "liberal" media made a temporary detour in attacking Bill and Hillary Clinton, let's take a look at how effectively the Republican right manipulated the media against Al Gore.

In her book with Paul Waldman, *The Press Effect*, Kathleen Hall Jamieson of the Annenberg School of Communications at the University of Pennsylvania documents just what a raw deal Al Gore got from the press in his 2000 campaign. Jamieson notes that the press framed the campaign as a contest between two caricatures: Bush the dim bulb and Gore the phony. Or, as she puts it, "Dumbo versus Pinocchio." While unfair to both candidates, the stereotypes were not equally unfair. After all, a not-so-bright president can put bright people around him. A dishonest president can't very well compensate by hiring honest people. Having modest intelligence is a shortcoming, but dishonesty is a character flaw—and a fatal one at that.

Al Gore is not a liar. Or rather, he's much less of a liar than most of the politicians we know. Our experiences with him proved him to be a straight shooter, and more so than most people. Yet time after time, the press twisted stories to make Gore look like a phony. Here are a couple of the more egregious examples:

"I Invented the Internet"

Al Gore never claimed he invented the Internet. Never said it. It's a myth. Here's what he actually said, in an interview with CNN's Wolf Blitzer: "During my service in the United States Congress, I took the initiative in creating the Internet." As Jamieson observes, "In fact, Gore's role in securing funds for expansion of the fledgling network in the late 1980s was substantial. . . . The truth of Gore's statement rests in part on whether one concludes that the Internet was 'created' by the computer scientists and engineers who designed the system, or by the politicians who provided the funding to turn a small network linking a few universities and military facilities into a global one. However, once the term 'invented' became inextricably attached to the claim, it was no longer a subject of debate but an unquestioned example of Gore's dishonesty. . . . A LexisNexis search seeking stories mentioning Al Gore and using the phrase 'invented the Internet' captures 1,684 articles between Gore's interview with Blitzer in March, 1999 and election day of 2000." [17] In truth, Gore sponsored the Supercomputer Network Study Act of 1986, and he first introduced the High Performance Computing Act in 1989. Vinton Cerf, the father of the Internet, said in 1999, "The Internet would not be where it is in the United States without the strong support given to it and related research areas by the vice president in his current role and in his earlier role as a senator." [18]

"Love Canal"

The story that Al Gore took credit for exposing the toxic disaster at Love Canal in New York was the result of a misquote, plain and simple. Gore was talking about hearings he'd held on a toxic waste site in his home state of Tennessee. Gore said of the Tennessee case, "That was the one that started it all." But both *The New York Times* and *The Washington Post* inaccurately told their readers Gore had said, "I was the one that started it all." The next day, when Gore tried to correct the record, the *Post* spanked him, saying, "He didn't quite mean to say he discovered a toxic waste site." This suggests that it was Gore who misspoke. But in truth it was the (liberal?) press that had misquoted him. [19]

"Love Story"

Here again, it was the press that made the mistake, but it was Gore who paid the price. Gore once said that a journalist in Tennessee interviewed author Erich Segal and reported that Segal had based his lead male character, Oliver Barrett IV, on Gore, and his female lead, Jenny Cavalleri, on Tipper. In 1997, *The New York Times* picked up on that but set the record straight after talking with Segal, writing that "when the author, Erich Segal, was asked about Gore's impression, he stated that the preppy hockey-playing male lead, Oliver Barrett IV, indeed was modeled after Gore and Gore's Harvard roommate, actor Tommy Lee Jones. But Segal said the female lead, Jenny, was not modeled after Tipper Gore." [20] So a Tennessee reporter mistakenly wrote that Oliver and Jenny were based on Al and Tipper, when the more accurate story was that part of Oliver was based on Al but that Tipper wasn't in the story at all. But that error—and a journalist's error, at that—led *The Washington Post* to call Gore "the man who mistakenly claimed to have inspired the movie *Love Story.*" [21]

"The Union Label Lullaby"

In September 2000, while campaigning with Teamsters, Gore joked that when he was a baby, his mother used to sing him to sleep with the lullaby "Look for the union label . . ." The Teamsters laughed. It was obvious to them that Gore was joking. After all, the song wasn't written until 1975, when Gore was twenty-seven. But the media pounced. Despite the fact that the speech was videotaped, and the laughter was clearly audible on the tape, Gore "lying" about the lullaby became part of the myth.

Why would the supposedly liberal press hammer Gore? After the election, Eric Boehlert of *Rolling Stone* talked to some of the people who had covered him. Their answer is startling—the reporters who had covered Gore hated him. Here's what they told Boehlert:

"The coverage seemed to be much more aggressive and adversarial than I'd ever seen before," says Scott Shepard, a veteran newspaper reporter who has four presidential campaigns to his credit and who covered the Gore campaign for the *Atlanta Journal-Constitution.*

"There was a fair amount of animus as time wore on with Gore," says James Warren, who was then Washington bureau chief for *The Chicago Tribune,* referring to the mood on the press plane. "People were overly hard toward him. He's a decent, honest fellow. He was not the greatest candidate, but he's not dishonest. And some in the press came perilously close to saying that."

Recalls one network television correspondent who spent lots of time on the presidential campaign, "There just developed among a certain group of people covering Gore, particularly the print people, a real disdain for him. Everything was negative. They had a grudge against [Gore]. I don't know how else to put it." [22]

A review of press coverage of Campaign 2000 in *The Columbia Journalism Review* came to this conclusion: "Gore's motives are frequently questioned, frequently framed in the most negative light—even in the lead of straight-news stories from some of the most respected and influential news organizations. . . . In contrast, Bush's proposals are not only treated straight, as they should be, in straight-news stories: he's often been given the benefit of the doubt on subjects where he could be vulnerable." [23]

The Press Was Pro-Bush in Campaign 2000

The reporters who covered George W. Bush liked him. They really liked him. Frank Bruni, who covered the Bush 2000 campaign for *The New York Times,* recalls that "up close and personal . . . [Bush] was most comfortable, nimblest and, not so incidentally, most impressive." Bruni calls Bush "instinctively bright, quick to the punch." [24] Right, Panchito. (Bush's nickname for Bruni, when he wasn't calling him "Brunei, my man from the *Times.*") Bruni also draws this contrast, suggesting why reporters were so much more fond of Bush than of Gore: "Bush, with his buoyancy of spirit, presented a perfect contrast to Gore, so turgid and tendentious." [25] Bush's buoyancy of spirit created a frat-rat esprit de corps on the campaign plane, with journalists jockeying for the approval of the coolest kid in class—the one with the big trust fund and the winning, self-deprecating style. This is obvious to anyone who watches Alexandra Pelosi's film, *Journeys with George.* Bruni, too, captures it, noting that in addition to bestowing nicknames on favored reporters, "the tactile element of Bush's interpersonal style, another possible holdover from his fraternity days, [was] another facet of a fraternity-house sensibility that had never wholly abated. He touched those of us around him a lot. . . . He pinched our cheeks or gently slapped them, in an almost grandmotherly, aren't-you-adorable way." [26]

It was a strategy, and it worked. Bush himself was thrilled with the puffy press he was getting, telling a magazine during the campaign, "I think probably the best thing I've done is interface with the press." [27]

Of course, some journalists are just plain easy. The people closest to him know that George W. Bush is not fond of journalists. Indeed, not knowing he was within microphone range, he famously described Adam Clymer of *The New York Times* as "a major league asshole." [28] But no matter what he said about them or their colleagues behind their backs, the reporters covering

Bush liked him. And they cut him breaks. While Gore was excoriated as a lying, phony stiff for every misstatement, real or imagined, Bush was cut some slack.

He was also cut slack on serious questions of character, competence, and qualifications. Compared to Bill Clinton or Al Gore, George W. Bush in 2000 got some of the softest treatment from the press of any recent presidential candidate.

A Pew Center study examined thousands of news stories and concluded that 76 percent of the media's coverage of Al Gore in the 2000 election included one of two themes: that Gore lied and exaggerated, or that he was marred by scandal. The most common theme about Bush, the study found, was that he was a "different kind of Republican." This theme was reflected in the plurality (40 percent) of all stories filed on Bush.[29]

Another study, this one by the Project for Excellence in Journalism and Princeton Survey Research, found that Bush received twice as much favorable coverage as Gore in the crucial months of September and October 2000.[30]

A Nexis search revealed there were 68,096 stories about Whitewater, Bill Clinton's penny-ante land deal. When there were credible allegations in the 2000 campaign that Bush had committed insider trading as an executive with Harken Energy, they generated only 110 stories.

Both Clinton and Bush had, shall we say, complicated histories on the issue of the draft. Yet Clinton's sojourn through Selective Service merited 13,641 stories, while Bush going AWOL from the Air National Guard for a year was mentioned in only 49 stories in Campaign 2000. True, the press picked up the coverage in the Vietnam-obsessed campaign of 2004, but by then Bush had already been commander in chief through two wars, and voters were less interested in his Vietnam-era draft dodging.

You may recall quite a few stories in 1998 alleging that President Clinton had lied in a civil deposition concerning his personal life. But you may not recall that when Governor Bush swore under oath that he had not discussed a funeral home investigation either with the head of the state agency charged with investigating funeral homes or with representatives of the funeral home corporation under investigation, his testimony was directly contradicted by both his appointee to head the funeral home oversight agency and the CEO and lobbyist of the funeral home company. That's because, in stark contrast to the forests that were denuded to tell the Clinton story, the allegation that George W. Bush lied under oath made it into only 22 stories. Maybe it really was about the sex after all.

FOX Is Guarding the Henhouse

The phrase "in the tank" comes from boxing. When a fighter is going to throw a fight—lose on purpose—he is said to be "taking a dive." You can see why: He's going to dive onto the canvas to lose on purpose. From there the phrase morphed into "going into the tank"—a tank being something into which one might dive—or just "tanking" the fight. Now the expression applies more broadly. In journalism a reporter or commentator is said to be "in the tank" if she or he leans toward a candidate or cause in his or her reporting.

Truth be told, some reporters really are in the tank, and a great many of those are in the tank for the Republicans. Let's be clear, being conservative in one's personal politics and being in the tank for the Republicans are two very different things. When Brit Hume was covering the Clinton White House for ABC, he made no secret of his conservative political views, even writing a piece for the ultra-right-wing, Clinton-hating, discredited *American Spectator*.[31] But as far as we could tell, when he was on the air at ABC, Hume displayed no ideological bias. Later, when he joined FOX News, his conservatism found its way on the air on a regular basis.

Why the change? We think the ethic at ABC News is still one of professionalism. Both liberals and conservatives work there, and they try to put their journalistic values of fairness ahead of their political views. But FOX News—how shall we say this?—is in the tank. It is a twenty-four-hour-a-day in-kind contribution to the conservative movement. It's run by Roger Ailes, for Pete's sake. Before he became a millionaire media big shot, Roger was a Republican political consultant. (In fact, he and Karl Rove once teamed up against Carville and Begala in the 1991 special election for the Senate in Pennsylvania. Suffice it to say the good guys won.) Ailes was the media consultant for President George H. W. Bush. And now he has his own news network.

We've got to admit it: We like Roger. We really do. How could we dislike a guy who's bombastic, fiercely loyal, and deeply committed to his political agenda? We admire his moxie and his brains. But the difference between Roger and us is that no one has put us in charge of a news network. Nor could they. If someone tried to do that, the right would howl (as Bill Clinton used to say) like a pig stuck under a gate. And yet Rupert Murdoch has given control of a news network to a right-wing political consultant, and no one says boo. That's because the right has been working the refs for decades.

Under Ailes—who "transitioned" from right-wing Republican political consultant to right-wing Republican news executive by producing Rush Limbaugh's ill-fated television show—the FOX News Channel has achieved dramatic ratings success. It has also been plagued by charges of right-wing bias. As David Brock copiously documents in his book *The Republican Noise Machine,* former FOX news staffers have been candid and specific about allegations of a right-wing slant. A number of FOX staffers complained to the *Columbia Journalism Review* of "management sticking their fingers in the writing and editing of stories to cook the facts to make a story more palatable to right-wing tastes." [32] Longtime newsman Jed Duvall, who joined FOX after a distinguished career at ABC, has said, "I'll never forget the morning that one producer came up to me and, rubbing her hands like Uriah Heep, said, 'Let's have something on Whitewater today.' That sort of thing doesn't happen in professional news organizations." [33]

Former FOX producer Charles Reina wrote a lengthy exposé of the network on the industry website maintained by Jim Romanesko of the Poynter Institute. Reina claimed he was all but ordered to produce a favorable special on Ronald Reagan. "You know," his boss told him, "how Roger feels about him." [34] While working on an environmental story, he was instructed thus: "You can give both sides, but make sure the pro-environmentalists don't get the last word." [35]

Lest you think these are one-off, isolated examples, Reina revealed the FOX method of controlling the slant of the news: The Memo. Each day FOX executives e-mail a memo telling their producers and reporters, in Reina's words, "what stories will be covered and, often, suggesting how they should be covered. . . . The Memo was born with the [George W.] Bush Administration, early in 2001, and, intentionally or not, has ensured that the administration's point of view consistently comes across on FNC." He said that on March 20, 2003, in the days leading up to Bush's invasion of Iraq, the memo said, "There is something utterly incomprehensible about [UN Secretary General]) Kofi Annan's remarks in which he allows his thoughts are with the Iraq people. One could ask where his thoughts were during the 23 years Saddam Hussein was brutalizing those same Iraqis."[36] Yes, one could. And one could just as easily ask where the Republicans were when Ronald Reagan was supporting Saddam Hussein, and when Donald Rumsfeld was sucking up to Saddam just after he'd gassed the Kurds. But The Memo did not suggest exploring Republicans' long support for the Butcher of Baghdad.

Another former FOX employee, Matt Gross, tells a similar tale. "Let me just say that the right-wing bias [at FOX News] was up-front and obvious, from the day a certain executive editor was sent down [to where he worked, at FoxNews.com] from the channel to bring us in line with their coverage. His first directive to us: Seek stories that cater to angry, middle-aged white men who listen to talk radio and yell at their televisions."[37]

David Shuster spent six years as an on-air political reporter for FOX. We came to know him when he covered Whitewater, and he covered it very aggressively. Looking back on that period, Shuster says, "At the time I started at FOX, I thought, this is a great news organization to let me be very aggressive with a sitting president of the United States [Bill Clinton]. I started having issues when others in the organization would take my carefully scripted and nuanced reporting and pull out bits and pieces to support their agenda on their shows.

"With the change of administration in Washington," Shuster continued, "I wanted to do the same kind of reporting, holding the [Bush] administration accountable, and that was not something that FOX was interested in doing. Editorially, I had issues with story selection. But the bigger issue was that there wasn't a tradition or track record of honoring journalistic integrity. I found some reporters at FOX would cut corners or steal information from other sources or in some cases, just make things up. Management would either look the other way or just wouldn't care to take a closer look. I had serious issues with that."[38]

While FOX News has undeniably succeeded at winning ratings, it has been less successful in actually informing its viewers. In October 2003 the

Program on International Policy Attitudes at the University of Maryland (on whose board of advisers sit John Ashcroft's pollster, Fred Steeper, and former Michigan Republican congressman Bill Frenzel) released a study on public misperceptions of the war in Iraq. It found that FOX News viewers were the least-informed, or rather, the worst-informed, of any media consumers. "Those who receive most of their news from FOX News," the study found, "are more likely than average to have misperceptions" about the war in Iraq. The study identified three "misperceptions," a polite term for falsehoods: first, that evidence has been found linking al Qaeda and Saddam Hussein's Iraq; second, that weapons of mass destruction have been found in Iraq; and third, that world public opinion supported the U.S. led invasion of Iraq. "FOX News watchers," the study found, "were most likely to hold misperceptions—and were more than twice as likely as [viewers of] the next nearest network to hold all three misperceptions."[39]

Fully 80 percent of FOX viewers believed one of those whoppers. Only 55 percent of CNN viewers did, and just 23 percent of National Public Radio listeners and Public Broadcasting System viewers did. This is not merely a partisan thing, it's a FOX thing. Unlike some Democrats, we don't believe we're smarter than Republicans. Indeed, while 78 percent of Bush supporters who watch FOX believe that evidence linking Saddam and al Qaeda has been found, just 50 percent of Bush supporters who watch PBS and listen to NPR believed this fiction.[40]

FOX understands that its viewers use the FOX News Channel the way a drunk uses a lamppost: more for support than illumination. And so FOX offers more affirmation than information.

FOX isn't the only media organ that's in the tank for the Republicans. Some of the most respected journalists and commentators in the nation have, at one time or another, taken a dive for President Bush.

In the closing days of the 2004 presidential campaign, Osama bin Laden roiled the race by releasing a videotape. Senator John Kerry declared that all Americans were united in their opposition to bin Laden. He also noted that he had for years criticized the Bush administration for "outsourcing" the capture or killing of bin Laden to foreign mercenaries when the terrorist leader was holed up in the mountains of Tora Bora.

Right-wingers in the media pounced. Echoing the preferred GOP line, they accused Kerry in unison of having previously endorsed Bush's tactics at Tora Bora. First in line was Charles Krauthammer, who wrote in his *Washington Post* column that "Kerry himself said on national television at the time of Tora Bora (Dec. 14, 2001): 'What we are doing, I think, is having its impact and it is the best way to protect our troops and sort of minimalize the proximity, if you will'—i.e., not throwing American lives away in tunnels and caves in alien territory. 'I think we have been doing this pretty effectively and we should continue to do it that way.' " [41] Note that Krauthammer helpfully added the phrase "i.e., not throwing American lives away in tunnels and caves in alien territory." As we shall see in a minute, Krauthammer had to add that phrase, because Kerry never said it. And Kerry never said it, because he didn't mean it, didn't believe it, and wasn't making that point at all.

The day after Krauthammer's column appeared, *The New York Times*'s David Brooks wrote this: "Back in December 2001, when bin Laden was apparently hiding in Tora Bora, Kerry supported the strategy of using Afghans to hunt him down. He told Larry King that our strategy 'is having its impact, and it is the best way to protect our troops and sort of minimalize the proximity, if you will. I think we have been doing this pretty effectively, and we should continue to do it that way.' " [42]

Right on cue, FOX News joined the parade. On *FOX News Sunday,* host Chris Wallace asked Kerry strategist Bob Shrum, "Has Kerry been consistent about that whole action and the way in which the bin Laden issue in Tora Bora was handled? The reason I ask is back in 2001 he was asked about the question of letting Afghan warlords try to capture bin Laden, and this is what he had to say: '[I]t is the best way to protect our troops and sort of minimalize the proximity, if you will. I think we have been doing this pretty effectively and we should continue to do it that way.' " [43]

Wow. Sure looks like Kerry was for the strategy at Tora Bora before he was against it. Except he wasn't. The folks at Media Matters for America (which is a must-read each day for everyone who cares about truth in the media) did a little digging. Turns out the three-year-old Kerry quote that mysteriously appeared in *The Washington Post* and *The New York Times* and on FOX News within a three-day period just before the election (imagine that!) was not about—as Wallace put it—"the question of letting Afghan warlords try to capture bin Laden." It was about the wisdom of bombing from above versus using flamethrowers. That's right, flamethrowers. Here's the question, from a caller to *Larry King Live,* and the responses from Kerry, as well as right-wing California Republican congressman Randy "Duke" Cunningham, and retired four-star general George Joulwan:

CALLER: Hello. Yes, I would like to ask the panel why they don't use napalm or flamethrowers on those tunnels and caves up there in Afghanistan?

KING: Senator Kerry?

CALLER: My golly, I think they could smoke him [Osama bin Laden] out.

KING: Senator Kerry?

KERRY: Well, I think it depends on where you are tactically. They may well be doing that at some point in time. But for the moment, what we are doing, I think, is having its impact and it is the best way to protect our troops and sort of minimalize the proximity, if you will. I think we have been doing this pretty effectively and we should continue to do it that way.

KING: [California] Congressman [Randy] Cunningham, what do you think of that question?

CUNNINGHAM: I think Senator Kerry is right on the mark. To use a flamethrower, you've got to get right into the area, close in. And plus, it doesn't penetrate that deep in those tunnels. You've got to go in there after him. So I think you have to neutralize that threat. And then you can get him out in a lot of different, various ways, including what the gentleman spoke about.

KING: [Retired] General [George] Joulwan, what are your thoughts?

JOULWAN: Well, I think what you are seeing here are laser-designated bombs going in that are highly effective. In fact, I think much more effective than napalm will be, given the extent of these tunnels. You may see some of this when the troops get in there; you have troops on the ground. But right now, I think the laser-designated bombs are doing a great job.[44]

Why would Krauthammer, Brooks, and Wallace—who are respected, serious men—all use the same dishonest argument? Where do you suppose they got it? Do you really believe all three of them, and countless of lesser imitators on the right, all independently decided to review and distort the same three-year-old transcript from *Larry King Live*? No. They were spoon-fed this misinformation, presumably by the Bush-Cheney campaign. And they in turn became the dutiful tools of the Republican Party, unquestioningly repeating the party line. That's called being in the tank.

The Media Have Been Bludgeoned into Believing Only Republicans Are Believers

We've written earlier in this book about the right-wing conceit of moral superiority. About how insufferable right-wingers like to claim, in their sanctimonious way, that they're better Christians or Jews or whatever; that they have the moral high ground. Frankly, we think that's a bunch of crap. What's interesting is how deeply that arrogant, elitist right-wing sanctimony has penetrated the press.

On the day of Pope John Paul II's funeral, CNN decided to have a brief discussion of Catholics in American public life. They asked Bob Novak and Paul to discuss the topic. It promised to be an interesting pairing. Paul is younger and a "cradle Catholic"; Bob is not as young, and he is a convert to Catholicism. But here's how Wolf Blitzer introduced them:

BLITZER: While they were united today in mourning the death of the pope, U.S. Catholics are a diverse group, as illustrated by two of our *Crossfire* co-hosts, the conservative Robert Novak, the liberal Paul Begala. Both good Catholics—I don't know "good" Catholics, but both Catholics. I'm sure Bob is a good Catholic, I'm not so sure about Paul Begala.

Paul's blood was boiling. It was by far the angriest, most outraged, most insulted he'd been on television. And this is a guy who hosted debate shout-fests for five years. Here's the exchange that ensued:

BEGALA: Well, now, who are you to pass moral judgment on my religion, Mr. Blitzer? My goodness gracious.
BLITZER: All right, go ahead, go ahead.

BEGALA: On the day of my Holy Father's funeral. My eldest son is named John Paul, after the pope.

BLITZER: So you are a good Catholic?

BEGALA: I'm serious, that annoys me. I don't think anybody should presume that a liberal is not a good Catholic.

At this point Bob Novak—a conservative *and* a good Catholic—found it incumbent on him to defend Paul's faith:

NOVAK: Paul, Paul, Paul is a good Catholic.

BEGALA: The Holy Father is liberal. And in fact, when [CNN contributor] Carlos [Watson] was speaking [earlier in the program], I was in the greenroom. Underneath, some producer had written, "Many Catholic doctrines are conservative." Absolutely correct. Many are liberal as well. The Holy Father bitterly opposed President Bush's war in Iraq. He came to St. Louis—and I was there—and he begged America to give up the death penalty. President Bush strongly supports it, as did President Clinton and others. Many of the Holy Father's views—my church's views— are extraordinarily liberal. The pope talked about savage, unbridled capitalism, not Bob Novak's kind—

BLITZER: I was certainly not questioning—I was only teasing.

BEGALA: Okay.

BLITZER: Don't be so sensitive.

BEGALA: Well, it's an important day for my faith.

BLITZER: It's a very important day—

BEGALA: It's the only pope of my adult lifetime, so I'm a little emotional tonight.[45]

Blitzer later sent Paul an e-mail in which he apologized and said he was just trying to make a joke. That's no doubt true; Wolf Blitzer is a good guy. But the incident sparked a small firestorm, because it touched a nerve. Progressive Catholics around the country were offended. Countless numbers of them e-mailed Paul, telling him they were tired of being insulted by right-wingers.

But the prejudice against progressives of faith in the media runs deep.

You can't imagine a newsperson saying, for example, that Republican Rudy Giuliani is a bad Catholic, despite the fact that Giuliani supports legal abortion, supports gay marriage, and has himself been married three times. No newsperson says Justice Antonin Scalia is a bad Catholic, despite the fact that Scalia champions the death penalty, which the late Pope John Paul II called part of the "culture of death."

So what do we need to do to take back the media? A few simple steps:

1. Work the Refs Yourself

That great Democrat Al Smith once said that all the ills of democracy could be cured by more democracy. He was right. And many of the ills of pro-conservative media bias could be cured by Democrats working the refs as aggressively as the GOP does.

This doesn't require money or organization or power. All it takes is a little time and some determination. So when you see a column that's false or dishonest, when a newsperson writes or says something you think is unfair to progressives, when you detect a pro-Bush slant or the absence of the progressive point of view, fire up your computer. Send an e-mail. Write a letter. Make a phone call. Then, once you've written your letter, circulate it. Send the offending news item, along with your letter, to your like-minded friends. Ask them to check it out for themselves and, if they agree, to join you in your grievance.

You would be astonished at the power and influence a few dozen e-mails can have on a news organization. They are especially powerful if they're organic, not scripted.

Democrats just don't do as good a job of complaining as Republicans do. We remember when ABC News asked George Stephanopoulos to host its Sunday-morning interview show *This Week*. George had been out of politics for several years, had proved himself as a journalist, and had written a book about his experiences with President Clinton that some liberals found disloyal. Despite the time and the distance from Clinton, the right freaked out when George was given hosting duties on *This Week*. The conservative Media Research Center excoriated "Boy George" as a "political partisan" and a "lib-

eral presidential aide," two things he had clearly been some years before joining ABC. Yet they did not seem to have the same concerns about former Republicans in the media, like ABC's Diane Sawyer (who once worked for
Richard Nixon) or former Republican congresswoman Susan Molinari (who
hosted a show on CBS).

We were especially amused when one right-winger said no network
would put a former aide from a Republican White House in charge of a Sunday talk show. I suppose he didn't notice that Tony Snow, a former aide to
President George H. W. Bush, was at the time hosting *FOX News Sunday.*
When Tony was asked to host *FOX News Sunday,* liberals didn't pounce.
They didn't whine. But when a former Clinton aide was assigned to a similar
program at another network, all hell broke loose. Such is the state of play. Republicans work the refs; Democrats do not.

The difference between the liberals' approach to the media and the conservatives' is instructive. Many Democrats believe journalists are their
friends. In their intellectual arrogance, they believe all smart people are—or
ought to be—liberal. And they're bitterly disappointed when a journalist
turns out not to be liberal but is instead fair-minded or even conservative.
Conservatives harbor no such illusions. For decades they have seen the media
as their enemy, an obstacle to be gotten around. So rather than seducing
journalists, the right intimidates them. They bludgeon and bully and bull-
doze them.

Frank Bruni covered the Bush 2000 campaign for *The New York Times.*
Bruni had never covered a presidential candidate before George W. Bush.
After writing an article noting that then-governor Bush's fading campaign in
the New Hampshire primary was causing some Republicans to worry
whether Bush had "the gumption and grit to go the distance," Bruni received
the full Bush intimidation treatment. As he recalled, "the article was published on the front page on a Saturday morning, and around midday, I had to
call campaign advisers for another story I was working on. I tried one senior
official, who was pronounced unavailable and never called back. I tried another; same deal. I finally reached one of the spokespeople, who told me, in
no uncertain terms, that everyone was displeased with me." Bush staffers
trashed Bruni to his colleagues and competitors behind his back.

Bush's belligerence works. Whereas too many Democrats simply, passively presume the press will be on their side (perhaps they've been reading and believing too many right-wing talking points), conservatives push, they criticize, they impugn the motives of journalists, they allege bias. The effect of all this pressure is often journalists who bend over backward to prove to conservatives they're not biased. This sometimes creates a pro-conservative tilt that suits the right just fine.

Democrats should learn another lesson from conservative press managers: Hit 'em where it hurts. The Bush press team has mastered this strategy. If a journalist writes or broadcasts a report they believe is unflattering to the president, there are consequences. Former Bush White House press secretary Ari Fleischer was infamous for calling reporters and muttering darkly that their impertinent question to the president "was noted in the building."[46] The recipient of such a call would frequently find that on his next story, normally helpful White House aides would shun him. Administration officials would refuse to return his calls. Republican sources in Washington would dry up. And oftentimes his competitor would mysteriously receive a killer scoop—one that he'd been frozen out of. The lesson was clear: If you write bad stories about the president, bad things will happen to you.

Conversely, if you write nice things about Bush, you'll be rewarded. On December 1, 1999, *The Washington Post* put a report on the soon-to-be-released tax-cut plan from Governor George W. Bush on page one, with this headline: BUSH TO OFFER $483 BILLION TAX-CUT PLAN; WORKING POOR, MIDDLE CLASS WOULD GET MUCH OF RELIEF.[47]

The story was a triumph for Bush on a variety of levels. First, the notion that Bush was proposing a $483 billion tax cut was baloney. The costs of tax cuts had always been estimated, by the Congressional Budget Office, the Office of Management and Budget, and every credible private sector analyst, over a ten-year period. Thus, to compare apples to apples, the only sensible way to describe the Bush tax cut's cost would be $1.14 trillion over ten years. The headline understated the size of the tax-cut proposal in a way that helped Bush considerably.

Second, the headline claimed that the working poor and the middle class would get "much" of the relief, whatever that means. This is the heart of the fabrication the *Post* fell for—that Bush, as a self-described "compassionate conservative," cared more about the poor and the middle class than traditional conservatives. This essentially gave away the game. One of the Democrats' principal concerns about Bush's tax cut was that it gave America's hard-earned surplus principally to the very rich. But the first sentence of the *Post*'s story looked more like a Bush press release—and a misleading one at that—than an article in a fiercely independent newspaper: "Texas Gov. George W. Bush will propose a $483 billion tax-cut plan today *that would focus its deepest reductions on the working poor and middle class* and become the centerpiece of the Republican front-runner's economic plan" (emphasis added). In the second paragraph, the *Post* told its readers that "roughly half of the overall relief would be targeted to middle- and lower-income families, according to campaign aides."

In point of fact, the proposal lavished over 60 percent of its benefits on the wealthiest 10 percent of taxpayers and, in a neat coincidence, gave just 10 percent of the benefits to the lowest 60 percent. By "lowest 60 percent," we mean the middle class and the working poor. Sixty percent of Americans would get to split just ten cents on the dollar, and yet the *Post* credulously claimed the Bush proposal "would focus its deepest reductions on the working poor and middle class."

How could the *Post* have gotten it so wrong? The Bush team bullied and buffaloed the paper into reporting the tax-cut plan without any comment from its critics. According to Jonathon Chait of *The New Republic*, the Bushies struck this secret deal with the *Post*: "When George W. Bush's campaign leaked his economic plan to the press . . . the lucky recipients were forced to accept a special condition: any reporter who wanted to see it had to agree not to share the details with other campaigns or, more importantly, outside analysts. 'This is between you, me, and your typewriter,' a Bush aide told one reporter." Chait went on to note that "the result of this clever leak strategy was an initial wave of reviews that dovetailed with Bush's efforts to cast himself as compassionate. The plan, according to *The Washington Post*, would 'focus its deepest reductions on the working poor and middle class' and 'mark a clear departure from more traditional GOP tax policy.' "

Thus did one of America's great newspapers turn from being watchdog over presidents to being George W. Bush's lapdog.

The next day the *Post* retrenched, reporting that, according to the experts at the progressive Citizens for Tax Justice, "Two-thirds of the benefits would go to the wealthiest 10 percent of Americans, who would receive tax cuts averaging $8,362 a year. . . . By comparison, taxpayers in the lowest 60 percent of the income scale would get only 11 percent of Bush's tax cuts, with an average cut of only $249."[48]

Let's be clear: We don't blame the Bush team for this. We blame the *Post* and the other media who bought the Bush line unquestioningly. We fault ourselves a little for lacking the chutzpah to come up with a scam like that, but we don't blame the Bushies. In fact, not long after that story ran, Paul shared a steak and a nice bottle of red wine with one of Bush's top strategists. The strategist chuckled all through dinner about the deal they'd cut with the media. Kind of like a carnival con man bragging about the bumpkin he ripped off for a big score in Smallville.

Mark Halperin, the political director of ABC News, is one of the smartest people we know in the media. He also has a gift for stating obvious but often unspoken truths. "Any objective person," he notes, "would say that in some ways Bill Clinton was covered too aggressively in some areas, and George W. Bush is not covered aggressively enough."[49] Why is that? In part, we believe it's because Bush adopted a much tougher tone with the press. We Clintonites tried to deal with the media, treating them like legitimate players in the policy and political process. Our critics would say we tried to co-opt them; we prefer the notion that we were cooperating with them. Team Bush has a very different press-management style: intimidation and confrontation. And it works.

Through a sophisticated understanding of the carrots and sticks that work on the press, and an audacity we find impressive, the Bush team was able to launch its central domestic policy proposal—and never was heard a discouraging word.

We're not advocating the same level of manipulation. Rather, Democrats should understand that access is a reporter's lifeblood. When we were hosting *Crossfire*, we grew quite fond of the Republicans who deigned to come on our show—especially after Tom DeLay tried to organize a Republican boycott. (Apparently, Mr. DeLay didn't like the fact that two Democrats were cohosting a show "from the left." Perhaps the show would have better suited Mr. DeLay if it had had only right-wingers presiding over a vigorous agreement.)

Journalists, like the rest of us, understand only two things: what you can do for them, and what you can do to them. The Bushies push and pull those two levers as artfully as the man behind the curtain in *The Wizard of Oz.* It wouldn't kill the Democrats to cut off access to a few reporters they believe are biased against them.

2. Support the Watchdogs

Media Matters for America is one of our favorite new organizations. Its website, www.mediamatters.org, is a daily diary of right-wing bias in the media. Media Matters was founded by David Brock, the self-described right-wing hit man who first reported on President Clinton's private life in the early 1990s. As he tells it in *Blinded by the Right,* Brock was an integral part of an effort by right-wing extremists to use the conventions of journalism to further a far-right, Clinton-hating agenda.

After being blinded by the right, Brock has seen the light. He now spends his time policing the media through Media Matters. He has a talented staff of researchers and analysts who set the record straight anytime a right-wing blowhard tries to use the media to mislead.

Eric Alterman, who writes about the media in *The Nation* and the altercation blog on MSNBC.com, is a one-man truth squad. We earlier described his book, *What Liberal Media?,* as important. We want to go further. It's essential; we hereby declare it required reading for the Carville-Begala canon. If you follow Media Matters for America and read Alterman's book and his columns, you will never again fall victim to the pernicious and pervasive right-wing attempt to dominate the media.

The Daily Howler is a terrific website as well. Edited by stand-up comic and Harvard-educated policy wonk Bob Somerby, www.dailyhowler.com chronicles what it calls the "clownish" behavior of the media. It is carefully researched, acidly accurate, and oftentimes pretty darned amusing.

3. Be a Populist, Not an Elitist

This is one more area where Democratic elitism hurts. Most Democrats we know want to be in *The New York Times* or on NBC; they don't want to do farm radio or be in a local paper. And that's why they're getting killed in the media. While the elite media are still influential, radio, regional papers, and the Internet are increasing in importance.

Democrats should understand this changing dynamic and adjust to it. The line of Washington Democratic big shots who want to appear on *Meet the Press* stretches out the door and a mile down the road. But the line for *Good Morning Cleveland* is empty. At least of Democrats. The reality is, more Americans get their news from local television than from any other single source. When Bill Clinton was president, he routinely granted interviews to local television stations. But try getting a nationally known Democrat on local news today. It's darn near impossible.

Howard Dean was the first politician to grasp the power of the Internet as a tool for fund-raising, organizing, and message delivery. What's disappointing is how few Democratic politicians have followed Dean's lead. Too many of them use the Internet as a place to post press releases and photos. To be truly effective, we believe Democrats have to adapt to the technology rather than trying to use print-era tactics online. At their simplest, the Democrats' websites should follow the style of the truly successful progressive websites, like Daily Kos, Buzzflash, and Talking Points Memo. Each of these sites delivers news, but all of them do it with attitude. Kos, especially, has created a vibrant, strong sense of community. Democratic officeholders and candidates should use their websites to receive information, not merely disseminate it. That is, they should be asking folks to share their opinions, their stories, their perspectives on the issues of the day. A thriving blog is a must. The key to it is a daily post that's actually written by the politician. It can't read like a press release drafted by an uptight twenty-two-year-old straight out of the Ivy League. It must be informal, folksy, and accessible. Democrats are the party of the people. They should be much more aggressive about using a medium that so dramatically empowers people.

Bill Clinton understood how to use media in a populist way. When Clinton was fighting his way through the New York primary in 1992, Don Imus was using his powerful microphone to ridicule him every day. Imus played the snippet of Ray Charles's "What'd I Say," in which Ray sings, "Tell your mama, tell your pa / Gonna send you back to Arkansas . . ." He called Clinton "Butter-butt" and—worst of all with a New York audience—"Bubba."

Another politician in another era would have been offended. Clinton was intrigued. Not that he enjoyed being pilloried, but he actually listened to Imus and understood his appeal immediately. In between jibes and comedy sketches, there were interviews with politicians like Senators Lowell Weicker and Bill Bradley. In those interviews, Imus impressed Clinton with his grasp of the issues and his uncanny ability to sum up a situation or a person with a single cutting phrase. And so Clinton got himself booked on the Imus show. We were with him in his hotel room the morning he did the call. Oftentimes politicians prepare exhaustively for big interviews, and in New York there was nothing bigger than Imus. Instead, Clinton had a brief workout and a big breakfast. Then he picked up the phone and called in, after only the briefest of conversations with us about the show. This made us a little nervous, as we were big proponents of Clinton going on Imus, and some of our campaign colleagues looked askance at the ploy. We knew if Clinton bombed, we'd be justifiably blamed. We needn't have worried. Clinton got off the line of the day, telling Imus he didn't mind being called Bubba. "Bubba is just southern for mensch," he said. Perfect pitch. He closed by serenading the New York press corps, all of whom he knew were listening to Imus. On the spur of the moment, he warbled a few bars of Elvis's "Don't Be Cruel."

We're not saying one appearance on Imus saved Clinton in New York. But we do believe that appearance made an enormous impression on voters and the media. He showed that this Arkansas traveler could thrust and party with the quickest wit in Manhattan.

Clinton later repeatedly used nontraditional media when he couldn't break into the mainstream press. In 1992, even after Clinton won the California primary, Ross Perot was dominating the media, and for good reason. He was a wisecracking billionaire with no political party, yet he was ahead in the polls, leading both the incumbent president of the United States and the likely Democratic nominee. Clinton was fit to be tied. There were no more primaries to win, and he had won more of them than any Democratic presidential candidate in history. This was supposed to be the time he was introduced to swing voters in glowing profiles. We expected him to be on the cover of *Time* and *Newsweek*. Nothing.

So, on June 3, the day after his largely ignored victory in the California primary, Clinton appeared on *The Arsenio Hall Show.* That's where the iconic image of Clinton playing "Heartbreak Hotel" on the saxophone (wearing Paul's sunglasses, by the way) was born. But what's been forgotten is that in addition to having fun, Arsenio and Clinton had a serious conversation about the Los Angeles riots, the lack of economic opportunity in the inner city, and Clinton's ideas for fighting poverty and bringing growth to poor neighborhoods. The appearance was pooh-poohed by the media mandarins of Manhattan. And that's one of the reasons it worked. Clinton understood that he had to go around and through the media elites to reach the people he needed. And when he did so successfully, the media elite followed. Clinton did wind up on the cover of *Time* and *Newsweek,* but he had to go on Imus and Arsenio first.

4. Engage on the Battlefield of Ideas

One of the striking pieces of advice Lewis Powell gave to big business was that to influence the media, they had to influence those to whom the media turned for information, advice, and commentary. And so the right has poured billions into think tanks over the past several decades. The Heritage Foundation, the American Enterprise Institute, the Cato Institute, and many more churn out policy positions, studies, and polemics. Some of them are garbage, real hackery. Others have substance and merit. But an astonishing number of them are covered by the media, and often in the most unquestioning way.

Belatedly, progressives are getting into the game. The Center for American Progress is, we believe, the best thing that's happened to progressive politics since Bill Clinton left office. Founded by John Podesta, Clinton's former chief of staff, the center has brought together some of the freshest minds in the country who analyze defense and national security, taxes and the deficit, energy and the environment, and more. It's a remarkable place and a remarkable success. In just its first two years, the center has grown into a multimillion-dollar organization with more than a hundred employees. Central to the center's success, though, has been its media strategy. It operates on the theory that a good idea no one knows about is not such a good idea. So Podesta has hired some of the top communications talent in Washington, and he's put them to work. The center's detailed policy analyses are accessible to read, even for state-school guys like us. And the center engages in the daily pull and tug of the media through its Progress Report, which analyzes the issues of the day every day, then links the reader to dozens of facts, news stories, and research documents. The Progress Report allows you to get a quick view of the news or do a deep dive, and it's written in a lively style. The center also has a daily blog—Think Progress—and it has a sizable stable of media-savvy experts, ready to be deployed on the talk-show circuit at a moment's notice.

If we seem enthusiastic about the center, it's because we are. But before we get too carried away, you should know our adversaries on the right were doing all this and more two decades ago. Still, we subscribe to the old saying that the best time to plant a tree is twenty years ago; the second best time is right now.

5. Develop Our Own Echo Chamber

The Catholic order the Christophers has a wonderful motto: It's better to light a candle than to curse the darkness. For years Democrats have simply cursed the darkness of the right-wing media. We've cursed the Republicans' ability to amplify their message across the media, from right-wing tabloids to right-wing websites to right-wing radio to the right-wing news channels. But in the last few years, a group of progressives has decided to quit cursing and start lighting candles. Liberal talk is now the fastest-growing format on the radio. Liberal radio hosts like Al Franken and Stephanie Miller and Janeane Garofalo and Ed Schultz and Bill Press and Christy Harvey and Randi Rhodes and Rachel Maddow and Jerry Springer (yes, that Jerry Springer) are setting the airwaves on fire with their combination of humor and outrage.

Progressive websites and blogs—still viewed with suspicion by some of the more Luddite Democrats in Washington—are extremely influential. Net-roots organizations like MoveOn.Org and Gold Star Mother Cindy Sheehan's instant national anti-war movement have created powerful message machines out of nothing. MoveOn originated as a vehicle for ordinary

Americans of both parties to express their disgust with the radical Republicans' attempts to impeach President Clinton in 1998. The name came from the group's initial proposal to censure Clinton and "move on" with the country's business. Years later, MoveOn is one of the most potent forces in the progressive movement.

Some fear a nascent civil war between the establishment Washington Democrats and the new net-roots activists. We'd like to propose a truce. Here are the terms: The net-roots activists are right when they say establishment Democrats have to get tough on President Bush and the Republicans. (We want to vouch for both Senate Democratic leader Harry Reid and House Democratic leader Nancy Pelosi; the two of them are absolutely unafraid of Bush, stronger than garlic in a milkshake.) Establishment Democrats will also have to listen to the activists' plea for new ideas. It seems to us an opposition party needs to do two things: oppose and propose. Too often, establishment Democrats have hesitated to tell folks exactly where they stand; they've been too timid to propose real solutions to global warming, or our dependence on Middle East oil, or the deficit, or Bush's disastrous foreign policy. Finally, establishment Democrats have to embrace reform as if their careers depended on it—because they do. Net-roots activists are properly disgusted when D.C. Democrats cave in to corporate lobbyists on tax cuts, or on the new bankruptcy that screws the poor, or on cuts in programs that help the working poor lift themselves up to the middle class.

Again, we're not trying to choose up sides. But if we come down on the side of the net-roots activists on many of these issues, it's because part of this book's purpose is to give our beloved Democratic donkey a kick in the ass. Here's what we ask of our fellow activists/agitators: Deal with reality. Support the Democrats, even when they're less than perfect. Our old boss Bill Clinton captured the difference between Democrats' pursuit of perfection and Republicans' pursuit of power perfectly when he observed that "Democrats want to fall in love; Republicans just want to fall in line."

So, folks, fall in line.

6. Challenge Corporate Concentration of the Media

We are under contract for television commentary to CNN, which is part of the vast Time Warner media conglomerate. This book is published by Simon & Schuster, which is part of the equally enormous Viacom media empire. In half a lifetime of working in and around the media, neither one of us has been told what to say or not to say—at least not for political reasons. To be sure, we've been reminded to keep our potty-mouth tendencies in check. And every television producer reminds us to keep it simple, not to get into the arcana of Social Security reform. But we can't think of a time when a corporate suit has ever told us what to say or write. Not that we'd listen, anyway.

So, if corporate America has never tried to silence us, why do we suggest that progressives challenge corporate concentration of media? Because control of the media is power, and no Democrat should want too much power in too few hands. Let's start with radio. Clear Channel Communications started with just one radio station in San Antonio. Its owner, Lowry Mays, soon bought a second—the powerful all-talk station WOAI. At the same time, Mays became more active in right-wing Republican circles. He was an investor with George W. Bush in the Texas Rangers—the deal that garnered Bush $14 million off a very small investment.[50]

Like any good businessman, Mays wanted to grow. But the law was in the way. Federal communications law prohibited any one entity from owning more than two stations in any market, and no one could own more than twenty-eight stations nationwide. This is where politics comes into play. When Republicans took over Congress in the mid-1990s, they set about loosening those restrictions. Just a tad. They succeeded, and President Clinton signed their bill into law. Today Clear Channel owns 1,200 radio stations, including stations in 247 of the 250 biggest markets in America. Its revenue is north of $3 billion.[51]

Concentrating such power in one set of hands has driven ad rates up, homogenized radio content, and ended radio's status as a forum for local news—and emergency information. In Minot, North Dakota, all six commercial radio stations are owned by Clear Channel. In 2002, the PBS program *NOW with Bill Moyers* reported, a train derailed in Minot, spilling 210,000 gallons of poisonous ammonia and sending a toxic plume into the air. Local authorities wanted to tell citizens to stay inside, so they called all six radio stations to spread the word.

Nobody was home. All six stations, owned by absentee landlord Clear Channel, have abandoned locally based programming in favor of preproduced, homogenized, beamed-in baloney. So instead of lifesaving emergency information, all Minot listeners got was a woman's voice chirping, "I'm Becky Wright—have a great weekend!!" You, too, Becky.[52]

Clear Channel's dominance—and its right-wing agenda—have clear political implications as well. In 2003, Texas native Natalie Maines of the Dixie Chicks had the temerity to say that President Bush's foreign policy was alienating the world and that "We're ashamed that the president of the United States is from Texas." Many Clear Channel stations pulled the Dixie Chicks from their playlist. Another radio giant, Cumulus Media, pulled the Chicks from all its stations.[53] Banning the Dixie Chicks was not a market-based decision; they were the number one act in country music. No, it was a political move—and one that President Bush apparently appreciated. He told NBC's Tom Brokaw that, while the Dixie Chicks had a right to speak their mind (awfully gracious of you, Mr. President), "They shouldn't have their feelings hurt just because some people don't want to buy their records when they speak out. . . . Freedom is a two-way street."[54]

We believe—and Democrats should argue—that the First Amendment calls for a greater diversity of voices, which can be possible only with greater diversity of ownership. This is not a new or radical notion. Justice Hugo Black said as much in the 1945 case of *Associated Press* v. *United States,* in which the Supreme Court ruled that the First Amendment supports, rather than prohibiting, the application of antitrust laws to media ownership. Why? Because the First Amendment "rests on the assumption that the widest possible dissemination of information from diverse and antagonistic sources is essential to the welfare of the public, that a free press is a condition of a free society."[55] Anti-competitive practices, which come with concentration of ownership, are antithetical to that purpose. If Democrats don't stand up against the increasing corporate control of the information we receive, the effects on our democracy will be great. Not to mention we'll have to listen to a lot of really crappy music.

7. Attack the Real Biases in Media

The media are biased. There's no question about it. They're just not biased in the ways right-wingers pretend they are. But there are several very real biases Democrats should attack:

The "Balance Bias"

Balance does not always equal fairness. Too often in partisan fights, the media plays the passive role of holding the combatants' coats. Instead, the press ought to be a referee—calling fouls, correcting errors, and making sure the fight doesn't get too dirty. In matters of opinion, simply letting two opponents have at it may be good enough, but when one side starts slinging falsehoods as facts, the media have a duty to get involved. We get the feeling that if a Republican said the moon was made of green cheese, and a Democrat said no, it's rock, the media would cover it with a headline saying, LEFT, RIGHT CLASH ON LUNAR MAKEUP. The press ought to call Neil Armstrong and ask him; he's been there.

In other words, when there is objective fact, or overwhelming consensus among experts, the media should not pretend there are two equally viable competing theories. The right exploits the balance bias brilliantly. Despite the fact that every single serious scientist recognizes evolution is a valid theory, the right has concocted a competing "theory"—so-called intelligent design—which the media then cover as if there were a legitimate debate. Nonsense. The right-wingers trying to force intelligent design into science curricula are really trying to inject religion; they're just not honest enough to admit it. But if we're going to start teaching religion as if it were science, we Catholics would like science teachers to instruct students that transubstantiation is a scientific fact rather than a miracle of faith.

Same with global warming. The case is closed. The debate is resolved. Climate change is real. It is caused by humans. It is endangering our planet. And yet the right, playing to the balance bias, comes up with some jackleg pseudoscience that pretends to claim global warming isn't happening. And so the press covers the "debate" between actual scientists and flat-earth dopes.

The Market Bias

Every consumer of news has by now heard the old saying on television, "If it bleeds, it leads." Corporate-owned media are under tremendous pressure to make profits. This distorts the news. Do you really think we're faced with an epidemic of bizarre pop singers molesting children? Or washed-up actors killing their wives? And you surely don't believe there's a rash of cute white girls disappearing in Aruba, do you? But if all you did was watch cable news, you'd think so.

To be sure, when a big story like Hurricane Katrina hits, cable news can rise to the occasion. Not to brag on the network that pays us, but CNN especially distinguished itself on that story. But without an actual big story, market forces exert enormous pressure to create one.

The Commentary Bias

Powerful forces pressure media to do more commentary and less coverage. If the president has a press conference, for example, every network has the same feed. But as soon as it ends, the real competition begins. If you want to see what Tim Russert thought of the president's performance, you've got to tune to NBC; for Stephanopoulos, ABC. Of course, if you want to see James put a garbage can on his head, you're pretty much limited to CNN. We love doing commentary, and we think it has an important place in the news business. But that's all we do on CNN; we don't cover stories, we just comment on them. For most journalists, the swinging door between those two functions—coverage and commentary—spins with stunning speed. No one should confuse commentators like us with reporters. But by the same token, reporters shouldn't be used as commentators.

The Strategy Bias

In his classic book *Out of Order,* Tom Patterson of Harvard argues that press coverage of campaigns has degenerated into a single question: "How are you going to win?" That's all the media want to know. Voters, on the other hand, don't much care about strategy. They care about substance. The question that's on their mind is "What will you do for me?" Patterson says reporters are trapped in a "game schema" in which every move is analyzed for its strategic import. Having spent a number of years both as campaign strategists and as media analysts, we find Patterson's description apt. When George W. Bush was first beginning his run for president in 1999, his spokeswoman, Karen Hughes, appeared on a cable show Paul was hosting on MSNBC. The producers told Paul to make some news—ask Hughes why she'd fired press aide David Beckwith; ask her how Bush would compete against Steve Forbes's big money; ask her whether Gary Bauer would capture Christian conservatives, or if John McCain would win among veterans. Paul asked Karen whether Bush would sign or veto an increase in the minimum wage. Karen dodged, showing viewers the Texas governor had not yet thought through the issue. Had Paul asked the questions about strategy, Hughes, a talented strategist, would have been more than prepared to answer them. But voters don't care about strategy. We've never met a single voter who said, "I like Candidate A on the issues, but B has a better strategy, so I'm going to vote for him."

The Scandal Bias

Bill Clinton began the 1992 campaign with a series of four ninety-minute policy addresses at Georgetown University. Although he gave them a stone's throw from the Beltway media, precious few deigned to cover them. (Those who did, including Joe Klein, E. J. Dionne, Jr., and Ron Brownstein, wound up with a much deeper sense of who Clinton was and what he stood for than did the latecomers.) But a few weeks later, when a woman called a press conference at the Plaza Hotel to allege that she'd had a twelve-year affair with the Arkansas governor, it was the biggest story on earth. Throughout the Clinton years, Republicans were ruthless about exploiting the media's scandal bias. During the Bush years, the Democrats have been toothless. We're not advocating that Democrats dig into Bush's (or anyone else's) private life. Rather, we're angry that, when they had control of the Senate, Democrats essentially turned a blind eye to allegations of cronyism and corruption—from Enron to the secretive energy task force to allegations that Halliburton had done business in Iran and Iraq while Dick Cheney was its CEO. And even after losing the power to call hearings and conduct investigations, too many Democrats were too passive in the face of scandals that Republicans would have forced onto page one.

The Conflict Bias

Journalists like a good fight. Nobody understood that better than Newt Gingrich. He threw bombs and hurled charges—and brought his party into power in the House for the first time in forty years. Too many Washington Democrats are congenitally incapable of picking a principled fight. They expect the media to do it for them. But (see "The Balance Bias," above) journalists would rather cover a fight than actually fight.

When Democrats, led by the steely new duo of Harry Reid in the Senate and Nancy Pelosi in the House, fought President Bush on his plan to privatize Social Security, they got plenty of coverage. And they won. Despite having only a minority of the votes in both the House and the Senate, Reid and Pelosi won a fight against a powerful president and strong majorities of Republicans in both chambers. They won in large measure because the American people were on their side. The American people were on their side because they'd been informed of the fight by the press. And the press covered the story because the Democrats gave them a fight to cover.

The Conservative Economic Bias

Next time someone tells you the press is liberal, you tell them no, the media are conservative. And we can prove it. Our own experience tells us that the media are in fact more liberal than most Americans on social issues. They're overwhelmingly pro-choice, pro–gun control, and pro–gay rights, for example. Conservative critics who attack these biases have a valid point—though, inexplicably, Bernard Goldberg, in his book, *Bias,* never alleges a pro-choice bias by the media. Perhaps that's because Goldberg himself is pro-choice. But on economic issues—meat-and-potatoes kitchen-table issues that affect a lot more people's lives than most social issues—journalists are markedly more conservative than most Americans.

A study conducted by Professor David Croteau of Virginia Commonwealth University for Fairness and Accuracy in Reporting (a progressive media watchdog) contrasted the views of Washington journalists with the general public. Turns out that journalists are what FDR called "economic royalists." Journalists are, for example, much less bothered by concentrations of corporate power than most Americans, and much less likely to support national health care than their fellow citizens.

The Croteau study found that, compared with most Americans, journalists were much less supportive of President Clinton's 1993 tax increase on the rich, much more supportive of NAFTA and "fast track" trade promotion, and much more supportive of cutting spending on entitlements like Social Security and Medicare. It stands to reason. Only 5 percent of journalists in the Croteau study reported incomes below $50,000 a year; most reported incomes over $100,000.[56]

The media's economically conservative consensus affects coverage in important ways. When Al Gore, whose southern populism was bred in the bone by his southern populist daddy, campaigned for "the people, not the powerful," the media elite universally declared him to be a phony—and, worse, a traitor to his fellow Beltway elites. But when George W. Bush—a true son of privilege, heir to a great fortune, legacy admittee to Yale and Harvard—posed as a rancher (on a piece of land he bought just before running for president), the press bought it. We've both spent a fair amount of time in the country, so believe us: If George W. Bush is a rancher, we're a pair of Hassidic diamond merchants.

Why this raw hostility to a message of economic populism? Because media elites are well off, and because, according to Croteau's study, they deeply disagree with attacks on entrenched economic power.

So, yes, Virginia, there is a liberal media—on sideshow issues of social policy. But on the bread-and-butter economic issues that truly drive this country—and on the coverage of politicians who dare to challenge the economic elite—there is a provable conservative bias. Somewhere, Spiro Agnew is smiling. The "nattering nabobs of negativism" have become the crooners of corporate conservatism.

In sum, we believe Democrats can take back allegations of media bias and correct the constant, grinding rightward tilt in the media. But to do that, we'll have to be more clear-eyed, more disciplined, more aggressive, and a whole hell of a lot tougher.

The Meeting

If you read our book *Buck Up, Suck Up . . . and Come Back When You Foul Up,* you know we hate meetings. We believe in the old saw "Those who can, do. Those who can't, meet." Well, we can't meet. Or rather, we can't stand to meet. Still, if you've spent decades in Democratic politics, you've spent years in meetings. We decided to boil them all down to one meeting—sort of like a reduction sauce. What follows are actual quotes from actual Democrats in actual meetings. Each quote illustrates something that's wrong with the Democratic Party.

The senior leadership of a Democratic campaign is gathered around a conference table in what was once a nice conference room. But time and the campaign have taken their toll. Still on the table from last night's meeting are a couple of half-full (recycled) paper cups of coagulating Starbucks mocha decaf whipped soy latte (with cinnamon). Around the table, some are in Phish T-shirts, others in Hermès scarves (with pizza stains). The men are unshaven. So are the women. BlackBerries and Treos at the ready, people settle in.

The CAMPAIGN MANAGER calls the meeting to order.

CANDIDATE'S SPOUSE: I'm sick of us being kicked around by the Republicans. Why don't *we* attack *them*?

CAMPAIGN MANAGER: Because swing voters hate negative campaigning. We just got a focus-group report back from Dayton, Ohio, and swing voters in swing states hate negative campaigning. So from now on, no attacks on the Republicans.

CANDIDATE: But they're killing me on taxes. We've got to say something about taxes.

POLLSTER: No. We're thirty points behind on taxes. Don't talk about taxes. Talk about health care and the Patients' Bill of Rights. We're thirty points ahead on the Patients' Bill of Rights. Or housing; we're way up on housing.

SPEECHWRITER: But don't say "housing." Say "homeownership." A house is a building; a home is a place. A house is made of bricks and beams, but a home is made of hopes and dreams. [He's interrupted by Carville throwing an organically grown, whole-grain, low-fat, gluten-free blueberry muffin—with berries picked by union farm workers—at his head.]

SCHEDULER: Speaking of housing . . .

SPEECHWRITER: Homeownership.

SCHEDULER: Whatever. My in-box is overflowing with invitations, including one from the Homebuilders. We've got to sift through these invitations and decide where we're going.

SPEECHWRITER: See? They don't call themselves the "Housebuilders."

SCHEDULER: I swear to God, I'm gonna kill you.

SPEECHWRITER: I thought you didn't believe in God . . . or the death penalty.

SCHEDULER: Then I swear to whatever Higher Power you turn to, if you feel a need to recognize some sort of Supreme Being, that I'm going to kick you out of our book club. Anyway, I don't care about the Homebuilders. But I've got invitations from NARAL, from the AFL-CIO, from People for the Ethical Treatment of Animals, Citizens for Sugar-Free Cereal. We can't afford to miss any of them—especially the People in Solidarity and Sisterhood with Elephants and Donkeys. They're already PISSED.

FIELD DIRECTOR: Well, I need him in western Pennsylvania. It's the swing part of a swing state. April 20 is the first day of trout-fishing season. Let's take him fishing in western PA.

CANDIDATE: I love fishing! My father used to take me.

POLITICAL DIRECTOR: I don't know. Sounds risky to me. I don't think women will react well if he's seen fishing. Women don't like fishing.

While this insanity is going on, PRESS SECRETARY *leans over and whispers to* COMMUNICATIONS DIRECTOR.

PRESS SECRETARY: Did you see The Note? We killed 'em in The Note this morning.

COMMUNICATIONS DIRECTOR: And we definitely won in The Hotline.

CANDIDATE'S SPOUSE: I don't care about fishing, and I don't think most women do. What I want to know is, what's our position on Social Security? My cousin in San Antonio says that's all she hears about in the hair salon where she works. Why don't we do a major speech on Social Security in San Antonio?

FIELD DIRECTOR: Social Security may be a big issue. But not in San Antonio. There are no old people in San Antonio.

CANDIDATE: You're all missing the point. We need a message. Here's what I want to run on. I'm for rising incomes in a growing economy. I'm for good jobs at good wages. I'm for a clean environment and making health care a right, not a privilege. I'm for the middle class, for a strong national defense, and I'll always protect Social Security. And most of all, I believe that children are our future. We must teach them well and let them lead the way.

POLLSTER: I've heard you say that before, so I tested it. It polls off the charts.

CANDIDATE'S DAUGHTER: But isn't that because it's just a bunch of platitudes? Don't we actually have to be against something? Don't we have to draw a contrast between our vision and the Republican vision?

CANDIDATE: But why should I divide people? I'm pro-environment and pro-growth. I'm pro-labor and pro-business. I'm pro-choice and pro-life; pro-police and pro-victim; pro-teacher and pro-accountability; pro—

CANDIDATE'S DAUGHTER *(muttering)*: Yeah, and I'm pro-football.

CANDIDATE'S WIFE: Very funny. But all that pro-this and pro-that doesn't give us an answer when the Republicans attack us. (*To* CANDIDATE) They're saying you coddled murderers when you were a prosecutor. How can they get away with that? You were so tough as a prosecutor you made Attila the Hun look like Richard Simmons!

CAMPAIGN MANAGER: May I answer that? Look, I know this upsets you, but you have to calm down. The attacks on your husband's record as a prosecutor are coming from a small right-wing independent group with a small ad campaign on cable TV. We must not dignify those attacks with a response.

VOLUNTEER COORDINATOR: I agree. The volunteers aren't talking about those attacks. You know what they're talking about—and what I, for one, think we ought to be talking about in this campaign? Historic preservation. The Republicans have a terrible record on that, and you, Senator, you cosponsored the Hickenlooper Amendment to provide deductibility for preserving historic buildings.

CANDIDATE: I did?

SPEECHWRITER: Well, we've got a big speech coming up at the National Association of Counties. Want to do historic preservation there?

CANDIDATE: No. I know county government. Man, that's where the rubber really meets the road, the county. Trust me on this. Those folks want to hear about sewers. I've funded more sewers for more local governments than anyone. Sewers. I'm telling you, the county folks care about sewers.

FUND-RAISING DIRECTOR: I don't care what you say to the county officials. But at some point, we'd better start to rehabilitate our party in the business community. My cousin represents the pharmaceutical industry, and she says there are more Democrats there than you'd think. You should definitely meet with the pharma folks and see what you can offer them. I'll tell you this: We have to stop demonizing the business community.

FIELD DIRECTOR: Screw the business community. What kind of a community are you talking about, anyway? A community is a group of people who care about each other and help each other. Why don't we cater to our own community?

We need to focus our time, money, and attention on our field organization. If we out-organize the Republicans, we can win. I don't know why you're spending all your time on "message" and "scheduling" and all. I just think we ought to get out there and knock on doors. Organize, organize, organize.

CANDIDATE'S COLLEGE ROOMMATE: She's right. We ought to return to our roots. And the best way to do that is to first fire all the consultants. They're just a bunch of greedy, self-interested hired guns. Fire 'em all.

COMMUNICATIONS DIRECTOR: Well, before we fire them, can someone please just tell me what our message is? The Republicans have a clear message. They're strong and we're weak; they're for lower taxes and we're for higher taxes; they're for less government and we're for more government; they're for family values and we're against them. What's our message?

CAMPAIGN MANAGER: Look, we have a textured, layered, complex message. It's not simple; that's for the Republicans. We have a more nuanced worldview.

I think we should take a vote to determine our message.

At this point, the meeting breaks up. James has left the room, weeping piteously and repeating, "We're gonna lose! We're gonna lose!" Paul is staring out the plate-glass window, thinking, "If I run full speed into that window right now, would I crash through it and plunge to a quick death ten stories below, or would I just bounce off, break my nose, and still be in this meeting?"

The Meeting, Dissected

Okay. Let's go over a few of the things said in that meeting, and take a hard look at how they reflect some of the fundamental problems facing the Democratic Party. Think of it as seventh-grade biology, when you cut that frog open. It was messy and smelly and gross, but it taught you something. Let's sharpen our scalpels.

When CAMPAIGN MANAGER said **"swing voters hate negative campaigning,"** she was like many Democratic strategists, relying too heavily on focus groups. Focus groups are a collection of strangers gathered in a meeting room at a suburban mall. They're asked questions, knowing they're being videotaped and observed through a one-way mirror. Focus groups sometimes produce interesting insights; we've used them. But too many Democrats take them too literally. The people in Dayton really did say they hate negative campaigning. The people in Dayton were lying. They said that because that's what decent people say, especially around strangers who are recording them. Ask 'em about negative campaigning, they'll say they hate it. But they devour negative ads and regurgitate the attacks—invariably citing the newspapers, not negative ads, as the source. As a reality check, in addition to asking them how they feel about negative ads, ask them what magazines they read. They'll all say *The New Yorker* or *National Geographic*. But somebody's buying *Playboy* and *People*. They just don't admit it in polite company. We actually once saw a Democratic media consultant jump up and down when a focus group approved of his ad by a 6 to 5 vote, and voted against his rival's ad by 5 to 6. You'd have thought he'd just pitched a no-hitter in the World Series. In truth, it was meaningless, certainly not anything you could base a decision on.

POLLSTER says, **"We're thirty points behind on taxes. Don't talk about taxes."** He fails to comprehend the transformational power of leadership. Just because you're behind on an issue today does not mean that you'll remain behind on it if you talk about it. When Bill Clinton met with us in 1991, he noted that Democrats were thirty points behind on welfare—welfare had been a stone winner for Republicans for decades. So he said, "Boys, they're killing us on welfare. We'd better talk about welfare." The first ad we ran in the 1992 race was about welfare reform. Same with George W. Bush. In 1998, when he first thought about running for president, one of the things he noted to close advisers was that Republicans were way behind Democrats on the issue of education. So he vowed to talk about education until he'd closed the gap on an issue that Democrats had been winning on for decades.

SPEECHWRITER is guilty of being way too literal when he says, **"Don't say 'housing.' Say 'homeownership.' "** Sure, "homeownership" may be more evocative, more poetic. But that kind of micro-editing in the absence of an overall message is not merely missing the forest for the trees, it's missing the tree for the veins in the leaf. This is a bigger problem for Democrats than for Republicans. Seems like every Democratic candidate still wants to sound like JFK. But rather than conveying the strength and certainty of JFK, they lamely try to mimic his rhetorical aerials. This, combined with excessive reliance on polling and focus groups, makes Democrats sound phony, scripted, and insincere. We've always marveled at how President Bush has made his inability to speak simple English into an asset, and we think it's because he instinctively knows how to contrast his incoherent ramblings with the Democrats' cautious, poll-tested nostrums. His subtle message (subliminable, really) is this: "I must be telling the truth. I'm too inarticulate to lie." Democrats should speak in simpler, clearer sentences.

We therefore empathize with SCHEDULER'S desire to kill SPEECH-WRITER, but he's dead wrong in thinking of the schedule as nothing more than sifting through invitations and responding. He's too reactive when he says, **"We've got to sift through these invitations and decide where we're going."** Democrats should be pro-active. Rather than responding to requests from interest groups, Democrats have to decide what it is they stand for. Also, rather than pandering to interest groups, Democrats should try a little counterscheduling. Hillary Clinton showed a ton of guts (and a ton of smarts) when she went to a conference of pro-choice activists and said there are too many abortions in America, and we should work with pro-lifers to reduce the number of abortions. That's being proactive, not reactive. Trouble is, Democrats are too dominated by pressure groups. To be sure, the Republicans have their special interests—hell, they're a wholly owned subsidiary of every dirtbag corporate criminal in America. But they do their whoring behind closed doors. Democrats grovel to every interest group they can find in public. How many times did George W. Bush appear in public before the National Rifle Association? Exactly zero. But the NRA knew he was their guy—and they threw their support to him without humiliating him in front of voters who may not be as pro-gun as they are.

The tyranny of political correctness continues, as POLITICAL DIRECTOR says, **"I don't think women will react well if he's seen fishing."** Don't forget, all these comments are real. Someone actually suggested in 1992 that Bill Clinton shouldn't go fishing in western Pennsylvania because women might not like it. We've always viewed the notion of "women's issues" as stupid and patronizing. Women's issues are jobs and health care and retirement and security. Why is breast cancer a women's issue? Men care just as much; they have wives and mothers and sisters and daughters they love. But POLITICAL

DIRECTOR thinks women worry about fish. Would it be okay, we wonder, if CANDIDATE caught only male fish?

Both PRESS SECRETARY and COMMUNICATIONS DIRECTOR have fallen into a common trap when they talk about winning in The Note or The Hotline. They're running the campaign to impress and please the gang of five hundred: the elite journalists and talking heads in Washington and New York. For these elites, The Note—edited by ABC News political director Mark Halperin—and The Hotline, edited by *The National Journal*'s Chuck Todd—are the Bible. Like any insider's dope sheet, they're fun and gossipy and smart. You can't do without them. We love them. But they shouldn't be the focus of the campaign. We bet Steven Spielberg reads *Variety* every day; it's indispensable. But he makes his movies for the multiplexes in the malls. One of the great strengths of the Bush campaign was that its leaders, from the president on down, truly did not give a rat's patootie what the elite press thought. They ran their campaign for the 99.99 percent of Americans who've never even heard of The Note. And they won.

We know you're doubting us when we say this, but yes, we were actually once in a meeting where someone said, **"Social Security may be a big issue. But not in San Antonio. There are no old people in San Antonio."** Too many Democrats rely on urban myths, old wives' tales, and folk wisdom rather than facts. So nonsense like this gets handed down for generations. By the way, we looked it up, and it turns out that San Antonio has a larger percentage of old people than the average city, because so many military families that pass through San Antonio wind up retiring there. More important, even if there were no old people in San Antonio, there are TV cameras there, and old people watch TV. It seems odd, but even a half century into the television age, too many Democratic candidates think they have to speak to the audience in the room, rather than to a broader audience. Yet another reason why voters think we pander to narrow interests rather than appealing to the national interest.

We can't tell you how many Democratic candidates have wanted to run on pablum like "good jobs at good wages." And yes, we even had a client who once said, **"I'm pro-environment and pro-growth. I'm pro-labor and pro-business. I'm pro-choice and pro-life; pro-police and pro-victim; pro-teacher and pro-accountability."** One of the biggest problems Democrats have is an unwillingness to draw distinctions. We want to be all things to all people, so we wind up being nothing to anyone. Rather than pleasing everyone, we piss off everyone. In the words of one of Al Gore's top advisers, "We actually convinced people that the principled positions we took on issues were nothing but crass political calculations." It's far better to have a message that polls at 55 percent but is credible than it is to have one that polls at 75 percent but isn't.

You know we didn't make up the quote from CAMPAIGN MANAGER: **"We must not dignify those attacks with a response."** It's been the epitaph of many a Democratic campaign. From Michael Dukakis and Willie Horton to John Kerry and the outrageous lies they told about his war record, Democrats perennially presume that no one will believe attacks on them. But voters can't process information they're not given. Even more important, Democrats shouldn't base their campaign on rapid *response*. How 'bout rapid ATTACK? General George Patton said, "No bastard ever won a war by dying for his country. He won it by making the other poor dumb bastard die for his country." Of course Democrats should answer the Republicans' attacks. And we should make the Republicans respond to some of our attacks. It's hard for your opponent to say bad things about you when your fist is in his mouth.

VOLUNTEER COORDINATOR has his heart in the right place, but his head is up his ass when he says the CANDIDATE should talk about **historic preservation.** Democrats' most common problem is not that we're seen as too liberal. It's that we're seen as too elite, too effete. We seem out of touch with the real problems of real people. And when we talk about elite issues like arts funding, public television, and historic preservation, we send precisely the wrong message. The notion that we lose NASCAR fans drives us crazy. Those are our people. Our ideas, our policies, our programs are what sustains middle-class life in America. And yet Democrats' intellectual and cultural elitism repels them.

We actually did have a client who said, **"Sewers. I'm telling you, the county folks care about sewers."** There's a reason voters think the Democratic Party is a collection of politicians who pander to a collection of interest groups; it's because we are. Or at least we are too often. Rather than sucking up to the most narrow interest of the audience, the CANDIDATE should be thinking about the message he wants to convey. Rather than viewing voters as members of special-interest groups, Democrats need to see voters as people. The voter we speak to as, say, a teacher, is also an Episcopalian, and a gun owner, and an environmentalist. And gay. Democrats have to stop treating folks as unidimensional automatons, and treat them like the complex, contradictory individuals they are.

Too many Democrats are wanna-be Republicans. That's what FUND-RAISING DIRECTOR sounds like when she says they should **suck up to the pharmaceutical lobby.** Do Republicans sit around in meetings pining about their lack of support among left-wing activists? We doubt it. So why do Democrats whine about their lack of support among the most Republican business groups? We're not advocating that Democrats abandon business; indeed, President Clinton had plenty of support among businesspeople. But the way to earn that support is by appealing to those businesspeople who understand that the best way for them to get rich(er) is to have a growing economy—and economic growth depends on a growing middle class. In other words, make the case for Democratic economic policies to the business community the same way you would to anyone else. And if they don't like it, if they think they'd be better off with special privileges for a few than with a growing economy for everyone, that's okay. That's why God made the Republican Party.

FIELD DIRECTOR gives voice to a perennial gripe—that **Democratic campaigns don't put enough emphasis on field organizing.** We strongly agree that the party needs to return to its grass roots. And we think it's great that Chairman Howard Dean has emphasized organizing voters and energizing people in neighborhoods and communities. Our problem is this: What are you trying to organize them around? A message, that's what. The greatest organizational tool ever conceived by the mind of humanity is a message. Running around a neighborhood, knocking on doors, is just going to annoy people—unless you have something interesting, relevant, salient, and credible to tell them when they open the door. Organizing people without first deciding what you stand for is like gassing up the car and gunning the engine on an iced-over parking lot. You make a lot of noise, generate a lot of motion, but don't get anywhere.

We have a lot less sympathy for the elitist nonsense a candidate's roommate spouts about **firing all the consultants.** As political consultants, we've been hearing this crap all of our careers. The folks who say it remind us of the stuffy old windbags at the country clubs who say, "Sport [they always call it "sport," as if they were upper-class British twits] was more pure when it was entirely amateur." Yeah, and it also was the exclusive playground of the mon-eyed elite. Professionalizing sports has certainly had its downside, but the quality of athletes today is immeasurably superior to the days of *Chariots of Fire*. Same thing with political consulting. Back in the old days, campaigns were managed by, say, the candidate's brother, which is fine if your brother is Bobby Kennedy. But most people don't have a brother who's a political ge-nius. No one pines for the days of amateur attorneys or amateur doctors. No one decries the professionalization of air traffic controllers. And have you ever noticed that the people who most commonly lament political pros are bigshot journalists and lobbyists—people who make a handsome living off politicians; people who think they should control the country's agenda and manipulate politicians for their own ends. The same idiots who decry the "win at all costs" mentality among political consultants scream for the head of the Redskins head coach every time he loses a game. We have a name for campaign managers who don't put winning ahead of other considerations (except, of course, the law and ethics): losers. And the Democratic Party is al-ready fully stocked with losers, thank you very much.

While the notion that Democrats shouldn't run professional campaigns is annoying but quaint, CAMPAIGN MANAGER'S comment—**"we have a tex-tured, layered, complex message. It's not simple; that's for the Republi-cans"**—is downright dangerous. That comment, by the way, didn't come from a first-time campaign manager for deputy water commissioner of Kokomo. It was made by the campaign manager of a Democratic nominee for president who shall remain nameless. There's no such thing as a "textured, layered, complex message." A message is brief. A message is emotional. A message tells a story. A message draws clear distinctions. Above all, a message is simple. "Love thy neighbor as thyself." That's a message—it's a religion, for crying out loud. And it's only five words. "As I would not be a slave, neither would I be a slave owner"—now, there's a message. Nothing nuanced or lay-ered or textured about that.

And finally, yes, we do know a CAMPAIGN MANAGER who once said, **"I think we should take a vote to determine our message."** Wrong. Even in a democracy, a campaign is not a democracy. Democrats are often too sensitive, too worried about offending anyone. And so we round the corners, we smooth the rough edges, we split the difference. No wonder people think we're a bunch of jelly-spined wimps. Again, look at the contrast with the Republicans. President Bush (who knows political strategy as well as any political consultant we know) put his faith in Karl Rove. And Karl doesn't take votes; he makes decisions. The strength and focus of the Bush campaign were a metaphor for how they wanted people to believe they govern—with strength and clarity and certainty. We think they're strong and wrong, but keep in mind what President Clinton said: Americans would rather you be strong and wrong than weak and right.

Taxes: The Heiress Versus the Waitress

Part of the Democratic Party died on September 23, 2004.

We know what you're thinking: What the heck happened on September 23, 2004? The usual back-and-forth on the campaign trail. More tragic news from Iraq. Raul Ibanez of the Seattle Mariners tied the American League record with six hits in a nine-inning game. All in all, just another day.[1]

So why do we choose that date as the day the music died for our beloved Democrats?

Because on September 23, 2004, Congress hurt the poorest children in America in order to help the wealthiest corporations in the world.

The bill, which cost you $146 billion, did some good things. It extended the middle-class portions of the Bush tax cut of 2001, just in time for the elections. But the bill also did a lot of bad. It gave $13 billion of your money to giant, greedy corporations in the form of tax breaks. And how did your Congress find the money for this giveaway?

By shafting the poorest, most vulnerable people in our country—poor kids. Leonard Burman of the Urban Institute estimated that more than 4 million impoverished families—with 9.2 million kids—would actually lose their child tax credit under the bill.[2] You see, the Republican Congress, in its wisdom, decided that the child tax credit should be taken away from families raising kids on the princely sum of $10,750 a year *or less.* We can't imagine how moms and dads raise their kids on $10,750 a year in the first place. Neither of us grew up rich, and trying to raise a child on $206.73 a week is unimaginable to us. Keep in mind, we're talking about *working* people here. The GOP Congress put their crosshairs squarely on people who are living the values they preach: choosing work instead of welfare, choosing to have babies rather than abortions.

So here's the deal: You're busting your butt, making less than $11,000 a year. The work is wearying, but you don't complain. There's dignity in work. It gives order and structure to your day. And despite its small size, you feel pride in every paycheck. You know you're never going to live like the folks you see on TV: people who have multimillion-dollar private ranches in Texas or exclusive mansions in Jackson Hole, Wyoming. But you take comfort in knowing you're rich in other ways. You've got kids. So you know the true meaning of the psalm that says, "Behold, children are a gift of the Lord" (Psalm 127:3). And for each child you have, the children's tax credit means you get an extra $1,000 a year to help make ends meet. That makes a huge difference. But then you pick up the paper one day—September 23, 2004, to be exact—and read that the Republican Congress is taking your children's tax credit away from you in order to pay for huge giveaways to energy companies and Caribbean rum-makers.[3] You put your head in your hands. Instead of thinking of the psalm that speaks to the joy in every parent's heart, the shortest verse in the Bible comes to mind; "Jesus wept" (John 11:35).

Here's the sad part: Democrats went along with it. The House passed the tax cut 339 to 65. And the Senate—that millionaires' club—passed it 92 to 3. To make it worse (if that were possible), two of the three senators who opposed this monstrosity were Republicans (Olympia Snowe of Maine and Lincoln Chafee of Rhode Island). Only one Democrat in the Senate, Ernest "Fritz" Hollings, had the good sense to vote against this truly evil act.[4] Sadly, Senator Hollings is now retired.

Defenders of the Democrats would note the die was cast long before the floor vote; and it was. As so often happens in Congress, the real fight was in the Conference Committee, where the differences between the House and Senate versions of legislation are worked out. Senator Blanche Lincoln of

Arkansas, a good red-state Democrat, led the fight to protect the working poor in the Conference Committee. "I am continually astounded that some members of Congress don't understand how challenging it is to raise a family in today's economy," she said. "While the cost of everything from milk to laundry detergent continues to rise, tax relief for low-income working families decreases."[5]

But Lincoln's appeal fell on deaf ears. Senators and members of the House earn $158,100 a year.[6] That's over three times the median family income of $43,4318.[7] Our best guess is that when you're making more money than three families in your district or state combined, it's kind of hard to understand the sacrifices and pain, the frustration and humiliation, the despair and despondency that goes with raising a child on less than $10,750 a year. And for some of them, their Senate salary amounts to a rounding error, so vast is their wealth. We'd like to see one senator spend one year raising even one child on $10,750 a year.

So our Congress, with the overwhelming support of Democrats, passed a tax cut that gave a little to the middle class, while giving big corporations the gold mine and giving the poor the shaft.

Paul was hosting *Crossfire* that day, and he 'bout blew a gasket. Here's how he summarized the bill:

"Well, there are some good things in the tax bill being voted on in the Senate today, principally tax cuts for the middle class. But one provision of that bill shows the true heart of the Republican Party in the age of Bush, and it's not a pretty sight.

"The bill takes away the child tax credit from 9.2 million of the very poorest children in America, while giving $13 billion in tax breaks to corporations. That's right. The rich get billions. The middle class gets a little something. It is, after all, an election year. But the poor, and I mean the poor, families making less than $10,750 a year, will actually lose some or all of their child tax credit. Sorry, you're out of the game, but thanks for playing.

"The savagery, selfishness, really sinfulness, of the Republicans hurting the most impoverished children in our country while helping huge corporations is just stunning. Friends, if this is compassionate conservatism, I guess Dick Cheney is Mr. Rogers."

Paul was only warming up. Before pundits were focusing on the "values voters" who would dominate the post-election analysis, Paul cast the issue in biblical terms: He went on to proclaim that anyone who would vote for such a "sinful" bill should go to hell. His right-wing partner and pal on *Crossfire,* Tucker Carlson, probably thought he was kidding. Maybe he didn't, but in any event, the following exchange occurred:

CARLSON: Okay, well, the sinfulness, huh? Well, thank you, Father Begala, for your— You're a holy man, and I appreciate you spreading a little of your holiness to the rest of us mere mortals.

BEGALA: It is sinful.

CARLSON: And I must say, Paul, when you get done with this gig, maybe you can apply for a job in the propaganda bureau of the North Korean government . . . because this is so stupid that it's sinful. It's a tax bill, man. Lighten up. It's not sinful.

BEGALA: No, they are screwing the poorest children in America while giving money to corporations.

CARLSON: Lighten up, Paul. Lighten up, man.

BEGALA: No.

CARLSON: You're going to have an aneurysm. Settle down, Paul.

BEGALA: That's the kind of stuff that gets you in hell.

CARLSON: You're making me worried. They're going to hell now? Going to hell now.

BEGALA: Yes, they are, for that stuff.

CARLSON: Ladies and gentlemen, the Republicans are going to hell, says Paul Begala.

BEGALA: Yes, they are. They can, as far as I'm concerned.

CARLSON: Woo! Buckle your salvation belts, baby. You're going to hell. Okay.

BEGALA: Absolutely . . .

CARLSON: Will you heal me after this show? Will you heal me after this show? Will you touch me and heal me, anoint me with oil?

BEGALA: You can mock it.

CARLSON: I am mocking it.

BEGALA: But there's no moral justification for hurting those children.

CARLSON: As long as you anoint me with oil, Paul, I'm all better. Going to hell.

BEGALA: You know what? You can mock my religion if you want, Tucker.

CARLSON: I am. I'm mocking your religion. If your religion is based on tax cuts, I'm mocking it. Going to hell, baby.

BEGALA: Jesus said suffer the children who come unto me, not suffer children, which seem to be the Republicans' point.

CARLSON: We're going to pass the plate later in the show.[8]

Set aside the fact that if a Democrat mocked a Republican for bringing his religious values into the public square, he'd be attacked for anti-religious bigotry. (Tucker himself is the least bigoted person we know, a practicing Christian and a good guy.) Focus instead on the utter lack of any defense of the legislation. Why didn't one of the smartest guys on the antigovernment right defend hammering poor kids and helping rich corporations? Because he couldn't. No one can. And yet the Republicans pushed it though anyway. The party that piously preaches family values slammed the most fragile families in America, all so they could give more of your money to big corporations and their wealthy contributors.

A few other Democrats were as outraged as Paul. The only reason Paul knew to raise the issue on *Crossfire,* for example, is that Representative Rosa DeLauro of Connecticut alerted him to the outrage. DeLauro was a tigress on the issue. She fired off a press release that mocked the Republican-chosen name of the bill and explained the outrage beautifully:

"The 'All American Tax Relief Act' raises the eligibility level for the child tax credit from $10,000 to $11,000 next year. Because household income has actually *declined* by more than $1,500 under the Bush Administration, many families whose incomes have gone down in the last four years will see their child tax credit shrink or even disappear next year, because of this bill.

"Debate over the tax legislation comes on the heels of a *Wall Street Journal* article naming 82 American corporations that have avoided federal income tax for at least one year of the last three. Under the 'All American Tax Relief Act,' U.S. corporations will see $13 billion in tax breaks.

" 'So, this is All American Tax Relief?' " asked DeLauro. "Eighty-two of our most profitable corporations pay nothing in income tax. $13 billion in tax breaks added at the last minute for businesses. And nine million children are left out in the cold? Those children are every bit as American as the rest of us."

Those kids—defenseless little children whose moms and dads make less than $11,000 a year—are not as American as big corporations. At least not in the eyes of the Republicans.

Too many Democrats—indeed, most Democrats—went along with screwing poor kids and sucking up to corporations. What the hell use is it to have a political party if you're not going to fight something like that? What the hell were the Dems waiting for, something more important? What the hell does this party stand for, anyway?

Why would Democrats go along with this? Ralph Nader might suggest it's because of corporate money polluting the Democratic Party, and there's some merit to his indictment—the money can have a corrupting influence. But we believe in the old adage a grizzled southern politician gave to a freshman: "If you can't take their money, drink their whiskey, screw their women, and then vote against 'em, you don't belong here."

We think that this cave-in had as much to do with gutlessness as it did with avarice. We sat in on meetings with top Democratic strategists in 2001 and 2002, begging them to take on the Bush tax cuts for the rich. We believed then—and now—that standing up against Bush's fiscal foolishness is not only good policy, it's good politics.

Democrats looked at the Republican advantage in polling on taxes, which is considerable, and decided not to fight on what they thought was the opponent's turf. The problem is that surrender is not often a successful strategy. In 2002, without an effective opposition on Iraq and taxes, the "Off the Table" strategy left Democrats defending civil service protections in the homeland security bill. Not exactly the most vital issue facing the republic. We lost the 2002 elections because we did not engage on the big issues, especially taxes.

How to Take Back the Tax Issue

In 1932, Franklin Roosevelt boldly declared that taxes were too low. In his acceptance address at the Democratic convention, he said corporate profits had soared under the Republicans, but that very little of that profit had been plowed into lower prices for consumers or higher wages for workers. "And, incidentally," he noted, "very little of it was taken by taxation to the beneficent Government of those years." He also spoke of a combination of fiscal responsibility and activist government.[9]

But FDR was a lifetime ago. And we all remember what happened to Walter Mondale when he said, truthfully, that we'd need to raise taxes to pay down the Republican deficit of the 1980s. It's important that we learn the right lesson about taxes. So let's take a look at the tax issue and how Democrats can win it.

As he has been so often in this book, Bill Clinton is our reference point. In his 1992 campaign, he offered a blistering indictment of Republican tax policy, telling the Democratic convention that the Republicans had "raised taxes on the people driving pickup trucks and lowered taxes on the people riding in limousines."[10] He called on voters to support him if they were "sick and tired of a tax system that's stacked against you."[11] He said he wanted "an America, yes, in which the wealthiest few, those making over $200,000 a year, are asked to pay their fair share. An America in which the rich are not soaked, but the middle class is not drowned, either. Responsibility starts at the top."[12]

Clinton's willingness to call for higher taxes on the most fortunate was not just an occasional applause line in an occasional speech. It was a central issue of his campaign. The first issue in his campaign brochure was, naturally, the economy. Under that, the first specific was this: "Bill Clinton will cut taxes for the middle class and make the rich pay their fair share."[13] Under the heading "Demanding Corporate Responsibility," Clinton wrote, "Ensure tax fairness by cracking down on foreign companies that manipulate our laws to evade taxes. Eliminate deductions for companies that ship American jobs overseas and reward outrageous executive pay."[14]

Clinton saw the tax code as an extension of America's moral code. That's why he called for dramatically expanding the earned income tax credit, a previously little-known provision created by Louisiana's cagey senator Russell Long. The EITC exempts low-wage working people from federal income taxes and provides a refundable tax credit to folks at the lowest end of the wage scale.[15] The conservative economist Milton Friedman first conceived of this as "negative income tax." The idea was that, just as wealthy people send more money to the IRS, the IRS would in turn subsidize low-wage working people—first by reducing their taxes, then, if they earned a really small income, by sending them a check.[16] When President Reagan signed an expansion of EITC, *The Wall Street Journal*'s Al Hunt called it "the most important anti-poverty measure enacted over the past decade."[17]

No wonder the EITC was Clinton's kind of tax policy. It was first and foremost rooted in values: It rewarded work; it boosted the incomes of people who choose work over welfare. And it worked. Here's how the political reporter Ron Brownstein of *The Los Angeles Times* summarizes Clinton's legacy on poverty:

"From 1993 through 2000, the poverty rate in America fell from 15.1 percent to 11.3 percent—a reduction of 25 percent, the biggest eight-year decline since the 1960s. As with income, the most vulnerable groups recorded the biggest gains. The poverty rate among blacks dropped by fully a third under Clinton; among Hispanics, the drop was just over 30 percent. For both groups, the poverty rate is now the lowest ever recorded. Poverty dropped faster for female-headed households than it did for married couples and is now, by far, at the lowest level ever recorded. Children registered the greatest gains of all. Under Clinton, poverty among children fell by nearly 30 percent, to the lowest level since 1978. During Clinton's tenure, the number of children in poverty fell by 4.1 million—compared with just 50,000 during the expansion under Ronald Reagan."[18]

Clinton made taxes a moral issue. So should we.

The Morality of the Estate Tax

Republicans say they love cutting taxes, but that's only part of the story. They actually love cutting taxes for the wealthiest Americans. Perhaps that's why they've never cut payroll taxes, the principal federal tax paid by 75 percent of working Americans. They prefer cutting taxes like the capital gains tax, which is paid by only 9.5 percent of Americans. Or the dividend tax, which is paid by a small portion of Americans. Or the income tax, which is disproportionately paid by the well off.

But the tax they love cutting the most—the tax they want to eliminate entirely—is the estate tax.

The estate tax has a long and rich (yes, the pun was intended) history. It was signed into law by the first Republican president, Abraham Lincoln. As one examination of the history of taxes notes, the inheritance tax "passed Congress with little debate because of the widespread demand in the North for sacrifice, especially from the wealthy." [19] (Lincoln also signed a progressive income tax, which taxed only the top tier of earners.)

If you were to tell schoolchildren these days that once there was a Republican who believed rich people should help pay for the wars fought principally by working people, they might not believe you. But Lincoln was not the only Republican president who had such dangerous ideas. Theodore Roosevelt, citing Lincoln as his role model, declared that there was a distinction between money earned from work and money received from inheritance or investment. In his classic "New Nationalism" speech, TR drew the distinction this way:

"No man should receive a dollar unless that dollar has been fairly earned. Every dollar received should represent a dollar's worth of service rendered—not gambling in stocks, but service rendered. The really big fortune, the swollen fortune, by the mere fact of its size acquires qualities which differentiate it in kind as well as in degree from what is possessed by men of relatively small means. Therefore, I believe in a graduated income tax on big fortunes, and in another tax which is far more easily collected and far more effective—a graduated inheritance tax on big fortunes, properly safeguarded against evasion and increasing rapidly in amount with the size of the estate." [20]

In calling for these taxes, TR rooted himself squarely in the tradition of Lincoln, quoting with approval from the Great Emancipator: "Labor is prior to, and independent of, capital. Capital is only the fruit of labor, and could never have existed if labor had not first existed. Labor is the superior of capital, and deserves much the higher consideration." [21]

Roosevelt then noted wryly, "If that remark was original with me, I should be even more strongly denounced as a Communist agitator than I shall be anyhow. It is Lincoln's. I am only quoting it." [22]

Sadly, there's little chance of a twenty-first-century Republican following in the footsteps of the greatest Republicans of the nineteenth and twentieth centuries. So Democrats should. Sure, Lincoln and TR are carved into Mount Rushmore. But they got there by being canny politicians. They didn't call for envy; they didn't call for punishing success or restricting initiative. But they did not shy away from appealing to patriotism and morality in insisting that the rich should pay a greater share of the nation's bills.

From Abe Lincoln to Paris Hilton

Today's Republicans have precisely the opposite view. That's why they've made a crusade of abolishing the tax Lincoln created: the estate tax. In 2004 over 99 percent of all American families were exempt from the estate tax. That means (bear with us here, we weren't exactly Rhodes Scholars) fewer than 1 percent of American families were subject to the estate tax. [23] They were, obviously, the wealthiest 1 percent of Americans. We're not talking about a lot of people here. In fact, the IRS estimated that half of the revenue generated by the estate tax was paid by just 2,900 hyper-wealthy families. [24] Where we grew up, that's not even an impressive turnout for a junior high school football game. But these folks have a lot more juice than your average guy in the bleachers. This is definitely the skybox crowd.

There may not be many people paying the estate tax, but they do pay a lot of money: $1 trillion over ten years. [25] A trillion dollars. That's money our country needs these days—to pay down the deficit, to pay back the Chinese central bankers who are financing our debt. Or we could use it to pay for armor for our troops, classrooms for our kids, inspectors for the border, rangers for the national parks, limo drivers for bigshot Republican politicians in Washington. But, despite fighting a war in Afghanistan, a war in Iraq, and a war against terrorism, the Republicans declared war on the estate tax.

All to help Paris Hilton.

The gifted writer and political observer E. J. Dionne, Jr., dubbed the effort to repeal the estate tax "the Paris Hilton Tax Cut." It's a brilliant image. Paris Hilton is the perfect embodiment of everything modern Republicans stand for. She became famous for a sex tape that Rebecca Traister of *Salon* magazine called "a poor-quality home video of two narcissist strivers dying to get noticed by the world." Traister said the video should have been called "When C-Listers Copulate."

But perhaps Ms. Traister was being too rough on young Paris. After all, no one should be judged on her worst moment—especially not for her sexual transgressions. We're not Ken Starr.

Not surprisingly, the Hilton family donates a lot of money to Republicans.[26] And why shouldn't they? The Republicans believe that Paris Hilton has a right to sit on her bony little tush, inherit a vast fortune, and pay not one dime in taxes on that fortune. Contrast that with the waitress who brings Hilton her double mocha skim decaf latte. That waitress can't even afford to stay in a Hilton, much less live like one. She makes, say, $25,000 a year, and she pays taxes on every penny of it. She pays state taxes, local taxes, property taxes, sales taxes, excise taxes, gas taxes; she pays Social Security tax, Medicare tax, and income tax out of every paycheck she earns. And that's the key word: "earns." In the Republicans' America, Hilton stands to inherit a vast fortune and won't have to pay a nickel in taxes.

The Republicans' vision is one that rewards wealth and punishes work. It holds waitresses in contempt and puts heiresses above the law, or at least beyond the reach of the taxman. Their vision also imperils America's long-term fiscal security—and your retirement security. As Dionne notes, if you kept the estate tax for just 1 percent of estates, it would raise enough money to pay for one fourth of the projected shortfall in Social Security.[27]

Who Would Jesus Tax?

Some of our friends like to wear bracelets that say WWJD, short for "What would Jesus do?" Al Gore has said it's a question he frequently asks himself.[28]

The idea is to have a constant reminder that a Christian's every action should be judged against the standard of Jesus Himself.

Alabama governor Bob Riley is no liberal. A conservative Republican, when he was in the Congress, he was one of the right-wingers who disgraced himself by voting for Bill Clinton's impeachment—even for the articles that failed to pass the Republican House.[29]

In 1992, Riley was elected governor of Alabama. A Sunday-school teacher and chairman of the board of trustees of the First Baptist Church of Ashland, Alabama, Riley seemed to take WWJD seriously.[30] Alabama Republicans thought it was just great when he told the Alabama Christian Coalition, "If we are going to save this country, if we are going to reestablish that belief in God, it's up to us. If we don't do it, who will?"[31] Riley's fellow Christian conservatives no doubt liked it when he compared the war in Iraq to the spiritual war he sees being waged in America: "There is another war going on in this country. This one is far more insidious. It's one that you just can't go and attack. It's a war for the absolute soul of this country."[32]

But the self-described Christian right was strangely silent when Riley applied Christ's teachings to tax policy. One analysis by *The Christian Science Monitor* said that "timber companies, which own over 70 percent of Alabama land . . . pay less than 2 percent of state property taxes. Here, timberland is taxed at 95 cents an acre; in neighboring Georgia, it's $5 an acre. Alabama compensates by placing an unusual share of the tax burden on the poor."[33]

Citing Christian teachings, Riley called for a $1.2 billion tax package that would have raised taxes on wealthy Alabamians and on prosperous timber companies and other corporate interests in order to finance tax cuts for the poor.[34]

Whoa, Trigger. That's when the Alabama Christian Coalition jumped off the Riley bandwagon. John Giles, the president of the Alabama Christian Coalition, said he liked the tax-cut part of Riley's proposal, but not the tax increases on the rich. That, he said, "is a separate issue."[35]

No, it's not. It's half of the same issue. Alabama, like a lot of states, has a tax system that protects powerful interests and overtaxes poor and working-class families. It's one system—and it's designed to reward the rich and punish the poor.

Riley's plan was influenced by Alabama law professor Susan Pace Hamill, who, while on sabbatical from a divinity school, came across an article that described Alabama's tax code as among the nation's most unfair.[36] Hamill, who teaches tax law and once worked for the IRS, put on her green eyeshade and took a fresh look at Alabama's tax laws through a moral lens. She found that while the poorest people in Alabama pay about 11 percent of their income in state taxes, the wealthiest pay only about 4 percent. "There is no defense for putting a greater proportional burden on the poor," she said.[37]

Professor Hamill wrote and agitated and preached. And Governor Riley acted. Noting that a family of four pays taxes on an income as low as $4,600 a year, he proposed eliminating the income tax for every Alabama family earning less than $20,000 a year.[38] Riley, who as governor was conducting Bible studies in the Capitol where George Wallace once preyed on racial animus, said he'd learned something from studying the teachings of Jesus. "I've spent a lot of time reading the New Testament, and it has three philosophies: Love God, love each other, and take care of the least among you. It is immoral to charge somebody making $5,000 a year an income tax."[39]

That, you would think, is hard to argue with. Not for the Alabama Christian Coalition. It strongly opposed Riley's Bible-based tax reform, allying itself with powerful corporate interests and against many Alabama churches. Grover Norquist, the leader of a powerful Washington anti-tax group, took a sudden interest in Alabama tax policy, if not in theology. He vowed "to make Riley the poster child for Republicans who go bad. I want every conservative Republican elected official in the United States to watch Bob Riley lose and learn from it."[40]

Grover delivered on his threat. In a state that is 90 percent Christian, Riley's Christian tax reform was trounced.[41] Drubbed. Beaten like a borrowed mule. Like a redheaded stepchild. Pounded like a bad piece of meat. Whipped like Jim Caviezel in a Mel Gibson movie.

And what lesson should we learn from this? The lesson Norquist sought—that tax justice is a loser? Hamill says the lesson is that the religious right is more powerful than the religious left for one reason: greed. "We are all greedy," she said in a speech a few months after the tax plan went down. "That's why simple charity—soup kitchens and all that—are not enough.

We can't substitute charity for economic justice, because we are too greedy. Justice requires more from those of us with the most, and those among us with the most don't want to hear that."[42]

Alabama is overwhelmingly Christian—and overwhelmingly Republican in presidential elections. Lots of good Democrats, presumably good Christians themselves, supported Riley's effort to put their religious values into action. But lots more Republicans chose to serve mammon instead of God.

Fairer, Simpler, More Progressive

We admire Governor Riley's efforts in Alabama. But he lost in part because only 55 percent of African-American Alabamians supported his reform.[43] This despite the fact that, being disproportionately poor, African-Americans would have been much better off under Riley's plan. Perhaps black Alabamians distrusted anything that state government proposed. Perhaps Riley's record as a conservative Republican caused them to be wary. (African-American leaders had recently split with Riley over voting rights for felons.)[44] It may also be the case that in all that arguing over rich versus poor, the folks Bill Clinton used to call "the forgotten middle class" felt forgotten.

Given Riley's debacle, Democrats can't sit back and wait for the Holy Spirit to move another Republican to call for fairer, more progressive taxes. So we should.

Tax reform has long been a pet project of the Republicans. Jack Kemp, who, as a congressman, wrote the Reagan tax cuts that plunged us into years of debt and deficit, still hasn't learned his lesson. He's the Energizer Bunny of GOP tax cutters. He campaigned for vice president in 1996, saying, "We are going to scrap the whole, fatally flawed internal revenue code and replace it with a fairer, simpler, flatter system. We will end the IRS as we know it."[45]

During his reelection campaign, President Bush said that replacing the federal income tax with a national sales tax was "an interesting idea."[46] Within days of the election Bush's aides were leaking to *The Washington Post* that they were planning to "push major amendments that would shield interest, dividends and capital gains from taxation, and expand tax breaks for business investment."[47] With the deficit out of control, Bush can ill afford any of these tax breaks for the upper class. So who do you think he's going to stick with the bill? You got it.

Those same Bush aides told the *Post* they'd make up the revenue lost by liberating the idle rich from taxes on their investments by possibly "eliminating the deduction of state and local taxes on federal income tax returns and scrapping the business tax deduction for employer-provided health insurance."[48]

We've got to hand it to the Bushies. They're like a dog with a bone. After cutting income taxes, dividend taxes, capital gains taxes, corporate taxes, estate taxes (did we miss any?), all for the most fortunate people in America, their second-term agenda is to shift *more* of the tax burden onto the backs of the middle class. Their philosophy is clear. They honor, value, revere, and reward wealth. And they want to burden, punish, and penalize work.

To his great credit, John Kerry stood strong on repealing the Bush tax cuts for the rich. (Despite the fact that, it should be noted, Kerry and his wife benefit greatly from them.) But Kerry's ideas on taxes, like most Democrats', were too derivative of Bush's. Democrats say, "I'll repeal this portion of Bush's tax cuts" or "I support continuing that part of Bush's tax cuts." We believe that's thinking too small.

Democrats' alternative should be bigger and bolder. We obviously can't afford to abandon the field as we did in 2002, with our Busboy Strategy. Nor should we demonize the rich. Americans are aspirational people; we all want to get rich. Democrats should propose tax reform that makes it easier for middle-class people to become rich, and easier for poor people to live the middle-class American Dream. That means rejecting the Republican strategy of pulling the ladder of opportunity away from the middle class. In their vision, the purpose of the tax code is to keep you in your place and keep them in theirs.

So when the Republicans come with their proposal to reward wealth and punish work, Democrats should be ready. We should answer their phony call for a tax code that is "fairer, simpler, and flatter" with a call for real tax reform that makes the tax system fairer, simpler, and more progressive.

A Progressive Proposal for Fundamental Tax Reform

The Center for American Progress is the best thing that's happened to progressive politics in the twenty-first century. The center is run by John Podesta, who was President Clinton's chief of staff. Podesta is whip-thin and Chicago-tough. He practically hums with a focused and formidable intellect. From nothing he's built the Center for American Progress into one of the premier think tanks in Washington, bringing together geniuses like Bob Boorstin, who served in the White House under Clinton, the Treasury Department under Bob Rubin, and the State Department under Madeleine Albright; Sarah Wartell, who was one of President Clinton's top advisers on domestic economic issues; Mort Halperin, a national security expert under Presidents Clinton, Nixon, and Johnson; Cassandra Butts, who was an attorney with the NAACP before becoming chief policy wonk to House Democratic leader Dick Gephardt; Gene Sperling, who was President Clinton's director of the National Economic Council; P. J. Crowley, a retired air force colonel and an official with the National Security Council; and Lawrence J. Korb, who served as a top Pentagon official in the Reagan administration. Needless to say, there are a lot of smart folks doing a lot of big thinking at Podesta's think tank.

Under Podesta, the Center for American Progress has come up with what we believe is the smartest, fairest, most progressive idea on tax reform we've ever seen. We commend it to every Democrat—and every Republican—who wants America to be more prosperous and more just. Because it's tax policy, you'd think it would be impenetrable. But it's not. Its genius lies in its simplicity, and in the fact that the proposal is rooted in core American values. The center's tax-reform proposal would make our tax code fairer, simpler, and more progressive.

Fairer

"Taxes," Oliver Wendell Holmes famously said, "are the price we pay for civilized society." Those words are carved on the IRS Building in Washington.[49]

If the Bush administration were honest, they'd replace Holmes's maxim with something that more accurately reflects the Republican view of taxes:

"Taxes Are for Suckers"

Taxes in America have never been more unfair. Largely bereft of other ideas to boost the economy, Republicans have used the tax code to lavish massive favors on the wealthiest people in America, while dumping more of the tax burden on middle-class families and the poor. How? By cutting the taxes that rich people pay, while refusing to cut the kinds of taxes paid by middle-class and poor families. Take the income tax, for example. Since President Bush took office, the income tax's share of total tax receipts has dropped from 49.9 percent to just 42.6 percent.[50]

The Tax Policy Center has estimated that if the Bush tax cuts are made permanent, the amount of taxes paid by the wealthiest 1 percent would drop from 24.3 percent of all federal taxes to 22.8 percent. But for the 59 percent of Americans who are in the middle class—families earning between $22,955 and $80,903—their share of the federal tax burden under George W. Bush would actually rise, from 25.5 percent to 26.1 percent.[51]

The income tax is not the only tax Bush and the Republicans want to cut. They've also proposed eliminating the estate tax, despite the fact that only a tiny fraction of the wealthiest people in America pay it. They'd like to end all taxes on dividends and reduce taxes on capital gains—the profits gained from the sale of stocks, bonds, yachts, and polo ponies. The only thing the Republicans don't want to cut taxes on is work. They've refused to cut the payroll tax, which funds Social Security and Medicare. Three fourths of Americans who file taxes pay more in payroll taxes than they do in income tax.[52] The payroll tax is regressive. It applies to every penny of income made by someone who earns up to $90,000 a year, but then it's capped.[53] High-income Americans thus pay much less in payroll taxes, as a percentage of their income, than middle-class folks. As the Tax Policy Center has noted, someone who earns $40,000 to $50,000 a year pays 12.2 percent of his income in payroll taxes. But someone making $500,000 a year pays just 3.5 percent of his income in payroll taxes.[54]

Back in 1970, payroll taxes accounted for 23 percent of federal revenue.

Today payroll taxes account for 40 percent.[55] But there's no hue and cry from the GOP to cut the payroll tax. That's because it's the tax *you* pay. It is, in their eyes, the tax paid by suckers, chumps, fools. In other words, working people.

If you thought Republicans have never met a tax cut they didn't like, you're wrong. They've never cut the payroll tax, because their philosophy is to tax work, not wealth. They pick winners and losers: Winners are folks with huge investment portfolios, massive dividend payments, and large inherited fortunes. Oh, and don't forget corporate America (Lord knows the Republicans never do). A study in the journal *Tax Notes* revealed that eighty-two of the largest corporations in America paid no taxes at all over a three-year period. Twenty-eight of those no-tax corporations had a combined profit of $44.9 billion.[56]

We bet—and, granted, we're just guessing here—that you and two dozen of your neighbors didn't make $44.9 billion over the last three years. And if you did, we bet you didn't get away scot-free when the taxman came calling. Only in America. Actually, only *offshore* of America. In the Age of Bush, corporations have made parking profits offshore into an art form, sending profits of foreign subsidiaries of U.S. corporations up from $88 billion in 1999 to $149 billion in 2002.[57]

Democrats can take back the tax issue by attacking the unfairness of the federal tax scheme under the Republicans. We should shift the debate away from the old charge that Democrats are for higher taxes and on to the more relevant and salient debate over who pays. We should point out that, under the Republicans, on the issue of taxes, we're being treated like the guy who got divorced in that old Jerry Reed country song: "She Got the Gold Mine, I Got the Shaft."

The Center for American Progress's tax-reform proposal goes a long way toward making the tax code fairer for working people. First and most important, it proposes doing something so fair that it's downright revolutionary: treating all forms of income alike. So if your money comes from working for a living, you're taxed at the same rate as someone whose money comes from sitting on his rear end and cashing dividend checks. Everything would be taxed at the same progressive rates: wages, tips, interest, dividends, capital gains, inheritance (after first allowing any couple to bequeath $5 million tax-free, which would exempt small businesses and family farms from any inheritance tax at all). Income is income, whatever its source. It's only fair.

Second, CAP's plan would abolish the payroll tax for working people, while maintaining the part of the payroll tax paid by employers. And employers would pay their share of the payroll tax on every penny of wages they pay, rather than capping it at $90,000 per year. This would make the payroll tax less regressive.

Third, Democrats should follow CAP's lead and call for making the tax code fairer for families by making sure that folks who get married still get to keep their earned income tax credit; by expanding and increasing the child tax credit; and by extending the child tax credit to folks who make as little as $5,000 a year—thereby reversing the sinful policy of denying help to the poorest parents in America.

Keep It Simple, Stupid

The next step in taking back the tax issue is for Democrats to make the tax code simpler.

Jimmy Carter, with his clear eye for moral outrage, looked at the complexity of America's tax code in 1976 and pronounced it "a disgrace to the human race."[58] Since then the tax code has doubled in size.[59] But since Carter, our conservative friends have done a better job than we have of tapping in to Americans' moral outrage at a tax system that's stacked against them. (The conservative solution is a system that's even *more* stacked against middle-class taxpayers, but we'll get to that in a minute.)

While they talk about making the tax code simpler, Republicans have actually been moving in the opposite direction. As with so many other issues, you've got to watch what the Republicans do, not what they say, because they say one thing and do another. Since they took over the Congress in 1995, Republicans have added a whopping ten thousand pages to the tax code.[60] The reference manual for tax pros, *The Standard Federal Tax Reporter,* is over sixty thousand pages long.[61] The Bible, by contrast, is 1,340 pages.[62] In 2000 the IRS estimated that it took 6.1 billion hours for Americans to comply with the federal tax code.[63] Tax compliance costs us $200 billion a year—about 10 percent of total tax revenues.[64]

For some conservatives, the answer to the tax code's maddening complexity is to scrap the whole thing entirely. One right-wing organization, Citizens for a Sound Economy, has devoted itself to a crusade to "Scrap the Code." CSE, which is headed by former House Republican leader Dick Armey, advocates a flat tax as a solution to the complexity of the tax code. Kind of like blowing up a skyscraper because the elevator's too slow.

As Mr. Republican, Bob Dole, has noted, a flat tax would "shift the tax burden from the super rich to the middle class."[65] The flat tax would eliminate taxes on interest, dividends, capital gains, and inheritance,[66] so it would be a boon for the super-rich Dole referred to. But if you're in the middle class, it's a bad deal, because it leaves in place all the taxes middle-class folks pay— payroll taxes and sales taxes and property taxes and excise taxes—and still hits you with an income tax. Back when Armey was in Congress, he proposed a flat 20 percent tax on income. The Treasury Department estimated that would be a tax increase for every American making less than $200,000 a year—and a huge tax cut for those making more than $200,000.[67]

Knowing the flat tax's fatal flaws, but still looking for a way to shift the tax burden from wealthy people to working people, other conservatives have called for a consumption tax. Basically, a consumption tax is a sales tax. The theory behind it is that the government should tax money when it's spent, not when it's earned. Supporters argue that this would encourage people to save and invest their money, rather than spend it, since savings and investment would not be taxed and spending would be.

That's the theory. Here's the reality: Like the flat tax, a consumption tax would shift the burden of taxes—you guessed it—away from the wealthy and on to working people. And that's not just our opinion. The Bush Treasury Department examined several tax-reform proposals and concluded, in an internal report, that both the flat tax and the consumption tax would be a boon to upper-income Americans and a burden to the middle class.[68]

Democrats should want this debate. We can win it. But in order to win a battle, you've got to be willing to wage the battle. Here's how Democrats can take back the issue of simplicity in the tax code.

The Center for American Progress's tax-reform proposal would simplify the tax code from six brackets down to just three. If you made up to $25,000 a year, you'd pay 15 percent. Income between $25,000 and $120,000 a year would be taxed at a 25 percent rate, and all income over $120,000 would be taxed at a 39.6 percent rate—the same top marginal rate we had in the Clinton economy.[69]

That's a good start.

Eliminating the alternative minimum tax, or AMT, is another step toward simplification that we believe Democrats should embrace. Created to ensure that wealthy Americans couldn't use loopholes to avoid taxes, the AMT was never indexed for inflation, so while it applied to only nine thousand people in 1970, it will soon hit one out of every three taxpayers.[70] The AMT complicates the tax code while burdening and annoying middle-class taxpayers. CAP proposes we eliminate it; we agree.

CAP would further simplify the code by closing $30 billion in loopholes used by corporations and the wealthy. Closing the "Bermuda loophole" would not only simplify our tax code, it would make companies that benefit from America's free-enterprise system bear their share of the cost of keeping America free. Cracking down on other offshore tax shelters and ending corporations' ability to "defer" taxes on overseas profits would save billions more.[71]

But tax loopholes are like cockroaches in a cathouse: No matter how many you stomp on, you know there are thousands more ready to crawl in. So CAP would institutionalize the war on loopholes by creating a bipartisan commission on corporate subsidies. The commission would act much like the Base Alignment and Relocation Commission, which requires Congress to vote up or down on closing military bases. Such a commission would be a Roach Motel for corporate loopholes.

Senator Ron Wyden of Oregon—a member of the influential Senate Finance Committee—has introduced legislation that tracks much of what the Center has proposed. The Wyden bill is called the "Fair Flat Tax Act of 2005." Democrats ought to get ahead of the curve and get behind Wyden's bill.

More Progressive

In one of our many debates with him on the subject of taxation, Bob Novak said the notion that the wealthy should pay more originated with Karl Marx. Well, being public school kids from the South, we'd never studied Marx. Groucho, yes; Karl, no. But we knew the notion that people who have the most should do the most predates Marx by about two thousand years. We noted to Novak, who is a faithful Catholic, that Jesus Himself taught, "From everyone who has been given much, much will be required; and to whom they entrusted much, of him they will ask all the more" (Luke 12:48).

It may be going too far for some to say we agree with the folks in Alabama who see progressive taxation as a religious obligation. But we certainly believe that the principle of progressivity is one worth fighting for. The Republicans plainly believe it's worth fighting against. That's why they love the flat tax, the VAT tax, the payroll tax, the sales tax—any tax that hits working people harder than the rich.

Democrats can take back the tax issue by making progressivity a matter of principle. Make Republicans explain why they think billionaire investor Warren Buffet should pay a lower rate of taxes than his secretary.[72] Sure, the Republicans will scream, "Class warfare!" Let 'em. Our answer should be to quote Buffet back to them: "If class warfare is being waged in America," he wrote to his shareholders in 2004, "my class is clearly winning."[73] It's winning in a rout. A 2005 IRS analysis revealed that the number of wealthy Americans who pay no tax at all has soared by 15 percent. Under President Bush and the Republicans, thousands of Americans who earn hundreds of thousands, even millions, of dollars pay no tax at all. None. Zip. Zilch. Nada.[74] We'll bet you can't say that.

The truth is, we have great needs in America. We have an enormous deficit and a looming, crippling debt caused largely by tax cuts, which went mostly to the rich. We owe trillions to Chinese and Japanese central bankers. Defaulting on that debt is not an option. We're America, not Argentina. Somebody's got to pay the bill. Isn't it only logical, isn't it only fair, to send the bill to the folks who ran up the tab?

Far from punishing the rich, we're protecting Americans, rich and poor, from a potential economic catastrophe. Paul Volcker, a man so deeply respected on both sides of the political aisle that he was appointed chairman of the Federal Reserve by both Jimmy Carter and Ronald Reagan, has predicted a 75 percent chance that the United States will be hit with a financial crisis in the next five years.[75] Saving America from such a crisis should be one of the top priorities of the Democratic Party. If the sort of crisis Volcker is warning of were to hit, you can rest assured that lots of rich people would lose a lot more than just their Bush tax cut. Conversely, despite paying a higher top marginal rate under President Clinton, the rich in America did quite well. Over time, rising-tide economics is best for everyone. It just requires political leaders who believe we're all in the same boat, rather than the current crop of Republicans, who seem to care only for the folks in the yachts.

If Democrats seize the tax issue and redefine it in big, broad, bold terms; call for a fundamental rewrite of the tax code to make it fairer, simpler, and more progressive; and propose paying down some of Bush's debt, putting our fiscal house in order, and ensuring that those who have the most pay the most, we can take back the tax issue.

When You've Got
Your Health . . .

When Toyota announced that it was going to build its seventh manufacturing plant in North America—a $1 billion investment—several suitors stepped up, offering tax incentives and other goodies to lure these good jobs their way. Reportedly, Alabama, Michigan, and Missouri all made bids for the factory, as did Ontario, Canada.[1]

Now, if you were just guessing where Toyota would go, you'd say they'd probably want low labor costs, so that would knock out Canada, which has much higher union participation than the United States. They'd probably want low taxes, so that would also knock out Canada, which has the highest tax rates of any of the bidders. They'd want to be as close as possible to their biggest market, so that, too, would knock out Canada. They'd probably want less big government regulation of how their plant operates; Canada has more than the U.S. You see where we're going here. In May, Toyota decided to build their new plant in Ontario, Canada.

What was Canada's big selling point? Health care. Because Canada provides health care for all of its citizens, it saves car manufacturers a huge amount of money. Today every General Motors car that rolls off the assembly line has your standard-option package built in. But also built in is something else: over $1,500 in health care costs for the folks who built the car. American automakers now spend more money on health care than they do on steel. Think about that: GM and Ford have become health care providers who happen to make cars on the side.

Health care is a jobs issue. The lack of a sensible, comprehensive system of health insurance in America costs us jobs. Our so-called health care system is a huge drag on our economy.

Most Democrats, and we're no different, believe that health care is a basic moral issue—ours is a country that should take care of the sick. It should be a cause of national shame that there are eighteen thousand unnecessary deaths among adults each year due to a lack of health insurance.[2] Health-related emergencies are the second leading cause of personal bankruptcy, and getting sick shouldn't mean going broke. But as the example of the Toyota plant shows, health care is more than just a moral issue; it's an economic issue, it's a jobs issue, and it's a competitiveness issue. For Democrats, it also should be a winning issue.

America spends more money on health than any other nation in the world. Today a full 15 percent of our economy is dedicated to health spending—$1.7 trillion a year.[3] Premiums are growing at the rate of 11 percent a year, five times faster than wages.

You'd think that for all that money, at least we were getting the best health care in the world. You'd be wrong. We currently rank thirty-seventh in overall health system effectiveness. Thirty-seventh. Can you believe that? What if we were thirty-seventh in basketball in the Olympics, losing not only to Germany and Britain but also to Slovenia and Snottsylvania? (Okay, we made up one of those countries, just to send President Bush to his atlas when he reads this.)

One of the best measures of the strength of a health care system is how we perform on the basic task of bringing infants into this world alive. In 2002 the U.S. infant mortality rate increased for the first time since 1958.[4] Today our infant mortality rate is higher than that of forty-one other nations, including South Korea, Slovenia, and all major European nations.[5]

Why aren't we doing something about it?

During the Clinton administration, Hillary Clinton tried to take on the issue of health care in a bold, comprehensive way. To make a complicated story simple, she got burned. It's time for Democrats to come back at the issue of health care in a visionary way. It's the right thing to do, it's the smart thing to do, and Republicans just ain't doing it.

The Republican Solution: Turn Your Head and Cough—or Just Turn Your Head

Republicans have spent a lot of time and energy—and made their allies spend a lot of money—making people think that there's a crisis in Social Security, even though there isn't.

At the same time, they've completely ignored the fact that there's a real crisis to be dealt with, and that's health care. In part, that stems from the Republicans' belief that helping people live healthy lives just isn't their party's business.

In one of the more telling moments way back in the 2000 campaign, George W. Bush was in South Carolina when a woman came up to him and told him about a disease her son had, and how medical insurance wasn't covering everything he needed. After hemming and hawing for a minute, he said, "I'm sorry, I wish I could wave a magic wand."[6]

What's that? Faith-based health care? The irony is that when George W. Bush got elected, he conveniently forgot that a $5.6 trillion surplus is nothing if not the political equivalent of a magic wand. Actually, he didn't forget that it was a magic wand, he just used it to perform one trick only—he magically made rich people richer while simultaneously making the surplus disappear.

And how about health care? In his time in office, George W. Bush has done nothing to increase the number of people who have access to health care, virtually nothing to bring down the cost of health care, and little to improve the quality of health care.

As a result, on his watch, five million Americans lost their health insurance from 2000 to 2003.

Now, you'll hear conservatives say a lot of stupid things about the uninsured—that they don't work, that they're largely young and healthy or older and wealthy, that they go without health insurance by choice, or that they're simply undeserving. Here are the facts: About seven million of the uninsured are poor children, and eight out of every ten uninsured people work—many of them at jobs that don't offer health benefits, or that make it difficult to get them.[7] It's not that they're too rich to need health insurance; it's that they simply can't afford it.

Some folks have the temerity to suggest that when the number of uninsured people goes up, health insurance gets cheaper, because we're taking the costs out of the system. The truth is, we all pay for the uninsured.

The other thing conservatives argue is that hospitals don't turn away people, so if you don't have insurance and you get hit by a bus, you'll get care. In one sense, they're right. Someone will call an ambulance, and it will pick you up and eventually find an emergency room that will take you in and patch you up. But don't think that's free. We all pay for it. It gets built in to the cost of our own health insurance. It gets built in to the cost of the procedures the hospital uses. It gets built in to everything. When people are uninsured, it isn't just bad for them, it's bad for all of us.

Here are the five key reasons insurance matters.

1. When you're uninsured, you don't get preventive care.

Uninsured adults are 30 percent less likely to have had a regular checkup, during which a lot of health problems can be caught early. Uninsured men are 40 percent less likely to have had a prostate exam, and uninsured women are 60 percent less likely to have had a mammogram. That means that when uninsured folks are diagnosed with diseases, it's at a later stage, when treating it costs more money but offers less hope. As a result, uninsured Americans are sicker and die earlier than those with insurance. Again, that makes health care more expensive for everybody.

2. When you don't have insurance, you put off getting the care you need until you end up in the hospital unnecessarily.

Uninsured people who know they are sick still go to the doctor less. For example: Uninsured people with heart disease go to the doctor's office 28 percent less than insured people. It's about the same for people with hypertension, diabetes, and other diseases. As a result, the rate of unnecessary hospital stays for uninsured adults has more than doubled. Over 10 percent of hospital stays for uninsured people could have been avoided if that person got treatment earlier—and those unnecessary hospitalizations cost, on average, $3,300. Again, bad for them, more expensive for all of us.

3. When you're uninsured, you're more likely to die.

As we noted before, a study by the Institute of Medicine found that every year, eighteen thousand deaths are associated with people not having health insurance. It doesn't get simpler than that.[8]

4. Medical care costs more for the uninsured than for the insured.

That's because, for starters, major insurers negotiate big discounts with hospitals and doctors. Uninsured people can't do that. The other reason is that the uninsured often have to cover big medical bills with credit cards, which can take a long time to pay off. In fact, paying for health care is the second leading cause of personal bankruptcy.[9] And when someone files for bankruptcy, those costs—you guessed it—get passed on to all of us.

5. When you're uninsured, going to the doctor means going to the emergency room.

Uninsured Americans are four times more likely to use the emergency room as a regular place of care. Uninsured children are five times more likely to do so. That makes health care more expensive for everybody. In fact, a recent study by the Kaiser Family Foundation found that hospitals provide $35 billion in uncompensated care every year.

So even if you're a cold, callous, heartless human being—that is to say, if you're a Bush Republican—you should recognize that even doing the selfish thing means doing the compassionate thing. It means making sure all Americans have access to health care.

So Republicans have been guilt-tripped into putting forward an idea for health care. Republicans are the party of one idea and one idea only—tax cuts. When the only tool you've got is a hammer, everything starts to look like a nail. So the only Republican idea on health care is to give people a tax credit so that they can go buy health care in the individual market. Sounds reasonable, right? Wrong. The individual market is the most unregulated, expensive, and discriminatory health care market we have in this country. It also has the worst benefits. Even if you get people into this market, there's no guarantee that they're going to get health care out of it.

The second problem is that providing tax credits for people to buy their own health care creates an incentive for employers to drop the health care coverage they do offer. If you give people a tax credit to pay for health care (ignoring the fact that the tax credit won't come close to covering the cost, and that to get health insurance in the individual market you basically need to prove that you've never been sick and don't plan on getting sick), businesses are going to say, "Hey, employee, now that you get this tax credit, we're going to stop providing health care, so why don't you take your tax credit and go buy health care for yourself?"

Some folks will, some folks can't, and many folks won't. Meanwhile, the government and businesses will have washed their hands of the moral obligation to provide for the health of their people. Congratulations, Republicans, only you could come up with a health care plan that could leave more people without insurance.

How to Take Back Health Care

Here's what a real solution to health care will include: not only improving our health care system but also improving the health of the American people. As with energy (see "Energy and the Environment"), there are a lot of little battles we can fight, and many of them are worth fighting. For example, the Patients' Bill of Rights is an important battle, and it's a popular one, but in the grand scheme of things, it's a little battle. We want to win the big war. Forty-five million Americans lack health insurance. Americans are becoming less healthy every year. That's the big stuff, and that's what we need to focus on.

1. Be Not Afraid

Three of the most powerful words in the Gospel are these: "Be not afraid." Too many Democrats for too long have been too afraid of the health care issue. That's understandable. As Newt Gingrich has asserted, health care is the real third rail of American politics—politicians from both the left and the right who have touched it have been burned. FDR couldn't get us to universal health care; neither could Truman. LBJ and Jimmy Carter both tried and failed. And, of course, President Clinton's most heartbreaking domestic defeat came on health care.

So we understand Democrats' trepidation. We just don't share it. We believe the time is right for Democrats to once again call for universal health insurance. First, because it's the right thing to do. Second, because it's the smart thing to do. And third, because we think it's the most politically beneficial thing to do.

We understand how difficult it is to get to universal coverage; we have the scars to prove it. But we believe it's even more damaging to Democrats that people don't think we stand for anything. The truth is, most Democrats—

nearly all Democrats, really—want America to include everyone in the health care system. So why don't we say it? People just might start to get the idea that we stand for something.

2. Make Health Care a Values Issue

Why is it that Democrats and the media lamely accept the Republicans' definition of values? Why is it that two gay guys making out in Massachusetts are a moral affront to Republicans, but two children turned away from a hospital because their parents can't afford health insurance are not?

Democrats should consistently present their commitment to health care as an issue of moral values. Every major religion teaches its followers to care for those who are less fortunate. We should not merely aim for people's heads when we talk health care. We should speak to their hearts and souls as well. If given the choice, always go for the heart. Good people make important decisions from the heart, not the head.

When Republicans attack us for being "too liberal" as we call for universal health care, we should tell 'em that means God is a liberal, too.

3. Keep It Simple

One of the reasons President Clinton's health care initiative failed is that it was just too darn complicated, though even at 3,700 pages, it was brief compared to some of the trade deals Congress passes routinely. Still, opponents were able to use the complexity of the proposal to sink it. Let's learn from that lesson. Whatever we do, let's keep it simple.

4. Build on What Works to Get Everyone Covered

One way to keep it simple is to build on what people already have, what they already know. Right now the majority of Americans get their health care from one of three places: their employers, Medicaid, or Medicare. Let's start with those systems as a foundation, then build on them.

The way we remember the difference between Medicare and Medicaid is that Medicare ends with an "e"—for "elderly." Medicaid ends with a "d"—for "destitute." Medicaid covers more than 52 million of America's most vulnerable children, low-income parents, people with disabilities, and seniors.[10] One of the problems in health care today is that there are a lot of people who make too much money to qualify for Medicaid, but they have jobs that don't provide health care and they can't afford it themselves.

Republicans are forever flapping their gums about how the private sector does everything right and the government couldn't effectively run a two-car parade. So here's our proposal for those Republicans. They can go get their health care coverage in the private-individual insurance market, and the rest of America can have the health plan they have.

See, every member of Congress gets to enroll in something called the FEHBP, the Federal Employees Health Benefit Program. With nine million federal employees and their families now getting health care through the FEHBP, it is the largest employer-sponsored group health care plan in the world. It's made up of a lot of plans (about 180) that offer all kinds of different health care packages. The government gets to say which plans participate, then negotiates prices, covered services, and other standards for care. Because health care companies want access to those nine million people, they go along with these requirements. As a result, it's a good system. Here's where the health care that America gets should truly be "good enough for government work"—we should let small businesses and individuals buy in to this program with tax credits that will make it affordable. And businesses that like the coverage they have can keep it. This isn't a new idea, but it's a damn good one.

Then we should expand Medicaid to make sure that all children and working poor get covered. Somewhere around seven million children nationally are eligible for Medicaid and the Children's Health Insurance Program but aren't enrolled. We should not *recommend* that they get enrolled, we should *require* it. And for those who aren't eligible for these programs because they make a little too much money, we should help them buy in to it. Sure, it'll cost money, but remember, our big goal is universal health care. That requires making the choices necessary to get us there.

4. Focus on Prevention

Getting everyone covered doesn't automatically translate into better health. Getting to better care means better prevention. Right now we're suffering from near-epidemics of preventable conditions like diabetes.[11] This is totally predictable, given that we spend under 2 percent of our health budget on prevention. This despite the fact that prevention is a big money-saver. If a child can get a $50 checkup that prevents her needing a $500 emergency room visit, we're out of our minds for denying it. Right now there is no national prevention agenda. We need one.

5. Bring Down Costs

When you stop and look at what is making the cost of health care increase, you see that it's really three big things: prescription drugs, doctors, and hospitals. Prescription-drug companies do a lot of good in this world; they come up with some amazing research, a lot of it underwritten by federal grants. They've reached the point, though, where they're spending more money on marketing than they do on research.

Drug companies that invest in research should be able to keep their patents until they've made back the amount they spent on research plus a reasonable profit. The problem is that drug companies are so hell-bent on keeping their patents—and preventing generic versions of the same drug from coming to market, introducing competition, and reducing price—that they've resorted to cajoling, conspiring with, and all but bribing congressmen and competitors. Senator Chuck Schumer of New York came up with a bill that would keep drug companies from gaming the patent system, and Democrats—while they were in control of the Senate—actually managed to pass it. Republicans love the concept of competition right until the moment it comes into conflict with the concept of rewarding your powerful contributors. So they blocked the bill from passing in the House.

Democrats need to be for bringing down the price of prescription drugs. This one idea will save billions of dollars each year.

We also need to reduce hospital and doctor costs. As much as one quarter of all the money America spends on health care doesn't go to health care at all; it goes to nonmedical costs like paperwork, advertising, and paying bills. No other industry in our country is this inefficient. Why aren't we—the party of change and progress—the ones championing the use of technology for something other than nudie pictures? Let's get behind the power of the Internet to bring down the cost of health care. Heck, as we saw in the chapter on "Working the Refs," the press thinks Al Gore invented the damn Internet to begin with.

One thing about health care is that nobody thinks there's such a thing as getting too much of it. Your doctor says you should have an X ray, good. An MRI? Even better. A CAT scan—great, just give me a shot of that barium. It's all good. Except that it's not. We are spending the largest amount of money in the world on our health care system, but we aren't getting the best health care results in the world. Medicine is about science, and sometimes you have to follow the science. Which means sometimes all that stuff isn't necessary. We should take all the information that we get from all the patients (keeping their privacy, of course) and really figure out what technologies are most effective; then we should use those standards for the government to do creative things like rewarding hospitals that achieve good outcomes. Researchers say that reducing unnecessary excessive health care could save Medicare alone 30 percent—that's about $70 billion.[12]

6. Improve Quality

A lot of times we hear about the really, really bad medical errors—the wrong leg gets amputated, the wrong organ gets transplanted, truly egregious stuff. What you don't often hear is that medical errors in hospitals across America are estimated to cost about ninety-eight thousand lives per year, according to a report by the Institute of Medicine. This is an arena where things like electronic medical records aren't just money-savers, they also improve quality for the silly but very real reason that it's impossible to read a doctor's handwriting. The other thing we should do is require health plans and providers to report performance data on quality and staffing levels so we can see what works best. There's the saying that when students enter medical school, they're told by the person in charge that "half of what we will teach you is wrong. Unfortunately, we don't know which half." With medical knowledge increasing so rapidly, doesn't it make sense for us to take some time and energy, and maybe even spend some money, to figure out what works so we can make it work better?

Right now the weaknesses of America's health system should make us all sick. Democrats have to be the ones showing us a way to get well.

The Flood: "Mr. Bill Was Better Informed Than Mr. Bush"

In the days after Hurricane Katrina flooded New Orleans, killing hundreds, displacing hundreds of thousands, James was in a state of absolute shock. Here he was, looking at the city where his beloved and departed mama and daddy had taken him as a child, the city that represented everything that was cosmopolitan and sophisticated and fun, the city where he was married, the city where he loved taking his children.

You can grieve for only so long before that grief becomes anger, and that anger goes in search of answers. It didn't take long for James's anger to find a target. On the morning of September 1, three days after the storm, George W. Bush, fresh from a month-long vacation, sat down with Diane Sawyer on *Good Morning America*.

Diane Sawyer asked President Bush the question on James's mind: "Given the fact that everyone anticipated a hurricane [of category] five, a possible hurricane five, hitting shore, are you satisfied with the pace at which this [help] is arriving?"

President Bush's response was "I don't think anyone anticipated the breach of the levees."

James went through the goddamn roof. The guy may have taken a month off, but his lying hadn't gotten the least bit rusty. Because everyone the president should have been listening to *did* anticipate a breach of the levees.

Bush's own federal government in 2001 designated a major hurricane hitting New Orleans as one of the three "likeliest, most catastrophic disasters facing this country."[1] Anyone in Louisiana could have told him that the levees were sinking, and that one storm hitting us just right would turn the city of New Orleans into part of the Gulf of Mexico and give everyone in a thirty-mile radius some unwanted waterfront property.

Here's what Senator Mary Landrieu had to say in March of this year, after Hurricane Ivan hit Alabama and Florida but months before that witch Katrina struck: "We could have lost a hundred thousand lives had Hurricane Ivan hit the mouth of the [Mississippi] river before it turned. . . . God has been good, but one of these days a hurricane is going to come, and . . . we're sitting ducks."[2]

Shoot, even Mr. Bill knew the levees were at risk. The clay character made famous on *Saturday Night Live* is a creation of New Orleanian Walter Williams. Williams made a public service announcement warning that, because of coastal erosion, a major storm could breach the levees and flood New Orleans. "How can it be," Senator Landrieu asked on the floor of the Senate, "that Mr. Bill was better informed than Mr. Bush?"[3]

Then, as with most of the president's lies, his advisers saw it—and raised it. White House spokesman Scott McClellan followed up by saying, "Flood control has been a priority of this administration from day one."

Now, you might say, "James and Paul can't help but politicize everything they see, and maybe we can at least forgive James for getting so hopped up on this one, because it is his home state, after all."

You don't need to take it from us, and in the next couple of pages, you won't have to. This storm was an act of God, yes. But so much of the damage it did was due to the incompetence of man. And the man we're talking about is George W. Bush.

George W. Bush has staked his presidency on saying to the American people, "You can have it all. You can have tax cuts and a war at the same time. You can drive your SUV and still enjoy low gas prices. You can rebuild cities in Iraq and levees in Louisiana."

Saying you can have it all is a big gamble, and big gambles mean you might lose big. When George W. Bush announced that we can have a war in Iraq and still invest in making Americans safer here at home, he said we could have it all. But he was actually making a choice. And if you measure things by money and manpower, he was choosing Iraq.

Here are the facts on which we base our indictment that George W. Bush is in part responsible for the devastation of a great American city.

He Outright Cut the Funds Needed to Prepare for Such a Storm

Now, was it the smartest thing in the world to build New Orleans in a sub-sea-level bowl between the Mississippi River and Lake Pontchartrain? Maybe not. Take it up with Alonso Álvarez de Pineda. He's the Spanish explorer and cartographer who was the first European to "discover" the area in 1518. By 1718 the French had decided it was a fine spot to build a city, and they named it after Philip II, the Duke of Orléans who was the regent ruling France at the time. Now, ol' Phil was a party animal. He hid copies of Rabelais's satires in his Bible and read them during Mass, and his parties are still remembered for their debauchery (kind of like the Deke House at Yale in the 1960s, come to think of it). He opposed censorship, made the Sorbonne tuition-free, and opened the Royal Library to the public. All in all, the kind of guy who would have loved New Orleans.

So for 287 years, New Orleans has been in that geologically undesirable but geographically indispensable location. Thomas Jefferson weighed the pros and cons and bought all of Louisiana—a third of the continent—in large part so he could have New Orleans and control the Mississippi.

In order to protect this strategic asset, the federal government built a system of levees to protect the city from the water. After a 1995 flood killed six people in New Orleans, President Clinton and the GOP Congress came together to create the Southeast Louisiana Urban Flood Control Project, through which the Army Corps of Engineers was to strengthen, improve, and update the levees and pumping stations that protected New Orleans.

But President Bush had other priorities. In a remarkable series of nine articles in 2004 and 2005, the New Orleans *Times-Picayune* documented how the basic responsibility to update and strengthen the levees in Louisiana was being sacrificed to pay for the war in Iraq. Here's what Walter Maestri, the emergency management chief for Jefferson Parish, Louisiana, had to say on June 8, 2004: "It appears that the money has been moved in the president's budget to handle homeland security and the war in Iraq, and I suppose that's the price we pay. Nobody locally is happy that the levees can't be finished, and we are doing everything we can to make the case that this is a security issue for us."[4]

In early 2004, as the cost of the conflict in Iraq soared, Bush proposed spending less than 20 percent of what the Army Corps of Engineers had said was needed for Lake Pontchartrain, according to a February 16, 2004, article in *New Orleans CityBusiness*:

"The $750 million Lake Pontchartrain and Vicinity Hurricane Protection project is another major Corps project, which remains about 20% incomplete due to lack of funds, said Al Naomi, project manager. That project consists of building up levees and protection for pumping stations on the east bank of the Mississippi River in Orleans, St. Bernard, St. Charles and Jefferson parishes. The Lake Pontchartrain project was slated to receive $3.9 million in the president's 2005 budget. Naomi said about $20 million is needed. 'The longer we wait without funding, the more we sink,' he said. 'I've got at least six levee construction contracts that need to be done to raise the levee protection back to where it should be [because of settling].' "[5]

For years, Louisiana's congressional delegation begged President Bush to help them shore up their state's coast. Bush gave them one sixth of what experts said what was needed.[6] One sixth. Meanwhile, Republicans were calling for the largest budget cut to New Orleans' Army Corps of Engineers funding in history.[7] As Landrieu said at the time, "I think it's extremely shortsighted. When the Corps of Engineers' budget is cut, Louisiana bleeds. These projects are literally life-and-death projects to the people of south Louisiana and they are [of] vital economic interest to the entire nation."[8]

In one of the more prescient statements made as Republicans were chopping New Orleans' ability to prepare for and respond to disasters, Terry Tullier, the New Orleans emergency preparedness director, said, "I'm all for the war effort, but every time I think about the $87 billion being spent on rebuilding Iraq, I ask: What about us? Somehow we need to make a stronger case that this is not Des Moines, Iowa, that we are so critical that if it hits the fan in New Orleans, everything this side of the Rockies will feel the economic shock waves."[9]

There is something especially galling about learning that Iraq was getting our flood control money. That country—or rather, Bush's invasion of that country—has already claimed the lives of 2,000 of our finest, bravest Americans. It has claimed the limbs and blood of 15,000 more troops. It has claimed $200 billion of our money. And now it's claimed our flood control funds?

Pardon us for stating the obvious, but *Iraq is a desert. How often does it flood?* In fairness, we looked it up. There was a terrible flood in Baghdad. Seven thousand homes in the Karkh district of Baghdad were destroyed. In 883 A.D. That would be 1,122 years ago.[10]

Put Incompetents in Charge and Cut the Ability to Respond

Once George W. Bush had successfully rendered Louisiana more vulnerable to a disaster, you'd think he would have at least made sure that his government was ready to respond to one. You'd be wrong. Now, we know that nobody likes a prophet—or maybe we're not prophets, and it's just that a blind squirrel finds an acorn every now and again—but long before Hurricane Katrina, both James and Paul predicted that putting political hacks in charge of the Federal Emergency Management Agency was a bad, bad idea.

Here's what Paul had to say about Michael Brown on *Crossfire* on September 17, 2003—almost two years before Katrina. Note especially that Bob Novak defended Brown as a "distinguished public servant."

BEGALA: Under President Clinton, the Federal [Emergency] Management Agency was run by experienced professionals. But when President Bush took office, he kicked the pros out and replaced them with his campaign manager and other political hacks. Today that agency is run by a man whose prior jobs included executive director of a lobbying group and a stint as a political staffer for the Oklahoma state senate. Disaster preparation, indeed.

Mr. Bush also, it seems, turned down a request from his own Army Corps of Engineers to replenish the corps's $60 million disaster assistance fund, which might come in handy when the hurricane strikes. It seems Mr. Bush plans for hurricanes just about as well as he planned for the occupation of Iraq.

(cheering and applause)

ROBERT NOVAK, COHOST: Paul, you once again have done an atrocious libel and smear on a distinguished public servant.

Michael Brown, who is the undersecretary of homeland security, has a distinguished record in local and state government, as did his predecessor, James Lee Witt, who was also a local politician appointed by Governor Clinton. Why can't you be straight? They're both politicians in the job.

BEGALA: That's not true. Because that's not true. James Lee Witt had four years of experience before he went to FEMA as an emergency disaster relief expert.[11]

And here's what Paul had to say on *Crossfire* on August 16, 2004, after FEMA responded sluggishly to Hurricane Charley in Florida. This time Tucker Carlson was in the unenviable position of defending political hackery.

BEGALA: Speaking about the president, the head of the Federal Emergency Management Agency today said that it could take weeks to search through all the debris and find all the victims of Hurricane Charley in Florida. Of course, one of President Bush's first moves as president was to fire James Lee Witt, the disaster relief professional who had turned FEMA from a basket case to showcase.

Mr. Witt was replaced by George W. Bush's campaign manager, Joe Allbaugh, who was in turn replaced by another political hack, Michael Brown, whose prior experience with disasters consisted of serving as a Republican staffer in the disaster of the Oklahoma legislature.

What's worse, from the very beginning of his term, Mr. Bush has sought to eliminate something called "Project Impact." Now, that was a Clinton FEMA initiative to help disaster-prone communities like Florida prepare for and reduce the damage they would inevitably suffer.

So, Floridians, help may be slow in coming from the Bush administration. Too bad political hacks can't rebuild communities.

CARLSON: I can barely even— That is so wrong in every way. This may blow your mind, Paul. But actually the president was not, in the end, responsible for Hurricane Charley. Second—

BEGALA: He is responsible for the disaster he has made of our federal government. . . . That's what the man from FEMA said . . . the political hack Bush put in charge. Just put competent people in charge.[12]

And here's what James wrote ten years ago, in his book *We're Right, They're Wrong,* about the importance of a professionally run FEMA.

Let me tell you the name of a person you will never find glorified in the media. He didn't go to the most prestigious school. You're not going to find him at a lot of Georgetown dinner parties. He doesn't get asked to editorial board meetings with major newspapers. His name even sounds a little bubba-ish. It's James Lee Witt, and he runs the Federal Emergency Management Agency, the agency that helps people when Mother Nature knocks down their door.

It wasn't too long ago that Sen. Fritz Hollings (D-SC) correctly called FEMA "the sorriest bunch of bureaucratic jackasses I've ever known." FEMA truly was one of the biggest stains on the federal government. In 1992, it turned in one of its worst performances ever when it took three days to show up to help the communities in Florida leveled by Hurricane Andrew.

Shortly after, President Clinton appointed Witt to head FEMA, and the agency has turned around completely. Over the past three years, FEMA has won universal praise for its handling of the Los Angeles earthquake, the midwestern flooding, and several southeastern hurricanes. In the words of *Washington Monthly,* the reinvention of FEMA is "the most dramatic success story of the federal government in recent years. Not only does it provide further evidence that government can work, it offers a blueprint for what it takes: strong leadership, energetic oversight, and, most importantly, a total reevaluation of its mission."

When Witt took over, the agency was still spending a ridiculous portion of its time and money preparing for a Soviet nuclear attack. Witt refocused it toward dealing with natural disasters. He also brought in quality people and cut about half of FEMA's internal regulations.

No, Mr. Witt's not much of a hero to the pontificating editorialists. But to people who just got the hell shaken out of them in an earthquake or damn near blown away in a hurricane, he's a pretty important guy.

So George Bush took an important agency and put an absolute political hack at its head. He must have had competent deputies, right? Actually, had Michael Brown been out that week (as opposed to just out of touch), things might have been even worse.

His chief of staff—the next in the line of succession at FEMA—was a guy named Patrick Rhode. Rhode's major distinction had been planning events for President Bush's campaign. He had no emergency management experience whatsoever. But maybe he's the one responsible for making sure the backdrop to President Bush's speech in New Orleans looked pretty.[13]

FEMA's deputy chief of staff, Scott Morris, had a similar dearth of emergency experience. Before he came to FEMA, Morris's work experience included a stint at Maverick Media, the advertising agency for the Bush-Cheney campaign.[14] In the interest of full disclosure, we should note that Maverick Media is run by Mark McKinnon, an old college buddy of Paul's and a good friend of James's as well. We love McKinnon (or M-Cat, as the president calls him). But we love our families on the Gulf Coast more. What are we supposed to do when the next hurricane bears down on our nieces and nephews in Texas and Louisiana—ask Morris to run a negative ad attacking the storm?

Almost unbelievably, Brooks Altshuler, FEMA's acting deputy chief of staff, also had no disaster management experience. But he is an experienced advance man for President Bush. Altschuler worked in the Office of National Advance Operations with fellow FEMA appointee Rhode.[15]

Let's be clear: We support jobs for political aides. How do you think Paul got his job at the White House? But you don't put unqualified political hacks in charge of disaster preparation and emergency response. Sure, give them a job. But that's why God made the Department of Commerce.

So now that the waters have receded and the damage is done, it's time for a clear look at what went wrong.

The Katrina Time Line: A Disaster

We're big fans of the old detective show *Dragnet*. We always loved it when Sergeant Joe Friday would give his best deadpan expression to a loquacious witness and say, "Just the facts, ma'am." So here are the facts. Here's what happened during those terrible and tragic days and what Bush and his unqualified political hacks did—and failed to do.

Friday, August 26, 2005

Bush Vacations at His Ranch in Crawford. "No public events are scheduled." [16]

Louisiana Governor Blanco Declares a State of Emergency. While President Bush enjoys his vacation, Governor Kathleen Blanco of Louisiana is already working to protect her state. With Katrina brewing in the Gulf, Blanco declares a state of emergency.

Saturday, August 27, 2005

Bush Radio Address Mentions Iraq Eight Times; Doesn't Mention Katrina Once. In his weekly radio address, President Bush says, "Our efforts in Iraq and the broader Middle East will require more time, more sacrifice, and continued resolve. Yet people across the Middle East are choosing a future of freedom and prosperity and hope. And as they take these brave steps, Americans will continue to stand with them because we know that free and demo-cratic nations are peaceful nations." [17]

Bush Declares a State of Emergency for Louisiana from Crawford. To his credit, President Bush declares a state of emergency in Louisiana, authorizing federal emergency management officials to release federal aid and coordinate disaster relief efforts. [18]

National Hurricane Center Issues Hurricane Warning: Katrina Likely to Approach the Area as a Category 4 or 5 Hurricane. "Katrina was expected to approach the area as a Category 4 storm, with winds of 145 mph, and it could build to a top-of-the-chart Category 5 storm, with winds of 155 mph or higher, National Hurricane Center Director Max Mayfield said Saturday afternoon. . . . The forecast projected the storm sweeping directly over the city. The Hurricane Center posted a hurricane warning from Morgan City to the Alabama-Florida line." [19]

Gulf Coast Oil Rigs Are Evacuated. "In anticipation of Hurricane Katrina's arrival, energy companies continued Saturday to shut down rigs and evacu-ate workers from the Gulf of Mexico." [20]

Gov. Blanco Implements Contraflow Evacuation Traffic Plan. "As Hurri-cane Katrina took aim at south Louisiana, Gov. Kathleen Blanco on Saturday ordered State Police to implement the state's latest 'contraflow' traffic plan as scores of New Orleans area residents drove north and west toward higher ground." [21]

Mandatory and Voluntary Evacuations Are Ordered. By midafternoon, officials in Plaquemines, St. Bernard, St. Charles, Lafourche, Terrebonne, and Jefferson parishes have called for voluntary or mandatory evacuations. New Orleans mayor Ray Nagin follows at five P.M., issuing a voluntary evac-uation. "Come the first break of light in the morning, you may have the first mandatory evacuation of New Orleans," Nagin tells WWL-TV. St. Tam-many officials ordered evacuations of the parish's low-lying areas by today at noon. [22]

Sunday, August 28, 2005

Bush Touts "Progress" in Iraq While Katrina Becomes a Category 5 Hurricane. Speaking to reporters at his ranch in Crawford, TX, President Bush talks about Hurricane Katrina quickly, before launching into an update on Iraq that lasts over twice as long as his comments on Hurricane Katrina. "Yesterday I signed a disaster declaration for the state of Louisiana, and this morning I signed a disaster declaration for the state of Mississippi. . . . On another matter, today Iraqi political leaders completed the process for drafting a permanent constitution. Their example is an inspiration to all who share the universal values of freedom, democracy, and the rule of law . . . we're making good progress toward making sure this world of ours is more peaceful for generations to come." [23]

Katrina, "a Once in a Lifetime Event," on Collision Course for New Orleans. "Hurricane Katrina is a massive, powerful storm, one that has the potential to eclipse Camille as the standard for killer hurricanes," writes the *Times-Picayune*, "and every map and forecast Sunday afternoon showed it on a collision course for our metro area. 'This is a once in a lifetime event,' Mayor Nagin said. 'The city of New Orleans has never seen a hurricane of this magnitude hit it directly.' " [24]

National Hurricane Center Warns Katrina Will Hit New Orleans as Category 5 Monday Morning, Will Flood New Orleans. At four P.M., National Hurricane Center meteorologist Chris Lauer says Katrina is still on track to hit the New Orleans area as a devastating Category 5 hurricane. A computer model by the Louisiana State University Hurricane Center indicates that even without waves, a Category 5 storm would flood most of eastern New Orleans, the Ninth Ward, Mid-City, much of downtown, and areas in St. Tammany close to Lake Pontchartrain. Kenner also will see severe flooding entering from St. Charles Parish. Areas outside the levee protection system, the *Times-Picayune* reports, are particularly vulnerable. [25]

National Hurricane Center Chief Personally Briefs President Bush. On a secure videoconference beamed into the presidential ranch in Crawford,

Max Mayfield, the director of the National Hurricane Center, personally briefs Bush on the oncoming storm and its potential for destruction.[26]

Monday, August 29, 2005

Bush in Arizona Campaigns Hard to "Pre-Sell" His Medicare a Political Victory. At noon Bush talks to an invitation-only audience of about four hundred people at the Pueblo El Mirage RV and Golf Resort. *The Arizona Republic* says Bush came to campaign hard for his new Medicare plan. Bush says he's in El Mirage " 'pre-selling' the importance of enrolling for the prescription drug benefit."[27]

Bush Stops to Celebrate McCain's Birthday at Luke Air Force Base. The president pauses on the tarmac at Luke Air Force Base in Arizona to celebrate Senator John McCain's sixty-ninth birthday. The cake melts in the Arizona sun before McCain can eat it.[28]

"Upbeat" Bush Continues Campaigning in Rancho Cucamonga, CA. The president tells a carefully selected audience of two hundred at the James L. Brulte Senior Center that his Medicare prescription-drug proposal is "a good deal."[29]

Katrina Moves Onshore as Category 4 Hurricane. At six A.M. the National Hurricane Center warns that "extremely dangerous Category 4 hurricane Katrina [is] preparing to move onshore near southern Plaquemines Parish, Louisiana. . . . Hurricane-force wind gusts occurring over most of southeastern Louisiana . . . and as far east as the Chandeleur Islands."[30]

At Least Fifty-Five Reported Deaths by Hurricane Katrina Throughout Gulf Coast. As *The Washington Post* writes, "Hurricane Katrina barreled into the Gulf Coast on Monday morning, its fierce winds cutting a 125-mile swath of destruction stretching from coastal Alabama across Mississippi to the French Quarter and the Superdome. At least 55 people were killed. The storm's leading edge, wielding winds up to 145 mph across the Gulf of Mexico, made landfall as a fearsome Category 4 hurricane at 7:10 a.m. Eastern time near the Louisiana bayou town of Buras, about 63 miles southeast of New Orleans. Katrina then wheeled into western Mississippi, bringing a 20-foot storm surge along the coast near Biloxi."[31]

Tuesday, August 30, 2005

Bush Boosts Iraq War in Coronado, CA. With the aircraft carrier U.S.S. *Ronald Reagan* as a backdrop, President Bush invokes the anniversary of the Japanese surrender in World War II to make the case for support of his occupation of Iraq.[32]

Bush Plays Guitar with Country Singer in Coronado. President Bush playfully laughs and strums a guitar given to him by country singer Mark Wills.[33]

Chaos in New Orleans. As Bush is strumming the guitar in the California sun, the *New Orleans Times-Picayune* reports, "Law enforcement efforts to contain the emergency left by Katrina slipped into chaos in parts of New Orleans Tuesday—with some police officers and firefighters even joining looters in picking stores clean. At the Wal-Mart on Tchoupitoulas Street, an initial effort to hand out provisions to stranded citizens quickly disintegrated into mass looting. Authorities at the scene said bedlam erupted after the giveaway was announced over the radio. 'We don't have enough cops to stop it,' an officer said. 'A mass riot would break out if you tried.'"[34]

Mayor of New Orleans Warns Floodwaters Will Continue to Rise Rapidly. New Orleans mayor Ray Nagin warns that efforts to plug the holes in the Seventeenth Street canal have failed. Floodwaters continue to rise rapidly. Eventually, Nagin says, the water could reach as high as 3 feet above sea level, meaning it could rise to 12 to 15 feet high in some parts of the city.[35]

Wednesday, August 31, 2005

Bush Returns to Washington, D.C. Working from his Texas ranch, President Bush participates via videoconference in a large meeting of federal, state, and local disaster management officials preparing for the storm's on-slaught. Separately, he speaks by phone with the governors of Louisiana, Mississippi, Alabama, and Florida. Bush then cuts short his vacation and flies back to Washington. As he flies over the Gulf Coast, he instructs the pilot to bring Air Force One low so he can observe storm damage. At five-fifteen P.M. ET, Bush meets at the White House with a task force established to coordi-nate the efforts of fourteen federal agencies that will be involved in respond-ing to the disaster.[36]

Bush Addresses Nation. Speaking from the Rose Garden, the president tells victims of the storm, "I'm confident with time you'll get your life back in order. New communities will flourish. The great city of New Orleans will be back on its feet and America will be a stronger place for it. The country stands with you."[37] *The New York Times* calls it "one of the worst speeches of his life . . . especially given the level of national distress and the need for words of consolation and wisdom. In what seems to be a ritual in this ad-ministration, the president appeared a day later than he was needed. He then read an address of a quality more appropriate for an Arbor Day celebration: a long laundry list of pounds of ice, generators and blankets delivered to the stricken Gulf Coast. He advised the public that anybody who wanted to help should send cash, grinned, and promised that everything would work out in the end."[38]

In New Orleans, Rescuers Push Bodies Back with Sticks. Lucrece Phillips, a resident of the Ninth Ward of New Orleans, tells the *Times-Picayune*, sobbing, "The rescuers in the boats that picked us up had to push the bodies back with sticks. And there was this little baby. She looked so per-fect and so beautiful. I just wanted to scoop her up and breathe life back into her little lungs."[39]

Superdome Resembles Apocalypse. According to the *Times-Picayune*, "The Superdome resembled a scene from the Apocalypse on Wednesday morning, with thousands of refugees trapped in a hellish environment of short tempers, unbearable heat and the overwhelming stench of human waste. Evacuees told horror stories of assaults and the apparent suicide of a man who leapt from a balcony. . . . The Dome situation had deteriorated noticeably from earlier days, as new swarms of refugees and rescuees arrived. On Wednesday morning, running water to the building was lost—as it was throughout the city—making the already overwhelming bathrooms downright noxious."[40]

Thursday, September 1, 2005

Bush Says No One Anticipated the Breach of the Levees. Appearing on ABC's *Good Morning America,* the president says, "I fully understand people wanting things to have happened yesterday. I mean, I understand that— anxiety of people on the ground. I can imagine—I can't imagine what it is like to be waving a sign saying come and get me now. So there's frustration. But I want people to know there is a lot of help coming. I don't think anybody anticipated the breach of the levees." Later in the day, Bush appears in the Oval Office with former presidents Bush and Clinton to announce their leadership of a private fund-raising effort similar to their effort after the tsunami earlier this year.[41]

Conservative *Manchester Union Leader* Criticizes Bush's Leadership on Katrina. " 'The cool, confident, intuitive leadership Bush exhibited in his first term, particularly in the months immediately following Sept. 11, 2001, has vanished,' said the paper's ultra-conservative editorial page. 'In its place is a diffident detachment unsuitable for the leader of a nation facing war, natural disaster and economic uncertainty.' "[42]

Local Officials Call Federal Effort Too Little, Too Late. The *Times-Picayune* reports, "The mounting relief effort did not allay concerns from local officials that it remained too little and mighty late. And Thursday offered continuing evidence that the city's flirtation with sheer chaos was not yet over: a medevac helicopter scared off by gunfire as it attempted to airlift patients from a downtown hospital; the Oakwood Mall reduced to charred rubble after looters broke in and set fires throughout the sprawling complex; corpses floating in flooded streets; scores of police officers simply abandoning their posts to flee a city gone at least temporarily mad."[43]

From there the Bushies were deep into damage-control mode. The president went to the Gulf region again and again. With St. Louis Cathedral lit up behind him like Cinderella's Castle at Disney World, he spoke about poverty and race and vowed to do better. But behind the curtain, things were politics as usual for Team Bush. The White House tried to blame the governor of Louisiana, the mayor of New Orleans, and anyone else they could think of. The crony-laden and discredited people at FEMA awarded hundreds of millions of dollars in no-bid contracts—some of which FEMA later rebid after congressional pressure and public outrage.

We can do better. The people of the Gulf Coast deserve better. Here's how we can take back the trust of the American people after Katrina.

1. It's About Class, Not Race

One of the more awkward moments in live television occurred during NBC's live concert fund-raiser for victims of Hurricane Katrina. The rapper Kanye West was slated to appear alongside the comedian Mike Myers to read a script about the breach in the levees around New Orleans. Myers stuck straight to the telePrompTer.

MYERS: The landscape of the city has changed dramatically, tragically, and perhaps irreversibly. There is now over twenty-five feet of water where there was once city streets and thriving neighborhoods.

Kanye West, however, wasn't about to read the network pablum.

WEST: I hate the way they portray us in the media. You see a black family, it says, "They're looting." You see a white family, it says, "They're looking for food." And, you know, it's been five days [waiting for federal help] because most of the people are black. . . . So anybody out there that wants to do anything that we can help—with the way America is set up to help the poor, the black people, the less well off.

West continued for a little bit and then threw it back to Myers—looking like a deer caught in the headlights; maybe because he's Canadian, he didn't feel like he had much skin in this game—who just kept reading.

MYERS: And subtle, but in many ways even more profoundly devastating, is the lasting damage to the survivors' will to rebuild and remain in the area. The destruction of the spirit of the people of southern Louisiana and Mississippi may end up being the most tragic loss of all.

Then Myers, sticking straight to script, gave West another chance.

WEST: George Bush doesn't care about black people![44]

Kanye West's comments were later cut out of NBC's West Coast feed, which is a shame. Because all they needed to do was change one word. It's not that George Bush doesn't care about black people. We're confident that he would have been just as indifferent, just as incompetent, just as inept if it had been poor *white* people clinging to their roofs. Kanye got it wrong—or half right: George W. Bush doesn't care about *poor* people.

Democrats should not make this an argument about race. It is an argument about class. When President Bush wants to do away with the prevailing wage in Louisiana for workers trying to rebuild their communities, we should point out the effect of that policy. Right now in New Orleans, the prevailing wage is $9.00 a hour. If you work 40 hours a week, for 50 weeks a year, that's $18,000 a year. Remember, that $18,000 has to pay for health care, filling up the car to get to the job site, and everything else. That's not much. But get this: *President Bush and the Republicans think $18,000 a year is too much.* That's why they want to do away with the prevailing wage. They don't give a damn about poor people—the effect of Bush's heartless policy will be to throw many people back into the same poverty that rendered them unable to escape from the flood in the first place.

2. Bold, Persistent Experimentation, Not Failed Right-Wing Quackery

As soon as President Bush started talking about reconstruction, we started hearing Republicans talking about using Louisiana as a test site for ideas that Americans have rejected—suspension of wage supports, school vouchers, wholesale deregulation, abandoning environmental regulation, and more tax cuts. Democrats need to be clear that there is no place in this recovery for political opportunism or right-wing social engineering.

We need progressive ideas that go beyond dusty New Deal–era programs. We should start with a reconstruction czar, someone from business or the military who can kick ass and take names. We're thinking Donald Trump or General Barry McCaffrey, someone who can cut through the bureaucracy and get things done.

The president, however, put Karl Rove in charge of Katrina reconstruction. The notion of the president's embattled (at this writing) chief political aide overseeing Katrina recovery would be laughable if the stakes weren't so high.

Democrats should heed Hillary Clinton's call to move FEMA out of the Department of Homeland Security. Under President Clinton, FEMA reported directly to the president. It should again.

To rebuild cities and towns, we should not merely fall back on the old social programs of the New Deal and the Great Society. Don't get us wrong, we love Social Security and Medicare and food stamps. But progressives have had some valuable and innovative new ideas in the last forty years. Gene Sperling, former chairman of President Clinton's National Economic Council, has written a thoughtful new book called *The Pro-Growth Progressive*. In it he advances new ideas for balancing work and family, for making pre-kindergarten universal, for helping young minority men become better fathers and workers, and for adapting new technologies to help bring more people into the economic mainstream. Sperling also calls for further expanding the earned income tax credit for people who choose low-wage work over welfare.

Other Democrats have called for innovative policies to rebuild the New Orleans police force and other community institutions by offering low- or no-interest mortgages to police officers, firefighters, teachers—the kinds of folks you can build a community around.

Democrats should also insist that displaced residents and local companies get first crack at the rebuilding jobs. We ought to fight for a dynamic on-site job-training program that can prepare folks to rebuild their communities while giving them the tools they'll need to earn a better living in their rebuilt neighborhoods. As we've said before, give someone a fish and you've fed him for a day; teach him to fish and you've fed him for a lifetime. Democrats ought to be in the business of teaching fishing lessons.

After the devastating hurricane of 1900 destroyed Galveston, Texas, and killed at least ten thousand people, the people of Galveston raised the level of their city seventeen feet and built a seawall that still stands. We have to think as big and as bold as that in rebuilding New Orleans. Like Galveston, New Orleans is uniquely vulnerable to a hurricane. This is a time for big ideas.

After a flood in the Netherlands killed two thousand people in 1953, the Dutch people spent $8 billion over a thirty-year period on a state-of-the-art system of dikes, dams, and levees. They built a hydraulic seawall 130 feet high and six miles long. Today the Dutch system is 150 times stronger than the system in New Orleans. And in the last fifty years, the Dutch have withstood everything Mother Nature has thrown at them.[45]

3. It's About Environmental Protection

In addition to all that construction, the Dutch made sure to preserve, protect, and defend their wetlands—the first line of protection against a flood. Democrats should do the same. Environmental protection, in the case of flooding, isn't about strapping on your Birkenstocks and then strapping yourself to a tree. Since wetlands are our first and best defense against flooding, good environmental policy is good flood-control policy. Today, due to the channeling of the Mississippi River and George W. Bush's pro-development/anti-wetlands policy, Louisiana loses twenty-five square miles of coast a year.[46] Democrats need to make the point that environmental protection is ultimately about protecting people.

And then we come to global warming. We're not climatologists. We have no idea if the upsurge in deadly hurricanes these past few years is because of climate change or if it's just a multi-decade fluctuation. But we know this, and it's pretty simple: Global warming is real. A warmer planet means warmer water in the Gulf of Mexico and the Atlantic. Warmer water in the Gulf and the Atlantic means bigger, stronger, meaner hurricanes. Warm water is to hurricanes what gasoline is to a bonfire. Even if what we're going through is just a normal fluctuation, can you imagine how much worse the next fluctuation will be in, say, thirty years, when global warming has superheated the oceans? Hello, Waterworld.

Democrats need not be alarmist. But we ought to recall that classic 1970s commercial for Chiffon margarine: "It's not nice to fool Mother Nature."

4. Get Rid of the Culture of Corruption

If you were troubled by the images of young men taking television sets during the flooding, just wait until you see what George Bush's friends have in mind. When billions in reconstruction funds start flowing, that's when the real looting begins.

Senator Barack Obama of Illinois had the right idea when he got together with Tom Coburn, a Republican senator from Oklahoma, to call on FEMA to get actual bids for the $1.5 billion in rebuilding contracts that were awarded with no competition at all.

Obama is also calling for a chief financial officer who would be responsible for the efficient and effective use of federal funds in all activities relating to the recovery from Hurricane Katrina. Every month the CFO would have to issue financial reports to Congress on how the federal funds were being used. These reports would include information about the extent to which federal funds have been distributed to persons most in need, the extent to which federal funds have been distributed to companies that hire local workers, and the use of no-bid and cost-plus contracts.

Republicans see disasters as opportunities to help themselves. We need to make sure they are opportunities to help the people most in need.

Progressive Patriotism

Americans don't like what Republicans stand for, but they don't know what Democrats stand for. And, as Grandma used to say, "If you don't stand for something, you'll fall for anything."

In this book, we are attempting to state plainly what we stand for—what we believe most Democrats stand for. We are also trying to persuade, cajole, force, shame, coax, wheedle, entice, sweet-talk, bully, charm, and threaten the Democratic Party into proudly proclaiming what it stands for. It's a hell of a lot easier to sit on the sidelines, as we do now, than actually to get in the game and make a difference. Having been in the arena for most of our lives, we know that. So we decided to take a crack at what we think Democrats ought to say—what we believe Democrats stand for. At least what these two Democrats stand for.

We are Progressive Patriots. As Democrats, we are the heirs of some of the greatest political leaders and thinkers the world has ever known. We have Thomas Jefferson's trust in the wisdom and decency of ordinary Americans rather than elites. We have Andrew Jackson's belief in a strong, unified nation. We have Franklin D. Roosevelt's strong and active faith that together we can fight poverty at home and oppression abroad. We have Harry Truman's determined internationalism, John F. Kennedy's call for patriotic sacrifice, Lyndon Johnson's passion for the poor, Jimmy Carter's commitment to peace, freedom, and human rights, and Bill Clinton's conviction that the best way for America to be freer, stronger, richer is to put people first.

This is our intellectual and political inheritance as Democrats. It must be reclaimed.

Republicans, too, are the heirs of a political tradition. They have not merely squandered their inheritance, they have rejected it, mocked it, and disgraced it. Abraham Lincoln, their party's founding genius, appealed to "the better angels of our nature." Today's Republicans devise "wedge issues" to divide Americans based on race and religion and region; gender and generation; education and income. At the turn of the twentieth century, Teddy Roosevelt railed against "the malefactors of great wealth." At the turn of the twenty-first century, George W. Bush looked out at a crowd of millionaires in white tie and tails and joked, "This is an impressive crowd: the haves and the have-mores. Some people call you elites; I call you my base." [1]

We believe the mortal sin of the Republicans under George W. Bush is that in the end, they appeal to our selfishness. Ronald Reagan famously asked, "Are you better off than you were four years ago?" Progressive Patriots ask, "Are *we* better off? Is *America* better off?"

Bush Republicans say you're on your own. Progressive Patriots say we're all in this together.

Bush looks at economic stagnation, social divisiveness, and international embarrassment and says we've never had it so good. Progressive Patriots say we can do better.

The unifying theme of so much of what President Bush stands for is selfishness.

His tax cuts have bankrupted our Treasury while enriching a privileged elite.

His deficits have driven us deep into debt, mortgaging our economic security to the tender mercies of Communist Chinese central bankers.

His Social Security proposal would be a boon to Wall Street but a bust for the millions of Americans whose benefits would be cut.

On health care, he supports so-called medical savings accounts, which are little more than an insurance policy with a $5,000 deductible: fine if you're healthy and wealthy and well, and great if you're an insurance company, but useless if you're a working American.

On education, the No Child Left Behind Act has left millions behind by insisting on higher standards without providing higher levels of funding. At the same time, Republicans want to send tax dollars to elite private academies instead of to struggling public schools.

On national security, Bush has sent hundreds of thousands of young men and women—overwhelmingly the sons and daughters of the middle class and the poor—to fight and kill and bleed and die for his ill-fated invasion of Iraq, while the sons and daughters of privilege are asked to do nothing but party on.

On the environment, he has allowed oil-company lobbyists and his Enron cronies to write his energy plan in secret; reneged on his promise to limit greenhouse gases, which cause global warming; and held hands with the Arab oil sheiks who are ripping us off at the pump.

It's all about selfishness—for Bush's base. No wealthy person has to give up his tax cut or his SUV or dig a little deeper to pay teachers more. John F. Kennedy famously told us to "ask not"; George W. Bush tells his prosperous supporters to "ask more."

After the terrorist attacks of September 11, President Bush had a historic opportunity to unite the country around a grand enterprise. Instead, he cynically manipulated that national tragedy to his partisan advantage. He didn't unite us, he divided us. He didn't challenge us, he patronized us. He didn't call on us to sacrifice, he called on us to shop.

The essence of being a patriot is loving your country enough to sacrifice for it. We don't believe Americans are one bit less patriotic today than were the colonials who nearly froze at Valley Forge, or the GIs who stormed the beaches at Normandy. We've been to Walter Reed Army Medical Center, and we've talked with young men who've lost limbs and are eager to go back to serving their country. But what about the rest of us? Are the middle-aged sons and daughters of the Greatest Generation really as selfish and greedy as President Bush and the Republicans seem to believe?

We don't think so. We think Americans today are every bit as patriotic as they were under FDR or JFK. The only difference is, no one's asked. We believe Democrats need to ask. We're asking tough questions about where the party we love has gone wrong. We're asking interest groups—some of the most powerful organizations on the left—to back off a bit. And we're asking you to think anew about what it means to be a Democrat, what it means to be a progressive, and most of all, what it means to be a patriot.

Unlike most great civilizations in history, America doesn't have a distinct race, or religion, or common ancient culture, except the one we've made here: the heritage and the history and the culture we remake every generation. Each generation asks itself what it means to be an American. To us, the central value of being an American—and a Progressive Patriot—is to be part of a cause that is larger than yourself. It is our sense of unity and community that makes us Americans, and in the absence of common racial or religious or ethnic bonds, that sense of unity is more important here than anywhere else on earth.

The oldest and most persistent question in human history comes to us from the biblical story of the first person born on earth. Cain, the eldest son of Adam and Eve, was jealous that God preferred his younger brother Abel's sacrifice of a firstborn lamb to Cain's sacrifice of some of the fruit of his fields. So Cain murdered Abel. Wanting to shame him into admitting his crime, God asked Cain where Abel was. And it was then that Cain asked the question that resounds through the millennia: "Am I my brother's keeper?" (Genesis 4:9).

Cain's question must be asked and answered by every person, especially these days. The Bush Republicans have an answer—a definitive and hard-hearted no. Progressive Patriots must answer with a strong and certain yes.

Let the Republicans be the party of Cain; we Democrats will be the party of our brother's keepers.

Not only is the common purpose we propose rooted in Judeo-Christian religious teaching, Progressive Patriotism is also in keeping with our strongest civic traditions. Those old, dead white men who wrote the Constitution knew something when they penned the first three words of our governing document: "We, the People." And they gave us a motto—three words that define what it is to be an American: *E Pluribus Unum*. From many, one.

The Founding Fathers did not tell us to build our nation on selfishness, any more than God told us to build our religions on ignoring our neighbors. We are Americans because we believe in certain shared values—and unity is at the heart of those values. Wise old Ben Franklin was displaying more than gallows humor when he told a querulous and quarrelsome Continental Congress that "we must all hang together or we will most assuredly all hang separately." He was appealing to that most American of values: community.

It was true when America was invented, and it remained true as America was expanded. When settlers left the comfort of the Eastern Seaboard or Europe and ventured out to build a nation "from sea to shining sea," they did so together. They formed wagon trains, pooled their resources, and looked out for one another. When a wagon train was attacked, they circled the wagons so everyone was mutually protected. Everyone who could was expected to grab a gun and defend his neighbors. And when they reached their destination, it certainly wasn't every man for himself. Neighbors helped one another. They cleared one another's land and built one another's barns. They all worked together to build a one-room schoolhouse, and they all chipped in to pay for a teacher.

Progressive Patriotism means not only that we're all in it together, but also that we each have to do our part. President Clinton used to say the values that informed his policies were opportunity for all, responsibility from all, and a community of all. As Progressive Patriots, we understand that our nation requires something from each of us. The age of something for nothing must end. Everyone must contribute, because every American must be a patriot.

Those who have the most have the opportunity to be the most patriotic. That was true at our founding, when the mostly well-off Continental Congress pledged to each other "our lives, our fortunes, our sacred honor." Many of them lost all three. This, too, is in our strongest religious traditions. Jesus Christ taught that from those to whom much has been given, much will be expected (Luke 12:48).

Truth be told, a lot is going to be expected of a lot of us in the years to come. Most of the smart people we know have all concluded that America's options on a host of fronts are pretty limited—and pretty scary.

America is faced with a huge fiscal crisis, a not particularly robust growth rate, continued pressure to maintain a divisive culture war that we'd prefer not to engage in, a horrendously overstretched military, and a tarnished reputation around the world.

Politically, the answer to the latter two is simple: neo-isolationist demagoguery. If a Democrat ran on a hard-core anti-immigrant, anti-trade, anti-international engagement, anti-multinational-corporation message, he or she would find a welcoming audience. That's just not what we believe in. We don't think those policies would be good for America, and if there's anything we learned from Bill Clinton, it is that over time, the best policy is the best politics.

And so, as Progressive Patriots, we're going to advocate the tougher course, the harder way, what the poet called the road less traveled. As people who believe in good government, we know that we've got to rebuild our military, pay down the debt, come to grips with our aging population, level out our trade imbalance, confront global warming, and help the families that are getting squeezed to death between the rising cost of health care and the rising cost of tuition.

Progressive Patriotism begins with a clear articulation that every American has to rise to meet the challenge of America's future—no one is exempt from participating in rebuilding a strong America. We have seen again and again that Americans will resent someone who talks down to them, but respect someone who calls on them to rise to a challenge.

Right now Republicans have embraced a regressive patriotism—if you run a wealthy and powerful corporation, you can incorporate offshore and avoid paying taxes to the United States Treasury. If you're a wealthy heiress, you can inherit a billion dollars and not pay a nickel in taxes on it. If you're powerful Republican politician, you can shake down special interests for campaign contributions, in exchange for which you will legislate special benefits for your wealthy donors. If you're a millionaire lobbyist for oil companies or polluters, you get special access to the powerful, and you get to shape—and cripple—the regulations under which you operate.

That's the antithesis of patriotism. We can do better. The first thing Progressive Patriots must do is reject the Bush-era ethic of selfishness.

The second imperative of Progressive Patriotism is rebuilding the military. Nothing represents U.S. patriotism more than our military. No one is more patriotic, more willing to sacrifice, more prepared to give their all, than the men and women and families of our military. Progressive Patriots must honor their service and endeavor to spread the military's culture of selflessness across civilian society. Traditionally, Republicans have held a huge advantage on military issues, and yet it is the Bush Republican policies that have done so much damage to the army and Marine Corps. We must reverse both those destructive Republican policies and the perception that somehow the Republican Party has cornered the market on support for our military.

Third, Progressive Patriots must reclaim self-government itself. Too often, Representative Rahm Emanuel has said, when the speaker's gavel comes down, it opens up an auction house instead of the People's House. Progressive Patriots support radical government reform. We reject the cronyism, criminality, and corruption of the Bush Republicans. We will replace self-dealing with service; we will replace patronage with patriotism; and we will replace dishonesty with decency.

Fourth, Progressive Patriots want a truce in the culture wars here at home. With Islamo-fascists around the world targeting Americans, we can't afford to attack our own people and our own culture. We have respect for those with whom we disagree on difficult social issues. We have reverence for religion and deference for people of faith. We also recognize that the Bush Republicans have cynically manipulated the heartfelt concerns of people of faith in order to demonize Democrats, discredit their ideas, and distract voters from their common concerns.

Finally, Progressive Patriots stand for big, bold ideas. All the great leaders of prior times stood for big ideas: George Washington and his colleagues created America and gave us self-government. Thomas Jefferson had the audacity to bet the Treasury on the Louisiana Purchase, which tripled America's size. Abraham Lincoln saved the Union, freed the slaves, and created land grant colleges. Teddy Roosevelt connected the world's two vast oceans and busted the trusts. Woodrow Wilson helped make America the emerging, dominant power of the twentieth century. Franklin Roosevelt—Lord, what didn't he do?—suffice it to say he saved the world from fascism and saved capitalism from collapse. John F. Kennedy sent us to the moon, and Lyndon Johnson confronted and defeated segregation.

In our time, Progressive Patriots must aim high, too. We will make America energy-independent. We will extend health care to every American. We will make college affordable. We will attack global warming and save our planet. We will reform our government and drive the money changers out of the temple of democracy.

Above all, Progressive Patriots are optimists. As Ronald Reagan, the ultimate American optimist, used to say, how can we not be? After all, we're Americans. On a policy and political level, there was so much about Reagan with which we disagreed. But his sunny, exuberant optimism, his limitless faith in America, his deep and determined belief in the goodness of the American people—these are traits shared by every Progressive Patriot.

We believe Democrats have better ideas and a better approach. We believe we can do better. We believe America will be stronger, freer, richer, cleaner, and smarter if each of us does more and if none of us is left behind. But we must find our voice again. And we believe that voice is to be found in Progressive Patriotism.

Notes

"Houston, We Have a Problem"

1. See http://www.hq.nasa.gov/office/pao/History/SP-350/ch-13-1.html.
2. See Dan Keating, "Fla. 'Overvotes' Hit Democrats the Hardest: Gore 3 Times as Likely as Bush to Be Listed on Tossed Ballots," *Washington Post,* January 27, 2001, for evidence that "overvotes" cost Gore three times more votes than Bush, with Gore losing 46,000 votes to Bush's 17,000. The *Post* also reported that the "butterfly ballot" of Palm Beach County cost Gore more than 7,000 votes.
3. See http://www.washingtonpost.com/wp-dyn/articles/A23636-2004Nov3.html.
4. Carson's bio is available online at http://www.odl.state.ok.us/usinfo/congress/107cong/carson107.htm.
5. See *Louisville Courier-Journal* editorial, quoted in *USA TODAY,* 10/22/04.
6. Associated Press, online at http://cnews.canoe.ca/CNEWS/Politics/US/2004/11/03/698453.html.
7. Ron Brownstein and Ric Rainey, "GOP Plants Flag on New Voting Frontier," *Los Angeles Times,* 11/22/04.
8. Ibid.
9. Ibid.
10. Greenberg-Quinlan-Rosner Research, January 2005, online at http://64.233.187.104/search?q=cache:QaNyzHqhjIwJ:www.wvwv.org/docs/WVWV_200

4_post-election_memo.pdf+greenberg+women+voices+votes&hl=en&client=firefox-a.

11. Center for American Women and Politics at Rutgers University, online at http://64.233.187.104/search?q=cache:sLMYmM7-yAYJ:www.cawp.rutgers.edu/Facts/Elections/GG2004Facts.pdf+demographic+analysis+2004+election&hl=en&client=firefox-a.

12. CNN, online at http://www.cnn.com/ELECTION/2004/pages/results/states/US/P/00/epolls.0.html.

13. *First Things,* February 1997, online at http://www.leaderu.com/ftissues/ft9702/opinion/mchugh.html.

14. Ibid.

15. *Washington Post,* 11/12/02.

16. Ibid.

17. Ibid.

18. Ibid.

19. *USA TODAY,* 7/22/04, online at http://www.usatoday.com/news/politics elections/nation/president/2004-07-22-poll-cover_x.htm.

20. AFL-C10, online at http://www.aflcio.org/yourjobeconomy/jobs/jobcrisis.cfm.

21. National Association of Manufacturers, online at http://www.nam.org/s_nam/sec.asp?CID=201507&DID=229891.

22. CNN, 10/14/04, online at http://www.cnn.com/2004/ALLPOLITICS/10/13/factcheck/index.html.

23. Census data, cited by Media Matters for America, online at http://media matters.org/items/200509130002.

24. See http://www.klkntv.com/Global/story.asp?S=2225488.

25. Congressional Budget Office, "Budget and Economic Outlook," January 2001.

26. Center on Budget and Policy Priorities, 10/28/03.

27. See http://icasualties.org/oif.

28. Lt. Gen. Lawrence P. Farrell, Jr., USAF (Ret.), National Defense Industrial Association, "Pentagon Feeling Pressure on the Budget," October 2004. Available online at http://www.ndia.org/Content/NavigationMenu/Resources1/Presidents_Corner2/October_2004.htm.

29. Exit poll: "How Are Things Going in Iraq?" Well=43; Badly=52.Online at http://www.cnn.com/ELECTION/2004/pages/results/states/US/P/00/epolls.0.html.

30. Interview with senior Bush-Cheney campaign strategist.

31. Ibid.

32. Ibid.

33. See http://archive.salon.com/politics/feature/2000/11/02/dumb/.

34. See http://www.u-s-history.com/pages/h201.html.

35. See http://www.u-s-history.com/pages/h822.html.

36. Joaquin L. Gonzalez III, "Christianity Returns to America," University of San Francisco, online at http://www.usfca.edu/TRIP/Gonzalez.pdf.

37. See http://www.u-s-history.com/pages/h830.html.

38. University of Virginia's Miller Center of Public Affairs, American Presidency, online at http://www.americanpresident.org/history/franklindelanoroosevelt/biography/CampaignsElections.common.shtml.

39. The conservative activist Phyllis Schlafly quotes this with approval in her column "Y2K and the Man of the Century," 1/12/00, online at http://www.eagleforum.org/column/2000/jan00/00-01-12.html.

40. Houghton Mifflin, Great American History Fact-Finder, online at http://college.hmco.com/history/readerscomp/gahff/html/ff_060641_elect1944.htm.

41. Ibid., online at http://college.hmco.com/history/readerscomp/gahff/html/ff_060648_elect1972.htm.

42. "American Rhetoric: George W. Bush, 2004 Republican National Convention Address," online at http://www.americanrhetoric.com/speeches/convention2004/georgewbushrnc.htm.

43. Ibid.

44. Ibid.

45. "Deficits Seen Through 2005: White House Budget Chief Blames Recession, War on Terrorism," CNN.com, 11/29/01, online at http://money.cnn.com/2001/11/29/economy/budget/.

46. Redacted president's daily briefing of August 6, 2001, online at http://www.thesmokinggun.com/archive/0409041pdb1.html.

47. Interview with senior Bush-Cheney strategist.

48. Adam Nagourney, "Bush's Aides Plan Late Campaign Sprint in '04," New York Times, 4/22/03, online at http://209.157.64.200/focus/f-news/897646/posts.

49. Washington Post, 5/31/04, online at http://www.washingtonpost.com/wp-dyn/articles/A3222-2004May30.html.

50. USA TODAY, 3/11/04, online at http://www.usatoday.com/news/politicselections/nation/president/2004-03-11-bush-ads_x.htm.

51. See http://www.factcheck.org/article152.html.

52. See http://www.oxxfordclothes.com/suntimes.asp.

53. See http://austin.about.com/cs/bushbiographies/a/crawford_ranch.htm.

54. See http://www.factcheck.org/article152.html.

55. See http://slate.msn.com/id/2067995/entry/2068076/.

56. See http://www.cbsnews.com/stories/2004/09/29/politics/main646435.shtml for all "flip-flops" except NAFTA, online at http://www.nojohnkerry.org/kerry.html/flipflops.htmNAFTA.

57. *Washington Times,* 9/28/04, online at http://www.washtimes.com/national/20040928-123834-6324r.htm.

58. Proceedings of the 1996 Democratic National Convention, online at http://www.4president.org/speeches/clintongore1996convention.htm.

59. Proceedings of the 2004 Republican National Convention, online at http://www.gopconvention.com/cgidata/speeches/files/v46q7+4op60p0109d9b8i8 373arhnn0r.shtml.

60. GIGA quotes by Mrs. Alice Roosevelt Longworth, online at http://www .giga-usa.com/gigaweb1/quotes2/quautlongworthalicerx001.htm.

61. Franklin Roosevelt, address to the 1932 Democratic National Convention, Chicago, online at http://shs.westport.k12.ct.us/jwb/AP/GrtDep/Roosevelt .htm.

62. Ibid.

63. Ibid.

64. Harry Truman, Address to the 1948 Democratic National Convention, online at http://www.trumanlibrary.org/publicpapers/index.php?pid=1060&st=&st =&st1.

65. John F. Kennedy, Address to the 1960 Democratic National Convention, online at http://www.americanrhetoric.com/speeches/jfk1960dnc.htm.

66. CNN *Crossfire,* 7/27/04, online at http://transcripts.cnn.com/TRAN SCRIPTS/0407/27/cf.00.html.

67. *Washington Post,* 9/1/04, online at http://www.washingtonpost.com/wp-dyn/articles/A51318-2004Sep1.html.

68. See http://www.dems2004.org/site/apps/nl/content3.asp?c=luI2LaPYG&b= 125919&ct=158734.

69. See http://www.pbs.org/newshour/vote2004/demconvention/speeches/carter .html.

70. *Boston Globe,* 11/14/05, online at http://www.boston.com/news/nation/articles/2004/11/14/on_the_trail_of_kerrys_failed_dream?mode=PF.

71. Ibid.

72. Committee for the Study of the American Electorate, online at http://www.fairvote.org/reports/CSAE2004electionreport.pdf.

73. Statistical Abstract of the United States, 2001, Federal Election Commission, online at http://www.infoplease.com/ipa/A0763629.html.

74. Northwestern University survey, online at http://www.yvoteonline.org/noshows2000_about.shtml.

75. Thomas Edsall and James V. Grimaldi, "Shrewd Spending Boosted GOP in Presidential Race, Study Finds," *Washington Post,* 12/30/04, online at http://www.washingtonpost.com/ac2/wp-dyn/A35062-2004Dec29?language=printer.

76. Ibid.

77. Ibid.

78. *U.S. News and World Report,* 8/20/01, online at http://www.usnews.com/us news/doubleissue/heroes/lovell.htm.

Moral Values: God Is a Liberal

1. Steven Hayward, "Reagan, Lott and Race Baiting," *National Review,* 12/29/02, online at http://www.nationalreview.com/comment/comment-hayward 121902.asp.

2. Franklin Roosevelt, Address to the 1936 Democratic National Convention, online at http://millercenter.virginia.edu/scripps/diglibrary/prezspeeches/roosevelt/fdr_1936_0627.html.

3. CBS News, "Woodward Shares War Secrets," 4/18/04, online at http://www.cbsnews.com/stories/2004/04/15/60minutes/main612067.shtml.

4. Lawrence B. Finer and Stanley K. Henshaw, "Estimates of U.S. Abortion Incidence in 2001 and 2002, Alan Guttmacher Institute, 5/18/05, online at http://www.guttmacher.org/pubs/2005/05/18/ab_incidence.pdf.

5. Glen Stassen, "The Pro-Life Movement and Economic Justice," *Sojourners,* 6/29/05, online at http://www.sojo.net/index.cfm?action=news.display_article&mode=C& NewsID=4864.

6. Ibid.

7. Glen Stassen and Gary Krane, "Why Abortion Rate Is Up in Bush Years," *Houston Chronicle,* 10/17/04, online at http://www.chron.com/cs/CDA/ssistory.mpl/editorial/outlook/2851283.

8. *Washington Post/*ABC poll, April 21–25, 2005, online at http://www.pollingreport.com/abortion.htm.

9. CNN/*USA TODAY/*Gallup poll, January 10–12, 2003, online at http://www.pollingreport.com/abortion.htm.

10. Ibid.

11. Ibid.

12. *Los Angeles Times* poll, January 30–February 2, 2003, online at http://www.pollingreport.com/abortion.htm.

13. Casey speech to National Press Club, 1993.

14. Bob Casey, *Fighting for Life* (Dallas: Word Books, 1996).

15. Carter-Reagan debate, October 28, 1980, transcript online at http://www.pbs.org/newshour/debatingourdestiny/80debates/cart4.html.

16. 2004 Republican Platform, online at http://www.gop.com/media/2004platform.pdf.

17. Charles Babington, "Two Opponents of Abortion Are Tapped for Senate Judiciary Panel," *Washington Post*, 12/21/04, online at http://www.washingtonpost.com/wp-dyn/articles/A14759-2004Dec20.html.

18. Ayelish McGarvey, "Carter's Crusade," *The American Prospect*, 4/5/04, online at http://www.prospect.org/web/page.ww?section=root&name=ViewWeb&articleId=7572.

19. Will Saletan, "Safe, Legal and Never: Hillary Clinton's Anti-Abortion Strategy," *Slate*, 1/26/05, online at http://slate.msn.com/id/2112712.

20. Ibid.

21. "Democrats Announce Plan to Reduce the Number of Abortions," Democrats for Life press release, 4/26/05, online at http://www.prnewsnow.com/PR%20News%20Releases/Politics/Democrats%20Announce%20Plan%20to%20Reduce%20the%20Number%20of%20Abortions.

22. J. Blackmun, dissenting in *Webster* v. *Reproductive Health Services*, 492 U.S. 490 (1989).

23. Associated Press, "Report: 30 States Ready to Outlaw Abortion," 10/5/04, online at http://www.foxnews.com/story/0.2933.134530.00.html.

24. Richard M. Aborn, "The Battle over the Brady Bill and the Future of Gun Control Advocacy," *Fordham Urban Law Journal* 22 (1995): 417.

25. Gary Langer, ABC Polling Director, May 1, 2003, online at http://abcnews.go.com/sections/us/Politics/poll_sillyseason030501.html.

26. See http://www.nraila.org/NEWS/read/InTheNews.aspx?ID=175.

27. Americans for Gun Safety, online at http://ww2.americansforgunsafety.com/the_issues_gun_loop.asp.

28. John Scalia, U.S. Department of Justice Bureau of Justice Statistics, "Special Report: Federal Firearms Offenders, 1992–1998, with Preliminary Data

from 1999," June 2000, online at http://www.ojp.usdoj.gov/bjs/pub/pdf/ffo98.pdf.

29. Jim Vandehei, "Democrats Give Up Gun Control Issue; White House Hopefuls Rarely Talk About Tougher Gun Laws," *Washington Post,* 10/26/03.

30. Americans for Gun Safety, op. cit.

31. Vandehei, *Washington Post,* op. cit.

32. Michael Janofsky, "New Program in Richmond Is Credited with Getting Handguns Off Streets," *New York Times,* 2/10/99.

33. Barbara L. Schwemle, "Salaries of Federal Officials: CRS Report for Congress," Congressional Research Service, 1/11/05, online at http://www.senate.gov/reference/resources/pdf/98-53.pdf.

34. Gallup poll, October 11–14, 2004, available online at http://www.pollingreport.com/guns.htm.

35. Preston Bryant, "Bush Win Bodes Well for Virginia GOP in '05," *Roanoke Times,* 11/8/04, online at http://www.roanoke.com/columnists/bryant/13508.html.

36. David Kirkpatrick, "In Secretly Taped Conversations, Glimpses of the Future President," *New York Times,* 2/20/05.

37. Ibid.

38. Ibid.

39. Dan Payne, "Dukakis-Bush Déjà Vu," Salon.com, 5/5/04, online at http://www.salon.com/news/feature/2004/05/10/attacks/index.html.

40. *Washington Post,* 12/30/04, online at http://www.washingtonpost.com/ac2/wp-dyn/A35062-2004Dec29?language=printer.

41. Ansolabehere and Stewart, "Truth in Numbers: Moral Values and the Gay-Marriage Backlash Did Not Help Bush," *Boston Review,* February/March 2005, online at http://www.bostonreview.net/BR30.1/ansolastewart.html.

42. Ibid.

43. *Boston Globe* poll, conducted by University of New Hampshire Survey Center, May 4–9, 2005, online at http://www.pollingreport.com/civil.htm.

44. Ibid.

45. Quinnipiac University poll, December 7–12, 2004, online at http://www.pollingreport.com/civil.htm.

46. Wendy Kaminer, "Gay Rites," *The American Prospect,* online at http://www.prospect.org/print/V11/8/kaminer-w.html.

47. Anti-Defamation League, "Fred Phelps and the Westboro Baptist Church," online at http://www.adl.org/special_reports/wbc/default.asp.

48. "Lott's Association with Supremacist Group Questioned," Scripps-Howard newspapers, 1/16/99, online at http://www.ferris.edu/isar/Institut/CCC/scripps.htm.

49. "State Republicans Obsessed with God and Gays," *The Texas Triangle*, 8/12/04, online at http://www.sodomylaws.org/usa/texas/txnews084.htm.

50. "Homo Hate: Kerry Loses to Rove's Anti-Gay Hysteria," *LA Weekly*, 11/5–11/04, 2004, online at http://www.laweekly.com/ink/04/50/election-ireland.php.

51. 1.2 million Americans are on active duty; another 1.3 million are in the Guard or ready reserve. U.S. Census Bureau, online at http://www.census.gov/Press-Release/www/2003/cb03-ff04se.html.

52. Okay, it's actually 296,497,519, not 300 million. Picky, picky. For total U.S. population statistics, see U.S. Census Bureau, online at http://www.census.gov.

53. Human Rights Campaign, citing data from the Gallup poll, online at http://www.hrc.org/Content/NavigationMenu/HRC/Get_Informed/Federal_Legislation/Employment_Non-Discrimination_Act/Background_Information/Public_Polls_Show_Strong_Support_for_ENDA.htm.

54. Human Rights Campaign, "Employment Non-Discrimination Act: Quick Facts," online at http://www.hrc.org/Content/NavigationMenu/HRC/Get_Informed/Federal_Legislation/Employment_Non-Discrimination_Act/Quick_Facts2/ENDA_Quick_Facts.htm.

55. Ibid.

56. *Dillon v. Frank*, 959 F2d 403, 6th Circuit, 1992.

57. ABC News Special, "Sex, Drugs and Consenting Adults with John Stossel," 5/26/98, transcript online at http://www.sodomylaws.org/usa/georgia/ganews10.htm.

58. Richard Lacayo, "Where the Right Went Wrong," by *Time*, 12/21/98, online at http://www.cnn.com/ALLPOLITICS/time/1998/12/21/right.html.

59. See http://www.lovewonout.com/.

60. MSNBC.com, "Healed by God: Evangelical Group Sponsors Conference on Nature of Gays," 6/23/05, online at http://www.msnbc.msn.com/id/8234503.

61. NBC, *Meet the Press*, 6/5/05, online at http://www.msnbc.msn.com/id/8062380/.

62. Vice presidential debate, October 5, 2000, online at http://www.debates.org/pages/trans2000d.html.

63. "The Compassionate Answer: Homosexuality Is Avoidable, Doctor Tells Parents," *San Francisco Faith: The Bay Area's Lay Catholic Newspaper,* July–August 1998, online at http://www.ldolphin.org/narth2.html.

64. "Cheney Differs from Bush on Amendment to Ban Gay Marriages," *Christian Century,* 9/21/04, online at http://www.findarticles.com/p/articles/mi_m1058/is_19_121/ai_n6355196.

65. "Rep. Frank Opposes Gay Marriage Effort," CNN.com, 2/19/04, online at http://www.cnn.com/2004/ALLPOLITICS/02/18/gay.marriage.frank.ap.

66. Dr. Martin Luther King, Jr., *New York Journal American,* 9/10/62, online at http://www.towson.edu/news/student/msg00583.html.

67. CNN/*USA TODAY*/Gallup poll, February 2–4, 2005, online at http://www.pollingreport.com/prioriti.htm.

68. Kennedy's Inaugural Address, January 20, 1961, online at http://www.americanrhetoric.com/speeches/johnfkennedyinaugural.htm.

69. From FDR's last speech, online at http://www.worldofquotes.com/author/Franklin-Delano-Roosevelt/1/.

70. Time line of George Wallace's life, *The American Experience,* online at http://www.pbs.org/wgbh/amex/wallace/timeline/index_2.html.

71. Paul M. Weyrich, "Honoring a Soldier of the Right," 2004, online at http://acuf.org/issues/issue22/041018cul.asp.

72. Ibid.

73. "Ted Turner Attacks Catholics . . . Again," *Daily Catholic,* 3/7/01, online at http://www.dailycatholic.org/issue/2001Mar/mar8nu1.htm.

74. Amy Sullivan, "Do the Democrats Have a Prayer?," *Washington Monthly,* June 2003, online at http://www.washingtonmonthly.com/features/2003/0306.sullivan.html.

75. Ibid.

76. ABC News/Beliefnet poll, June 20–24, 2004, online at http://abcnews.go.com/sections/us/DailyNews/beliefnet_poll_01071.8html.

77. "GOP Congressman Calls Democrats Anti-Christian," *Washington Post,* 6/21/05, online at http://www.washingtonpost.com/wp-dyn/content/article/2005/06/20/AR2005062001194.html.

78. "Republicans on the Judicial Anack," FOX News, 4/17/05, online at http://www.foxnews.com/story/0.2933.153616.00.html.

79. See United States Department of Justice Office of Legal Policy website for bi-

ographies of judicial nominees, online at http://www.usdoj.gov/olp/brown
resume.htm.

80. See Pryor's official bio on the Alabama attorney general's website, online at
http://www.ago.state.al.us/bio_pryor.cfm.

81. See Judge Owen's official bio on the Department of Justice Office of Legal Policy website, http://www.usdoj.gov/olp/owenbio.htm.

82. George Washington bio online at http://www.americanpresident.org/
history/GeorgeWashington/.

83. "Episcopalian Presidents of the United States," online at http://www.grace
churchprovidence.org/uspres.htm.

84. "Largest Religious Groups in the United States," online at http://www.adher
ents.com/rel_USA.html.

85. Richard Hofstadter, "The Paranoid Style in American Politics," *Harper's*, November 1964, online at http://karws.gso.uri.edu/JFK/conspiracy_theory/the_
paranoid_mentality/The_paranoid_style.html.

86. ABC, *This Week with George Stephanopoulos*, 5/1/05.

87. Associated Press, "Conservatives Are Trying to Put Religion Back into Christmas Season," 12/14/04, online at http://www.freenewmexican.com/news/
7949.html.

88. Ibid.

89. Ibid.

90. "Democrats in Red States: Just Regular Guys," *New York Times*,
8/22/04.

91. Thomas Frank, "What's the Matter with Liberals?," *New York Review of Books*,
5/12/05.

92. Amy Sullivan, "Do Democrats Have a Prayer?," op. cit.

93. *Ladies Home Journal*, August 2004, online at http://www.meredith.com/News
Releases/Mgz/LHJ/lhj0804quotes.htm.

94. Brent Bozell, "Kerry's Catholic Problem," 7/7/04, *Town Hall*, online at
http://www.townhall.com/columnists/brentbozell/bb20040707.shtml.

95. Buzzflash.com interview with Jim Wallis, 2/22/05, online at http://www
.buzzflash.com/interviews/05/02/int05008.html.

96. "Clinton Honors Reverend Billy Graham at Final US Revival Meeting," Voice
of America News, 6/26/05, online at http://www.voanews.com/english/2005-
06-26-voa15.cfm.

97. "Gay Tinky-Winky Bad for Children," BBC, 2/15/99, online at http://
news.bbc.co.uk/1/hi/entertainment/276677.stm.

98. John McKay, "Shrek Character Is Target of Traditional Values Religious Group," Canadian Press, 2/22/05, online at http://www.peterhansen.com/fundamentalist_christian_moralit.htm.

99. Buck Wolfe, "Muppet Sex Rumor: Ernie and Bert Just Ducky: Felt Puppets Shoot Down Personal Scandal," ABC News, 1/21/04, online at http://abc news.go.com/Entertainment/WolfFiles/story?id=430945&page=1.

100. Eric Boehlert, "Paralyzed Broadcasting System," Salon.com, 2/3/05, online at http://www.salon.com/news/feature/2005/02/04/pbs_and_conservatives/index.html.

101. Zogby International, 11/12/04, press release online at http://www.zogby.com/soundbites/ReadClips.dbm?ID=10389.

102. "Life Support? Stem Cell Support Holds at Six in Ten," ABC News poll, August 3, 2004, online at http://www.abcnews.go.com/sections/politics/DailyNews/poll010803.html.

103. "CMA Doctors Oppose California Proposition 71," Christian Medical Association press release, 9/3/04, online at http://www.cmdahome.org/index.cgi?BISKIT=2584450544&CONTEXT=art&art=2746.

104. Transcript: Second Presidential Debate, Washington University, St. Louis, October 8, 2004, online at http://www.washingtonpost.com/wp-srv/politics/debatereferee/debate 1008.html.

105. Ibid.

106. Ibid.

107. Ibid.

108. "How Many Frozen Embryos Are Available for Research?," RAND Corporation Law and Health Research Brief, online at http://www.rand.org/publications/RB/RB9038/.

109. Jim Wallis, online at http://www.sojo.net/index.cfm?action=about_us.display_staff&staff=wallis.

110. "The Sleuth Behind the Temple Bombing," Atlanta Journal-Constitution, 5/29/96, online at http://melissafaygreene.com/pages/author.html.

111. Zogby International, November 12, 2004, press release online at http://www.zogby.com/soundbites/ReadClips.dbm?ID=10389.

112. CBS News, "GOP: 'Liberals' Will Ban Bible," 9/24/05, online at http://www.cbsnews.com/stories/2004/09/24/politics/main645393.shtml.

113. Ibid.

114. Bill Press, How the Republicans Stole Christmas (New York: Doubleday, 2005).

115. Santorum interview with Associated Press, April 7, 2003, transcript printed in

USA TODAY 4/23/03, online at http://www.usatoday.com/news/washing ton/2003-04-23-santorum-excerpt_x.htm.

116. Ibid.

117. Michael Sokolove, *The New York Times Magazine,* 5/22/05, "Rick Santorum: The Believer."

118. Ibid.

119. *Congressional Quarterly,* Vote #55, March 16, 2005.

120. Since 1998, Santorum has voted against a raise in the minimum wage at least six times: Vote #76, April 7, 2000; Vote #356, November 9, 1999; Vote #239, July 30, 1999; Vote #94, April 28, 1999; Vote #77, March 25, 1999; Vote #278, September 22, 1998. Facing a tough reelection fight, Santorum proposed a minimum-wage "increase" that the Economic Policy Institute said would have excluded 250,000 Pennsylvanians from being eligible for the minimum wage. Santorum's proposal would have required that tips be counted toward the employer-paid minimum wage, and it would have eliminated overtime benefits for tens of thousands of employees.

121. Rick Santorum, online at www.santorumexposed.com/serendipity/archives/ 67-Countdown-Names-Santorum-Worst-Person.html.

122. Keith Olbermann, *Countdown* MSNBC, 9/8/05, online at www.santorumex posed.com/serendipity/archives/67-Countdown-Names-Santorum-Worst-Person.html.

123. Chris McGann and Kathy Mulady, "Gay Sex Scandal Rocks Spokane: Mayor Denies He Abused Boys in 1970s or Misused His Office," *Seattle Post-Intelligencer,* 5/6/05, online at http://seattlepi.nwsource.com/local/223201_ west06.html.

National Security

1. Bob Dole, vice presidential debate with Walter Mondale, Houston, Texas, October 15, 1976, online at http://www.super70s.com/Super70s/News/1976/ campaign76/VP_Debate.asp.

2. "Debating Our Destiny," Public Broadcasting System, Jim Lehrer interview with Bob Dole, November 10, 1999, online at http://www.pbs.org/news hour/debatingourdestiny/interviews/dole.html.

3. 1976 vice presidential debate transcript, op cit.

4. Yvonne Abraham, "Dean Supporters Reject Comparison to '72 McGovern," *Boston Globe,* 12/26/03, online at http://www.boston.com/news/politics/

president/dean/articles/2003/12/26/dean_supporters_reject_comparison_to
_72_mcgovern.

5. "Nixon, Richard M.," *Reader's Companion to American History*, online at
http://www.college.hmco.com/history/readerscomp/rcah/html/ah_065200_
nixonrichard.htm.

6. "A Journey into the Wild Blue Yonder with WWII Pilot George McGovern,"
http://www.bookpage.com/0108bp/stephen_ambrose.html.

7. McGovern Campaign Brochure, "What President George McGovern Would
Do," online at http://www.4president.org/brochures/mcgovern72.pdf.

8. American Chamber of Commerce in Vietnam, online at http://www.am
chamvietnam.com/.

9. Jeffrey Lembcke, "Debunking a Spitting Image," *Boston Globe*, 4/30/05, online at http://www.boston.com/news/globe/editorial_opinion/oped/articles/
2005/04/30/debunking_a_spitting_image/.

10. "Memorable Quotes from *The Man Who Shot Liberty Valance*," Internet Movie
Database, online at http://www.imdb.com/title/tt0056217/quotes.

11. Editorial, "A New Presidency: How Bush Should Spend His Windfall of Political Capital," *Wall Street Journal*, 9/19/01, online at http://www.opinion
journal.com/editorial/feature.html?id=95001169.

12. Ibid.

13. Ibid.

14. Phillip Gordon and Michael O'Hanlon, "September 11 Verdict: Yes to
Missile Defense, but Don't Alienate Russia or China," *Los Angeles Times*,
10/17/01, online at http://www.brookings.edu/views/op-ed/gordon/20011017
.htm.

15. Mike Allen, "Bush Cites 9/11 on All Manner of Questions; References Could
Backfire," *Washington Post*, 9/11/03, online at http://www.washingtonpost
.com/wp-dyn/articles/A57456-2003Sep10.html.

16. "President Urges Tax Relief Aimed at Recovery," White House website,
10/5/01, online at http://www.whitehouse.gov/news/releases/2001/10/2001
1005-6.html.

17. Remarks of the president to the Fiscal Responsibility Coalition, April 16,
2002, online at http://www.whitehouse.gov/news/releases/2002/04/2002
0416-8.html.

18. NBC News, *Meet the Press*, 6/9/01.

19. DeFrancis quote from CNN, September 15, 2004; Labor Department's Bu-

reau of Labor Statistics report, "Impact of the Events of September 11, 2001, on the Mass Layoff Statistics Data Series," both cited on Americablog.com, online at http://www.americablog.blogspot.com/archives/2004_09_12_america blog_archive.html.

20. "The Impact of Bush Linking 9/11 and Iraq," *Christian Science Monitor,* 3/14/03, online at http://www.csmonitor.com/2003/0314/p02s01-woiq .html.

21. *Washington Post* poll, reported by Associated Press, 9/26/03, online at http://www.usatoday.com/news/washington/2003-09-06-poll-iraq_x.htm.

22. *Washington Post,* 6/18/04, online at http://www.washingtonpost.com/ wp-dyn/articles/A50679-2004Jun17.html.

23. Glen Kessler and Dana Priest, "Iraq, 9/11 Still Linked by Cheney," *Washington Post,* 9/29/03, online at http://pages.zdnet.com/trimb/id169.html.

24. Ibid.

25. CNN, 6/29/05, online at http://www.cnn.com/2005/POLITICS/06/29/ hayes.911/.

26. *Washington Post,* 6/18/04, online at http://www.washingtonpost.com/ wp-dyn/articles/A50679-2004Jun17.html.

27. "Kerry Tora Bora Comments Rankle Troops," FOX News, 11/1/04, online at http://www.foxnews.com/story/0.2933.137209.00.html.

28. Barton Gellman and Thomas Ricks, "U.S. Concludes Bin Laden Escaped at Tora Bora Fight," *Washington Post,* 4/17/02, online at http://www.washington post.com/ac2/wp-dyn?pagename=article&contentId=A62618-2002Apr16& notFound=true.

29. Ibid.

30. "Kerry Tora Bora Comments Rankle Troops," FOX News, 11/1/04, online at http://www.foxnews.com/story/0.2933.137209.00.html.

31. Associated Press, "Report Says bin Laden Eluded U.S. Forces in Tora Bora," *USA TODAY,* 3/22/05, online at http://www.usatoday.com/news/washing ton/2005-03-22-bin-laden-report_x.htm.

32. Barton Gellman and Thomas Ricks, "U.S. Concludes Bin Laden Escaped at Tora Bora Fight," op. cit.

33. Michael Hirsh, "Exclusive: CIA Commander: U.S. Let Bin Laden Slip Away," *Newsweek,* 8/15/05, online at http://www.msnbc.msn.com/id/8853000/site/ newsweek.

34. Howard Fineman, "Gore Loyalists Are Relieved That Bush Is the Man: Re-

publican Has More Room to Maneuver, Less Baggage," msnbc.com 10/3/01, online at https://netfiles.uiuc.edu/ro/www/OrangeandBlueObserver/archive/vol11/issue2/obiter.html.

35. Richard Berke, "A Nation Challenged: The Democrats; Bush Winning Gore's Backer's High Praise," *New York Times,* 10/21/01.

36. John McCain, "How the POW's Fought Back," *U.S. News & World Report,* 5/14/73.

37. South Carolina Democratic Party press release, August 24, 2004, online at http://www.scdp.org/blog.php?blog_id=22.

38. David Corn, "Bush Politics 101: How to Make Someone Else's Smear Work for You," davidcorn.com, 8/23/04, online at http://www.truthout.org/docs_04/082504E.shtml.

39. South Carolina Democratic Party press release, op. cit.

40. Ibid.

41. Phillip Gailey, "Georgia Republicans Pander to Those Who Prefer the Ignoble Past," *St. Petersburg Times,* 11/17/02, online at http://www.sptimes.com/2002/11/17/Columns/Georgia_Republicans_p.shtml.

42. Michael Crowley, "Former Sen. Max Cleland: How the Disabled War Veteran Became the Democrats' Mascot," Slate.com, 4/2/04, online at http://slate.msn.com/id/2098171/.

43. Kerry Silver Star citation, reprinted in Douglas Brinkley, *Tour of Duty* (New York: William Morrow, 2004).

44. Timothy Noah, "How Dick Cheney Is Like Dan Quayle," slate.com, 7/27/00, citing a 1989 interview Cheney gave *The Washington Post,* online at http://slate.msn.com/id/1005761/.

45. CBC News, "9/11 Chair: Attack Was Preventable," 12/17/03, online at http://www.cbsnews.com/stories/2003/12/17/eveningnews/main589137.shtml.

46. The August 6, 2001, president's daily briefing is available in its redacted, de-classified version online at http://www.thesmokinggun.com/archive/0409041pdb1.html.

47. Global Security, online at http://www.globalsecurity.org/security/ops/millenium-plot.htm.

48. The Smoking Gun, op. cit.

49. Doug Struck, Howard Schneider, Karl Vick, and Peter Baker, "Borderless Network of Terror," *Washington Post,* 9/23/01, online at http://www.washington

post.com/ac2/wp-dyn?pagename=article&node=&contentId=A10543-2001
Sep22.

50. Maria Ressa, CNN, "U.S. Warned in 1995 of Plot to Hijack Planes, Attack
Buildings," 9/18/01, online at http://archives.cnn.com/2001/US/09/18/inv
.hijacking.philippines.

51. "White House Commission on Aviation Safety and Security: Final Report to
President Clinton, February 12, 1997," online at http://www.fas.org/irp/
threat/212fin-1.html.

52. Ibid.

53. Democrats.com, online at http://archive.democrats.com/view.cfm?id=4532.

54. Ibid., citing *Newsday* news account from 1996.

55. Josh Meyer, "Moussaoui Memo Says FBI Stalled Probe After Attacks," *Los Angeles Times,* 5/28/02, online at http://foi.missouri.edu/whistleblowing/mous
saouimemo.html.

56. Kevin Whitelaw, "With Plenty of Screw-ups to Go Around, the 9/11 Panel
Digs Deeper," *U.S. News & World Report,* 4/26/04, online at http://www.us
news.com/usnews/news/articles/040426/26commish.htm.

57. Bob Woodward and Vernon Loeb, *Washington Post,* 9/14/01.

58. Michael Elliott, "Special Report: The Secret History: They Had a Plan," *Time,*
8/12/02.

59. Ibid.

60. Ibid.

61. Robert Scheer, "CIA's Tracks Lead in Disastrous Circle," *Los Angeles Times,*
9/17/01, online at http://www.robertscheer.com/l_natcolumn/01_columns/
091701.htm.

62. Hart-Rudman Report, quoted in *Yale Bulletin,* 10/12/01, online at http://
www.yale.edu/opa/v30.n6/story2.html.

63. All of Clarke's proposals in the imagined briefing to "President Gore" were actually presented by Clarke to Condoleezza Rice before Bush was inaugurated.
Michael Elliott, "Special Report: The Secret History: They Had a Plan," *Time,*
8/4/02, online at http://www.time.com/time/covers/1101020812/story.html.

64. Ibid.

65. Jane Mayer, "The Search for Osama: Did the Government Let bin Laden's
Trail Go Cold?" *The New Yorker,* 8/4/03, online at http://www.newyorker
.com/fact/content/?030804fa_fact.

66. Barton Gellman, "A Strategy's Cautious Evolution: Before Sept. 11, Bush
Anti-Terror Effort Was Mostly Ambition," *Washington Post,* 1/20/02, online

at   http://www.washingtonpost.com/ac2/wp-dyn?pagename=article&node=
&contentId=A8734-2002Jan19.

67. In his comments at Emma E. Booker Elementary on September 11, 2001, Bush ordered "a full-scale investigation to hunt down and to find those folks who committed this act." CNN, 9/12/01, online at http://archives.cnn.com/2001/US/09/11/bush.statement.

68. David Corn, "Did Bill Wag the Dog?," Salon.com, 8/21/90, online at http://www.salon.com/news/1998/08/21newsc.html.

69. Rep. Tom DeLay, "Removal of United States Armed Forces from the Federal Republic of Yugoslavia," *Congressional Record*, 4/28/99.

70. Tim Weiner, "Crisis in the Balkans: The Debate," *New York Times*, 5/4/99.

71. R. G. Ratcliffe, "Bush Toughens His Stance on NATO Bombing," *Houston Chronicle*, 4/9/99.

72. "Senate Approves Iraq War Resolution," CNN, 10/11/02, online at http://archives.cnn.com/2002/ALLPOLITICS/10/11/iraq.us/.

73. Clerk of the House of Representatives, Roll Call 455, H.J. Res. 114, 10/10/02, online at http://clerk.house.gov/evs/2002/roll455.xml.

74. "Senate Approves Iraq War Resolution," op. cit.

75. "Congress Approves Iraq Resolution," FOX News, 10/11/02, online at http://www.foxnews.com/story/0.2933.65395.00.html.

76. "Joint Resolution to Authorize the Use of United States Armed Forces Against Iraq," 10/2/02, online at http://www.whitehouse.gov/news/releases/2002/10/20021002-2.html.

77. Ibid.

78. Alan Eisner, "Iraq War Costs More Per Month Than Vietnam—Report," Reuters, 8/31/05, online at http://www.alertnet.org/thenews/newsdesk/N30297215.htm.

79. David Corn, "Is Bush's Iraq War a 'Brain Fart'?" *The Nation*, 9/26/03.

80. Paul Wellstone, "Statement by Senator Wellstone Regarding Military Action Against Iraq," 10/3/02, online at http://www.wellstone.org/news/news_detail.aspx?itemID=2778&catID=298.

81. Mark Zdechlik, "Wellstone States Opposition to Iraq War," Minnesota Public Radio, 10/3/02, online at http://news.minnesota.publicradio.org/features/200210/03_zdechlkm_wellstoneiraq/.

82. Edward Epstein, "Troops in Iraq Face Pay Cut," *San Francisco Chronicle*, 8/14/03, online at http://sfgate.com/cgi-bin/article.cgi?file=/c/a/2003/08/14/MN94780.DTL.

83. "Delegates Mock Kerry with 'Purple Heart' Bandages," CNN, 9/1/04, online at http://www.cnn.com/2004/ALLPOLITICS/08/30/gop.purple.hearts.

84. David L. Phillips, *Losing Iraq: Inside the Postwar Reconstruction Fiasco* (New York: Westview Press, 2005); excerpted online at http://shows.airamericaradio .com/alfranken.show/archive/2005/06/06.

85. Margaret Talev and Jerry Allegood, "Jones Seeks Iraq Exit Plan," *Raleigh News & Observer,* 6/17/05.

86. Chris Mazzolini, "Jones: U.S. Has No Iraq Playbook," *Daily News,* Jacksonville, North Carolina, 8/4/05, online at http://www.idnews.com/Site Processor.cfm?Template=/GlobalTemplates/Details.cfm&StoryID=33966& Section=News.

87. AP, "Jones Backs Timetable on Iraq," *Raleigh News & Observer,* 6/13/05, online at http://www.newsobserver.com/nation_world/iraq/story/2497896 p-8902275c.html.

88. Chuck Hagel, "Address to the Nebraska American Legion Annual Convention," 6/24/05, online at http://hagel.senate.gov/index.cfm?FuseAction= Speeches.Detail&Speech_id=19&Month=6&Year=2005.

89. John D. Banusiewicz, " 'As Iraqis Stand Up, We Will Stand Down,' Bush Tells Nation," U.S. Department of Defense, American Forces Press Service, 6/28/05, online at http://www.dod.mil/news/Jun2005/20050628_1894.html.

90. John Diamond and Dave Moniz, "Iraq Has Single Self-Sufficient Battalion, U.S. Generals Say," *USA TODAY,* 9/29/05, online at http://www.usatoday .com/news/world/iraq/2005-09-29-iraq-withdrawal_x.htm.

91. John D. Banusiewicz, Armed Forces Press Service, op. cit.

92. "National Insecurity Is the New Reality," interview with Zbigniew Brzezinski, *Newsweek,* 3/31/04, online at http://www.msnbc.msn.com/id/4640604/.

93. "Bush Vows to Rid the World of 'Evil-Doers,' " CNN, 9/16/01, online at http://archives.cnn.com/2001/US/09/16/gen.bush.terrorism/.

94. "War by Any Other Name," *On the Media,* National Public Radio, 7/29/05, online at http://www.onthemedia.org/transcripts/transcripts_072905_name .html.

95. "Bush: 'You Cannot Show Weakness in this World,' " NBC *Today* show, 9/2/04, online at http://www.msnbc.msn.com/id/5866571/.

96. Abraham Lincoln, Second Annual Message to Congress, 1862, online at http://home.att.net/~rjnorton/Lincoln78.html.

97. CBS News, "Clarke's Take on Terror," 4/26/04, online at http://www .cbsnews.com/stories/2004/03/19/60minutes/main607356.shtml.

98. Joe Klein, "Saddam's Revenge," *Time*, 9/18/05, online at http://www.time.com/time/magazine/printout/0.8816.1106254.00.html.

99. Associated Press, "Army Chief: Force to Occupy Iraq Massive," *USA TODAY*, 2/25/03, online at http://www.usatoday.com/news/world/iraq/2003-02-25-iraq-us_x.htm.

100. Rowan Scarborough, "Wolfowitz Criticizes 'Suspect' Estimate of Occupation Force," *Washington Times*, 2/28/03, online at http://www.drumbeat.mlaterz.net/Jan%20Feb%202003/Wolfowitz%20critical%20of%20occupation%20estimate%20022803a.htm.

101. Biography of General Eric Shinseki, online at http://ifpafletchercambridge.info/oldsite/speakers/shinseki.htm.

102. Biography of Paul Wolfowitz, Department of Defense, online at http://www.defenselink.mil/bios/wolfowitz.html.

103. Joe Klein, "Saddam's Revenge," *Time*, 9/18/05, online at http://www.time.com/time/magazine/printout/0.8816.1106254.00.html.

104. Francis X. Taylor, "A Global Perspective on Terrorism and Organized Crime," Keynote Speech to the International Conference on Asian Organized Crime and Terrorism, 4/12/04, online at http://www.state.gov/m/ds/rls/rm/31861.htm.

105. "Albright on Development Assistance, Globalization," United States Mission to the European Union, 4/24/00, online at http://www.useu.be/ISSUES/albr0424.html.

106. "National Insecurity Is the New Reality," interview with Zbigniew Brzezinski, op. cit.

107. State of the Union Address, January 20, 2004, online at http://www.whitehouse.gov/news/releases/2004/01/20040120-7.html.

108. Tony Blair biography, online at http://www.number-10.gov.uk/output/Page4.asp.

109. "War by Any Other Name," *On the Media*, National Public Radio, 7/29/05, online at http://www.onthemedia.org/transcripts/transcripts_072905_name.html.

110. CNN, "Bush: Iraq Crucial in War on Terror," 10/7/05, online at http://www.cnn.com/2005/POLITICS/10/06/bush.iraq.

111. Analysis by Richard Kogan of the Center for Budget and Policy Priorities.

112. John Mintz and Spencer Hsu, "Capitol Cleared over Errant Small Plane," *Washington Post*, 6/10/04, online at http://www.washingtonpost.com/wp-dyn/articles/A28863-2004Jun9.html.

113. Barry McCaffrey, "Failure Isn't an Option," *Wall Street Journal*, 7/1/05.

114. Sarah Schweitzer and Peter Canellos, "Military Recruiters Find the War a Difficult Sell," *Boston Globe*, 7/5/05, online at http://www.boston.com/news/local/massachusetts/articles/2005/07/05/military_recruiters_find_the_war_a_difficult_sell.

115. CNN, 9/3/03, online at http://www.cnn.com/2003/SHOWBIZ/Music/09/03/cnna.spears.

116. College Republicans Press Release, 7/23/04, online at http://www.crnc.org/resources/Press%20Releases/Field%20Release.pdf.

Don't Just "Clean Up" Washington; Fumigate It

1. Robert Novak, "Mission to Niger," 7/14/03, online at http://www.townhall.com/opinion/columns/robertnovak/2003/07/14/160881.html.

2. David Corn, "A White House Smear," *The Nation*, 7/16/03, online at http://www.thenation.com/blogs/capitalgames?bid=3&pid=823.

3. Larry Johnson, "Why Patrick Fitzgerald Gets It," Talking Points Café, 10/14/05, online at http://www.tpmcafe.com/section/politics.

4. CNN, "Sources: Tenet Says He Never Read Final Draft of Bush Speech," 7/29/03, online at http://www.cnn.com/2003/ALLPOLITICS/07/17/white.house.tenet.

5. "Fun Text: U.S. v. Libby Indictment," Office of Special Counsel, 10/28/05, Online at http://www.washingtonpost.com/wp-dyn/content/article/2005/10/28/AR2005102801086.html; Rove identified as "Official A" by Associated Press, see Pete Yost, "AP: Mysterious 'Official A' is Karl Rove," Associated Press, 10/28/05, online at http://www.editorandpublisher.com/eandp/news/article_display.jsp?vnu_content_id=1001392393.

6. CNN, "Wilson Wants Leak Culprit 'Frog-Marched,' " 10/6/03, online at http://www8.cnn.com/2003/ALLPOLITICS/10/05/cia.leak.

7. *Daily News*, October 30, 2003.

8. *The White House Bulletin*, 10/7/03.

9. David Corn, "CIA Leak Scandal: Rove Defied Bush's Command?," *The Nation*, 10/12/05, online at http://news.yahoo.com/s/thenation/20051012/cm_thenation/328485;_ylt=A86.12fcXk1DSxQBhhf9wxIF;_ylu=X3oDMTBjMHVqMTQ4BHNIYwN5bnN1YmNhdA.

10. Ibid.

11. Ibid.

12. *White House Bulletin,* 10/7/03.

13. Jake Tapper, "Boomerang," ABC News, 10/1/03, online at http://abcnews.go .com/sections/wnt/US/CIAleak031001_tapper.html.

14. David Corn, *The Nation,* op. cit.

15. Anne Mulkern, "When Advocates Become Regulators: President Bush Has Installed More Than 100 Top Officials Who Were Once Lobbyists, Attorneys or Spokespeople for the Industries They Regulate," *Denver Post,* 5/23/04, online at http://www.commondreams.org/headlines04/0523-02.htm.

16. Ibid.

17. Ibid.

18. CBS News, "Medicare Cost Cover-Up?," 3/5/04, online at http://www .cbsnews.com/stories/2004/03/15/eveningnews/main606477.shtml.

19. Robert Pear, "Inquiry Confirms Medicare Chief Threatened Actuary," *New York Times,* 7/7/04, online at http://www.nytimes.com/2004/07/07/politics/ 07medicare.html?ex=1129089600&en=a3e264872aed0cc0&ei=5070 &8br.

20. Anne Mulkern, *Denver Post,* op. cit.

21. Ibid.

22. Ibid.

23. Ken Cook, "Brain Food," Environmental Working Group, online at http://www.ewg.org/reports/brainfood/foreword.html.

24. Philip Babich, "Shafted," Salon.com, 12/11/03, online at http://archive.salon .com/tech/feature/2003/12/11/griles.

25. Jayson Stevenson, "Earth Shakers: The Counter-Enviro Power List: J. Steven Griles, Lobbyist," *Outside,* May 2005, online at http://outside.away.com/out side/features/200505/counter-enviroment-power-list-18.html.

26. Anne Mulkern, *Denver Post,* op. cit.

27. Ibid.

28. Jeffrey Birnbaum, "The Road to Riches Is Called K Street," *Washington Post,* 6/22/05, online at http://www.washingtonpost.com/wp-dyn/content/article/ 2005/06/21/AR2005062101632.html.

29. U.S. Census, 2000.

30. Jonathon E. Kaplan, "Lobbying Reform Targeted at DeLay, Abramoff Issues," *The Hill,* 4/21/05, online at http://www.hillnews.com/thehill/export/The Hill/News/Frontpage/042105/delay.html.

31. Jeffrey Birnbaum, *Washington Post,* op. cit.

32. Nicholas Confessore, "Welcome to the Machine," *Washington Monthly*, July/August 2003, online at http://www.washingtonmonthly.com/features/2003/0307.confessore.html.

33. Ibid.

34. Ibid.

35. Lou Dubose, "Broken Hammer?," Salon.com., 4/8/05, online at http://www.salon.com/news/feature/2005/04/08/scandals/index.html.

36. James Verini, "The Tale of 'Red Scorpion,' " Salon.com., 8/17/05, online at http://www.salon.com/ent/feature/2005/08/17/abramoff/.

37. James Harding, "Jack Abramoff: The Friend Tom DeLay Can't Shake," Slate.com, 4/7/05, online at http://slate.msn.com/id/2116389/.

38. Associated Press, 6/8/05.

39. *Wall Street Journal*, 7/3/01.

40. Susan Schmidt, "Insiders Worked Both Sides of Gaming Issue," *Washington Post*, 9/26/04, online at http://www.washingtonpost.com/ac2/wp-dyn/A50258-2004Sep25?language=printer.

41. Ibid.

42. Maria Recio, "Cornyn Denies Ties to Lobbyist," *Fort Worth Star-Telegram*, 4/17/05, online at http://www.tpj.org/page_view.jsp?pageid=838&pubid=603.

43. Peter Stone, "Ralph Reed's Other Cheek," *Mother Jones*, November/December 2004, online at http://www.motherjones.com/news/outfront/2004/11/10_400.html.

44. Maria Recio, *Fort Worth Star-Telegram*, op. cit.

45. Susan Schmidt, *Washington Post*, op. cit.

46. Ibid.

47. Ibid.

48. Ibid.

49. Kristin Jensen and Michael Forsythe, "Former Bush Official Indicted on Obstruction," Bloomberg News, 10/5/05, online at http://www.bloomberg.com/apps/news?pid=10000087&sid=aOSX2cl6rNOM&refer=top_world_news#.

50. James Grimaldi, "Abramoff Indicted in Casino Boat Purchase," *Washington Post*, 8/12/05, online at http://www.washingtonpost.com/wp-dyn/content/article/2005/08/11/AR2005081101108.html.

51. Ibid.

52. Ibid.

53. Ibid.

54. Harding, Jake, Slate, op. cit.

55. Peter Stone, "Lobbying & Law: Abramoff's and DeLay's Foreign Adventures," *National Journal,* 2/26/05.

56. *New York Times,* 4/3/02.

57. Peter Stone, *National Journal,* op. cit.

58. *New York Times,* 6/11/02.

59. Jonathon D. Salant, "DeLay Indictment May Be Overshadowed by Looming Abramoff Probe," Bloomberg News Service, 9/29/05, online at http://www .bloomberg.com/apps/news?pid=10000087&sid=auNbMNxcIEJU&refer= top_world_news.

60. Timothy Noah, "What Did You Do in the War, Hammer?" Slate.com, 5/4/99, online at http://slate.msn.com/id/1002713/.

61. *The Hill,* 3/2/05.

62. *Washington Post,* 4/6/05, and *New York Times,* 4/6/05.

63. Mark Shields, "The Real Scandal of Tom DeLay," CNN.com, 5/9/05, online at http://www.cnn.com/2005/POLITICS/05/09/real.delay/.

64. Ibid.

65. "Welcome to the Marianas," http://www.destmic.com/mariana.html.

66. Shields, CNN, op. cit.

67. CNN, "DeLay Faces Money Laundering Charge," 10/3/05, online at http:// www.cnn.com/2005/POLITICS/10/03/delay.indictment.

68. Candy Crowley, "Tom DeLay Rose to Power the Old Fashioned Way," CNN, 10/5/05, online at http://www.cnn.com/2005/POLITICS/09/28/DeLay.pro file/.

69. Stephen Pizzo, "Tom DeLay in His Own Words," Alternet, 5/16/02, online at http://politicalhumor.about.com/gi/dynamic/offsite.htm?zj=1/XJ&sdn= politicalhumor&zu=http%3A%2F%2Fwww.alternet.org%2Fstory% 2FJ3152.

70. Ibid.

71. *Houston Chronicle,* 9/9/05, online at http://blogs.chron.com/domeblog/ archives/2005/09/delay_to_evacue.html.

72. Jim VandeHei, "GOP Whip Quietly Tried to Aid Big Donor," *Washington Post,* 6/11/03, online at http://www.washingtonpost.com/ac2/wp-dyn/ A41839-2003Jun10?language=printer.

73. Citizens for Responsibility and Ethics in Washington (CREW), online at http://beyonddelay.citizensforethics.org/summaries/blunt.php.

74. Ibid.

75. VandeHei, *Washington Post,* op. cit.

76. CREW, op. cit.

77. Jonathon M. Katz, "Senator Sold Stock Before Price Dropped," *Washington Post,* 9/21/05, online at http://www.washingtonpost.com/wp-dyn/content/article/2005/09/20/AR2005092001767.html.

78. Jeremy Pelofsky and Richard Cowan, "Probe Widens of Sen. Frist's HCA Stock Sale," Reuters 9/23/05, online at http://news.yahoo.com/s/nm/20050923/pl_nm/hca_dc.

79. Ibid.

80. Ibid.

81. Larry Maraca and Jonathon M. Katz, "Frist's Holdings Raise Questions of Conflict," Associated Press, 10/12/05, online at http://articles.news.aol.com/news/article/adp?id=20051101117050990013.

82. Mike Madden, "Frist Was Notified of HCA Stock in Trusts," *USA TODAY,* 10/24/04.

83. Ibid.

84. Ibid.

85. "Beyond DeLay: The 13 Most Corrupt Members of Congress: Duke Cunningham," Citizens for Responsibility and Ethics in Washington, online at http://beyonddelay.citizensforethics.org/summaries/cunningham.php.

86. *North County Times,* 6/13/05; *Los Angeles Times,* 6/29/05; *Roll Call,* 6/22/05; *North County Times,* 6/28/05.

87. CREW, op. cit.

88. Copley News Service, 6/12/05; *San Diego Union-Tribune,* 6/25/05; *Washington Post,* 6/28/05; http://www.mzminc.com/index.cfm.

89. CREW, op. cit.

90. Ibid.

91. Kevin Phillips, "The Company Presidency," *Los Angeles Times,* 2/10/02, online at http://www.commondreams.org/views02/0210-04.htm.

92. CNN, "Bush-Lay Letters Suggest Close Relationship," 2/17/02, online at http://archives.cnn.com/2002/US/02/17/bush.lay.

93. Charles Lewis, "The Enron Collapse: A Financial Scandal Rooted in Politics," Center for Public Integrity, 2/25/02, online at http://www.bop2004.org/report.aspx?aid=214.

94. Kevin Phillips, op. cit.

95. CNN, "Waxman Says Cheney Task Force Helped Enron," 1/16/02, online at http://archives.cnn.com/2002/ALLPOLITICS/01/16/enron.waxman.

96. Lou Dobbs, "Lobbying Against America," CNN, 8/12/05, online at http://www.cnn.com/2005/US/08/11/lobby.america.

97. Jonathon E. Kaplan, "Lobbying Reform Targeted at DeLay, Abramoff Issues," *The Hill*, 4/21/05, online at http://www.hillnews.com/thehill/export/The Hill/News/Frontpage/042105/delay.html.

98. Thomas Jefferson to Baron Humboldt, as quoted in Rayner's *Life of Jefferson*, online at http://www.worldofquotes.com/topic/Public-Trust/1.

99. Joseph E. Canter, "United States Elections, 2004," online at http://usinfo .state.gov/products/pubs/election04/campaign$.htm.

100. "Drunk on Ethanol," Taxpayers for Common Sense, 7/1/05, online at http://www.taxpayer.net/TCS/wastebasket/environment/2005-07-01drunkonethanol .htm.

101. Zachary Coile, "House OKs Energy Bill Laden with Tax Breaks," Associated Press 4/22/05, online at http://www.sfgate.com/cgi-bin/article.cgi?file=/c/a/ 2005/04/22/MNG45CDDBS1.DTL.

102. U.S. Capitol Historical Society, online at http://www.uschs.org/04_history/ subs_exhibit_c/04c_05.html.

A Declaration of Energy Independence

1. Energy Information Administration, Annual Energy Review, 2003, online at http://www.eia.doe.gov/emeu/aer/pdf/pages/sec5.pdf.

2. John Cassidy, "Pump Dreams," *The New Yorker*, 10/11/04.

3. See http://www.wired.com/news/technology/0,1282,66651,00.html.

4. U.S. Department of State, U.S. Climate Action Report 2002, p. 81.

5. Peter Schwartz and Doug Randall, "An Abrupt Climate Change Scenario and Its Implication for United States National Security (2003)," 1–3.

6. Natural Resources Defense Council, online at http://www.nrdc.org/global Warming/default.asp.

7. Earl Lane, "Bush: Moon Return by 2015," *Newsday*, 1/14/04, online at http://www.newsday.com/news/nationworld/nation/ny-bush-space-0114,0,4190003 .story?coll=ny-nationalnews-headlines.

8. NRDC, "Summary of Harmful Provisions in the Energy Bill," and H.R. 6, Energy Policy Act of 2005; The Green Scissors Campaign, "The Chopping Block," 10/6/05.

9. "Congress Dons the Mask of Big Oil," *Atlanta Journal Constitution*, 10/11/05; *Los Angeles Times*, "House Passes Bill to Boost Construction of Refineries,"

10/7/05; *New York Times,* "Refinery Construction Bill Is Drawing Broad Criticism," 10/7/05.

10. Pelosi press release, 10/7/05.

11. Zachary Coile, "House OKs Energy Bill with Tax Breaks," *San Francisco Chronicle,* 4/22/05.

12. H. Josef Herbert, "Oil Execs to Be Asked to Justify Profits," Associated Press, 11/1/05.

13. "Tracking the Payback: Energy/Natural Resources," The Center for Responsive Politics, 8/23/05, online at http://www.opensecrets.org/payback/issue.asp?issueid=EN5&CongN=109.

14. CBS News, "Woodward Shares War Secrets," 4/19/04, online at http://www.cbsnews.com/stories/2004/04/15/60minutes/main612067.shtml.

15. Center for American Progress, American Progress Report, 8/30/04.

16. Ibid., 8/30/04 and 8/2/05.

17. "Green Electric? GE Unveils Eco-Strategy," MSNBC, 5/10/05, online at http://www.msnbc.msn.com/id/7791657/.

18. "New Fuel Economy Standards Proposed," *Washington Post,* 8/24/05.

19. The American Council for an Energy-Efficient Economy, online at http://www.aceee.org/energy/cafe.htm.

20. See http://www.aceee.org/energy/cafe.htm.

21. Sen. Dianne Feinstein, "Senators Urge Stricter Fuel Economy Standards for SUVs and Light Trucks," 8/23/05, online at http://feinstein.senate.gov/05releases/r-fuelcon.htm.

22. Union of Concerned Scientists, online at http://www.ucsusa.org/clean_vehicles/fuel_economy/questions-and-answers-on-fuel-economy.html.

23. See http://www.ase.org/powersmart/.

24. See http://www.ase.org.

25. Amory Lovins et al., *Winning the Oil Endgame,* (City Rocky Mountain Institute, 2004), xiii.

26. Ibid.

27. Texas Department of Transportation, online at http://www.dot.state.tx.us/gsd/altfuel/altfuelvehicles.htm.

28. Steven Harmon, "Robert F. Kennedy Jr. Rips 'Crony Capitalism,'" *Grand Rapids Press,* 9/29/05, online at http://www.mlive.com/news/grpress/index.ssf?/base/news-25/1128007332252160.xml&coll=6.

29. Michael P. Armstrong, "A Fishery Survey of the Middle Brazos River Basin in North-Central Texas," U.S. Fish and Wildlife Service, Region 2, December

1998, p. 4, online at http://72.14.207.104/search?q=cache:lyeOgwOhI24J:
www.fws.gov/arlingtontexas/pdf/Brazos.pdf+middle+bosque+river+polluted
&hl=en&client=firefox-a.

Work the Refs

1. Lewis Powell, "Attack on the Free Enterprise System," 8/23/71, online at http://www.mediatransparency.org/story.php?storyID=22.
2. Eric Alterman, "What Liberal Media?," adapted from his book of the same name, *The Nation,* 2/24/03, online at http://www.thenation.com/doc/20030224/alterman2.
3. Ibid.
4. Eric Alterman. "Liberal Media, RIP," *The Nation,* 3/13/00, online at http://www.thenation.com/docprint.mhtml?i=20000313&s=alterman.
5. Ibid.
6. David Brock, *The Right-Wing Noise Machine: Right-Wing Media and How It Corrupts Democracy* (New York: Crown, 2004).
7. Media Research Center, "Top Ten Gumbel Stumbles," October 1999, online at http://www.mrc.org/projects/gumbel/stumbles.asp.
8. Alterman, op. cit.
9. Brock, op. cit., p. 98.
10. Joe Conason, "Starr Troopers," Salon.com, 6/22/98, online at http://www.salon.com/col/cona/1998/06/nc_22cona.html.
11. Media Research Center, "The Liberal Media: Every Poll Shows Journalists Are More Liberal Than the American Public—and the Public Knows It," 6/30/04, online at http://www.mediaresearch.org/SpecialReports/2004/report063004_pl.asp.
12. Conason, Joe, "Starr Troopers," op. cit.
13. Editorial, *New York Times,* 2/12/01, online at http://archives.cnn.com/2001/ALLPOLITICS/02/12/clinton.controversy.
14. Howard Kurtz, "Mainstream Media, R.I.P.," *Washington Post,* 1/13/05, online at http://www.washingtonpost.com/wp-dyn/articles/A6164-2005Jan13.html.
15. Dana Milbank, quoting from Ari Fleischer's book *Taking Heat,* "My Bias for Mainstream News," *Washington Post,* 3/20/05, online at http://www.washingtonpost.com/ac2/wp-dyn/A48952-2005Mar19?language=printer.
16. Mark Fabiani, "The Communication Stream of Conspiracy Commerce," Democratic National Committee, July 1995, quoted by Michael Goldfarb,

"Our President, Their Scandal: The Role of the British Press in Keeping the Clinton Scandals Alive," Joan Shorenstein Barone Center on the Press, Politics and Public Policy, Harvard University, 1999, online at http://www.ksg .harvard.edu/presspol/Research_Publications/Papers/Working_Papers/2000_ 5.pdf.

17. Kathleen Hall Jamieson and Paul Waldman, *The Press Effect* (Oxford: Oxford University Press, 2003), 48–49

18. John Schwartz, "Gore Deserves Internet Credit, Some Say," *Washington Post,* 3/21/99, online at http://www.washingtonpost.com/wp-srv/politics/cam paigns/wh2000/stories/gore032199.htm.

19. Jamieson and Waldman, op. cit., page 50.

20. *New York Times,* 12/14/97.

21. Cecil Connally, "First Love Story, Now Love Canal," *Washington Post,* 12/2/99.

22. Boehlert, *Rolling Stone,* op. cit.

23. Jane Hall, "Gore Media Coverage: Playing Hardball," *Columbia Journalism Review,* September/October 2000, online at http://archives.cjr.org/year/00/3/ hall.asp.

24. Frank Bruni, *Ambling into History* (New York: HarperCollins, 2002), 35.

25. Ibid, p. 33.

26. Ibid., pp. 25–26.

27. *Brill's Content,* September 2000.

28. Jake Tapper, "A Major League Asshole," Salon.com, 9/4/00, online at http://dir.salon.com/story/politics/feature/2000/09/04/cuss_word/.

29. Jane Hall, "Gore Media Coverage: Playing Hardball," op. cit.

30. See politicalwire.com/archives/media_buzz/.

31. "The Fox News Gamble," *American Enterprise,* September/October 2003, on-line at http://www.findarticles.com/p/articles/mi_m2185/is_n5_v8/ai_2003 2345.

32. David Brock, *The Republican Noise Machine* (New York: Crown, 2004), 318.

33. Ibid.

34. Ibid., p. 319.

35. Ibid.

36. Ibid., p. 320.

37. Ibid.

38. Mike Leonard, "Bloomington Native Reports the News," *Bloomington Herald-*

Times, 10/2/05, online at http://www.heraldtimesonline.com/stories/2005/10/02/column.1002-SH-A3_CMK35541.sto.

39. Program on International Policy Attitudes, "Misperceptions, the Media and the War in Iraq," 10/2/03, online at http://www.pipa.org/OnlineReports/Iraq/Media_10_02_03_Report.pdf.

40. Ibid.

41. Charles Krauthammer, "Kerry's Afghan Amnesia," *Washington Post*, 10/29/04, online at http://www.washingtonpost.com/wp-dyn/articles/A7885-2004Oct28.html.

42. David Brooks, "The Osama Litmus Test," *New York Times*, 10/30/04, online at http://www.nytimes.com/2004/10/30/opinion/30brooks.html?ex=1256875200&en=ef0b1c594e62c829&ei=5090&partner=rssuserland.

43. FOX News Sunday, 10/31/04.

44. *Larry King Live*, CNN, 12/14/01, online at http://mediamatters.org/items/200411010004.

45. CNN, 4/8/05.

46. Eric Boehlert, "Ari Fleischer: Still Saying Nothing After All These Years," Salon.com, 3/14/05, online at http://www.salon.com/news/feature/2005/03/14/fleischer/.

47. Eric Pianin and Terry Neal, "Bush to Offer $483 Billion Tax-Cut Plan; Working Poor, Middle Class Would Get Much of Relief," *Washington Post*, 12/1/99.

48. *Washington Post*, 12/2/99.

49. Brock, op. cit., p. 14.

50. Damien Cave, "Inside Clear Channel," *Rolling Stone*, 8/13/04, online at http://www.rollingstone.com/news/story/_/id/6432174?rnd=1128445270750&has-player=unknown.

51. Eric Beohlert, "Radio's Big Bully," Salon.com, 4/30/01, online at http://www.salon.com/ent/feature/2001/04/30/clear_channel.

52. Rick Karr, "Big Media," *NOW with Bill Moyers*, PBS, 4/4/03, online at http://www.pbs.org/now/transcript/transcript_bigmedia.html.

53. Brian Mansfield, "Dixie Chicks' Chart Wings Get Clipped," *USA TODAY*, 3/18/03, online at http://www.usatoday.com/life/music/news/2003-03-18-chicks-chart_x.htm.

54. Interview with Tom Brokaw aboard Air Force One, NBC News, 4/25/03, online at http://www.nytimes.com/2003/04/25/international/worldspecial/25BUSH-TEXT.html?ei=5070&en=a6aa2fd74be635db&ex=1128571200&ad

xnnl=1&pagewanted=all&adxnnlx=1128449312-JYn8GmXT2iiEeKO0Q
71QSA.

55. J. Black, *Associated Press* v. *United States,* 326 US 1 at 20 (1945).

56. David Croteau, "Examining the 'Liberal Media' Claim: Journalists' Views on
Politics, Economic Policy and the Media," Fairness and Accuracy in Media,
1998, online at http://www.fair.org/index.php?page=2447.

Taxes: The Heiress Versus the Waitress

1. See http://sports.espn.go.com/espn/page2/quickie?date=040923.

2. *Washington Post,* 9/23/04, online at http://www.washingtonpost.com/wp-
dyn/articles/A43278-2004Sep22.html.

3. Ibid.

4. *Washington Post,* 9/24/04, online at http://www.washingtonpost.com/
wp-dyn/articles/A45603-2004Sep23.html.

5. *Washington Post,* 9/23/04, online at http://www.washingtonpost.com/ac2/
wp-dyn/A43278-2004Sep22?language=printer.

6. Congressional Research Service, 6/25/04, online at http://64.233.161.104/
search?q=cache:CueVDJ68ENAJ:www.senate.gov/reference/resources/pdf/9
8-53.pdf+senate+salary+house&hl=en.

7. U.S. Census Bureau, online at http://64.233.161.104/search?q=cache:yqXFg
Coctk4J:www.census.gov/prod/2004pubs/p60-226.pdf+median+family+in
come+2004&hl=en.

8. CNN, *Crossfire,* 9/23/04.

9. Franklin Roosevelt, Address to the 1932 Democratic National Convention,
online at http://shs.westport.k12.ct.us/jwb/AP/GrtDep/Roosevelt.htm.

10. Bill Clinton, Address to the 1992 Democratic National Convention, online at
http://www.americanrhetoric.com/speeches/billclinton1992dnc.htm.

11. Ibid.

12. Ibid.

13. Clinton for President campaign brochure, online at http://www.4president
.org/brochures/billclinton92.pdf.

14. Ibid.

15. "Reagan's Liberal Legacy," *Washington Monthly,* January/February 2003, online at http://www.washingtonmonthly.com/features/2003/0301.green.html.

16. Concise Encyclopedia of Economics, "Negative Income Tax, online at http://
www.econlib.org/library/Enc/NegativeIncomeTax.html.

17. "Reagan's Liberal Legacy," op. cit.

18. "The Best of Times: America in the Clinton Years," *American Prospect*, February 2002, online at http://www.findarticles.com/p/articles/mi_go1661/is_200202/ai_n6759927.

19. Steven Weisman, *The Great Tax Wars*, cited by Ron Brownstein, *Los Angeles Times*, 1/13/03, available online at http://www.house.gov/georgemiller/lineoftheday31303.html.

20. Historic Speeches, Theodore Roosevelt, "The New Nationalism," 8/31/10, online at http://www.presidentialrhetoric.com/historicspeeches/roosevelt_theodore/newnationalism.html.

21. Ibid.

22. Ibid.

23. *Washington Post*, 4/12/05, online at http://www.washingtonpost.com/wp-dyn/articles/A45305-2005Apr11.html.

24. IRS data, cited by Isaac Shapiro, Iris J. Lav, and Jim Sly, Center for Budget and Policy Priorities, 2/26/01, online at http://64.233.187.104/search?q=cache:EFaBmf76znMJ:www.cbpp.org/2-26-01tax2.pdf+estate+tax+citizens+for+tax+justice&hl=en&client=firefox-a.

25. *Washington Post*, 4/12/05, online at http://www.washingtonpost.com/wp-dyn/articles/A45305-2005Apr11.html.

26. Federal Election Commission records, online at www.opensecrets.org.

27. *Washington Post*, 4/12/05, online at http://www.washingtonpost.com/wp-dyn/articles/A45305-2005Apr11.html.

28. "God in the Campaign," Northwestern University Medill School of Journalism panel, 9/26/00.

29. Vote of the House of Representatives on Article 2 and Article 4, 12/20/98, reported in the *Milwaukee Journal-Sentinel*, online at http://www.jsonline.com/news/president/1220roll2.asp and http://www.jsonline.com/news/president/1220roll4.asp.

30. Riley biography online at http://www.netstate.com/states/government/al_government.htm.

31. Americans United for Separation of Church and State, citing news coverage of Riley's speech in the *Mobile Register*, 3/8/03, online at http://www.au.org/site/News2?abbr=cs_&page=NewsArticle&id=5523&security=1001&news_iv_ctrl=1085.

32. Ibid.

33. *Christian Science Monitor*, 9/8/05, online at http://www.csmonitor.com/2003/0908/p03s01-uspo.html.

34. Religion News Service, online at http://www.beliefnet.com/story/129/story_12980_1.html.

35. Ibid.

36. Ibid.

37. Ibid.

38. *Washington Post,* 8/24/03, online at http://www.tallahassee.com/mld/democrat/news/opinion/6587024.htm.

39. Ibid.

40. Ibid.

41. Ibid.

42. *San Francisco Chronicle,* 12/12/04, online at http://www.sfgate.com/cgi-bin/article.cgi?file=/chronicle/archive/2004/12/12/MNGN9AAPG11.DTL.

43. Dr. Jim Seroka, Director, Center for Governmental Services, Auburn University, 12/5/03, online at http://www.auburn.edu/outreach/cgs/publications/Alabamataxvote2003.pdf.

44. Ibid.

45. Jack Kemp, Address to the 1996 Republican National Convention, online at http://www.usembassy-israel.org.il/publish/press/society/archive/august/bk2_8-19.htm.

46. *Washington Post,* 11/18/04, online at http://www.washingtonpost.com/wp-dyn/articles/A58554-2004Nov17.html.

47. Ibid.

48. Ibid.

49. Urban Institute Report, "Contemporary U.S. Tax Policy," online at http://www.urban.org/pubs/CTP/chapter1.html.

50. Center for American Progress, "A Fair and Simple Tax System for Our Future: A Progressive Approach to Tax Reform," 1/31/05, online at http://www.americanprogress.org/site/pp.asp?c=biJRJ8OVF&b=310260.

51. Dana Milbank and Jonathon Weisman, "Middle Class Tax Share Set to Rise; Studies Say Burden of Rich to Decline," *Washington Post,* 6/4/03.

52. *Boston Globe,* 1/10/04, citing Tax Policy Center statistics.

53. "Payroll & Tax Management: Social Security Taxes," Hancock Bank 2005, online at http://partners.financenter.com/hancockbank/learn/guides/smbizpayroll/sbfica.fcs?portal=home.

54. *Boston Globe,* 1/10/04, citing Tax Policy Center statistics.

55. Center for American Progress, citing Tax Policy Center Statistics, "Historical

Percentage of Revenue by Source," 2004, online at http://www.taxpolicycen ter.org/TaxFacts/TFDB/TFTemplate.cfm?Docid =204.

56. Center for American Progress, citing Citizens for Tax Justice, "Bush Policies Drive a Surge in Corporate Tax Freeloading," 9/22/04, online at http://www .ctj.org/corpfed04pr.pdf.

57. Center for American Progress, citing Martin Sullivan, "Data Show a Dramatic Shift of Profits to Tax Havens," *Tax Note,* 9/13/04, p. 1190.

58. Jimmy Carter, Address to the 1976 Democratic National Convention, online at http://www.americanrhetoric.com/speeches/jimmycarter1976dnc.htm.

59. Institute for Policy Information, Report #168, February 12, 2002, online at http://www.ipi.org/ipi%5CIPIPublications.nsf/PublicationLookupFullText/ A80226753C1131B286256B4D007B8FE4.

60. Rep. Jim McDermott, "Republicans Have Made Our Tax Code More Complex," 7/21/04, online at http://www.house.gov/mcdermott/sp040721a .shtml.

61. Center for American Progress, "A Fair and Simple Tax System for Our Future," op. cit.

62. *San Francisco Chronicle,* "Tax Code Still Too Complex," 11/1/05, online at http://www.sfgate.com/cgi-bin/article.cgi?file=/chronicle/archive/2000/11/ 01/BU118278.DTL.

63. Ibid.

64. Ibid.

65. Robert McIntyre, "Flat on Our Backs," *The Nation,* February 1996, online at http://www.ctj.org/html/flatwrng.htm.

66. Ibid.

67. Ibid.

68. *New York Times,* "A Clash of Goals in Bush's Efforts on the Income Tax; Pro- posals Would Shift Burden from Wealthy to Middle Class," 10/6/04.

69. Center for American Progress, "A Fair and Simple Tax System for Our Future," op. cit.

70. Ibid.

71. Ibid.

72. Warren Buffett, "Dividend Voodoo," *Washington Post,* 5/20/03.

73. Warren Buffett, letter to Berkshire-Hathaway shareholders, 3/8/04, online at http:money.cnn.com/2004/03/06/pf/buffett_letter/?cnn=yes.

74. David Cay Johnston, "The Nontaxpaying Affluent Grew by 15% in One

Year," *New York Times,* 7/1/05, online at http://www.nytimes.com/2005/
07/01/national/01tax.html.

75. "The Gospel According to Paul," *Financial Times,* 10/23/04.

When You've Got Your Health . . .

1. Barbara Schecter, "Toyota Reportedly Chooses Canada for New Plant: Lower Labour Costs Cited by Japanese Newspaper," *Financial Post,* p. FP1.

2. Institute of Medicine, Insuring America's Health: Principles and Recommendations (2004): 46.

3. U.S. Census Bureau, Current Population Report, p. 60–226, *Income, Poverty, and Health Insurance Coverage in the United State: 2003* (Washington, D.C.: U.S. Government Printing Office, 2004); Henry J. Kaiser Family Foundation/ Health Research and Educational Trust, *Employer Health Benefits Survey: 2003* (Menlo Park, Calif: KFF/HRET, 10/9/03); J. Appleby and S. S. Carty, "Ailing GM Looks to Scale Back Generous Health Benefits," *USA TODAY,* 6/24/05; C. Smith et al., "Health Spending Growth Slows in 2003," *Health Affairs* 24, no. 1 (2005): 185–94.

4. NCHS, *Health, United States, 2004,* Table 22, online at http://www .cdc.gov/nchs/data/hus/hus04trend.pdf#exe (August 12, 2005).

5. Central Intelligence Agency, "Rank Order–Infant Mortality Rate," *The World Fact Book, 2005,* online at http://www.cia.gov/cia/publications/factbook/ rankorder/2091rank.html (August 12, 2005).

6. M. Charles Bakst, "In GOP Primaries, Both Bush, McCain Are Looking Smaller," *The Providence Journal,* 2/22/2000, p. 1B.

7. "Health Insurance Coverage: 2001," published September 2002, from the 2001 Current Population Report, U.S. Census Bureau, online at www .coveringtheuninsured.org.

8. Institute of Medicine, *Care Without Coverage: Too Little, Too Late,* Committee on the Consequences of Uninsurance, Board on Health Care Services (Washington, D.C.: National Academies Press, 2002) p. 162.

9. E. Warren, T. Sullivan, and M. Jacoby, "Medical Problems and Bankruptcy Filings," *Norton's Bankruptcy Adviser* (May 2002).

10. Kaiser Commission on Medicaid and the Uninsured, "Medicaid at a Glance," January 2005, online at http://www.kff.org/medicaid/7235.cfm.

11. Ali H. Mokdad et al., *Actual Causes of Death in the United States, 2000,* 291 *Journal of the American Medical Association* 1238 (2004).

12. Elliott S. Fisher et al., "The Implications of Regional Variations in Medicare Spending. Part 2: Health Outcomes, and Satisfaction with Care," *Annals of Internal Medicine* 138, no. 4 (February 18, 2003): 288–98.

The Flood: "Mr. Bill Was Better Informed Than Mr. Bush"

1. Kevin Drum, "Political Animal," *Washington Monthly,* 9/1/05, online at http://www.washingtonmonthly.com/archives/individual/2005_09/007023.php.
2. Juliet Eilperin, "Shrinking La. Coastline Contributes to Flooding," *Washington Post,* 8/30/05.
3. Mark Leibovich, "Senator Bears Witness and Bares Emotions," *Washington Post,* 9/9/05, online at http://www.washingtonpost.com/wp-dyn/content/article/2005/09/08/AR2005090802014.html.
4. See http://www.pnionline.com/dnblog/attytood/archives/002331.html.
5. In the immediate aftermath of the storm, these stories were assembled by William Bunch, a senior writer for the *Philadelphia Daily News.*
6. Newhouse News Service, 8/31/05.
7. *New Orleans City Business,* 6/6/05.
8. Ibid.
9. New Orleans *Times-Picayune,* 9/22/04; *New Orleans City Business,* 6/6/05.
10. Amina Elbindary, "They Came to Baghdad," *Al-Ahram Weekly,* April 17–23, 2003, online at http://weekly.ahram.org.eg/2003/634/bo2.htm.
11. CNN, *Crossfire,* 9/17/03.
12. CNN, *Crossfire,* 8/16/04.
13. Center for American Progress, "Top FEMA Deputies Make Brown Look Qualified," *Think Progress,* 9/6/05.
14. *Chicago Tribune,* 9/7/05.
15. Ibid.
16. *Washington Times,* 8/26/05.
17. Whitehouse.gov, 8/27/05.
18. New Orleans *Times-Picayune,* 8/28/05.
19. Ibid.
20. Ibid.
21. Ibid.
22. Ibid.
23. Bush remarks, August 28, 2005.
24. New Orleans *Times-Picayune,* 8/29/05.

25. Ibid.

26. *St. Petersburg Times*, 8/30/05.

27. *Arizona Republic*, 8/30/05.

28. *Washington Post*, 8/30/05.

29. *Whittier Daily News*, 8/30/05.

30. Hurricane Center, http://www.nola.com/hurricane/?/hurricane/feed/active_storm2.html.

31. *Washington Post*, 8/30/05.

32. *Los Angeles Times*, 8/31/05.

33. Associated Press, August 30, 2005.

34. New Orleans *Times-Picayune*, 8/31/05.

35. Ibid.

36. Associated Press, 8/31/05; KOMO Radio-TV, 9/1/05.

37. Associated Press, 8/31/05.

38. Editorial, *New York Times*, 9/1/05.

39. New Orleans *Times-Picayune*, 9/1/05.

40. Ibid.

41. ABC, 9/1/05.

42. Associated Press, 9/1/05.

43. New Orleans *Times-Picayune*, 9/2/05.

44. Lisa de Moraes, "Kanye West's Torrent of Criticism, Live on NBC," *Washington Post*, 9/3/05, p. C1.

45. ABC News, "Dutch Can Relate to New Orleans Disaster," 9/17/05, online at http://abcnews.go.com/WNT/HurricaneKatrina/story?id=1131764&page=1&CMP=OTC-RSSFeeds0312.

46. Juliet Eilperin, "Shrinking La. Coastline Contributes to Flooding," op. cit.

Progressive Patriotism

1. CBS News, 10/20/00, online at http://www.cbsnews.com/stories/2000/10/18/politics/main242210.shtml.

Acknowledgments

More than any other book we've written, this one took a village. James has always had a rule that if you start thanking people in public you're going to wind up hurting someone. Still, at the risk—no, with the certain knowledge—that we're leaving some people out, here goes:

Paul's assistant, Jessie Lyons, and James's assistant, Sarah Sturdevant, were invaluable. Whether the request was for an obscure LexisNexis search or rejiggering our schedules to make time to write, they were always there.

Jeff Nussbaum is a good Democrat and a good friend. We thank him for his contributions to this book.

Bob Boorstin of the Center for American Progress read and edited several chapters—you'll know which ones; they're the ones that are the clearest and most cogent. Madhu Chugh, who is the daughter Paul and Diane always wanted but never had, also took time away from Yale Law School to give detailed edits and helpful comments on several chapters. David Palombi was enormously helpful to Paul, offering good advice and sound judgment. Jon Morgan and Eric Berman also offered their thoughts and assistance, although we generally ignored them. Our friend Mark Weiner has always been there for us, and we thank him for his assistance on this project. Peter and Jon Orszag, two of the brightest economic minds in America, shared their insights with us. And John Podesta and his entire crew at the Center for American Progress—fast becoming America's premier think tank—were absolutely invaluable. If Democrats are going to win the battle of ideas, the folks named above will be the reason why.

In the course of writing this book we had hundreds—possibly thousands—of conversations with Democrats all across the country. Some were insightful and earnest exchanges with people we didn't know—guys who grabbed us at the ballpark or women who came up to us when we were dropping our kids off at school. Democrats across the country are tired of losing and sick of the sanctimony, corruption, and incompetence of the Bush Republicans. Their thoughts inform every page of this book. Other Democrats we met with are more famous. They include President Bill Clinton and Senator Hillary Rodham Clinton, Bob Rubin, Roger Altman, Governor Ann Richards, Senator John Kerry, Steve Bing, Donna Brazile, Reverend Jim Wallis, George Lakoff, Senator Harry Reid, Senator Edward Kennedy, Senator Evan Bayh, Senator Ken Salazar, Governor Mark Warner, Representative Rahm Emanuel, Representative Harold Ford, Jr., Bob Casey, Jr., Tony Sanchez, Gene Sperling, Susan McCue, Anne McGuire, Karen Finney, Stan Greenberg, Doug Sosnik, Jim Margolis, Mike McCurry, Al From, Maggie Williams, Mandy Grunwald, Patti Solis-Doyle, Keith Mason, Steve Wrigley, Sid Blumenthal, and many more. We also talked with several leading members of the Bush-Cheney '04 campaign team. They were candid and cooperative, but requested that their names not be used because, like any good politician, President Bush doesn't like his political strategy discussed in public.

Of course, we are not the first people to take a hard look at the current sad state of American politics. And so we leaned heavily on the work of smarter people and better writers. Tom Frank's *What's the Matter with Kansas?* was influential, as was E. J. Dionne's *Stand Up, Fight Back*. Our chapter on the media was deeply influenced by the work of Eric Alterman, David Brock, Kathleen Hall Jamieson, and Thomas Patterson. We believe good ideas are like the fruitcake in Johnny Carson's classic joke—there are only a few of them and everyone keeps passing them around. We don't claim that this book contains brilliant flashes of insight, but we hope we've collected some of the brilliance of others and brought it together in one place for the reader.

Our lawyer, Bob Barnett, once again proved why he's the most respected and effective attorney in the publishing world. Geoff Kloske, our editor, and

ACKNOWLEDGMENTS 349

David Rosenthal, our publisher, were patient beyond any reasonable expectation, allowing us to adjust the text as the political currents shifted. We would also like to thank Laura Perciasepe and Elisa Rivlin of Simon & Schuster, whose keen eyes and good judgment have contributed greatly to this work. Our CNN colleagues (past and present)—Bob Novak and Tucker Carlson, Jon Klein, Sue Bunda, David Bohrman and Sam Feist, Kristy Schantz, Kate Farrell, Heather Date, Steven Samaniego, Abbi Tatton, Howie Lutt, and all the gang—have been wonderful and understanding about giving us time to work on this book.

For all the help from all the above-named people we are deeply grateful. Still, we want to stress that the views contained herein are our own. Some of the people we talked with agreed with us; others deeply disagreed. We alone should be held responsible for the contents of this book. The mistakes and misjudgments contained herein (and we're sure there are many) are ours alone.

Finally, and most important, our families. James's wife, Mary, and their girls, Matty and Emma, give him endless supplies of unconditional love.

Paul's wife, Diane, and their boys, John, Billy, Charlie, and Patrick, are not just the light of his life. They are his life. They were indulgent and inspirational.

About the Authors

JAMES CARVILLE has managed more political campaigns than anyone in history. For his role in Bill Clinton's election to the presidency in 1992, he was honored as Campaign Manager of the Year by the American Association of Political Consultants. He is the author or coauthor of the best-selling books *All's Fair; We're Right, They're Wrong; . . . And the Horse He Rode in On; Buck Up, Suck Up . . . and Come Back When You Foul Up; Stickin';* and *Had Enough?*, and is a frequent political commentator on CNN. He lives in Virginia with his wife and two daughters.

PAUL BEGALA, former counselor to President Clinton, served as a senior strategist to the 1992 Clinton-Gore campaign and has helped run political campaigns across America and in several foreign countries. He helped John F. Kennedy, Jr., found *George* magazine, where he was one of the original contributing editors. He has also written articles for *Esquire* and *Washington Monthly*, and opinion columns for *The New York Times* and the *Los Angeles Times* magazine. He is the author of the best-selling books *Is Our Children Learning?: The Case Against George W. Bush* and *It's the Economy, Stupid*, and coauthor of the best-seller *Buck Up, Suck Up . . . and Come Back When You Foul Up* with James Carville. He is also a research professor of public policy at Georgetown University's Georgetown Public Policy Institute, and a political commentator on CNN's *The Situation Room*.